Rhetorics of Fantasy

Rhetorics of Fantasy

Farah Mendlesohn

Wesleyan University Press • Middletown, Connecticut

Published by Wesleyan University Press, Middletown, CT 06459
www.wesleyan.edu/wespress

Printed in the United States of America

10 9 8 7 6

Library of Congress Cataloging-in-Publication Data

Mendlesohn, Farah.
Rhetorics of fantasy / Farah Mendlesohn.
p. cm.
Includes bibliographical references (p.) and index.
ISBN-13: 978–0–8195–6867–0 (alk. paper)
ISBN-10: 0–8195–6867–8 (alk. paper)
ISBN-13: 978–0–8195–6868–7 (pbk. : alk. paper)
ISBN-10: 0–8195–6868–6 (pbk. : alk. paper)
1. Fantasy fiction, American—History and criticism—Theory, etc. 2. Fantasy fiction, English—History and criticism—Theory, etc. 3. Science fiction, American—History and criticism—Theory, etc. 4. Science fiction, English—History and criticism—Theory, etc. 5. Fantasy fiction—Authorship. I. Title.
PS374.F27M46 2008
813'.0876609—dc22 2007033559

Dedicated to the staff of Birmingham Children's Hospital, who allowed me to finish The Lion, the Witch and the Wardrobe *before turning out the lights.*

And to Edward James in salutation of the first time we met.

HEALTH WARNING:

This book is not intended to create rules.
Its categories are not intended to fix anything in stone.
This book is merely a portal into fantasy, a tour around the skeletons and exoskeletons of genre.

Taxonomy: Theory and practice of classification.

Classification: Any method of organizing and systematizing the diversity of organisms, living and extinct, according to a set of rules (*Penguin Dictionary of Biology*, 9th ed., 1994).

Taxonomy is no longer typological. It's now systematics, consciously based in the axiom "The observer is part of the system." —Richard Erlich, e-mail, 2003

Formal critics all begin with a truth that ideological critics too often neglect; form is in itself interesting, even in the most abstract extreme. Shape, pattern, design carry their own interest—and hence meaning—for all human beings. What some critics have called "human meanings" are not required; nothing is more human than the love of abstract forms. —Wayne C. Booth, introduction to M. M. Bakhtin's *Problems of Dostoevsky's Poetics*

Contents

Acknowledgments

This work has been a long time in the making. It began as an impromptu way to arrange a presentation on modern children's fantasy at the Children's SF and Fantasy conference organized by the Association for Research in Popular Fiction and the Science Fiction Foundation in January 2002, and I am indebted to Nickianne Moody for providing that opportunity. It continued because my audience showed immediate interest; this interest has been extended by too many other audiences to thank them all, but if you have been one of my interrogators in the past, I thank you. Every one of you has assisted in honing my thoughts. In the process of writing I rambled on to many people, but thanks are especially owed to Jon Courtenay Grimwood and Karen Traviss for their conviction that writing is a craft, to Craig Jacobsen (for his comment on "gossiping about theory"), Brian Attebery, Dave Clements, John Clute, Steve Cockayne, Stefan Ekman, Neil Gaiman, Elizabeth Hand, Nalo Hopkinson, Edward James, Greer Gilman, M. John Harrison, Roz Kaveney, Ken MacLeod, China Miéville, Justina Robson, Graham Sleight, Peter Straub, Steph Swainston, and Gary K. Wolfe—all listened to me as I tried to work out what I wanted to say, and all, at some stage, commented on some part of the work. One consequence is that this book has a great many references to conversations and e-mails. This book is intended to function as a jumping-off point for discussion; I consider it very important that the discussions that took place be adequately acknowledged, even if it is impossible for future readers to track them all.

Many people helped me in small ways: finding definitions, checking references, making suggestions for further reading, or just asking the right question. I hope I have included them all here.

Zara Baxter
Bernadette Bosky
Tanya Brown
Andrew M. Butler
Elizabeth Billinger
Paul Billinger
Judith Clute
Tony Cullen
Neil Easterbrook
Richard D. Erlich
Glenda Guest
Niall Harrison
Dan Hartland
Tim Holman
Kathryn Hume

Kari Maund
Kevin McVeigh
Clare Mendlesohn
Potchka Mendlesohn
Cheryl Morgan
Stephanie Moss
Graham Murphy
Jess Nevens
Faye Ringel
Heidi Robbins
Veronica Schanoes
Brian Stableford
Jennifer Stevenson
Robert Van Osten
Greer Watson
Gary Westfahl
Shana Worthen

And special thanks to William Senior of the *Journal of the Fantastic in the Arts*, and to David Hartwell, Kathryn Cramer, and Kevin J. Maroney; and to the Wiscon Committee, who have all published my thoughts-in-progress as they have developed and to Suzanna Tamminen at Wesleyan University Press.

My gratitude also to Mike Houghton and James Bloom for keeping me fit enough to write; LiveJournal friends for encouragement in the final days; the staff of the British Library who cheered me with their recognition; and all the hotel staff in various hotels in Dublin who supplied me with tea, positive support, and a power socket when I couldn't find anywhere else to work.

Parts of this book have been published previously:

"Towards a Taxonomy of Fantasy." *Journal of the Fantastic in the Arts* 13, no. 2 (2002): 173–187.

"*Conjunctions 39* and Liminal Fantasy." *Journal of the Fantastic in the Arts* 15, no. 3 (2005): 228–239.

An application of the ideas expressed in this book can be found in my *Diana Wynne Jones: Children's Literature and the Fantastic Tradition* (New York: Routledge, 2005).

Introduction

This book is not about defining fantasy. The debate over definition is now long-standing, and a consensus has emerged, accepting as a viable "fuzzy set," a range of critical definitions of fantasy. It is now rare to find scholars who choose among Kathryn Hume, W. R. Irwin, Rosemary Jackson, or Tzvetan Todorov: it is much more likely they will pick and choose among these and other "definers" of the field according to the area of fantasy fiction, or the ideological filter, in which they are interested.

I want to reach out for an understanding of the *construction* of the genre; specifically, I wish to consider its language and rhetoric, in order to provide critical tools for further analysis. During the research for this book I became aware that while there are many single author or single text studies in genre fantasy criticism, there is relatively little comparative criticism beyond the study of metaphorical and thematic elements. There is almost nothing dealing with the *language* of the fantastic that goes beyond aesthetic preference.[1] My contention is that if we do not have a critical tool that allows us to collate texts in any yielding way (note that I do *not* insist on "meaningful"), we cannot engage in the comparative research that illuminates a genre.

I believe that the fantastic is an area of literature that is heavily dependent on the dialectic between author and reader for the construction of a sense of wonder, that it is a fiction of consensual construction of belief. This expectation is historical, subject to historical change, and is not unique to fantasy. Wayne C. Booth has written that "for experienced readers a sonnet begun calls for a sonnet concluded; an elegy begun in blank verse calls for an elegy completed in blank verse" (*Fiction* 12). This dialectic is conditioned by the very real genre expectations circling around certain identifiable rhetorical techniques that I will be describing. Intrinsic to my argument is that a fantasy succeeds when the literary techniques employed are most appropriate to the reader expectations of that category of fantasy. Understanding the broad brushstrokes of plot or the decoration of device is less fundamental to comprehending the genre; all of these may be tweaked or subverted while still remaining firmly within the reader's expectation of the text.

I came to this project as a science fiction critic, and that perspective has shaped the way I understand the structures and rhetorics of fantasy. Crucially, it led me to focus on an issue that both W. R. Irwin and Brian Attebery (Attebery, *Fantasy Tradition*) have raised: the way in which a text becomes fantasy or, alternatively, the way the fantastic enters the text and the reader's relationship to this.[2]

In science fiction, how the reader is brought into the speculative world influences the ways in which that world can be described. The incredible invention story rapidly gives way to the completed future, because the incredible invention permits only one level of emotional response, that of ritualized amazement or ritualized horror. In contrast, as Robert A. Heinlein argued and practiced, the completed future—the enclosed world or pocket universe—permits the author to elicit increasingly complex responses but demands much more sophisticated narrative techniques. But the question remains, what is the precise reader relationship to these futures? There is a clear difference between the imaginary society, which we enter riding on the shoulder of the otherworldly visitor (a construct most common to utopian fiction),[3] and the society we encounter as a hidden observer for whom no allowances are made: the first demands—and usually offers—explanations; the second requires the reader to unpack the intertext. The consequences of these reader relationships for science fiction have been explored by John Clute, Samuel R. Delany, John Huntington, Edward James, and Brian Stableford, among others. My approach therefore is not new. I am building on work already done, but work that has primarily been done for science fiction. My intention is to turn the same critical gaze on fantasy, to take up Roger Schlobin's challenge, implicit in his claim that the "key to the fantastic is how its universes work, which is sometimes where they are, but is always why and how they are" ("Rituals" 161). Attebery argues that most fantasy writers create clearly defined frames: "Narrative devices that establish a relationship between the fantasy world and our own while at the same time separating the two" (*Strategies* 66)—which is of course what my book is about: how these strategies work and their impact.

In this book I argue that there are essentially four categories within the fantastic: the portal-quest, the immersive, the intrusive, and the liminal. These categories are determined by the means by which the fantastic enters the narrated world. In the portal-quest we are invited through into the fantastic; in the intrusion fantasy, the fantastic enters the fictional world; in the liminal fantasy, the magic hovers in the corner of our eye; while in the immersive fantasy we are allowed no escape. Each category has as profound an influence on the rhetorical structures of the fantastic as does its *taproot* text or genre. Each category is a mode susceptible to the quadripartite template or grammar—wrongness, thinning, recognition, and healing/return—that John Clute suggests in the *Encyclopedia of Fantasy* (338–339).[4] Each mode places its emphasis on a different note within this four-note bar; within the mode, consistencies exist in the use of these templates that demonstrate coherence in the categories.

The construction of these groups strongly suggests a taxonomy and it would be disingenuous of me to attempt to fudge this issue. Taxonomy, however needs to be understood as a tool, not as an end in itself, and it needs to be understood in the modern context that taxonomical practices are increasingly polysemic and multiplex, generated by acknowledged questions and capable of existence alongside other configurations. It is not my intention here to argue that there is only one possible taxonomic understanding of the genre. The purpose of the book is not to offer a classification per se but to consider the genre in ways that open up new questions. It is a tool kit, not a color chart.

If the taxonomy I suggest is to succeed as a critical tool kit, it must work across the more commercial definitions of fantasy, as well as the categories of children's and adults' fantasy, dark fantasy, and light and comic fantasy. It must help to explain some of the more anomalous texts: those that find their genre coat of the wrong cut or color, rough to the touch or tight around the sleeves. In essence, my contention is that the failure to grasp the stylistic needs of a particular category of fantasy may undermine the effectiveness of an otherwise interesting idea. Eleanor Cameron wrote that fantasy is "a very special category of literature that compares with fiction as a sonnet compares with poetry. Either you have a sonnet if you have written your poem in a certain way, or you don't if you haven't" (165). To use my own terms, which are outlined below, an *immersive* fantasy told with the voice of *portal* fantasy will feel leaden; a *liminal* fantasy written with the naïveté of the *intrusion* fantasy will feel overcontrived.

Inevitably, there will be texts that appear to cross categories, but these exceptions test the rule: where authors move from one category to another within the text, they invariably assume new techniques; the cadence shifts, and both metaphor and mimetic writing take on different functions to accommodate the new category. This shift is at times inadvertent and at other times subject to the manipulation of more ambitious and skilled writers. Yet while many books move internally from one category to another, very few authors produce a single text that exists simultaneously within multiple categories (although as we shall see, immersive fantasy can host an intrusion). These exceptional few will be discussed in chapter 5, and their achievements provide an important caveat for this book: no theory that claims universal applicability is worth a damn. Here I take serious exception with Stanley Fish's argument that "theories always work and they will always produce exactly the results they predict, results that will be immediately compelling to those for whom the theory's assumptions and enabling principles are self-evident. Indeed, the trick would be to find a theory that *didn't* work" (68). This statement, however amusing, encapsulates much of what is wrong with current "schools" of literary criticism.[5] This observation may seem egregious, but it is essential when reading this book to know that its author does not necessarily *believe* in these structures. They are observations, not diktats, and they are powerful only to the degree that they remain arguable.

This book is very much grounded in a love of forms, but form cannot be wholly abstracted from content or ideology. Furthermore, I have come to believe that form may act to constrain ideological possibilities. Consequently consideration is given to interpretation where the issue is *how* a particular mode of writing helps to generate, intensify, or twist meaning. A great deal of this book will consider how particular rhetorics deliberately or unavoidably support ideological positions and in so doing shape character, or affect the construction and narration of story. Generally speaking this is a book about structure, not about meaning.

When I began this book I believed the issue to be taxonomy. Halfway through, I was convinced that I was working within narratology. Later, rhetoric became my principal concern. In the concluding stages I realized I was working within what is described as poetics. Finally, I realized that the most illuminating metaphors came from the world of landscape painting. This book is the result of an extended thought experiment. It is not intended to fix subcategories of genre (as I hope chapter 5 will make clear), or to say, "this is how you do *x* kind of fantasy." It is intended solely in terms of "this is what I observe over a wide range of texts." It is an exercise in almost pure Reason—a rather old-fashioned approach to criticism, I am aware. I have used other critics where I found them helpful, but there is surprisingly little written on the rhetoric or poetics of the fantastic. I am, however, indebted to the work of John Clute and Brian Attebery, whose writings have served as compass poles, and to the "How to Write Science Fiction and Fantasy" books and blog discussions of many active fantasy authors. Wherever this text fits, I hope that it provokes more questions than it answers.

A Note on the Selection of Texts

No *system* of selection has been applied to the choice of texts in this book. At best, the selection builds on Attebery's notion of the fuzzy set—the idea that there are core likenesses around which we can construct ever more distant perimeters—but with one significant caveat. I argue here that rather than a single fuzzy set, from which fantasy moves from genre to slipstream, we can actually identify several fuzzy sets, linked together by what John Clute has termed *taproot* texts (*Encyclopedia* 921–922). Inevitably, some forms of fantasy appeal to me more than others and I have yet to find a reader who claims to enjoy all of the kinds I have outlined: to give just one example, readers who like portal-quest fantasies rarely seem to enjoy the liminal fantasies, and vice versa. I have not been able to keep this coloration entirely absent from the text, although where I knew my own tastes might predetermine my analysis, I tackled the problem in part by asking those more enthusiastic for the forms to select my reading. This outside selection is particularly evident in chapter 1 (portal-quest fantasy) and chapter 3 (intrusion fantasy) where all the texts chosen came recommended by friends and members of the International Association of the Fantastic in the Arts online discussion list. In contrast the books selected for chapters 4 and 5 are works I had already read, and that had fascinated me. A consequence is that some writers central to the field do not appear in this book: in each case the omission is entirely because my personal taste does not extend in their direction. For these reasons, and aware that the passive academic voice has a tendency to reinforce reification, I have chosen to retain the first person.

I am not myself always convinced my assignments are appropriate. Some books have been wrangled back and forth between chapters as I have tried to decide in which mode they were written. Dividing between immersive fantasies (which just happened to have intrusions as part of their plot but whose rhetoric emphasized the immersive qualities of the text) and those fantasies set in other worlds (in which intrusion is the source of the fantastic) was not always easy. Whether the choices have been correct or not, the very engagement with them has generated questions about the ways in which the fantastic is written; any disputes as to where I have placed each book will, I hope, generate more.

Finally, where possible—and unless stated otherwise—I have referenced all texts to the first editions. The major exception to this is in chapter 3 where the classic Gothic novels are all referenced to current Penguin Classics for the ease of both author and reader.

The Categories

This book is constructed as a set of interlocking essays: with the exception of chapter 5 each of the essays stands alone while leaning against the arguments and definitions of the other chapters. The critical questions in each chapter are: How do we get there? How do we meet the fantastic? In what ways does this meeting affect the narrative and rhetorical choices? How does this affect the choice of language and in what way does the choice of language affect the construction of the fantastic and the position of the reader? What ideological consequences emerge from the rhetorical structures? Perhaps the most crucial question is, Where are we asked to stand in relationship to the fantastic? It is important to understand that I am not discussing point of view, or what Gérard Génette labeled *focalization*. Focalization is a matter internal to the story and there is no common choice within any of the categories (although one cannot but notice the extensive use of first person in the liminal fantasy). What I am interested in is the reader's relationship to the framework. Bijoy H. Boruah, in trying to rationalize the empathic emotions of the reader, wrote, "To appreciate fictions is, to some extent, also to fictionalize ourselves" (126), an activity he called "metaphoric participation." His phrase is peculiarly apt for what I am arguing. That "reader position" to which I will keep pointing, while on the one hand a reference to our ideal and implied reader, is also an invitation to construct a fictionalized self who can accept the construction of the rhetoric of a particular fantastic text. But the invitation is not free and open: it is an exercise in which the author continually seeks the upper hand. In his reader's report on this book Brian Attebery wrote, "Characters can be categorized variously as being immersed in, or wandering through, or fighting off invasions of the fantastic; readers, however, can take any or all of these positions at once, since they are constantly mediating between the fantasy world and their own experience" (Reader's report, 2006). Yet what I shall argue here is that the author seeks to control these choices, even while understanding the polysemous and proactive position of the reader. For many authors the task is to anticipate readers' strategies as part of their own poetics. The core rhetorical strategy of fantasy remains the same: fantasy is constructed *with precision* through point of view. Like a perspective puzzle, if the reader stands in "the wrong place," the image/experience will not resolve.

It is almost impossible to deal with each category discretely; thus there will be constant comparisons between the forms I identify in order to show the differences between their workings and tone.

The Portal-Quest Fantasy

A portal fantasy is simply a fantastic world entered through a portal. The classic portal fantasy is of course *The Lion, the Witch and the Wardrobe* (1950). Crucially, the fantastic is *on the other side* and does not "leak." Although individuals may cross both ways, the magic does not.[6]

Closest in form to the classic utopian or alien planet story (sometimes, but not always, a first contact tale), portal fantasies require that we learn from a point of entry. They are almost always quest novels and they almost always proceed in a linear fashion with a goal that must be met. Like the computer games they have spawned, they often contain elaborate descriptive elements. Yet while the intrusion fantasy must be unpacked or defeated, the portal fantasy must be navigated. Frequently, portal fantasies become more mysterious, rather than less. The reliance on destiny in so many portal fantasies may reflect the need to create rational explanation of irrational action without destroying this mystery. The language of the portal fantasy is often elaborate, but it is the elaboration of the anthropologist or the Pre-Raphaelite painter, intensely descriptive and exploratory rather than assumptive. It is a rare portal fantasy that achieves the Gothic (although David Lindsay's *A Voyage to Arcturus* [1920], comes to mind, as does *Alice's Adventures in Wonderland* [1865]) and when it does, the need to describe and explain remains a driving force behind the narrative and the language used. Most significant, the portal fantasy allows and relies upon both protagonist and reader gaining experience. Where the stock technique of intrusion is to keep surprising the reader, portal fantasies lead us gradually to the point where the protagonist knows his or her world enough to change it and to enter into that world's destiny. One way to envision this technique is that we ride alongside the protagonist, hearing only what she hears, seeing only what she sees; thus our protagonist (even if she is not the narrator) provides us with a guided tour of the landscapes. Diana Wynne Jones's *Tough Guide to Fantasyland* (1996) both mocks this technique and reduces it to its purest form: the travel guide.

When we think of portal fantasies, we commonly assume that the portal is from "our" world to the fantastic, but the portal fantasy is about entry, transition, and negotiation. Much quest fantasy, for all that it builds the full secondary world, fits better with the portal fantasy. Characteristically in quest fantasy the protagonist goes from a mundane life—in which the fantastic, if she is aware of it, is very distant and unknown (or at least unavailable to the protagonist)—into direct contact with the fantastic, through which she transitions, to the point of negotiation with the world via the personal manipulation of the fantastic realm. In chapter 1 I shall trace precisely this process in *The Lord of the Rings*. The discussion in chapter 1 will help to distinguish the creation of a convincing rhetorical secondary world from the techniques of immersive fantasy. In the quest fantasy we see the world through this transitional narrative: despite the assertion that this world has *always* existed, the technique remains identical to that of the portal fantasy and the effect on the language of the text is the same, forcing the author to describe and explain what is seen by the point of view character as she negotiates the world. The result, when done poorly, is didactic, but as I hope to demonstrate, even the most creative writers find it difficult in this form to avoid impressing upon the reader an authoritative interpretation of their world.

The Immersive Fantasy

The immersive fantasy invites us to share not merely a world, but a set of assumptions. At its best, it presents the fantastic without comment as the norm both for the protagonist and for the reader: we sit on the protagonist's shoulder and while we have access to his eyes and ears, we are not provided with an explanatory narrative. The immersive fantasy is that which is closest to science fiction; as such, it makes use of an irony of mimesis, which helps to explain why a sufficiently effective immersive fantasy may be indistinguishable from science fiction: once the fantastic becomes assumed, it acquires a scientific cohesion all of its own. In 2000, this problem of genre led to endless debates about the status of both Mary Gentle's *Ash* (2000) and China Miéville's *Perdido Street Station* (2000). The effectiveness of the immersive fantasy, however depends on an assumption of realism that denies the need for explication.

The immersive fantasy seems to be described in part by what it is not. We do not enter into the immersive fantasy, we are assumed to be of it: our cognitive estrangement is both entire and negated. The immersive fantasy must be sealed; it cannot, within the confines of the story, be questioned. While an intrusion narrative may drive the plot, as in *Perdido Street Station*, the setting is already fantastic so that the intrusion is not in itself the source of the fantastic. Most important is that the fantasy be immersive for the point of view characters: unlike the characters of quest fantasies, which I have argued above are better fitted to the category of portal fantasy, the point of view characters of an immersive fantasy *must* take for granted the fantastic elements with which they are surrounded; they must exist as integrated with the magical (or fantastic) even if they themselves are not magical; they must be "deeply competent with the world they know" (Clute, *Strokes* 34). As we shall see in chapter 2, successful immersive fantasy consciously negates the sense of wonder in favor of an atmosphere of ennui. M. John Harrison's *The Pastel City* (1971) both achieves this negation and uses this trope to mock our expectations.

The use of the immersive mode can undermine the intentions of an author. One might presume that Laurell K. Hamilton's vampire novels (beginning with *Guilty Pleasures* [1993]) were intended as horror. They contain the requisite actors: the vampire, the vampire hunter, several nasty monsters, and later a werewolf. But the fantastic elements are not in themselves frightening, and they are most definitely not horrific. The potential horror of the Anita Blake novels is subverted by the structures and language native to immersive fantasy: although a horror novel is read with expectation, the immersive fantasy places much of that expectation on contextual difference, rather than the intruding event. Immersion, with its ironic realism, normalizes the horrific and prevents the sense of attrition that Clute identifies as essential to Horror (personal communication). That these novels ended up in chapter 3 (intrusion fantasy) has nothing to do with the accoutrements of the fantastic by which they are usually categorized; their placement arises, rather, from the trajectory of escalation that shapes both the individual books and the series.

Perhaps most interesting is that it is most commonly in the immersive fantasies that one finds oneself in a fantasy world in which no magic occurs. Sometimes this absence is because the magic takes place elsewhere. But there are many immersive fantasy novels that differ from science fiction only in that they are set in apparently archaic worlds that are not connected to ours: in Mervyn Peake's *Titus Groan* (1946), the fantastic is embedded in the linguistic excesses of the text, or in the interaction between the setting and the protagonists. In the immersive fantasy, the plot may be the least fantastical element.

Intrusion Fantasy

In intrusion fantasy the fantastic is the bringer of chaos. It is the beast in the bottom of the garden, or the elf seeking assistance. It is horror and amazement. It takes us out of safety without taking us from our place. It is recursive. The intrusion fantasy is not necessarily unpleasant, but it has as its base the assumption that normality is organized, and that when the fantastic retreats the world, while not necessarily unchanged, returns to predictability—at least until the next element of the fantastic intrudes.

Fantasy and "reality" are often kept strictly demarcated: in some fictions, those set apart from the protagonist may not be able to perceive the fantastic even as they experience its effects. These structural characteristics of intrusion fantasy are mimicked by the language we can associate with this form. Because the base level is the normal world, intrusion fantasies maintain stylistic realism and rely heavily on explanation. Because the drive of intrusion fantasy is to be investigated and made transparent, description is intense, and it is assumed that we, the readers, are engaged with the ignorance of the point of view character, usually the protagonist. One consequence of this ignorance is that the language reflects constant amazement. Unlike the portal fantasy, which it otherwise strongly resembles, the protagonists and the reader are never expected to become accustomed to the fantastic.

The required awestruck or skeptical tone is tricky and may contribute to the preference for stylistic realism in order to maintain the contrast between the normal world and the fantastic intrusion. It also may explain the tendency of the intrusion fantasy to continually introduce new protagonists, and to up the ante on the nature or number of the horrors. Horror, amazement, and surprise are difficult to maintain if the protagonist has become accustomed to them. Escalation—of many kinds—is an important element of the rhetoric.

Intrusion fantasy, although usually associated with "real world" fantasy, can be set within the immersive. If such is the case, the same rules apply: there is a clear line between the constructed "normality" and the intrusion. Protagonists know what is normal even if we do not and express this clearly and forcefully; the intrusion must be defeated, and the actors remain acted upon. The innocence of the protagonists, however, is combined with their competence within the immersive fantasy; because their negotiation of their own world is fundamentally interesting to the reader, characters become actors within the immersive fantasy as well acted upon by the intrusion. The technique can be seen in Alexander Irvine's *A Scattering of Jades* (2002) in which an Aztec god is reintroduced to 1840s New York. Here, the historical city is our fantasy land.

The Liminal Fantasy

The liminal fantasy is perhaps the most interesting because it is so rare. M. John Harrison has spoken of the existence of the transliminal moment, the point where we are invited to cross the threshold into the fantastic, *but choose not to do so.*[7] The result is that the fantastic leaks back through the portal. One such manifestation can be the leakage of the monster into the narrated world—Philip Pullman uses this motif to create horror in *The Subtle Knife* (1997)—more subtly, however, the portal itself may be the intrusion. Harrison notes this motif in Wells's "The Door in the Wall" (1906), in which a man is three times tempted by a green door leading to a garden, and three times refuses the portal. While the metaphorical role of the green door may be significant to the critic, here its position as representative of the fantastic is more important. This seemingly ordinary story *feels* like fantasy. We somehow know that it is the fantastic. What I contend is that in this story the fantastic is the temptation framed by the door. The anxiety and the continued maintenance and *irresolution* of the fantastic becomes the locus of the "fantasy." The liminal moment that maintains the anxiety around this material temptation assists the creation of the tone and mode that we associate with the fantastic: its presence is represented as unnerving, and it is this sense of the unnerving that is at the heart of the category I have termed liminal. I prefer *liminal* to Tzvetan Todorov's *hesitation* or *uncertainty*, because I think that hesitation is only one strategy employed by these writers. Todorov's (1973) concern with "the fantastic" as something distinct from fantasy means that his ideas are encompassed within this section but do not describe the whole. Liminal fantasy as discussed here is very clear that magic, or at least the possibility of magic, is part of the consensus reality, a position rather different from, but not in conflict with, Todorov's more specific interests.

In the liminal fantasy we are given to understand, through cues to the familiar, that this is our world. When the fantastic appears, it *should* be intrusive, disruptive of expectation; instead, while the events themselves might be noteworthy and/or disruptive, their magical origins barely raise an eyebrow. We are disoriented. The enclosed nature of the immersive fantasy is absent: the hints and cues are missing. Yet, as in immersive fantasy, the protagonist demonstrates no surprise. It is the reaction to the fantastic that shapes this category, as well as the context of the fantasy.

The tone of the liminal fantasy could be described as blasé. An excellent example may be found in Joan Aiken's Armitage family stories, in which the family all remain remarkably calm when unicorns appear on their lawn

("Yes, But Today is Tuesday" [1953]). The tone of Aiken's work is matter-of-fact and casual; unlike James Thurber's "The Unicorn in the Garden" (1940), it is not trying to trick anyone. The protagonist in M. John Harrison's "I Did It" (2001) spends a great deal of time discussing why he put an axe in his head, and whether it looks good, but neither he, nor anyone else, questions the viability of its presence. While liminal fantasy casualizes the fantastic within the experience of the protagonist, it estranges the reader. The situation is odd, and it is our reaction to oddness that is being exploited. Whereas in the portal fantasy we ride with the protagonist, in the liminal fantasy we sit in the subconscious of the point of view character, quietly screaming, "But something is wrong," a dream on the point of becoming lucid. While the intrusion fantasy is fascinated with the monster, the liminal fantasy wallows in ennui. To cross the portal is to confront the illusion, but confrontation (as we shall see in chapter 1) reduces rather than intensifies the fantastic. The transliminal moment, which brings us up to the liminal point and then refuses to cross the threshold, has much greater potential to generate fear, awe, and confusion—all intensely important emotions in the creation of the fantastic mode.

Liminal fantasy may rely on conscious exaggeration of the mimetic style. Indeed, in defiance of the conventional understanding of the fantastic as straight-faced, the effectiveness of this category may rest with its adoption of the ironic mode. It seems clear that this category is shaped as much by doubts and questions as by assertions. It is perhaps the most interesting, though also the most elusive, of the categories proposed here. The liminal fantasy relies on a number of different techniques, but central to its construction of the Absurd are (1) irony and equipoise, (2) the twisting of the metonymic/metaphorical structures of fantasy, and (3) a construction of a point of balance right at the edge of belief.

This kind of fantasy may be the most demanding of the four categories outlined here and the one that most requires for its effectiveness the understanding and subversion of our expectations of the fantastic. Of all the categories it is the one that depends most on my notion of multiple fuzzy sets. Far from being at the edge of genre, the least fantastical of texts, liminal fantasy is the fuzzy set supported by and between the other modes that I am discussing. Liminal fantasies distill the essence of the fantastic.

The Irregulars

Chapter 5, considering as it does texts that warp and distort the patterns I have observed (and that may well have produced patterns I cannot yet see), is essential to this book. This book is about rhetorics, not taxonomic phyla. Genre markers (whether tropes or patterns) are useful analytical tools but they are constructions imposed on a literary landscape. The same landscape may be susceptible to quite a different cartography. The books discussed in this chapter may point the way to that other cartography.

I have no category title for the works in chapter 5. "Hybrid forms" would both reify the categories in a way I find uncomfortable and suggest that these texts are "between" things. I am also wary of terminology that implies a link between nonformulaic fantasy and quality. Quality is to be found in every one of the rhetorics I outline and much of this quality has to do with how formulas are exploited. In addition, these texts are, if anything, hyperaware of formula. The texts considered in chapter 5 straddle the forms I have outlined, folding, twisting, and reweaving the material of the fantastic in order to produce texts that depend on our understanding of these forms, yet do something "other." Each of the books in chapter 5 demonstrates the incredible potential that exists in the genre.

Rhetorics of Fantasy

Chapter 1

The Portal-Quest Fantasy

In both portal and quest fantasies, a character leaves her familiar surroundings and passes through a portal into an unknown place. Although portal fantasies do not *have* to be quest fantasies the overwhelming majority are, and the rhetorical position taken by the author/narrator is consistent.

The position of the reader in the quest and portal fantasy is one of companion-audience, tied to the protagonist, and dependent upon the protagonist for explanation and decoding (see also Branham, who makes the same connection). This reader position is quite different from the one we shall see in the immersive fantasy: there the implied reader, although dependent on the protagonist's absorption of sight and sounds, is not required to accept his or her narrative. One way to distinguish the two, is that despite the illusion of presence (the tales are usually told in the third person) the listener is represented as if present at the telling of a tale. Although I hesitate to describe the position constructed in the portal-quest fantasy as infantilizing—some of the novels I shall discuss demand significant intellectual commitment—it is perhaps not coincidental that the classic portal tale is more common in children's fantasy than in that ostensibly written for the adult market.

As Clute defines portals (*Encyclopedia* 776), they litter the world of the fantastic, marking the transition between this world and another; from our time to another time; from youth to adulthood. The most familiar and archetypal portal fantasy in the United Kingdom is *The Lion, the Witch and the Wardrobe* (1950), while in the United States the *Oz* tales are perhaps better known.[1] In both, and crucially, the fantastic is *on the other side* and does not leak. Nonetheless, there are differences in the placement of the protagonist, and in the role the elements of transition and exploration play. The extent to which the mode of narrative shifts as we traverse the portal from the frame world to the other world influences the degree to which we shall settle into the fantasy world and accept it as both fantasy and as "real." Different authors have handled the transition in different ways, and in the early period of the development of this form of fantasy there was little consensus.

Modern quest and portal fantasies rely upon very similar narrative strategies because each assume the same two movements: transition and exploration. The portal fantasy is about entry, transition, and exploration, and much quest fantasy, for all we might initially assume that it is immersive (that is, fully in and of its world), adopts the structure and rhetorical strategies of the portal fantasy: it denies the taken for granted and positions both protagonist and reader as naive. Characteristically the quest fantasy protagonist goes from a mundane life, in which the fantastic, if she is aware of it, is very distant and unknown (or at least unavailable to the protagonist) to direct contact with the fantastic through which she transitions, exploring the world until she or those around her are knowledgeable enough to negotiate with the world via the personal manipulation of the fantastic realm. There is thus little difference between Belgarion in David Eddings's *Pawn of Prophecy* (1982), who only discovers his magic when he leaves his village, and Andrew Carr, in Marion Zimmer Bradley's rationalized fantasy[2] *The Spell Sword* (1974), who discovers his telepathy on the world of Darkover.

Although individuals may cross both ways, the fantastic does not. Such an effect would move the fantasy into the category of *intrusion*, which (as I shall discuss in chapter 3) uses a very different grammar and tone. Very occasionally both categories may occur in the same book, but while immersive fantasies may contain intrusion, it is relatively rare for portal-quest fantasies to do so. One of the few crossovers are the Harry Potter novels, which typically begin as intrusion fantasies—the abrupt arrival of the owls in Privet Drive in *Harry Potter and the Chamber of Secrets* (1998), causing chaos and disturbance—but very rapidly transmute into almost archetypal portal fantasies, reliant on elaborate description and continual new imaginings.

Despite its reputation as a "full secondary world," the most familiar quest fantasy, J. R. R. Tolkien's *The Lord of the Rings*, follows the structure outlined: Frodo moves from a small, safe, and *understood* world into the wild, unfamiliar world of Middle-Earth. It is *The Silmarillion*, the book told from within the world, about people who know their world, that is the immersive fantasy. And as *The Lord of the Rings* (1956) contains within it the portal from the Shire into the big wide world, so *The Lion, the Witch and the Wardrobe* (1950), *The Wonderful Wizard of Oz* (1900), and many of their portal fantasy successors contain the journey and the goal of the quest narratives.

Typically, the quest or portal fantasy begins with a sense of stability that is revealed to be the stability of a thinned land—Michael Ende's *The Neverending Story* (1979) is the most explicit[3]—and concludes with *restoration* rather than *instauration* (the making over of the world). Most portal-quest fantasies associate the king with the well-being of the land,[4] and the condition of the land with the morality of the place. These thematic elements may seem coincidental, but they serve to structure the ideology of a narrative that is directive and coercive, and that narrows the possibilities for a subversive reading.

The origins of the quest fantasy, if not strictly speaking the portal fantasy, lie in epic, in the Bible, in the Arthurian romances, and in fairy tales. From the epic, portal and quest fantasies draw a certain unity of action, the sense that we follow characters through their beginning, middle, and end. This unity holds even where there are numerous characters. Robert Jordan's *Wheel of Time* sequence (1990 to present) rapidly disperses its cast, but we follow each character through their adventures in turn. The disunity of narrative is illusory; while it may appear to challenge the primacy of the single hero in the epic, in actuality this device operates to create linked epic narratives. The plot—while containing many convolutions—retains the essential simplicity of the epic. It is perhaps worth noting that of my suggested categories only the plots of portal-quest fantasies and intrusion fantasies seem indicated by their form.

Toohey suggests that epic, like tragedy, should contain reversal, recognition, and calamity, a structure that is instantly identifiable in the modern, three-volume quest fantasy and that often lurks in the background of the portal fantasy, as do the elements of glorification and nostalgia. Similarly, chronicle epics usually concentrate on the fortunes of a city or a region (Toohey 1–5), which in the modern fantasy may be transmuted into *the land*. The classic city epic is relatively uncommon in modern fantasy, although K. J. Parker's *Colours in the Steel* (1998; discussed in chapter 2) is precisely an account of the rise and fall-through-hubris of a city-state.

From epic, and from its descendants, the portal-quest fantasies have drawn ideas of sequenced adventures, journeys as transition, and the understanding that there is a destiny to follow.[5] But it is in the New Testament and from later Christian writings that we find the notion of a portal:

what else is a posthumous heaven (a notion almost completely absent from the Old Testament) other than the ultimate in portals? But while portal and quest fantasies have been heavily influenced by these taproots, the transition is neither seamless nor without consequence.

Most modern quest fantasies are not intended to be directly allegorical, yet they all seem to be underpinned by an assumption embedded in Bunyan's *Pilgrim's Progress* (1678): that a quest is a process, in which the object sought may or may not be a mere token of reward. The real reward is moral growth and/or admission into the kingdom, or redemption (although the latter, as in the Celestial City of *Pilgrim's Progress*, may also be the object sought). The process of the journey is then shaped by a metaphorized and moral geography—the physical delineation of what Attebery describes as a "sphere of significance" (*Tradition* 13)—that in the twentieth century mutates into the elaborate and moralized cartography of genre fantasy. The journeyman succeeds or fails to the extent he listens to those wiser or more knowledgeable than him, whether these be spiritual, fantastical, or human guides. It is of course quite possible to argue that the connection between *Pilgrim's Progress* and the portal-quest fantasy is tenuous: in *Pilgrim's Progress*, the pilgrim knows where the Celestial City is, so that it is a journey, rather than a quest; the point is simply to get there through many perils. Yet the same is true of a number of quest fantasies where the goal is to reach the city: Lewis Carroll's *Through the Looking Glass* (1871) charts a path to the crown that lies at the end of the chessboard; C. S. Lewis's *The Last Battle* (1956) concludes with a journey to the celestial city, as does—in a more mundane sense—*The Lion, the Witch and the Wardrobe* (1950), in which the children must reach Caer Paravel. Later books with the same structure include Marion Zimmer Bradley's *Thendara House* (1983), Sheri S. Tepper's *Marianne* sequence (1985–89), and Jeff Noon's *Vurt* (1993), where escape through the portal is the ultimate end of the novel, and the result disappointing. And where it is not true, we should accept that many writers believed themselves to be emulating the structures of much favored books while in reality doing quite the opposite: hundreds of "Tolkienistas"[6] have failed to notice that *The Lord of the Rings* is not a quest for power, but a journey to destroy power.[7] In any event, the very presence of maps at the front of many fantasies implies that the destination and its meaning are known.

Similarly, many of the differences between the structures laid down by Bunyan and those created in the shared world of the quest fantasy are due to a reworking of expectations and codings to produce a moral rhetoric and moral geography more acceptable to modern tastes. It is commonly assumed that the opposition to *The Wonderful Wizard of Oz* that has emanated from many Christian fundamentalists in the United States centers simply on the use of magic and of the telling of untruths. There is a partial truth in this interpretation today, but the original opposition to *The Wonderful Wizard of Oz* was directed at the highly individualistic morality of the main character. For the generation brought up on the film and modern ideas of American individualism, it is easy to miss the fact that Baum's Dorothy is *not* a nice child and that the message of the book has little to do with the communitarian values that prevailed in America's Christian heartland at the turn of the century,[8] before the individualism of the West became the dominant discourse of the United States. This is encoded in the journey Dorothy undertakes. Unlike Bunyan's Pilgrim, Dorothy's journeys do not result in her own moral growth—she herself is a representation of a new morality—but in the moral growth of those she influences. She is *grace*, a concept quite offensive to those who believe that grace can be bestowed only by the Redeemer.

What underpins all of the above is the idea of moral expectation. Fantasy, unlike science fiction, relies on a moral universe: it is less an argument with the universe than a sermon on the way things should be, a belief that the universe should yield to moral precepts. This belief is most true of the portal-quest narratives, and of the intrusion fantasies. But if intrusion fantasies are structured around punishment and the danger of transgression (see chapter 3), the portal-quest fantasies are structured around reward and the straight and narrow path. The epic and the traveler's tale are closed narratives. Each demands that we accept the interpretation of the narrator, and the interpretive position of the hero. The hero may argue with the gods, or with the rules of the utopia, but it is assumed that we will accept the paradigms of his argument. In modern fantasy this element is maintained even where, as in *A Voyage to Arcturus* by David Lindsey (1920) and *The Scar* by China Miéville (2002), we are dealing with an anti-quest.

Portal-quest fantasies have other, less visible, taproots. These others have contributed to the fantasies' rhetorical and moral structure and in particular have tended to reinforced this closed narrative. Most significant among these is the *club narrative,* a cozy discourse that emerged at the end of the nineteenth century and that profoundly shaped the portal-quest fantasy in the second half of the twentieth century.

The Club Story is simple enough to describe: it is a tale or tales recounted orally to a group of listeners foregathered in a venue safe from interruption. Its structure is normally twofold: there is the tale told, and encompassing that a frame which introduces the teller of the tale—who may well claim to have himself lived the story he's telling—along with its auditors and the venue. . . . At all levels of sophistication, the Club Story form enforces our understanding that *a tale has been told.* (Clute, *Conjunctions 39:* 421–422)

The last point, the understanding of the completeness of story, is perhaps the most crucial contribution of the club story to the portal-quest fantasy. The story made is one that is bounded by the rules of the club rhetoric. *The Canterbury Tales* is a club story, and so too, although less obviously, are *Pilgrim's Progress*, George MacDonald's *Lilith* (1895), and *The Lion the Witch and the Wardrobe*. In each of these cases, a tale is *recounted* as if it has happened in the past. Elsewhere, the club story is embedded within the frame narrative.

In the club story, the storyteller, whatever his designation, is possessed of two essential qualities: he is uninterruptible and incontestable; and the narrative as it is downloaded is essentially closed. Although not entirely relevant here, it is hard to avoid the acknowledgment that the club story has a gendered origin, and that there are consequences embedded in these foundations. The club narrative is diegetic, a denial of discourse, an assertion of a particular type of Victorian masculinity, a private place uninterrupted by the needs of domesticity or even self-care (there are always servants in the club), combined with a stature signaled by the single-voiced and impervious authority. This sense of authority matters because, as we shall see, the modern portal-quest narratives are hierarchical: some characters are presented with greater authority than others—authority that is intended, destined, or otherwise taken for granted—and this hierarchy is frequently encoded in speech patterns and the choice of direct or indirect speech. Although a tenuous connection, the tendency of portal-quest fantasies to ignore the personal needs of the protagonists may be less a mere accident of poor writing, than a direct consequence of the link with this mode of storytelling. As their personal needs will be ignored, so too will be the needs of characterization. What matters is that there be no chinks in the story entire. Discussing Joseph Conrad's "Heart of Darkness" (1899), John Clute has written:

Like any Club Story, "Heart of Darkness" is both a story and a device to mandate its reception. The impurity of this is obvious—what we're describing here is in a sense a form of reportage—and may help account. It may be the "impurity" of this element of reportage at the heart of the Club Story form that accounts for the fact that no literary theorist has ever mentioned it. Critics of the fantastic, dealing as they do with a set of genres intensely sensitive to the world, should have no such compunction. (*Conjunctions 39*: 422–423)

As in the true club story, it is the *unquestionable purity* of the tale that holds together the shape of the portal-quest narrative. In the club narrative, the ability to convince and to hold the floor is the sign of success, but the risk is always that the whole will not be sustained. In order to sustain it, the impurity and unreliability to which Clute alludes must be consistently denied and the authority and reliability of the narrator must be asserted. Either the story is accepted in its entirety, or it is entirely vulnerable; there is no room for the delicacies of interpretation. This structure and its attendant denial has a significant effect on the language of the portal-quest fantasy: in order to convince, to avoid too close analysis, the portal and quest fantasies attempt to convince through the accumulation of detail.

Fantasyland is constructed, in part, through the insistence on a received truth. This received truth is embodied in didacticism and elaboration. While much information about the world is culled from what the protagonist can *see* (with a consequent denial of polysemic interpretation), history or analysis is often provided by the storyteller who is drawn in the role of sage, magician, or guide. While this casting apparently opens up the text, in fact it seeks to close it down further by denying not only reader interpretation, but also that of the hero/protagonist. This may be one reason why the hero in the quest fantasy is more often an actant than an actor, provided with attributes rather than character precisely to compensate for the static nature of his role.

In the quest and portal fantasy much of the narrative is delivered in this club-story mode among a group of friends isolated in a context in which they will not be interrupted. Although "the journey" is a recognized function-trope in portal-quest fantasies, it is usually interpreted as a metaphor for a coming of age—it provides a space for the protagonists to grow up. But "the journey" also serves to divorce the protagonists from the world, and place them in a context in which they cannot question the primary narration because there is no evidence against which they can test the veracity of their source. Diana Wynne Jones manipulates this path in *The Crown of Dalemark* (1993): the quest journey is begun precisely to avoid exposing an imposter. This approach, however, is not usual. More commonly, the journey is where information is discovered, interpreted, and disseminated, safe from the awkward questions the outside world might provoke. The resemblance to the isolation inflicted on Kate in *The Taming of the Shrew* is not coincidental. In *The Lord of the Rings*, after Gandalf 's "death," the questors are even more willing to follow his interpretation of the adventure. Jones, again, makes the connection explicit in another Dalemark tale, the short story "The True State of Affairs" (1995), in which a woman traverses a portal only to find herself seized as a spy and locked in a tower. She can build a picture of the world she is in only by what she is allowed to know. The process of the quest or portal fantasy works, in one way or another, to construct an element of isolation and a focus on "the club." In contrast, and as I shall demonstrate, the intrusion fantasy is structured to encourage the protagonist to break out of the monologue.

There are almost always two clearly identifiable narrators in the portal-quest fantasy: the narrator of the microcosm (the world within a world) that we call the point of view character; and the narrator of the macrocosm, she who "stories" the world for us, making sense of it through the downloaded histories so common to this form of fantasy, or in the fragments of prophecy she leaks to us throughout the course of the text. Usually, but not always, this person is the implied narrator.

Let us consider first that point of view or diegetic character, for it is she who conditions our relationship to the fantasy world. She exemplifies the Bakhtinian insight that the narrator-focalizer dispenses the authoritative ideology. One of the defining features of the portal-quest fantasy is that we ride with the point of view character who describes fantasyland and the adventure to the reader, as if we are both with her and yet external to the fantasy world. What she sees, we see, so that the world is unrolled to us in front of her eyes, and through her analysis of the scene. One result is that the world is flattened thereby into a travelogue, a series of descriptions made possible by the protagonists' unfamiliarity with it. Terry Brooks's *The Sword of Shannara* (1977), a text to which I shall be referring frequently in this chapter because of the degree to which it is *the* generic quest fantasy, illustrates the point neatly. At the beginning of the novel, Flick, one of the two heroes, is a stranger in his own land. He should be so familiar with the area that all is taken for granted but instead: "the young man noticed immediately the unusual stillness that seemed to have captivated the entire valley this evening." Immediately the world is new to both him and us, even though it is new only in terms of what he is accustomed to. Such defamiliarization is necessary in order to justify the explanation of the world to the reader, and prepares us for the process of familiarization that takes place throughout the novel.

This extract characterizes the mode of engagement within the portal-quest fantasy: the hero *moves through* the action and the world stage, embedding an assumption of unchangingness on the part of the indigenes. This kind of fantasy is essentially imperialist: only the hero is capable of change; fantasyland is orientalized into the "unchanging past." This rejection of change is particularly noticeable in David Eddings's *The Belgariad* (1982–84), where we meet one culture dedicated to preserving the past (the faux-medievalist Arends) and one whose idea of preparing for the future is very much rooted in preservation (the Rivans). The Rivans have spent the previous centuries preserving their culture *precisely* for the appearance of our protagonist. This allows the protagonist not merely to insist upon his interpretation as he relays it to us, but to insist that it will always be valid. In this context, Garion's confusion ensures that we accept his realizations unquestioningly. To counteract such blind acceptance one might expect that a fantasy would work by making the *unfamiliar* strange, and we shall see just this effect in George MacDonald and David Lindsay's work. More commonly, however, the quest fantasy works by familiarization (Scholes 84), creating a world through the layering of detail, and making that detail comprehensible. Given the need for comprehensibility, the only way to continually create the sense of wonder needed by the portal and quest fantasy is to embroider continually, to prevent the accretion of comfort. When taken to excess we see the likes of the Harry Potter novels in which almost all of the imaginative material is in the world-building (the adventures themselves are game sequences and rather derivative)—or, as Colin Manlove has pointed out, the work of Lord Dunsany, of whose descriptive passages he writes, "Dunsany knows he is into a good thing here . . . and goes on for three more pages making it rather too much of a good thing" (*Impulse* 135). Michael Rifaterre describes this device as *diegetic overkill,* in which the representation of ostensibly insignificant details—in the case of the texts I'm discussing it could be jumping frog chocolates, lembas bread, or clothes that change color[9]—becomes a feature of realism (29–30).

This mode mediates between us and the protagonist. In seeing what he narrates to us, we are prevented from seeing *him.* The solution adopted by most writers in this genre—although not, interestingly, by Tolkien—is the *reverie*, a form of mimetic excess (Rifaterre 29–30). Bakhtin calls this form "the continuous hidden polemic or hidden dialogue with some other person on the theme of himself," but reverie is easier in the long term (207). The reverie is that moment when the protagonist (or on occasion another character) meditates on his own character, usually in terms of a flashback, to achieve a "profound dialogic and polemical nature of self-awareness and self-affirmation" (207). This meditation should not be confused with a moment of memory, which tends to focus on the emotion felt, rather than the story (McCabe and Peterson 165). What characterizes these reveries is that they are fully narrativized: pages 2–4 of Mindy Klasky's *The Glasswright's Apprentice* (2000), for example, tell us of the heroine's entry into the guild and the conditions pertaining to that place. Later, Rani worries about a theft she has committed:

> The theft made Rani nervous—she had been hired to clean the captain's quarters and she would be the most likely suspect when the soldier discovered his loss. She had become enough of a fixture in the Soldiers' Quarter that any of the girls who consorted with the guards would know to find her in Garadolo's lair. . . .
>
> Even now, she looked back to her life as an apprentice with blinding fondness. She'd been so lucky then, so privileged that her most difficult task had been scrubbing a whitewashed table. (184–185)

What should be already known to us, the context of the world, is delivered as memory, and more specifically, as story.[10] Because we cannot stand outside the narrative, the "omniscient narrator" is compromised: it is able to tell us only what Rani knows. We both see into her mind but are not, as in the first-person narrative, inside her head. The "omniscient narrator" limits our vision while asserting that we have privileged insight.

Occasionally these reveries are expressed as mutual revelation, a device Deborah Tannen suggests in real life is intended to show rapport: "By this strategy, the speaker expects his or her statement of personal experience to elicit a similar statement from the other." Unfortunately, authors rarely seem to remember that the "effectiveness of this device is dependent upon the sharedness of the system" (79). The single direction of information works instead to indicate the status-within-the-story of the speaker.

To steal yet again Clute's idea of "making storyable," I note that these reveries make storyable character and characteristics. Indeed, reverie and self-contemplation, far from creating depth, break the sense of immersion in a society, and are fundamentally antithetical to either character development or an immersive structure. It is a false mimesis that reminds us that we are in a narrated text and that *the protagonist's version must be true.* To doubt the validity of the reverie would be to destroy the impermeable nature of the club discourse: either the reverie is "true" or the entire structure collapses. Such is the case even where, as in Tad Williams's

The Dragonbone Chair (1989), the reverie that describes the protagonist is actually that of another person; it is Rachel (31–38) who—with improbable detail—remembers Simon's childhood for us. On the other hand, Robin Hobb, in the opening pages of *The Farseer: Assassin's Apprentice* (1996), acknowledges the persistent doubts: "on that day they [memories] suddenly begin, with a brightness and detail that overwhelms me. Sometimes it seems too complete and I wonder if it is truly mine. Am I recalling it from my own mind, or from dozens of retellings by legions of kitchen maids and ranks of scullions and herds of stables boys as they explained my presence to each other" (2).

Memory does not have to be delivered this way. Lloyd Alexander gets to the heart of the matter in *The Black Cauldron* (1965), a quest fantasy that is also a rite of passage novel, but is *not* a portal fantasy inasmuch as Taran is always familiar with his world. When Taran tries to buy the cauldron from Orddu, Orwen, and Orgoch in the marshes of Morva, one suggested price is a warm summer's day. Memory here is sense and feeling, yet this suggestion and its alternative—that they take one of his memories of Eillonwy—tell us much more about Taran than does a recounting of his childhood. Similarly, Tad Williams does not need to have his hero Simon think about being curious; his actions tells us that he is. Simon "could never understand how rooms that seemed as small as the doctor's did from outside—he had looked down on them from the bailey walls and paced the distance in the courtyard—how they could have such long corridors" (*The Dragonbone Chair* 14). At this point Simon is in the world in which he grew up, and Williams demonstrates neatly that in this—pre-quest—world he is fully immersed.

The reverie is a commodification of memory: one aspect of this ritualization of memory is that it reduces characters to that which can be described in terms essentially photographic. Stephen R. Donaldson, in *Lord Foul's Bane* (1977), provides us with a good example: "But where Lena was fresh and slim of line, full of unbroken newness, Atiaran appeared complex, almost self contradictory" (51). This kind of description tells us more than we can possibly know *or that the observing character* can possibly know. There are two aspects to this formulation. To begin with, the narrative structure of the portal-quest fantasy, in which we move through the map, posits many characters as mere signposts. In this context we do not have time to truly learn about people, any more than we would "learn" about the tree we passed. The second, and related, aspect is that we are therefore forced to rely on intuition. The portal-quest fantasy is thus often the last resting place of physiognomy, a tradition the sf writer

Jeffrey Ford has mocked brilliantly in *The Physiognomy* (1997). This tradition is usually discussed in terms of race and fantasy, but the "racing" of heroes and villains is in part a consequence of a rhetoric that posits insight in terms of visual perception.

The narrativization of memory also affects the description of action. It is not action that is of interest but response; action has to be "seen" by the protagonist and the protagonist cannot see "his" own physical movements. In this form, expression and feeling cannot be interpreted; they must be described, pinned down for the reader. They must also maintain primacy in the narrative drive of the novel. In this mode of fantasy, action is there to carry emotive weight, so that fighting is "valiant" (see Brooks again) rather than "wild" (see Howard's *Conan the Barbarian*). This emphasis on emotion is a distinct shift from, for example, the worlds of Conan the barbarian. The shift is from an externalized discourse of action—what we usually mean when we refer to the omniscient narrator—to the internalized discourse. Even the moment of recognition can be shaped by this demand. Toward the end of *Lord Foul's Bane*, Thomas Covenant learns some of what was intended for him, but it is framed not as action, but as self-regard: "Then, with a sickening vertiginous twist of insight, he caught a glimpse of Lord Foul's plan for him, glimpsed what the despiser was doing to him. Here was the killing blow which had lain concealed behind all the machinations, all the subterfuge" (353).

This raises the question as to whether this internal narrative is *intended* to parallel the external narrative of exploration and observation. Can one have an internal quest that does not require the protagonist to move through a physical and internal landscape? There are very few portal fantasies that are not succeeded by journeys.[11] The implication of what I have set out above is that the journey through the mind, while not absolutely necessary to the format, is one way that has emerged to handle the need to create closed and reliable characters—reliable only in the sense that we must trust their own assessment of themselves in order for the veracity of the story to hold. Thomas Covenant is a twist, not an exception to the rule. His misinterpretation of his role, his refusal to accept responsibility, is the surety of his character's narration. We believe him because Doubting Thomas is, in the final analysis, the most reliable witness—a double bluff.

This discourse and the insistence on the narrative and descriptive competence of the protagonist—even when we are told that they do not understand what is happening—thins the complexity of the world and makes of it a poorly painted stage set. The portal-quest fantasy by its very nature needs to deny the possibility of a polysemic discourse in order to validate the "quest." There can be only one understanding of the world: an understanding that validates the quest. And yes, that is recursive, a point I shall discuss further on.

There are some exceptions: the original grail stories offer polysemic narratives and question the reality, desirability, and possibility of "goal," as do some modern quest fantasies (which I shall discuss at the end of the chapter). More generally, however, this issue is extended into the world-building of fantasyland. Nonspecific landscape is unrolled like a carpet in front of the character. This landscape even embraces the contrived design of Romantic landscape painting.[12] Note this comment from Raymond J. O'Brien: "Viewers, whether river travellers or gallery-goers, were commonly impressed with the importance of foreground. In landscapes, the foreground—although not always available to steamboat passengers—was the means by which the observer entered the scene (e.g., a path, a stream or falls, a river road, a railroad track, a cleft in the rocks). And while the middle ground contained the subject matter or object (mountain, river, or townscape), a distant background was also imperative to create a hazy, far-away panoramic effect" (171). The entrant into the portal-quest fantasy is precisely this kind of tourist—and as an aside, in so many they are tourists in an American landscape painting, moving through and into the grandeur of the landscapes—"Imagining forth vastness" (R. Wilson 5). In the British equivalent the viewer is more likely positioned gazing at a vista (Wilton).[13] But in the absence of real depth, history, religion, and politics must receive a similar treatment. The difficulty is balancing the requirement that such matters *must always have been there* with the ignorance of the protagonist.

To some extent, almost all portal and quest fantasies use the figure of a guide to download information into the text. Here is where the classic portal fantasy has an advantage, in that those traveling through a declared portal are expected to be ignorant: it is perfectly plausible for the dwarf to fill in the children about the past few hundred years of Narnian history in *Prince Caspian* (1951). But in many quest fantasies, the portal is merely a move from the familiar village to the unfamiliar world. An impromptu civics class always seems unnatural. Most people, however ignorant, know a little about most matters, enough to interrupt, to argue, to disturb the narrative. Yet these narratives, including the one described in *Prince Caspian*, are distinctive because they are delivered entirely in the authoritarian mode. These narratives are uninterruptible, unquestionable, and delivered absolutely in the mode of the club discourse: the travelers group around the narrator and listen to his (less commonly her) description of great events or political structures. When the narratives are delivered by a guide figure, the result is that the guide usurps the narrator-focalizer role that might usually be supposed to belong to the protagonist (Rimmon-Kenan 83).

This form of fantasy embodies a denial of what history *is*. In the quest and portal fantasies, history is inarguable, it is "the past." In making the past "storyable," the rhetorical demands of the portal-quest fantasy deny the notion of "history as argument" which is pervasive among modern historians. The structure becomes ideological as portal-quest fantasies reconstruct history in the mode of the Scholastics,[14] and recruit cartography to provide a fixed narrative, in a palpable failure to understand the fictive and imaginative nature of the discipline of history.

Tolkien set the trend for maps and prehistory, establishing a pattern for the quest narrative in which the portal is not encoded solely in the travelogue discovery of what lies ahead, but in the insistence that there is past and place *behind*, and that what lies behind must be thoroughly known and unquestioned before the journey begins. As Diana Wynne Jones has pointed out, maps are a substitute for place, and an indication that we have to travel; they also, however, fix the interpretation of a landscape. Maps are no more geography than chronology and legend are history, but in portal-quest fantasies, they complete the denial of discourse.

Since the late 1970s, genre fantasy has frequently been signaled by these two devices: the map—which, as Diana Wynne Jones sarcastically observed, lists *everywhere* we will be visiting (*Guide* 10)—and the fixed and narrated past. Far too many post-Tolkien portal-quest fantasies begin with a download of legend. Their very anonymity creates the status that the closed club narrative requires. Occasionally, they are signed by a legendary figure, or by "a historian," but the presentation of these extracts is rarely placed against other, disputatious sources. Authors of these fantasies write as if Mark Twain had never pointed out the danger of trusting the presentable document. Jones puts it memorably:

> Scrolls are important sources of information about either HISTORY or MAGIC, and are only to be found jealously guarded in a MONASTERY or TEMPLE. You will usually have to steal your copy. Against this inconvenience is the highly useful fact that the Information in the Scroll will be wholly correct. There is, for some reason, no such thing as a lying, mistaken or inaccurate Scroll. (*Guide* 166)

See also her entry for PROPHECY (148–149). The consequence is that the found document is in the chair relating the club story; either all of it is correct, or none of it is. We can no longer debate history, in the sense of interpretation, analysis, discovery; we can only relate the past. This scholasticism permits only macronarratives: the past in these books is always what has been recorded about the greats, and it has always been recorded *somewhere.*

Yet concomitant with this is a reverence for *the* book, even while seeing books as alien artifacts to be decoded. This returns us once more to Bunyan and to generations of evangelicals for whom the Bible was not an ethical discussion but a book of riddles and challenges (Keeble xxiii).

Things that seem to be hid in words obscure,
Do but the Godly mind the more allure;
To Study what those Sayings should contain,
That speak to us in such a Cloudy strain.
(*Pilgrim's Progress*, 130)

This verse might come straight from the prologue of a modern fantasy. Susan Cooper's *The Dark is Rising* (1965–77) sequence is structured around rhymes to be deconstructed; *The Belgariad* has its Codex capable of predicting the coming of the Rivan King; Jeff Noon's feathers in *Vurt* are encoded fantasy-game riddles that offer a way out into otherworld. Each, like *Pilgrim's Progress*, constructs *the text* as a portal into a promised world. Running alongside this is an ideology of heroism that denies current authority in favor of an omnipresent power, yet prizes specifically the ability of the common man to decipher the code that will lead one through the gate. External means of testing veracity are closed off, and we are further sealed into the story.

As Keeble describes it: "The regenerate are distinguished from the unregenerate not by any exceptional abilities or virtue but by their faith: they keep on going" (xvii). Such describes both the regenerate Christian and the predestined hero in modern quests (and crops up most in Philip Pullman's *His Dark Materials* sequence [1995–2001]). Keeble points out: "The saint only gains final assurance of perseverance when he has persevered" (xix). Similarly evident in many modern portal-quest fantasies is the Puritan belief that "it is by playing a full part in this world that salvation is won" (xiii). Yet perseverance is defined in part by the ability to stay on the straight and narrow path, to follow the words of prophecy and the delivered interpretation—in effect, for the hero to maintain his own position-as-reader.

The idea is picked up in a number of fantasies, but perhaps most explicitly at the end of Lloyd Alexander's *The High King* (1968), where Taran is informed that he was only ever a collection of "ifs." In fantasy sequences such as *The Belgariad*, *Assassin's Apprentice* and its sequels, *The Chronicles of Thomas Covenant*, and many others, there is an overwhelming sense of this predictive narrative shaping the text, of the book of riddle interpreted only in the light of the successful conclusion. *Lud-in-the-Mist* (1926), which I shall otherwise be considering predominantly as an immersive fantasy, could be read as a reply to *Pilgrim's Progress*—and to the classic portal fantasy, as will subsequently emerge, because of its message accept what *is* and contextualize your evidence; do not rely on only one source. Even anti-quest fantasies such as *The Scar* seem able only to fight against this structure; with their dead ends and celestial cities rejected, they cannot construct anything else.

The assumptions that "the past" is unarguable, that it just *is*, and that "knowledge" is to be rediscovered rather than generated, has narrative consequences. Binabik, the historian-mage of Tad Williams's *Dragonbone Chair* (1988), assumes that in order to *learn* anything, he must return to the archives for research. Robin Hobb's *Assassin* sequence is structured within the writing of a history that depends for its backstory on material found in other, written histories. Each chapter begins with a memoir not dissimilar to the Venerable Bede's history: recollection and gossip masquerading as an accurate description of the past. The argument is circular, but nonetheless valid; yet the consequence for the author is that in order to preserve this sense, any history narrated must be done so in an authoritative fashion. The moment one introduces argument, one also introduces research and experimentation: portal-quest fantasies are full of learned people, who have read many books. Knowledge is fixed and it is *recursive*, and in this it demonstrates the peculiar and specific Christian heritage of the modern portal-quest fantasy. As Northrop Frye wrote, "How do we know that the Gospel story is true? Because it confirms the prophecies of the Old Testament. But how do we know that the Old Testament prophecies are true? Because they are confirmed by the Gospel story. Evidence, so called, is bounced back and forth between the testaments like a tennis ball" (*Code* 78). This circularity creates a reductiveness that utterly undermines any real notion of learning in the portal fantasy and has led me to muse on what a truly *Jewish* fantasy—with all the argument endemic to my religion—might look like. Peter David's *Sir Apropos of Nothing* (2001), whose sidekick refuses his predestined role, who spends much of the time raging at fate, and who frequently finds his achievements unapplauded, is one candidate.

But to get back on track, this one element, the insistence of the fixedness of history and of learning, divides quest fantasy from immersive fantasy.

Miéville's *Perdido Street Station* (2000) can make room for the experimental method (as, interestingly, can the later and more immersive Discworld novels) but *The Scar*, also by Miéville, must send people looking for a lost book and a lost scientist. Very occasionally, there is an understanding displayed that history cannot be written and preserved with fixative. Delia Sherman and Ellen Kushner's *The Fall of the Kings* (2002) is a book about the writing of history, whose protagonist is a scholar who wishes to return to the documents, to reconstruct history from source materials, and to argue with the belief of a fixed past, a found narrative. But the tale betrays the reader and the protagonist: at the end, history is again "found," the past revealed to us through dreams and through magic, rendering the research pointless and restoring "the past" to its rightful place above mere history. The historian's craft is swapped for the club-story narrative, fully hermetic.

The nature of the club story is that it valorizes the control of the narrator. This one factor may help to explain why, although many quest fantasies claim to be about a remaking of the world, few can be considered genuine instauration fantasies. A contributing factor is the portal-quest fantasies' denial of argument with the universe. It is a truism that fiction is about conflict, but in the portal-quest fantasies the possibilities for such conflict are limited by the ideological narrative that posits the world, as painted, as *true*. Consequently, it is this closed narrative that restricts the plot possibilities for most quest and portal novels. If multiple interpretations are to be denied, if the narrative is to be hermetic, then the novel becomes locked in the patterns that Clute observed in the full fantasy: wrongness, thinning, recognition, and healing/return (defined in Clute and Grant's *Encyclopedia of Fantasy*.) Such patterns, rather than being a coincident archetype, become fundamental to the structure. The genre accrues formalisms, and authors negotiate with these forms; one aspect of this negotiation is experimenting with which positions and rhetorics best familiarize (or defamiliarize) the reader with the fantastic.

Given the huge number of books written in this category, the books discussed below have been selected according to their historical significance, to their status as archetypes. (They are also the consequence of a trawl among the recommendations of a number of readers, to ensure that the choices presented here would not be entirely self-justifying.) While Tolkien and Lewis may have provided the archetypes of modern fantasy, the taproots of the genre are rather different. The emergence of a rhetoric to accompany this position can be traced to the earliest of the portal fantasies. Therefore, if we are to consider the development of the rhetorical styles and grammar of this mode of fantasy, we should begin by considering the condition of portal and quest fantasy before Tolkien and Lewis. The best known are George MacDonald's *Lilith* (1895), Lewis Carroll's *Alice's Adventures in Wonderland* (1865), L. Frank Baum's *The Wonderful Wizard of Oz* (1900), and David Lindsay's *A Voyage to Arcturus* (1920). When we lay these alongside one another, and in the company of John Bunyan's *Pilgrim's Progress*—a book that has had an immense if unconscious influence on the structure of quest fantasies and that shows many of the traits that later emerge of markers of this particular subgenre—certain patterns emerge.

Early Quest and Portal Fantasies

For Bunyan, the fantastic was that which was made up, rather than that which was supernatural, and it is in this context that we need to consider the dream sequences that provide the contextual structure of *Pilgrim's Progress*. In the modern fantasy, the dream sequence is conventionally seen as a distancing from the fantastic, a means of denying belief. When taken at face value in a text—such as *Alice's Adventures in Wonderland*—it has very specific consequences for the grammar of the fantastic. A consideration of *Pilgrim's Progress*, however, suggests that, in its religious context, dream as an entryway to the fantastic functioned rather differently.

Although Bunyan felt compelled to use dreaming to contextualize his allegory (perhaps because of the Puritan suspicion of fiction), that dream is closer to a vision of the prophetic than to the modern idea of the dream as unreal. It brings the afterlife *closer*, making the consequences of sin manifest. Bunyan's Pilgrim comes to him in a dream because the story is more than allegory; it is a spiritual gift, an aspect of visionary fancy.

Yet within *Pilgrim's Progress*, the dream structure is under attack from the needs of the narrative. The "Dream" as vision is a reminder of the reality of heaven; as *dream* it deprives us of completeness. While Bunyan avoids much of the exposition of landscape and personnel that will mark the portal fantasy and prevents full immersion in the fantastic, the repeated lines "and in the Dream" serve the same purpose, to distance the reader and to remind us that we are mere *external* observers of Christian's quest, not part of his company. The tale is being narrated to us. At other times, our immersed participation is demanded as a spiritual exercise. The effect on the tone of the fantasy is to create an unevenness, an alternation of description and immersion, of distancing and familiarity. At times we walk beside Christian, at other times we observe him from afar. But while in a dream we may be ineffectual, there is nonetheless the sense that we are at the center of the dream.

The vision is of elsewhere; it presumes that the frame world (our world) is already thinned, and provides the moment of rupture in which elsewhere becomes here. In *Pilgrim's Progress* it is the moment of recognition, where the man becomes Christian "(for that was his name)"; we know that we are now fully in the tale (10). The one significant difference in the second part of *Pilgrim's Progress* (which narrates the tale of Christiana's search for her husband, and for God through him) is that the dream becomes a matter of doubt. Although it is couched as a dream at the beginning of the act, it is also phrased as "Travels into those Parts" (143). An ambiguity creeps into the text, an ambiguity remade at the close, "Shall it be my Lot to go that way again, I may give those that desire it, an Account of what I here am silent about." For Bunyan, it might have been a sign to the reader that he was "fantasizing" in the second book, making up what came to him as divine inspiration in the first. To secular eyes, however, the narrative has become a greater part of reality because the power of vision is no longer reliable—or has, perhaps, become more metaphorical. The challenge to future fantasists is to make that vision more real, and they do so by making the portal of dream into a material portal of wood and wardrobe.[15] What proves less easy is to move beyond the positioning of reader as recipient of the tale told.

Bunyan's own insistence that *Pilgrim's Progress* is allegory reinforces the problem. Attebery argues that allegory "continually points beyond itself to the moral or metaphysical truths under examination" (*Tradition* 180). But in order to do this, Bunyan must strain his narrative structure. We cannot merely follow Christian, because that would be to risk that we do not understand the message. Instead both the omniprescient narrator (by lapsing out of the dream sequence) and Christian (in a pattern of telling and retelling as he meets each signpost character) guide our interpretation of the quest. In this narrative, it is the telling thereof, the rethinking of it, that is significant, rather than the adventure itself. Some of this rethinking remains in *The Lord of the Rings*: Bilbo's writing of his and Frodo's story will have resonance; Pippin and Merry will relate their tales to Treebeard, who will become part of the narrative and will be convinced. This element remains only hesitantly in the modern tradition, expressed, as we shall see, within the club story. The point is, the fantasy is made fantasy in part by *being related*.

In the periodic absences of the omniscient narrator, the text proceeds as a Socratic dialogue. Although this dialogue is to some extent feigned—Christian almost always has the correct answers, and the book he carries "was made by him that cannot lie" (11)—in the conversation between him and Faithful, and later Hopeful (104 and 205), we proceed to the Truth of the quest through a narrative more open than those of many modern fantasies. The structure, when between equals, is of question and answer, each drawing out the other's spiritual journey, using the questions to exhort as well as to query. However, when it is not between equals, Bunyan signals status through direct and indirect speech, by the abrupt changes in tone, from the mimetic, personal address of Christian, to the diegesis of reported reactions of the crowds or opposition. Form and Hypocrisie, "made him but little answer; only bid him look to himself" (33). Repeatedly, speech is given to that person who holds the higher countenance, while the one who is to listen, or learn, is described and distanced. The diegetic mode is used to create both status and differing levels of reality. This rule holds true even of Christian, who is reduced to a reaction shot in his conversation with Evangelist:

> *Evan.* Then, said *Evangelist*, How hath it fared with you, my friends, since the time of our last parting? *What* have you met with, and *how* have you behaved your selves?
>
> Chr. *Then* Christian, *and* Faithful, *told him of all things that had happened to them in the way; and* how, *and with what difficulty they had arrived to the right place.* (71)

The entire description of Vanity Fair, because it concerns those who are inferior and not in conversation with Christian and Faithful, is told in this diegetic mode so as to happen, in effect, offstage, to be less real. We have been evicted from our spectator seats. Less consistently, we frequently see the same technique in modern fantasy, most recently in Philip Pullman's *Northern Lights* [*The Golden Compass*] (1995), which drops into reported speech when the point is to communicate interpretation rather than events (see chapter 11, "Armour"). It reminds us again that this is a tale being *told.*

Pilgrim's Progress's omniscient narrator is ultimately a ruse. The point of view *is* Christian's: we experience only Christian's doubt, are told that of Faithful. But once the narrator admits that this is allegory, he hastens to explain things to us, not through Christian's eyes, but through his own: "I saw then that they went on their way to a pleasant River, which *David the King* called *The River of God*; but John, *The River of the water of life*" (90). Omniscience is asserted, and with it the fantasy is ruptured: omniscience as a vehicle for *explanation*, proves hostile to the portal-quest fantasy.

Although there are two centuries between Bunyan and George MacDonald, *Lilith* (1895) is actually less certain in its form. Although a portal fantasy, the portal structure of *Lilith* is unsupported by the narrative tone. An example of a portal novel written before the conventions of the form were settled, in its experimentation with register and with focalization, *Lilith* reveals patterns we can identify in its successors.

Lilith repeatedly veers between the Gothic style, as commonly found in the intrusion fantasy or the liminal fantasy, and the detailed creation and description of landscape and people that is more common to the portal fantasy. The reader is forced into a variety of positionings vis-à-vis the text and the protagonist. The use of the Gothic, of estrangement and intrusion in the frame-world sections of *Lilith*, is disruptive to the acceptance of the otherworld. It makes strange the familiar, denying the increasing comfort usually found as we proceed through the tale, and runs contrary to the balance that is normally associated with the portal fantasy. The otherworld of the portal fantasy relies on the contrast with the frame world, on the world from which we begin the adventure, an understanding manipulated by authors such as Diana Wynne Jones and Barbara Hambly.[16] Instead MacDonald makes the present world strange.

We begin *Lilith* in an environment that is unfamiliar to us but should be familiar to the protagonist: his family home. We should be in a fully immersed, taken-for-granted setting that we decode from the cues and sensibilities of the protagonist. Instead, the setting is made strange by a process of deliberate defamiliarization in which the protagonist, to bring us into his tale, describes in detail the library that is at the heart of his story, leaving vague the conformations of the house itself. It becomes an edifice, more complex in its interior than its facade. Nothing is taken for granted, and the result of this excessive detail, as in a medieval painting, is a distortion of perspective that pushes us outside the fantastic realm, making of us audience.

In the introductory sections of the book, the disruption is portrayed initially as nebulous. It is a sense, a feeling: "The garret at the top of it pervaded the whole house! It sat upon it, threatening to crush me out of it! The brooding brain of the building, it was full of mysterious dwellers, one or other of whom might any moment appear in the library where I sat!" (17). The alliteration, the emphasis on movement, on the activity of the presence, combine to create a sense of the protagonist under attack.

This sense is increased by his focus on his own reactions: "The mere words, however, woke in me feelings which to describe was, from their strangeness, impossible" (18). Elsewhere in the novel, when the focus becomes exploration, the role of emotion is diminished; here, however, the emphasis is on regaining control of the present world. The fantastic is signaled by a loss of that control rather than, as in the classic portal fantasy and in later sections of the text, the movement through the fantastic.

If *Lilith* contained but a single portal, the effect of this might be minimal: once one had left the frame world, the rhetoric of the portal fantasy would take over and the sense that the frame world was itself a fantastic place might recede. But *Lilith* is multiply portalled, so that we are shuttled between fantastical worlds narrated in different modes. The second chapter offers an example of this in the exploratory, complex neorealism—the making real through intense description of the landscape—of the portal fantasy in which the protagonist describes his landscape, a wood of tall, slender pine trees: "I spied before me something with a shine, standing between two of the stems. It had no colour, but was like the translucent trembling of the hot air that rises, in a radiant summer noon, from the sun-baked ground, vibrant like the smitten chords of a musical instrument" (16).

Then, and almost immediately, the protagonist is rejected, thrown back into his own world, a world no longer impervious to the fantastic, but penetrated and made unsafe by its presence: "Terror seized me, and I fled. Outside the chamber the wide garret spaces had an *uncanny* look. They seemed to have long been waiting for something; it had come, and they were waiting again! A shudder went through me on the winding stair: the house had become strange to me!" (16–17). The rendering of the frame world as uncanny, means that MacDonald must struggle harder to make his other world fantastical. He cannot rely on the contrast of realism and fantasy.

Because the uncanny is a mode focused on emotion—the fantasy as expressed experience—the first person is a logical choice of focalization. In *Lilith* (particularly prior to the revelation that the raven is in fact Adam) the first person is deployed to confuse and to place a barrier between ourselves and the fantasy world. The portal-quest genre as it develops will demand the illusion that the protagonist ride with the reader by his side, decode and understand the fantasy world in which they exist. But the spiral structure of *Lilith*, its multiple portals and frequent "return to start," and its insistence on the creation of the fantastic in terms of emotional response, makes the focalization much clearer: we are forced to acknowledge that we are mere recipients of the tale.

What we are privy to is recorded emotion: we can feel only what Vane *says* he feels. This is first person *narrated.* To make an obvious point, it cannot be clear whether this is a reliable or unreliable narration. On the one hand, what is the point of an unreliable narrator? On the other, it is made clear that Vane *does not understand* and that he himself cannot express everything he sees and is aware of this. The raven assures Vane—duplicitously—that he can give no guidance because "you and I use the same words with different meanings. We are often unable to tell people what they *need* to know, because they *want* to know something else, and would therefore only misunderstand what we said" (58–59). This concept, unsurprisingly, structures the novel, but it does so by convincing us of the incompetence of the narrator who cannot understand and therefore must trust, and of the incomprehensibility of the world—a notion at fundamental variance to the ideology of any text of exploration. At the conclusion of *Lilith,* we really know very little more of this fantasy world than we did at the start.

The outright statement of confusion and meaninglessness fractures the creation of the otherworld and prevents the accretion of familiarity associated with the modern portal fantasy. Vane is continually subjected to riddles and told that his judgment is valueless.[17] The process of decoding is denied: "it involves a constant struggle to say what cannot be said with even an approach to precision, the things recorded being, in their nature and in that of the creatures concerned in them, so inexpressibly different from any possible events of this economy, that I can present them only by giving, in the forms and language of life in this world, the modes in which they affected me—not the things themselves, but the feelings they woke in me. Even this much, however, I do with a continuous and abiding sense of failure" (60–61).

The emphasis is on the emotional response. Instead of mimesis, we receive allusion. Modern portal fantasies rely on the false belief that the reader interprets the world, but here MacDonald denies this: we cannot see what our narrator sees. We can only truly understand the world either through simile (all is described in likenesses, for example, "a head as big as a polar bear"), or in its effect upon him ("I dared not turn my eyes from them"; "I strove to keep my heart above the waters of fear" [64]), or through his reactions. The emphasis in this book is less on what passes or is passed through, but on how the protagonist *feels* about these movements. There are exceptions but they are oddly inserted into metastories (such as Vane's encounters with the skeletons), moments when Vane watches an event and tells it, not as part of his experience, but almost as a fireside tale.[18]

In later portal-quest fantasies, although the guide may be mysterious, he is usually comforting, offering guidance and wisdom. But in the first part of *Lilith*, Mr. Raven offers not guidance but disquiet and disorientation. He is an intruding alien who challenges the reality of the world. When he digs for a worm and it turns to a butterfly, he challenges what is and where is the fantastical. He is the alien to be met and decoded, to be revealed as Adam in the last section of the book. This unmasking is his undoing; he ceases to perform as a portal for dissonance and disruption from the moment that his identity becomes clear. The shift from disrupter to unreliable guide takes place from the moment that Vane decides to place his trust in Mr. Raven, to accept that it is Mr. Raven, not Vane, who is capable of judging his character growth (24–25). The issue of trust is crucial to the construction of the portal-quest fantasy; it is this that leads us into the closed, unquestioning narrative. *Lilith* enfolds us doubly into this closed narrative.

Once trust is established (around chapter 7), the rhetorical structures of *Lilith* shift from the description of nebulous fears, sensations, and emotions to the creation of a fantastical landscape, and an exploration of its geography. This landscape is constructed of people, as well as places, or moralities as well as landmarks. Mr. Raven's wife is part of this construction: "It was as if the splendour of her eyes had grown too much for them to hold, and, sinking into her countenance, made it flash with a loveliness like that of Beatrice in the white rose of the redeemed" (40). But the landscape remains constructed of likeness, often coined in the negative: the moon "is not like yours" (44); "Fatigue or heat she showed none"; "It was nearly noon, but the sense was upon me as of a great night" (149). Alongside this is the insistence that everything is done in great emotion: "The light, like an eager hound, shot before me into the closet, and pounced upon the gilded edges of a large book." In turn, the narrator springs to his feet and cries aloud (47). The use of simile indicates the shift to the neorealism of the portal fantasy: where metaphor estranges, simile seeks to make familiar. We are now inside the portal more fully, yet the reality of the world is cast into doubt by the continual references to the framing world, and to the insistence on an unusual intensity of emotion.

Equally experimental, *A Voyage to Arcturus* by David Lindsay (1920), comes nearer to the rhetoric of the full portal-quest novel, even while, in its inconsistencies and baroque style, demonstrating the ruptures of grammar of the early form. *A Voyage to Arcturus* continually shifts tone, from the supernatural (the fantastic as *felt*) through the descriptive (the fantastic as *seen*) at various points throughout the text. Unlike *Lilith*, there is no clear division between the mode of the frame world and the mode in which the otherworld is related. Instead, there are continual shifts among the Gothic, the baroque elaboration of fantasy exploration, and unnerving moments of apparent realism. These latter moments are usually dropped into the conversational structures of the book; in avoiding the mock medievalism used at other moments, they approach the plain puritan delivery of Bunyan. Yet in *Voyage to Arcturus* much is hidden in words that seem open. All is reversals and negatives.

We begin with a séance delivered in the low-toned popular style, essentially mimetic, reminiscent of Conan Doyle. Lindsay can conjure up unease without relying on the intonations of horror, because the séance itself is understood, both familiar yet semiscandalous. The opening of *A Voyage to Arcturus* is the opening into a club story. It is matter-of-fact, prosaic. But the sudden shifts in tone are a source of unease: there are attempts to deliver a travel fantasy through emotion rather than description, and the odd lapse into colloquialisms when the discussion is something which can relate to our own world (such as the use of "Thanks" when blood is shared). In order perhaps to put Maskull at his ease, Krag addresses him, "Oh, you will get your twenty four hours, and perhaps longer, but not much longer. You're an audacious fellow, Maskull, but this trip will prove a little serious, even for you" (18). But the offhandedness is deceptive: it is dismissive, it closes down the questions, begins the sealing off of the fantasy that ensures that none of the questions Maskull asks will challenge his received impressions, and that he will trust all the answers given.

But chapter 2 begins with the semi-Gothic. It leads to the supernatural, not to the portal: "The three men gathered in the road outside the house. The night was slightly frosty, but particularly clear, with an east wind blowing" (15). For this one moment in time, Maskull is presented as an inhabitant rather than an explorer of the world, and the tone conjures the latency crucial to the intrusion fantasy (see chapter 3, this volume). In the tower, things begin to get more sinister. The jovial tone is dropped and what is observed—the beating of the drums—is increasingly phrased not as an event but as an indicator: they "seemed somehow to belong to a different world" (29).

Unlike *Lilith* and subsequent portal fantasies, the actual portal is almost irrelevant to this fantasy. Like Edgar Rice Burroughs's John Carter, Maskull is transported instantaneously to the new world. With this alteration, we have shift of tone and focalization. On awakening, Maskull describes not what he sees but his bodily feelings: "he was unable to lift his body on account of its intense weight. A numbing pain, which he could not identify with any region of his frame, acted from now onwards as a lower, sympathetic note to all his other sensations" (40). He becomes aware of changes, of the fleshy protuberance on his forehead, and a tentacle on the region of his heart. Maskull's first experience of the new world is physical, of himself as landscape and as fantastical. As the presence or absence of various limbs proves crucial to the narrative, the morality of the tale is shaped on and with his body. The language is pregnant with the fantastic, but does not build the stage set I associate with this kind of fantasy. With Maskull, we explore not the world he is in, but his reactions to it. The description of landscape, although in the third person, is through perception. "When it came near enough he perceived it was not grass. . . . Some uncanny, semi-intelligent instinct was keeping all the plants together, moving at one pace, in one direction, like a flock of migrating birds" (48–49). Like MacDonald, he uses avoidance in the face of the realized fantastic: the "sense-impressions caused in Maskull by these two additional primary colours can only be vaguely hinted at by analogy" (49).

Conversation in *A Voyage to Arcturus* shows similar stylistic shifts. As with Vane, Maskull's interpretative agency is repeatedly denied. Although this is ostensibly a novel of exploration, he must not ask questions about the cut on his arm because "the effect is certain, but you can't possibly understand it beforehand" (34). Joviality is used to ensure compliance not just of Maskull, but of the reader. It is we who are being chivvied along into the fantasy through a denial of explanation—a lack of information is buried in apparent volubility. This denial wouldn't matter but, like many adventurers in the portal fantasy, he accepts whatever he is told (especially when it contradicts what he has been told before). We see this most clearly toward the end when he briefly follows a new prophet, only to change when his bodily configuration changes. It is unclear why this happens. A query about Crystalman results in the lesson that he is called Shaping and has many names (46). This mode later emerges as central to the uncanny, but is antithetical to the delivered mode of the modern portal-quest fantasy. When information is actually exchanged we move to excessive formality:

> "And well you may, for it's a fearful thing for a girl to accept in her own veins the blood of a strange man from a strange planet. If I had not been so dazed and weak I would never have allowed it."
>
> "But I should have insisted. Are we not all brothers and sisters? Why did you come here, Maskull?"

When what is to be delivered is not description, but a genuine discussion of a problem, Lindsay reverts to a more colloquial style: "It begins to look like a piece of bad work to me. They must have gone on, and left me" (45). Anything that discusses the fantastical is described in the slow, measured language of poetry. Anything that is about the "real" slips back into the colloquial and takes the fantasy characters with it. Joiwind is asked if she is being weakened: "'Yes,' she replied, with a quick, thrilling glance. 'But not much—and it gives me great happiness'" (54). It is that "not much" that seems rather odd. When Digrung is slandering Tydomin he again slips into the vernacular, because his slander is not a matter for fantasy: "I see into you, and I see insincerity. That wouldn't matter, but I don't like to see a man of intelligence like Maskull caught in your filthy meshes" (118). Digrung continues in much the same style, because he is talking about the mundane. When told not to kill someone he says "Thanks for that" (120). But as soon as he gets onto the subject of sin, he is back to excessive formalism "As for you, woman—sin must be like a pleasant bath to you" (120).

Although the séance is ended with a sudden rush into the room, action is rare. The predominant pace is slow, meandering; the planet Arcturus is the principal character whom Maskull must get to know. But Lindsay, like MacDonald, feels that landscape is not enough: the emotion, the effect of the fantastic on the soul should be the heart of the matter and our attention directed to it. The result is that the adventures often seem weak and almost irrelevant. When Maskull fights Crimtyphon, the whole is rushed, made small of. The "duel of wills" lasts only one paragraph (102). This is neither heroic or adventure fantasy.

Similar issues are at stake with *Alice in Wonderland, Through the Looking Glass,* and *The Wonderful Wizard of Oz.* Of the three novels, Carroll's work is clearest that it is the portal and the space beyond that is of intrinsic interest, and this emphasis is reflected in the confidence of tone with which the tale is delivered. To begin with, the portal is both a passage and a space. When Alice falls through the rabbit hole, it is lined with cupboards and shelves. The transition is not instant but is to be explored as much as other places. The second Alice book, however, is composed almost wholly of Alice moving into, assessing, and moving beyond a place/incident. Each time the mise-en-scène is described, Alice engages with it, but in the absence of a task, she then chooses to leave it behind. This form of encounter is quite different from most portal and quest fantasies, where such moves necessitate that tasks be performed, but markedly similar in that the emphasis is on place rather than an adventure, a happening. As with

The Wonderful Wizard of Oz, it reinforces the notion that the heart of the portal fantasy is always *the land* and not the adventure.

Perhaps the strangest aspect of the Alice books (in terms of their rhetoric) is that Alice proceeds as if she understands the world around her. In a reversal of the usual structure, Alice understands the rules of society and seeks to implement them, coming unstuck because those around her do not seem to understand them, while very superficially implementing them. Alice imposes herself on fantasyland, anticipating while puncturing the straight-faced "stranger/savior" politics of modern portal fantasies. The most obvious example is the Mad Hatter's Tea Party, to which Alice invites herself, although she knows this to be rude, while condemning the party for being unwelcoming. Despite the chaos, Alice does not act as a stranger in the world in quite the way we expect in a portal fantasy. Crucially, however, there is nothing she needs to find out, no place she needs to go, or quest to achieve. The result is that she asks relatively few questions. And when she does question, it is usually about the nature of the one she confronts who is equally interested in her. A question we might ask of *Wonderland* (as indeed Alice asks it in *Looking Glass*) is just *whose* adventure this is. It is clear from the balanced nature of interrogations between Alice and the caterpillar, Alice and the pigeon, and Alice and the Cat, that they each regard this as their adventure, and Alice merely someone they have met on the way.

Before leaving the Alice books, it should be noted that although the entrance to the rabbit hole does not signal a shift in Carroll's style—we might argue that this is because Alice is already asleep, is already in the fantasy—at the end of the book there is a very obvious break. Forced back into reality, into the frame world, Carroll opts for reverie. It is quite possible to regard this as a slippage into the conventions of the time, the rather sentimental tone adopted toward children that saw them all as potential adults, and childhood as a charmed rather than a fantastical time. Yet the reverie alerts us to something: in creating *Alice,* Carroll opted for an ironic macrorealism, in which the brutality of society is made fantastical as the language of society is revealed to be brutal. That refreshing tone is crucial to the creation of an unquestioned fantasy—which may suggest that *Wonderland*, for all the presence of that rabbit hole, is a precursor not to the portal fantasy but to the immersive.

As I write, I am increasingly convinced that the primary character in the portal fantasy is the land. In Baum's *The Wonderful Wizard of Oz* (1900) we can see this element emerging. Baum understood that the fantastic can be intensified if contrasted with the most mundane Real possible. Attebery writes: "Baum is doing what a painter does when he paints a large, flat, colorless area on a canvas: he is creating negative space which acts to make any positive design all the more vivid. Kansas is gray, so we begin to think about color. It is flat, so we long for contour. It is vast so we wish for something on a human scale. . . . Before the paragraph is done, we have been given, by contraries, a picture of Oz" (*Tradition* 84). This effect is intensified because in that very first (Kansas) segment, what is perhaps most noticeable is that the text is all description. There are only two lines of conversation, in which Dorothy is commanded to take refuge from the cyclone. The bleakness of Kansas is in part the absence of sound, paralleling that absence in the landscape. Dorothy's voice is a shock as much for being a voice as it is for its merry tone, but it is also a reminder that Kansas is a set of ideas as well as a place, and that Dorothy will be taking it with her.

Once in Oz, however, conversation becomes the crux of the dynamic. Questions drive the narrative, and give rise to narrative. Speech in *Oz* is relatively egalitarian: one cannot tell the status of someone from the use of direct or reported speech (although Attebery points out that it is encoded in who is described and in what detail (*Tradition* 100).[19] Reported speech is used only to relate something that we have already seen happen. In this book there is very little introspection from Dorothy; only occasionally does she feel the need to relate her tale or her emotions/reactions.[20] In contrast, all the characters she encounters introduces themselves with a tale, not of where they are going or what they are doing, but of who they are. Dorothy's narrative position, her domination of the story, comes in part from the conversational offerings of those wishing to make her acquaintance. There are four actors here, but only one is interpreting the world for us, even though the other three interpret the world for her.

Like *Alice*, *Voyage to Arcturus*, and *Lilith,* the book is a series of sequential movements through a landscape in which it is the landscape and its effects, rather than an adventure per se, that fascinates. As Attebery has pointed out, the journey itself is the plot (*Tradition* 87). The adventures are often the weakest part of the book—why use mice to pull a truck that the woodman and the scarecrow could pull?—because they are the elements closest to fairy tale. This form of fantasy, in which the adventures are often discrete and are added to until the author decides it is time to move to an ending, or a change of direction, I term a "bracelet" fantasy. Many of the links/adventures could simply be removed without fundamentally altering the tale.

What is most interesting about this book is that although landscape is the center of the book's wonders, Dorothy is oddly uncurious and takes much of it for granted. Take, for example, the Emerald City, where she does not question the use of the spectacles (117–118). It is the omnipresent narrator who notices the lack of animals (122); Dorothy herself does not comment upon it. Similarly she does not comment on the throne room, the narrator does (126). Her discovery of the Tin Woodman (54) shows little astonishment at the enchantment. Dorothy is happy to accept what she is told of the world by those she meets, she does not herself interrogate it. Dorothy accepts the fantastic while marveling at the colors and brightnesses (much, perhaps, as the magic of the storefront window was accepted while simultaneously a source of marvel). As we see more than Dorothy inquires about, or demonstrates curiosity for, we are not positioned as Dorothy's companion per se. We are frequently taken into an immersive fantasy, as we wonder at things she accepts. One explanation for this is that Dorothy has already traversed one portal, in moving from an eastern city to Kansas.[21] She is practiced at dealing with the unknown. Alternatively, this story is simply a very unusual portal fantasy, one that shifts the reader position from continually requiring explanation through the senses of the naive protagonist, to shifting through those senses in order to interpret what the heroine herself takes for granted.

Tolkien and Lewis

The classic quest fantasy, as I now envisage it, was set into its "final" form by J. R. R. Tolkien. *The Lord of the Rings* (1954–1955) codified much of how the quest fantasy deals with landscape, with character, with the isolation of the protagonists into the club-story narrative and with reader positioning. More or less contemporaneous with *The Lord of the Rings* was the publication of the first in the Narnia series, *The Lion, the Witch and the Wardrobe* (1950), a classic portal fantasy. These novels set the pattern for what Clute describes as the full fantasy: the novels presume a thinned world, one in which wrongness already exists—a motif absent from *Lilith* or *Wonderland* but already present in *Oz*—and a consolatory healing or restoration (rather than transmutation), in which the participants are fulfilling an agon, "a context conducted in accordance with artistic rules" (*Encyclopedia* 12).

It is rather useful to compare the ways in which each approach the problem of creating a satisfactory and entire otherworld, to illuminate what it was that Tolkien achieved and how, and how each of the elements I have described are constructed. *The Lion, the Witch and the Wardrobe* is not an inferior novel, but in terms of the creation of the fantastic it is far more visibly aware of the juxtapositions of its two worlds. Consistent with my argument throughout has been that the portal and the quest fantasy use essentially the same means of entry into the fantastic, and thus are required to take up the same narrative position: essentially one that posits the reader as someone to whom things are explained through explanations offered to the protagonist.

The opening of *The Lion, the Witch and the Wardrobe*, perhaps because it is a children's story, is much more self-consciously narrated than we have seen previously. The frame world is a story to be told, as much as the fantasy world is: "Once there were four children whose names were Peter, Susan, Edmund and Lucy" (9). It is narrated as if it were further in the past than the adventure itself: "It was the sort of house that you never seem to come to the end of, and it was full of unexpected places. The first few doors they tried led only into spare bedrooms, as everyone had expected that they would; but soon they came to a very long room full of pictures and there they found a suit of armour" (11).

This use of the past tense to create the frame world is also employed by Tolkien, but here the purpose and direction of the technique is rather different. Tolkien deploys this distanced past to build the history of his world, to create depth for the fantasy. Lewis is using it to create depth for the frame world, to make that real. Consequently, the unfanciful tone of Tolkien's prologue makes real, not the fantasy between the "there and back again," but the frame world of the Shire, which in turn makes real the adventure. By framing the Shire and the outside world with a viable past, a real, potential, future of the Shire is projected that is interwoven with ours.

Both Tolkien and Lewis feel the occasional need to rupture their fantasy lands. For Lewis, Narnia is unstable. It needs to be made more real by being rooted in our own world. By speaking directly with his readers, Lewis simultaneously breaks the fantasy and reminds us that it is real. So, for example, "This was bad grammar of course but that is how beavers talk when they are excited; I mean, in Narnia—in our world they usually don't talk at all" (100). Narnia is made the more real because the frame world from which Narnia is accessible is made the more real by this reminder.

In contrast, Middle Earth is rendered stable by the relationship of the Shire to the rest of the world. This dynamic depends entirely on the structure of registers that Tolkien has developed for his epic. The Hobbit sections are written in the immersive style (which I shall discuss later).

Much is taken for granted and the conversation is chatty, while neither interrogative nor excessively informative. What is particularly noticeable is that Gandalf is a questioner as well as questioned. He is not the source of all knowledge in this early part of the book (*Fellowship* 49, 50). However, while Frodo and Sam do not explain the Shire to us because they already know it, they *do* explain it to Gandalf, Aragorn, and to others they meet. Unusually, at these moments we look back through the portal to have the frame world described to ourselves as audience.

The difference of registers influences the shaping of the past. There is a clear difference between history as it is delivered in Tolkien's Prologue, and that delivered, often in rolling tones, by those with information to pass on, whether it be Gandalf narrating the history of the Ring, or the poetic prophecies interrupting the otherwise demotic narratives of the Faun Tumnus and the Beaver. High formality is reserved for delivering history and status, for establishing shots of relationships and characters. It distances not just us, but the hobbits and the four children, and reminds us that this is not their world either. And because it is not their world, they are reliant on what they are told. Tolkien and Lewis use different ways of closing the discourse down. Lewis simply puts doubt into the mouth of Edmund, whom we already know to be unreliable. We can trust the robin, because it is Edmund who casts doubt on its trustworthiness (61). Tolkien uses another, less coercive method, ensuring that all the kind people that the hobbits meet once they are dispersed from the fellowship accord with the dominant interpretation—what we might call a *conspiracy of companionship*. In both cases, this closure is for our benefit. As readers we are positioned to be dependent upon what we are told, but both Tolkien and Lewis recognize that if the internal narrative is to convince, it must be sealed from within, not without.

Many of the "histories" we receive are oral retellings, which might alert the reader to unreliability. In the hands of Tolkien and Lewis, however, they do the opposite. The first example is when Gandalf visits Frodo to tell him of what the Ring portends, " 'Ah!' said Gandalf. "That is a very long story. The beginnings lie back in the Black Years, which only the lore-masters now remember' " (*Fellowship*, "The Shadow of the Past" 60).[22] We then segue rapidly into the formal, the gloomy atmosphere conjured up by the capitals in the sentences. And it is here that language is used to convince us: "The Enemy still lacks one thing to give him strength and knowledge to beat down all resistance, break the last defences, and cover all the lands in a second darkness. He lacks the One Ring" ("The Shadow of the Past" 60). There is no space for doubt here, no question that there might not be an enemy. Others may doubt later in the book—particularly in the bar at Bree—but no one who has spoken to Gandalf will do so, just as the word of Aslan is by its very nature the Truth. Whereas Lewis achieves it by positing Aslan as a sacred figure, who cannot be challenged, Tolkien constructs a style that defies the doubter. The style shifts: it becomes impersonal, in part because Sauron's name may not be spoken, but also to give the sense of a Built Past. From Strider:

> In those days the Great Enemy, of whom Sauron was but a servant, dwelt in Angband in the North, and the Elves of the West coming back to Middle-earth made war upon him to regain the Silmarils which he had stolen; and the fathers of Men aided the Elves. But the Enemy was victorious and Barahir was slain, and Beren escaping through great peril came over the Mountains of Terror into the hidden Kingdom of Thingol in the forest of Neldoreth. There he beheld Luthien singing and dancing in a glade. (*Fellowship*, "A Knife in the Dark" 206)

The cadences are those of oral telling. The very seamlessness of it maintains the momentum that makes it sound formal but also sung. The narrative use of "and," as in Old Testament language and the narratives of the Anglo-Saxon Chronicle, provides the story with extra authenticity. Language in Tolkien is directed to the telling, that they be seen to be told. Stories, not just language, are in and of themselves convincing. When Bombadil speaks,

> The hobbits did not understand his words, but as he spoke, they had a vision as it were of a great expanse of years behind them, like a vast shadowy plain over which there strode shapes of Men, tall and grim with bright swords, and last came one with a star on his brow. Then the vision faded, and they were back in the sunlit world. (*Fellowship*, "Fog on the Barrow-downs" 157)

The vision compels belief, and this visionary element is present whenever History is retold. As reportage it takes on elements of the club narrative: impervious and protected by the reputation of the teller, and reinforced by the isolation in which the story is told. In contrast, we can consider the role of demotic language in *Lord of the Rings*. Although much information is delivered in formal storytelling sessions, many of the really significant decisions, observations, and pieces of information are actually exchanged in the low vernacular of the hobbits.

Sam, who operates as the voice of the narrator does in *The Lion, the Witch and the Wardrobe*, is the one who reminds us that he is a real person moving through the fantasy. Thus while Aragorn or Gandalf worry about the historical significance of actions taken or not taken, Sam reminds us of the realities of a cross-country trek, even down to a forgotten rope. This one small paragraph, and others like it, is crucial to the success of the quest. That it is told in an unspectacular style, drawing no attention to itself save as a bit of comic business, is marvelous. Hayakawa talks of the "value of unoriginal remarks" as both mood setters, and ways in which to control an atmosphere (80–81). Tolkien has embraced this understanding: much of what is really going on is hidden by the high-flown rhetoric of the "politicians." Nowhere is this understanding more evident than on page 419 where Sam is explaining Frodo to Pippin.

> "Begging your pardon," said Sam. "I don't think you understand my master at all. He isn't hesitating about which way to go. Of course not! What's the good of Minas Tirith anyway? To him, I mean, begging your pardon, Master Boromir." (*Fellowship*, "The Breaking of the Fellowship" 419)

Without deploying the ringing tones of authority, Sam cuts through the campfire discussion of politics, diplomacy, and strategy. But this change of voice is momentary. Elsewhere the book is dominated by the interpretive voice of Gandalf and Aragorn, who, while they may not control the movements of the hobbits, control their meaning. Later authors, however, have misunderstood the role of this material. Mistaken for an aspect of character, phatic discourse—the chats about cooking, about weather, the general reaffirmations of existence—becomes a mere attribute. Tolkien uses these moments to remind us what is *real* in both the metaphorical and fantastical sense.

If the role of the guide is increasing, and the understanding of the protagonist is increasingly molded by the presence of the guide, we as readers are also under increasing pressure to pay attention to the moral significance of landscape, that semiosis that encodes the feelings of actors and readers (Rifaterre 14). For both Lewis and Tolkien, landscape was validated as adventure and character in and of itself. Landscape for Lewis must have purpose: it is there to be useful and to be reacted to. When the children see the beaver house, "you at once thought of cooking and became hungrier than you were before" (69). Although the passage concludes with description of the rushing water, frozen as it falls, this apparently purely aesthetic description provides vital information about the nature and magnitude of the witch's power. At the same time: "Edmund noticed something else. A little lower down the river there was another small river which came down another small valley to join it. And looking up that valley, Edmund could see two small hills, and he was almost sure they were the two hills which the White Witch had pointed out to him when he parted from her at the lamp-post that other day" (69).

Elsewhere, landscape is not expected to speak; it merely accompanies the events. Although the characters interact with the landscape it is in the sense that they act with and upon it. The landscape is there to be moved through. The "aliveness" of Lewis's Narnian landscape with its dryads and hamadryads reduces the moral agency of the scenery: even in *Prince Caspian* (1951) where the land's aliveness is most at stake, it is acted upon, it is not an actor. In contrast, Tolkien's technique—and the one that will come to dominate the quest fantasy tradition—is to present the landscape as a participant in the adventure. It can indicate evil: "That view was somehow disquieting: so they turned from the sight and went down into the hollow circle"; "They felt as if a trap was closing about them" (*Fellowship*, "Fog on the Barrow-downs" 148, 149). The indication is that it is the landscape that actively traps them, pulling them down toward the barrow wights. Or, the landscape can simply influence: "The hearts of the hobbits rose again a little in spite of weariness: the air was fresh and fragrant, and it reminded them of the uplands of the Northfarthing far away" (*The Two Towers*, "Of Herbs and Stewed Rabbit" 257). Emulating a number of myth structures, Tolkien ties the land to the king/leader or to the virtue of the people: Gondor's townlands "were rich, with wide tilth and many orchards, and homesteads there were with oast and garner, fold and byre, and many rills rippling through the green from the highlands down to Anduin" (*Return of the King*, "Minas Tirith" 22). Pippin describes the feeling of connection thus:

> "One felt as if there was an enormous well behind them, filled up with the ages of memory and long, slow, steady thinking; but their surface was sparkling with the present; like sun shimmering on the outer leaves of a vast tree, or on the ripples of a very deep lake. I don't know, but it felt as if something grew in the ground—asleep, you might say, or just feeling itself as something between root-tip and leaf-tip, between deep earth and sky had suddenly waked up, and was considering you with the same slow care that it had given to its own inside affairs for endless years." (*The Two Towers*, "Treebeard" 66–67)

Lewis never attempts this marriage of mise-en-scène with emotion, virtue, or character (with the exception of the martyrdom of Aslan, which presents a scene redolent with grief and horror, surrounded by cold and dark). Later writers, as Attebery points out, use landscape to fill the gaps of actual experience, "to rehistoricize fantastic assertions by placing them within an approximation of the most accessible milieu in which such statements could have been made" (*Strategies* 132). Vital to this substitution is the intense *concentration* on landscape, the insistence on a level of detail that is almost distorting. Brian Stableford wrote, "Descriptive prose *can* be like a pre-Raphaelite painting, attempting to specify the colour, position and texture of every object which the hypothetical observer would see" (*The Way to Write* 28). The metaphor can be extended into landscape painting as a whole, in which the "natural" is actually a clever contrivance that encodes specific messages about what the Land should be. The more I consider it, the more obvious this link to Pre-Raphaelite painting seems. Dalí once cited the Pre-Raphaelites for "their precise rendering of detail and the equal focus accorded each element of reality. The technique rendered their paintings awkward in some ways, since sharp-focused clarity of each part works against the illusion of perspective" (Mathews 39). Similarly, the "microscopic natural detail [which] appears at the expense of space, atmosphere or any feeling of light and shade . . . seems to belong to a world of dreams and enchantments"—as Allen Staley conjures Millais's *Ferdinand Lured by Ariel* he also conjures the elaborate but curiously thin stage sets of so many quest fantasies (15). On the subject of the same picture, Staley quotes the 1851 *Art Journal*: "The emphasis of the picture is its botany, which is made out with a microscopic elaboration, insomuch as to seem to have been painted from a collection of grasses, since we recognise up to twenty varieties" (176). Exactly. As we shall see later, the insistence on a monosemic understanding of the world in so many quest fantasies works against the illusion of reality that this detail strives so hard to conjure.

What there is surprisingly little of in the work of both Lewis and Tolkien, is the action adventure rhetoric that one associates with modern heroic fantasy. A rare moment is on page 337, at the start of "The Choices of Master Samwise".

> Sam did not wait to wonder what was to be done, or whether he was brave, or loyal, or filled with rage. He sprang forward with a yell, and seized his master's sword in his left hand. Then he charged. No onslaught more fierce was ever seen in the savage world of beasts, where some desperate small creature armed with little teeth, alone, will spring upon a tower of horn and hide that stands above its fallen mate. (*The Two Towers*)

The language appears to have leaked in from the sword and sorcery genre that increasingly influences the quest narrative as the century proceeds. We can see it in the Conan stories of Robert E. Howard and Fritz Leiber's Grey Mouser stories. Both of these, like most sword and sorcery novels, are better considered when we turn to immersive fantasy,[23] but because in the post-Tolkien era sword and sorcery comes to influence the writers of quest fantasy—particularly Terry Brooks—the comparison of language is worth noting.

Howard's Conan is interesting because Howard focuses the reader's attention upon the action. Whereas in Tolkien, the emphasis drives the reader through the action, Howard is interested in the action itself. To take just one example, from "The Tower of the Elephant" (1933): "Steel flashed and the throng surged wildly back out of the way. In their flight they knocked over the single candle and the den was plunged in darkness, broken by the crash of upset benches, drum of flying feet, shouts, oaths of people tumbling over one another, and a single, strident yell of agony that cut the din like a knife" (16–17). Take note of the hyperbole in the adjectives, "flashed," "surged," and "strident." Although we do see hyperbole in Tolkien, it is rare. For Howard, the action itself is the point; the finding of the object sought after, or the completion of a task is almost irrelevant. Accompanying this style of writing is the sense that action is about what is felt. It is important that Conan reacts by instinct, and that when Murilo, Conan's employer, is frightened, we feel "his blood congeal in his veins." We are reading here to feel these emotions, to thrill with the hero, to fear with the onlooker.

Fritz Leiber aims for a similar impression, although writing with greater delicacy. While his descriptions of swordplay match those by Tolkien of landscape, his attention is on the beauty—and hence internal morality—of the action: "The Mouser made a very small parry in carte so that the thrust of the bravo from the east went past his left side by only a hair's breadth. He instantly riposted. His adversary, desperately springing back, parried in turn in carte. Hardly slowing, the tip of the Mouser's long, slim sword dropped under that parry with the delicacy of a princess curtseying and then leaped forward and a little upward" ("Ill-Met in Lankhmar" 9). Infusing the text is the sense that little can be done without emotion. Although more sparing with his adjectives than later imitators, Leiber allows Fafhrd to respond "gruffly, at the same time frantically" (151). Attention to action and emotion is much more specific, is much more a focus for the reader's attention than what we usually see in the portal and quest narratives. I do not consider it a coincidence that it is Sam for whom Tolkien writes these moments. He is the character most *of* the world and most physically engaged with it. Lewis is even coyer than Tolkien. Even when he presents action, there is no shift to the action adventure style with its emphasis on wild emotions and forceful movements. Instead, action is simply "a horrible, confused moment like something in a nightmare" (122).

But what are the consequences in all of this vis-à-vis the position of the reader? Lewis, the writer of an acknowledged portal fantasy, keeps the reader almost continually on the outside of the action. His double distancing of feelings and of action remind the reader that these events happened some time ago. If we are in danger of forgetting it, Lewis breaks the spell by reminding us of the differences between Narnia and our world, a technique that may be one of the distinctions between the true portal fantasy and the classic quest fantasy. Neil Gaiman's *Neverwhere* (1996), a recent full portal fantasy, uses a similar technique, creating dissonance quite deliberately by overlaying the fantasy world on the familiar diagram of the London Underground system. We are never fully in the other world. In contrast Tolkien uses a range of tones to create the effect of embedded realities and to convince us that we are in a fully real otherworld, in which there is no door to elsewhere. When Sam breaks the fantasy with his pragmatism, we are thrown back a step into the Shire, not into our own world, a Shire built by history and narrative. When the rolling rhetoric of Elrond, or Aragorn, or Gandalf becomes too much, one or another will launch into a story that both deepens the tale and—by its use of the oral narrative—pulls us to the fireside with the other listeners. Crucially, while we are capable of moving between the parties, we only ever know as much as we have been told. The degree to which this process is compelling is dependent in part on the extent to which both speakers seal the internal narratives from challenge by a continual reminder that the senior narrators are worthy of trust.

The Modern Era: Brooks and Donaldson to the 1990s

The two writers who most thoroughly articulated the pattern for quest and portal fantasies for the post-Tolkien era are Terry Brooks and Stephen Donaldson. *The Sword of Shannara* (1977) and *Lord Foul's Bane* (1977), are contemporaries. With the exception of *Lord of the Rings*, most fantasies prior to 1977 were short to mid-length books. After Brooks and Donaldson, the portal and quest genre would begin to sprawl. This is not a coincidence. Although very different writers, each homed in on certain aspects of Tolkien's technique in such a way as to emphasize reader positioning, and to ensure the length of the book. What Tolkien does, by creating both world and landscape as character, may be impossible to do in a short book (although, as we shall see when we consider immersion and liminal fantasies, there are other ways in which these elements can be constructed). Brooks and Donaldson each attempt the same thing, although with quite different effects and degrees of success.

Prior to 1977, the fantasy genre was popularly represented by two types: the stylists (Beagle, Anderson, Harrison, Lindsay, and so forth.) and the adventure writers (Burroughs, De Camp, Howard). In 1977 a new third type of writer entered the fray: the romance writer. Of these three categories of fantasies, romance is the most inherently deterministic, in that the structure of the plot is intrinsic to its definition. The other aspect of romance is one of style: emotion is writ, not sensed; action is only a vehicle for emotion and reflection upon emotion. We have seen hints of this in Howard and Leiber, and even occasionally in Tolkien, but as Brooks and Donaldson influenced the genre, this stylistic quirk would come to play a particular part in the positioning of the reader.

Even though *The Sword of Shannara* is horribly overwritten ("was dumbfounded," was "incredulous" that someone knew the way; adjectives are piled upon adjectives), what is immediately evident, and rather disconcerting, is that from the very beginning Flick, the protagonist, is a stranger in his own land. Nothing is taken for granted, everything is described in minute detail. For example, "Because he had traveled this same route a hundred times, the young man noticed immediately the unusual stillness that seemed to have captivated the entire valley this evening" (2).[24] Immediately the world is new to both him and us, even though it is new only in terms of what he is accustomed to.

This sense of the newness of discovery is extended to character and to the world. Brooks extends a technique that will permeate modern quest and portal fantasies: the reverie. Shea, Flick's adopted brother, is introduced to us through Shea's own internal reverie (20–21). The effect of the many reveries is that the characters are tourists in their own mind. Another example: "Menion also knew that he was not a part of this adventure for the sake of friendship alone. Flick had been right about that. Even now he was unsure exactly why he had been persuaded to undertake this journey. He knew he was less than a Prince of Leah should be. He knew that his interest in people had not been deep enough, and he had never really wanted to know them" (124). The effect is peculiar. It is intended to draw us into the mind of the character; instead, it reinforces the sense that we are tied companions. This is not real internal dialogue that is fragmented, or flashbacks that are confused, but rather Menion sitting with us, explaining to us his concerns. Reverie and self-contemplation break the immersion.

Self-contemplation is one aspect of the romance of adventure that Brooks inserts into the telling of the tale. The use of hyperbole in the description of action is the other. Where Leiber regarded adventure as an aspect of the baroque trappings of his world, for Brooks it is a source of emotive imagery, too often actually substituting for emotion: "But for the second time the hopelessly numbed humans were saved, this time from complete madness, as the powerful will of Allanon broke through the crazed sound to cloak them with protective reassurance. . . . The men stumbled mechanically through the heavy darkness of the tunnel, their minds groping at the safety line of coherence and calm that the Druid held out to them" (259). Because action is drawn in this highly emotive language[25] (each emotion is visited, much as each place on the map or in history is visited) there is no *room* to show emotional growth (plus the little problem of downloads substituting for phatic discourse of affirmation). So we have to be told: "Flick had changed considerably since his first meeting with Allanon weeks earlier in Shady Vale, developing an inner strength and maturity and confidence in himself he had never believed himself capable of sustaining" (541). I am amused to note that this approach is recorded by Bakhtin as one of the strengths of Dostoevsky's writing.[26]

The same effect is seen in the world-building. All necessary description is delivered by the wizard (Allanon) to the naive and ignorant Shea, who relies entirely on that conspiracy of companionship to which I have already referred (24–25).[27] Allanon thoroughly usurps the role of narrator-focalizer. Unlike Tolkien, however, Brooks does not use history to create a frame world that makes his fantasy world more real. Instead, history becomes a series of clues that thins the world by making the present less real than the past that must be fulfilled—the classic structure of Christian eschatology.

Although Brooks's protagonists explore their land, what they mainly explore is their own inner landscape, hence the use of reverie to indicate change and development in the plot. Donaldson, a more subtle writer, makes the same connection, but here the protagonist and the land are much more self-consciously and intimately linked. Donaldson writes fantasy as "one long wild discharge of energy that seemed to create the landscape of the earth out of nothingness by the sheer force of its brilliance" (4). Our attention is first drawn to this in the narration of the frame world. In a sense, this too is fantasy, the construction of an alien world. As a consequence, it is far more convincing: the village is made fantastic as the intrusion—Thomas Covenant—is isolated and corralled. It is an intrusion fantasy written from the point of view of the monster. As the monster, Covenant knows the world to be strange and therefore can accept almost any strangeness; in forcing himself into the town, he also becomes the pilgrim negotiating the landscape in a way that is replicated later on. His relationship to the place he is *in* is crucial to the construction of the fantasy, and Thomas Covenant *is* a stranger in the land—both the frame world and otherworld he enters through the portal. His connection to the Land is written into his body: "The fog and the attar-laden air seemed to weaken Covenant, as if the strength were being absorbed from his blood" (26). As Benjamin Laskar points out, *The Chronicles* "literalizes the metaphor of the realization of existential dislocation into a sickness or ailment" (411). The care of leprosy depends on discipline and the surrender of the self to routine and ritual, and *also* to a dependency on authority for both information and care. Covenant subsumes his self into a round of rituals designed to ensure his physical (but not mental) well-being. One cannot but think of the rituals of Gormenghast. Donaldson's work is successful in part because the construction of leprosy supports the demand of the narrative that we the reader will expect Covenant to have to listen and learn.

Nevertheless, the requirement that Covenant be the learner is a restriction on the creation of a full world. Having passed through the portal, he is at the mercy of whomever he meets and whatever he is told. Donaldson is cleverer than Brooks, whose sole concession to the problematic is to allow a moment of distrust to enter Shea's mind.[28] Covenant doubts. Doubting is his mythic purpose, and his doubts facilitate the continual loading of information into the mind of the reader. Covenant's continual denial supports the structure: we might doubt what we are told, but that Covenant doubts is confirmation that *we* should believe. W. A. Senior places this in a more positive light: "Covenant is the sole source of authority in *Lord Foul's Bane*, so narrative tension grows from the narrator's initial inability to provide any coordinate perspective. Any external criteria or evidence of the Land's validity would serve only to expunge the necessity for Unbelief and make Covenant into a cantankerous and pitiful cynic, not an epic figure fighting for his life and sanity" (138).

The result is, in the end, a recapitulation of the self-referential "New Testament" structures I discussed earlier. We are as much tied into a closed narrative as we are when we follow the innocence of Shea. The increasing use of prophecy in quest fantasies, from Brooks and Donaldson onward, is clearly linked to this. Prophecies allow knowledge to be imparted, so that in fact the goal is "known" even though its meaning is not understood (which might also be said about Bunyan's Celestial City). The hero does not have free will in a narrative driven by prophecy, and which might explain why the moment of *recognition* (Clute, *Encyclopedia* 804–805), the point at which the hero realizes his place in the story and loses free will, is usually displayed in snapshots rather than in gradual change. The hero cannot emerge, cannot slowly win the allegiance of colleagues, but must demonstrate fitness in some display; for example, Covenant displaying his white-gold ring. This recognition or analepsis seems vital even where the hero ostensibly wins allegiance through respect. Taran in Lloyd Alexander's *Chronicles of Prydain* must still display the *right* (the wielding of Drynwyn) to prove his kingliness and kingship and fulfill the prophecy. The scene tells us what to think. Typically, in this structure, the moment of recognition is for others rather than for the hero himself.

The naive hero, however skeptical, ensures that the structure is geared to "show and tell" with the Land as the subject. Donaldson, however, by deliberately acknowledging and exploiting the reader position of the portal and quest fantasy can also offer us a hero who narrates his own moment of recognition, pulling us momentarily into a moment of solipsism: "with a sickening vertiginous twist of insight, he caught a glimpse of Lord Foul's plan for him, glimpsed what the despiser was doing to him. Here was the killing blow which had lain concealed behind all the machinations" (353). In *Lord Foul's Bane* the omniscient narrator seems to be seeing only through Covenant's eyes, so is perhaps limited-omniscient. This limiting affects both the presentation of the hero and of that which he moves through. In this kind of fiction descriptions must tell us more than we can possibly know because we do not have time to learn about people, nor do we believe that minor characters can change, because they are as much scenery as is a tree. Just as a tree is described, so are people: Lena's "face bore the signs of that truce; her forehead seemed prematurely lined, and her eyes appeared to open inward on a weary battleground of doubts and uneasy consolations" (69). One consequence of this shorthand is that the characters who surround Covenant do not become real to him. Instead, they are merely information sources: Lena explains hurtloam, Altarian tells stories (80) and, on page 158 and elsewhere, Lena reveals that she has secret knowledge. In part this distancing is because Covenant cannot have proper discussions with other people: they are not real, they are simply devices. The alienation is exaggerated in *Lord Foul's Bane* where that unreality is partially the point. The result, however, is to insist that any real sense of Covenant's alteration comes not through how we see him behave but again through reverie, or through what he tells us of himself: "Of course he could not play the hero in some dream war. He could not forget himself that much; forgetfulness was suicide. Yet he could not escape this dream without passing through it, could not return to reality without awakening" (83). The overall effect, as it was in *The Sword of Shannara*, is to render the reader as therapist, required to accept this continuing internal analysis.

W. A. Senior points out, quite rightly, that this structure is prone to exhaustion. How long can a character *remain* new to a world? Donaldson revives the intensity of the books as he moves further into the sequence, by moving the Illearth Chronicler from the site of a portal fantasy, to the location of immersive fantasy with a fully immersed protagonist (Hile Troy). Just as Donaldson used leprosy as his driving metaphor in the first part, he comes to use "belief" as the controlling paradigm for the sequence as a whole, in neat parallel of form and content:

> the narrative of the entire trilogy falls into three discrete parts, each matched to a book and predicated on the current value of Covenant's Unbelief as its importance to him wanes: in *Lord Foul's Bane* Covenant's rejection of the Land is total, so the narrative does not diverge from his perception in any way; in *The Illearth War* his system of Unbelief begins to erode and fully one-third of the events of the Land are narrated from Hile Troy's point of view in Covenant's absence; finally, in *The Power that Preserves*, the narrative in the Land begins without Covenant present and separates into three tracks as Covenant's Unbelief becomes a moot point, and he ceases to dispute with himself the Land's reality or unreality. The evolving alteration of perspective within the text confirms, from our exterior understanding, the reality of the Land and concomitantly denies Covenant's beginning premise of dream." (Senior 140)

Having established the formula, we can begin to look at the degree to which authors are able to play with the form. From 1977 onward, quest fantasies in particular came to dominate the bookshelves of many bookstores, to the degree that in many minds, it was thought of as the default form of fantasy. Even the conventional portal fantasy diminished in popularity, while the shift between the mundane world of the quest hero and that of his fantasy world often became more marked. What remains of interest here, however, is the extent to which a number of very fine books were written in this period that, while often stretching the genre in terms of content conventions, continue to show the markers I have been discussing. For example, in Guy Gavriel Kay's *The Summer Tree* (1985), which is both a portal and a quest fantasy, Kay deals with the problems of the negotiated fantasy, the stranger in the land phenomenon, by developing one of his characters as a seer. Kim has foreknowledge and familiarity with the world she is in and is thus able to be the competent character of the immersive fantasy: we can see the world through her accumulated understanding rather than riding beside her as she greets it for the first time. However, it also means that Kay can download the history we are going to need through Kim's initiatory dreams: "And as she was whirled away from that bright vision, she came abruptly face to face with the oldest Dark in his stronghold of Starkadh . . . and she knew him for Rakoth the Unraveller" (97).

The vision, of course, is unquestionable. In the hierarchy of quest fantasy, street conversation is the least reliable, information given by a guide is very reliable, and visions generally unchallenged; because the vision is buried in the learning process, however, it is less ostentatious than someone sitting down to narrate a prophecy. To balance this, to make this approach work, Kay has also constructed Kevin. A rather relaxed character, Kevin is able to accept things without explanation. Between Kim's visionary knowledge and familiarity with the fantasy world, and Kevin's acceptance of it, Kay is able to sidestep at least some of the miniature show and tell sequences that form the backbone of his world-building. Elsewhere, because we still only know of the world what the characters learn as they travel, the world-building is not so easy. Dave and Paul, our primary guides in *The Summer Tree*, part company at least to some degree to expand our knowledge of the world: the more complex their routes, the more we shall come to understand the Land. Although each, individually, constructs a fellowship, and seals himself off from those external to that fellowship, these groups are linked so that the "conspiracy" or the club narrative is not entirely sealed.

At times Kay is forced to retreat to prediction within the tale, the narration of understanding rather than its depiction. When Paul and the King play a game of chess, they reach a point of almost understanding: "It was not to happen, but something else was born that night, and the fruit of that silent game would change the balance and the patterns of all the worlds that there were" (69). This narration succeeds in being simultaneously clumsy and subtle. Clumsy in that the import of the future is oversignaled; this is a novel so we expect something of import to happen. Subtle in that we are misdirected: we expect this to be a change of adventure; instead, the change is internal to Paul. As readers, however, we are dependent on a directed gaze. We are not allowed to look for significance elsewhere.

Tad Williams's *The Dragonbone Chair* (1988) is technically an alternative world in which everything seems to have slipped sideways (the savior is hung upside down on a tree, and one of the swords was made from the meteorite that hit the temple when he died). Because Williams narrates his tale almost entirely through the story of Simon, we are tied to Simon's side in what should be a rigid form of the reader positioning. We can see only what Simon passes through, understand the world only through his comprehension. At first, Williams seems to tackle this conventionally enough: "[Simon] could never understand how rooms that seemed as small as the doctor's did from outside—he had looked down on them from the bailey walls and paced the distance in the courtyard—how they could have such long corridors" (14). Although this is the conventional inner musing as download, it also functions to tell us that we have a complex space (which will be significant later), and that Simon is capable of independent thought, curiosity, and the research to satisfy such curiosity. Williams has taken a conventional trope, the reverie, and embedded within it the castle as character (at least the doctor's rooms) and a sense of who Simon is. Accompanying this, we also learn about Simon first in his own actions—the fascinated observation of a beetle (3–4)—then through the use of the castle as a foil to Simon (5–6), and later through the mind of Rachel (22–26), contextualized in terms of her frustration, sense of duty, and of love. While in part this method of description is an indication of the quality of the writer, it is also a subtle shift of the reader position. Although we shall walk through this quest with Simon, observing mainly what he observes, we are focused not only on his interests, but on Simon himself. Simon is to us as he is to the beetle. To add to the interest, when Simon does consider himself, in the way used in *Sword of Shannara*, he does so in a way that does not merely download information, but moves the discussion on: "When you stopped to think about it, he reflected, there weren't many things in life one truly *needed*. To want too much was worse than greed: it was stupidity—a waste of precious time and effort" (603). Simon has changed; this reverie contrasts with the earlier Simon who complained that he was hard done by. But the reverie does not say this, it shows it.

In the same manner, Williams manipulates Simon to supply backstory and history to build his world. Tolkien demonstrated the nature and form of the oral tradition as delivered, but for Williams a crucial question seems to be *why* it is delivered. We do not just listen to Simon, we are grateful to him: in *The Dragonbone Chair* we learn what we do because Simon asks questions, an aspect of the character established very early on. Simon is hungry for stories, demanding them throughout. His curiosity is what brings him in reach of the adventure. His status as child renders acceptable his dependence on his companions for information, as it does for Garion in David Eddings's *The Belgariad* and in hosts of other quest fantasies centered on youthful protagonists. Consequently, while in *The Dragonbone Chair* there are a number of delivered prophecies, there is no pretense that they are anything other than sealed narratives, a notion supported by the Scholasticism that dominates this book.[29]

In contrast, Robert Jordan's *The Eye of the World* (1990) makes a fetish of the techniques of the quest fantasy. Reader positioning in this book is rigid. We always ride with the protagonist, and this positioning is mitigated, not by any sleight of hand or subtle technique as developed by Williams or Kay, but instead by creating an inordinate number of travelers whose conversations and experiences we are allowed to try on throughout the novel. Dispersal becomes essential because it is the only route that Jordan allows us out of the claustrophobia of fantasy companionship.

Similarly, Jordan embraces the narrated world. Once, we hear rumors of a "false Dragon" (36) from a peddler, staged as a conversation between the peddler and his customers. Unreliability is built into the delivery, and unreliable it does indeed turn out to be. But elsewhere, information is delivered sealed: Rand learns that he may be adopted as his father lies deathly ill and he is given no opportunity to question. In its own way, this is "club" discourse, the uninterruptible and therefore "sealed" narrative—although in this case, its truth is held in question as his mother too was a stranger to the village so there is no one to corroborate the story (88). When Moiraine tells of the Aes Sedai, we are back to downloads, and a world that knows less than it once did: "In the Age of Legends . . . some Aes Sedai could fan life and health to flame if only the smallest spark remained. Those days are gone, though—perhaps forever" (92). The villain, Ba'alzamon spends a page and a half gloating, providing us with useful information at the same time (170–172); Moiraine tells Nynaeve about the symptoms she experienced as she broke through into her magic. At no point does Nynaeve intervene, although she does accuse Moiraine of lying when she has finished talking. There is no questioning, no actual discussion (269). The text is dotted with these deliveries. And the downloads in this book (and in others considered so far) are linked with a sense that the past is *better*, more knowledgeable, suggesting that the ideology is part of the form. The club narrative contains within it a melancholy of structure, a mourning, or at least nostalgia, for the past that makes it particularly useful for the expression of thinning: "So much was lost; not just the making of *angreal*. So much that could be done which we dare not even dream of" (92). As Tad Williams demonstrates, when Binabik declares, "there seems only one thing to do . . . it is back to the archives and searching again," nothing truly new can be made in a fully Built world.

The Subversion of the Portal-Quest Fantasy

Having outlined the rhetorical structures of the portal-quest fantasy tradition in its early stages and at its most typical, I shall now test this outline against deliberately challenging and subversive versions of the form. If the strategies I have outlined are fundamental to the genre, then they will exist to some extent or other in these more subversive novels, even where that existence is self-consciously challenged.

One route to subversion is to refuse the portal. Jeff Noon structures *Vurt* (1993) around a search for a portal. The fantasy as a whole is immersive: told in the first person, we sit in Scribble's brain and, for the most part, must work out what this modern Manchester looks like by the hints and clues dropped in the course of his search for the yellow Vurt feather and his sister Desdemona. When we are invited into Scribble's thoughts, he is usually considering a problem, not contemplating who and what he is—although we do receive some backstory through dream sequences. But these are dream sequences or flashbacks and are presented as such, not as reverie; they are rarely narrativized. There are moments of intrusion, in that the Vurt leaks, but because there is little surprise enacted, this is not an intrusion fantasy. The intrusion has become proper to this frame world. It is not in itself the means by which the fantastic enters the text.

But the portal lurks; it is an actor in the drama; the fantasy is a crosshatch and we slip and slide between states (Clute, *Encyclopedia* 237). Some Vurts contain the metaVurts, that can link Scribble to the fantasy world on the other side. MetaVurts are looking-glass Vurts, infinitely recursive. But when we are in a Vurt we can immediately see the difference in the way it is written. Despite the complexity of the nature of the portal as it is depicted, the difficulty of finding the portal, of being sure that it *is* a way through, and not simply a fantasy, the Vurt world is still described, whereas Manchester is taken for granted. It can be described from the outside—"Dreamsnakes came from a bad feather called Takshaka. Any time something small and worthless was lost to the Vurt, one of those snakes crept through in exchange" (25)—or it can be described from the inside,

> The garden was serene and beautiful, quintessentially English, just like I remembered, with burbling fountains and a mass of flowers growing wild, overflowing their beds . . . its heady perfume was caressing my senses, and a burst of pleasure was choking me, like every drop of blood in my veins had taken a sap-ride to my cock. (121)

Noon is sensitive to the "rules": only when he is in the Vurt, is through the portal, does Scribble give us this kind of florid description. Even the description of the Dog hang out does not match it in aesthetic intensity, for it is much more purpose driven:

> Along one wall were nailed the carcasses of dozens of dream snakes, shimmers of green and violet. Three dog men were eating there. . . . The smell was sweet to my nostrils. (301)

The first quotation makes of landscape a character; buried in the second quotation is information to be unpacked. Yet it is only at the very end that Scribble makes it through into the portal world, and when he does, it is a world reduced to the very essence of the portal fantasy. The Game Cat and Scribbler sit in a room piled high with objects. The Scribbler is now just one of them, as undifferentiated as all the other props in fantasyland.

Michael Swanwick takes the refusal of portal even further. An immensely complex novel, *The Iron Dragon's Daughter* (1993) barely belongs in this category. (I shall discuss this novel in much greater detail in chapter 2.) But for the moment we should consider briefly the way in which Swanwick evades the imperative of the portal fantasy.

The portal in *The Iron Dragon's Daughter* is so far in the protagonist's past that Jane is a full citizen of the otherworld. A changeling, she functions in fantasyland as if a native. She *is* a native, and the rhetoric and language of the novel is that of the immersive fantasy, with information leaked in the interstices of the building site that is the fantasy. The portal is denied almost until the very end of the book: although there are leaks and slippages, only in chapter 23 does Jane finally enter the portal in Spiral Castle. There, for the first time, she is granted a guide, a self-declared cicerone (333) who baffles her with a description of his Trans Am and the Springsteen on the radio. According to the conventions, Jane should learn from this, but she does not: language cannot communicate meaning in the absence of a reference (MacDonald and Lindsay were right about that), and Jane is not the hero of a quest fantasy, conditioned by isolation to trust. Then, in chapter 24, Swanwick fully rejects the rhetoric of the portal fantasy. "Restored" to her own world, to the ostensible frame world that has not framed this narrative, Jane acts as if she has always been there. We know she has not, and she knows she is a stranger in the land, but she has learned to act as if she is competent in her world and she takes this learning with her into the new world. Jane will provide us with no more explanation than she did in her previous world: we must decode, rather than passively receive, a reader position disguised by our knowledge of the new world.

Perhaps the easiest way to subvert the portal fantasy is to reverse the direction of travel. Two very good examples are in Diana Wynne Jones's *Howl's Moving Castle* and Barbara Hambly's *The Magicians of Night* (the second book in The Sun-Cross sequence).[30] *Howl's Moving Castle* contains within it a portal fantasy that underlines the differences in language for immersive and portal texts. Although the book as a whole is clearly an immersive fantasy, toward the end Howl, Sophie, and Howl's assistant (Michael) travel through the entrance of the Moving Castle into Wales. Immediately we are into the conventions of portal fantasy. The characters obey a guide (Howl), ask questions, and describe to us what they see. No longer must we just exist and interpret a foreign language; instead, they are our (mis-)translators in a world we know better than do they. Despite the book's diversion into *our* primary world, it never ceases to be high fantasy because this glimpse of our primary world is contextualized through Sophie's eyes as fantastic, creating in the reader "a feeling of awe and wonder" (Zahorski and Boyer 57). This moment, what M. John Harrison has described as "counter-trajectories of the counter-liminal,"[31] is in itself a critique of the genre: with her inversion Jones challenges reader acceptance of the protagonist-interpretation intrinsic to the functioning of portal fantasy. It is also—and incidentally—interesting because it answers the question of whether a quest fantasy can take place in a "known space." While the superficial answer is in the affirmative—all the characters find their treasure close to home—in reality only one of the characters actually knows the John Donne poem that forms the intellectual, or cognitive, space through which they move.

Barbara Hambly takes a slightly different approach. Here our protagonist, Rhion, knows that he is entering a different world. Yet in the opening chapters of *The Magicians of Night*, Rhion arrives ready to trust the guide. But Hambly *wants* to collapse this edifice, and she does this in part with the intense language of the portal fantasy: the language is both deceptive and revealing. Clues to Rhion's real situation are planted in the shaping of the world around him: he is led at the very beginning to trust in the "glow of candles, a constellation of six small flames" (1) because they are a key to familiarity. He is welcomed by "the pitiless beauty of a god carved in ivory" (2), a phrase that warns both Rhion and ourselves. And elsewhere, Hambly is deliberately deceptive, severing the link between landscape and morality. The hills that are splashed with golden sunlight, covered in wild ivy and buttercups, shelter evil, not elves (12). Later, Rhion will be alerted to evil through the material objects he touches: it is interesting that in Hambly's world, the psychic traces are attached to *made* objects. The world itself is not an active participant in the fantasy.

One critical difference that reshapes the entire fantasy is that we do not, in this case, ride exploring with Rhion. Except in the details of the plot, we are more familiar than is he with the environment he is exploring. We are displaced from our customary position. Consequently, when Hambly offers the usual little explanations of the customs and practices of the country ("Most of the people in this world were addicted to the inhaled smoke of cured tobacco leaves, and everything—cars, house, furniture, and clothing—stank of it" [13], she is playing a double game. Where in the conventional quest fantasy this detail is intended to familiarize us with the world, to make us feel increasingly at home, here the same tactic estranges us, reminds us that the "we" that is Rhion are strangers here.

Donaldson used the doubt of Thomas Covenant to convince the reader to trust. Hambly sets out to challenge the entire ideological edifice of the portal fantasy that assumes trust and constructs stupidity and passivity in the response of the protagonist in order to support that construction. Rhion is never a passive protagonist: once he is fully conscious, he interrogates the world around him. In other quest fantasies, the assertion that a gang of prisoners deserved to die, or to be used to test a drug (18–19) might be perfectly acceptable until conclusively proved otherwise[32] (usually by a counternarrative delivered by a competing party). Rhion, however, from the first glimpse of an ethical dilemma, begins to doubt, and by chapter 4 is in a case of permanent suspicion. Estranged from the usual source of learning in the portal fantasy, he must do that which the hero of this subgenre is usually not required to do: he must analyze. In this fantasy Rhion learns not from what he is told but from newsreels, from newspapers, and from the behavior of those around him (69). There are no shortcuts, no physical markers of evil, no guide (unless we count the Jewish barmaid, Sarah) to absolve him from interpreting the world as best he can.

This content is reflected in the rhetorical structure that Hambly deploys. Only those accounts of the world that are most unreliable, most despicable, are delivered as a closed narrative, whether an account of the disappearance of magic (11) or von Rath asserting the inferiority of women (68). It is not a coincidence Hambly has Rhion reject the "rediscovered" scholarship of past ages with its claim to be copied from yet older documents: "This was a usual claim made by occult societies, in Rhion's world as well as this one" (134). Nor that the coven consists of men who will not listen either to Rhion or to each other: books and men are each engaged in constructing and delivering their own sealed narrative, impervious to experimentation or to reason. Both elements are usually critical to the success of the portal fantasy. Here, dismantling them becomes the quest.

Samuel R. Delany's *Neveryóna* (1983) begins with a dragon flight; it follows a young girl's adventures, but at the end leaves her neither with a quest achieved nor returning home. But despite this, and although his appendix B rather undermines my case—Delany states that he took the structure from Frank Romeo's *Bye Bye Love*—there is a rather startling resemblance to the structure of *The Wonderful Wizard of Oz*,[33] starting with Pryn's ride on the dragon, a veritable whirlwind: "Flying, she saw the crazy tilting mountains rise by her, the turning clouds above her, the rocking green, the green-licked rock" (6). Pryn leaves behind her aunt, in a place of poverty, but thinks about her constantly. Being the person her aunt brought her up to be is at least part of the reason for her journey. She is inquisitive and self-centered, much as her aunt was in her obsession with developing the loom. As desperate as she is to leave, there remains a sense of "There is no place like home."

Once Pryn arrives in the world, the action seems to take place over a year. And yet, as with Dorothy, there is very little development of Pryn (what happens to the pregnancy?); we actually learn very little about her. Instead, she becomes the vehicle through which we ride through the fantasy. The world is narrated to Pryn in much the way it is narrated to Dorothy. There is one solitary moment where we might be seeing the world through an omniscience narrator: in chapter 8, "Of Models, Mystery Moonlight, and Authority," Madame Keyne, and Jade are talking in the garden. For nine pages (159–168) it seems as if we see them separately from Pryn. Then:

Somewhere a branch fell, off in the bushes . . .
Certainly it was no more than a branch.
But it made Pryn pull sharply back from the window's edge. (166)

It has been an illusion. Even in this private moment, we have seen the world through Pryn's eyes.

But Delany is not using his protagonist to create an impermeable narrative. *Neveryóna*, like *Oz*, is a bracelet tale, each section linked at the beginning and end but otherwise with relatively little overlap: each section is a discrete adventure and the incidents are frequently less important that the understanding of the world that is communicated. This need to understand the world is perhaps clearest in chapter 3, "Of Roads, Real Cities, Streets and Strangers," in which Pryn is taken around the city by Gorgik. His narrative of the city takes up two-thirds of an approximately fourteen thousand–word chapter. Yet what disturbs the reader is the ease with which Pryn moves from one truth to another. She is always slightly distrustful: what do each of the free liminals want from one another? She specifically breaks the rule that says the protagonist of the quest narrative must trust those who interpret the world on her behalf. But equally, the links of the bracelet are constructed of those moments when she carries the desires of each person encountered over into the next sequence.

The critique of the quest narrative that structures the book. *Neveryóna* is a discussion of the structures of narrative and the epistemological conventions of fantasy. It begins when Pryn first meets the storyteller at the end of the dragon flight. The storyteller's tale is polysemic, and shaped by this polysemy. What is told is mutable. And the tale is understood, not because it is right, or prophetic, or handed down from an authority, but because it is *constructed*. We are made to understand that neither storytelling nor oral traditions are natural; they are learned, and the rolling phrases of the high oral narrative, the understanding of the importance of reader response, is as yet uncoded in Neveryóna: "You want to know the outcome—I think it's very important to alert your listeners to the progress of their own reactions. I can foresee a time, after lots more tales have been told, when that won't be necessary. But for now it's a must" (15). Pryn's reactions are shaped in part by the rudimentary nature of storytelling. We may be able to judge her choices, but that is because, as we are told, "it was all a *very* long time ago, so that many tales that have nudged you to such a reading had not yet been written" (56).

There is also an issue of ownership of the tale: in a market that is, arguably, driven by reader demand for sequels and continued worlds, Pryn considers, "it was the teller's tale; the teller ought to know what happened in it, for all her multiple versions" (15). This attitude carries over to Pryn's reception of Gorgik's guided tour. She accepts the version of the city he narrates for her, yet notes: "Occasionally the huge slave's monologue had seemed to coincide with the real market they walked through; more times than not, however, it seemed to exist on quite another level" (55). Gorgik sees a promising young musician, pretty and talented, where Pryn sees a young woman, shabby, ill-kempt and not quite in touch with the world. Both Gorgik and Pryn are making story, but—atypically for quest fantasies—Gorgik's authority and role as a leader/counselor does not give him the authority to force his story upon Pryn; it is her freedom to resist that allows her to apparently switch sides at various points in the tale. She does not. It is rather that others view her as a pawn, to be engaged and captured; in Carroll's terms, she is in fact a Queen, self-directed and ultimately only on her *own* side.

In a pastiche of the quest tale, many of Pryn's tales are "abbreviated" into a lengthy narrative of what might have been told in another kind of tale:

> Were this another story, what we have told of Pryn's adventures till now might well have been elided or omitted altogether as unbelievable or, at any rate, as uncharacteristic. In that other story Pryn's next few weeks might easily have filled the bulk of these pages.
>
> Such pages would tell of a dawn's waking in the public park. . . . They would describe the two young women Pryn met working there [in the market] who dissuaded her from her plan for the next day: to go to the New Market and ask for a job as a bucket carrier. (188)[34]

Instead of listening to Pryn's experience day by day, we are allowed, for a while, to have been there, to have seen it happen. The diegetic ellipsis is used here to divide the Real from the Unreal, the true fantasy from the mundane life; the unity of the epic is broken. Delany does not tie us to his character with handcuffs, but he acknowledges the presence of such detail in other such novels. At the same time, the structure offers another function. Given that Delany's historical narratives of invention are *always* questioned and permeable, in that first short paragraph, and others like it, he builds his world out of denial. This is not *this* kind of story, it is another.

The epistemological ideologies of fantasy are challenged and challenged repeatedly in *Neveryóna* (as they will also be in *The Scar*). The storyteller claims to have invented a syllabary (9); Belham and Venn seem, between them, to have invented so much that one comes to wonder if they were indeed contemporaneous geniuses, or if a variety of inventions have come to bear their mark as a kind of catchall. Yet even that claim is challenged as we hear that this wonder "humankind will know and forget" (153 and again from another speaker on page 306): inventions are repeatedly reinvented, continuously disappear and reappear, so that there may be nothing new in the world. But we also hear that this is a tale told to account for the spread of knowledge. And tales and their telling are a rooted part of the system of knowledge. The making of double soup becomes first magical and then believably a thing of magic. The astrolabe that Pryn carries travels in the opposite direction, to stand first as a tool of mystical power, and later to be denied even the status of tool, or key, map, or coded message. The revealed knowledge endemic to the quest fantasy is denied; the nature of knowledge becomes transmuted. History does not carry power in quite the same way it does in other quest fantasies: most specifically, it does not carry authority. People find it difficult or undesirable to keep the past organized unlike the Scholastic and impermeable histories passed down in many quest fantasies. Tratsin, a carpenter, does not wish his memories of a suppressed rebellion to be to passed to his child; memories such as these are restrictive, not empowering. A lost battle in the past is not an incentive to fight more in the future. A fallen empire, its monasteries and courts emptied, will not suddenly spring up, revived. Knowledge must be invented, not found in old books. This fantasy world is built looking forward, not backward. Yet it is still built using the same components we have seen elsewhere.

The narration of fantasyland when done poorly is often didactic, but even the most creative writers find it difficult in this form to avoid impressing upon the reader an authoritative interpretation of their world. An interesting test case, because it is so otherwise divorced from the usual quest fiction, is the work of China Miéville. *The Scar* (2002), in which the protagonist is running away from her own society, while as elegantly written as *Perdido Street Station* (2000: see chapter 2, this volume, where is it discussed as an immersive fantasy), requires that much more be explained. Bellis Coldwine, the protagonist, acts as our guide to the world, whereas there is no such role in *Perdido Street Station*, and the descriptions are of what is seen, rather than what is. The result is that *The Scar* is less baroque; because the baroque functions best in the taken for granted, the immersive: while overdescribed in the quest fantasy, its function is to create landscape rather than tone.

In *The Scar*, these intense moments of description are almost always employed when either Bellis Coldwine, or Tanner Sack, the protagonists, see something new. They are moments of alienation, rather than impressions of familiarity. But they are marked for us: "Later, when she thought back to that miserable time, Bellis was shaken by the detail of her memories" (7–8). Reverie here is a device that deliberately impresses memory onto the traumatized; Tanner, at moments of stress, is told in the first person: "All black on black but still I can see hills and water and I can see clouds. I can see the prisons on all sides bobbing a little like fishermen's floats. Jabber take us all I can see clouds" (17). This is not the smooth, narrated reverie we have seen elsewhere. Miéville uses these moments to demonstrate the fragmented nature of observation; to demonstrate that what we see is not a painting, but abstracted, a personal construct.

Alienation is one of the keys to what Miéville achieves. In most quest and portal fantasies, the process of the novel requires the protagonist to become ever more comfortable with the fantasyland that she has entered. Yet Bellis Coldwine never does. Her alienation is expressed; explicitly; her culture shock is profound (see page 78 for an example). This alienation enables Miéville to give to Bellis the role of describing the world she can never take for granted because she cannot engage with it. Thus we never see Armada through the eyes of Shekel, who has adapted, become *immersed*, but predominantly through the eyes of Bellis, who learns much of what she knows through books (predigested, reported, alienated description); and secondarily through the eyes of Tanner, whose own understanding is distorted by gratitude. It means Miéville can mostly avoid the conversations that explain the landscape or the politics of Armada (although he does have two, one with Carianne, and another with Uther Doul) and instead present it in negatives, the things that Bellis encounters and is repelled by or does not understand.

Consequently it is those scenes in which neither Tanner Sack nor Bellis Coldwine appear that are written most like those of the classic quest fantasy. For example, "Below the waist, the crays' armoured hindquarters were those of colossal rock lobsters: huge carapaces of gnarled shell and overlapping somites. Their human abdomens jutted out from above where the eyes and antennae would have been" (41). Here Miéville has no choice but to simply describe, to pause the action while the characters are outlined. He has no one in place to mediate for him. In contrast, when Bellis observes the inhabitants of Armada, the Cray are simply "sluggish on their armoured legs" (79). We see what she notices, and only what she notices. Yet Miéville manipulates this rhetoric. Much later, he uses a moment of removal, a moment where there is no observer with whom we are identified, to deliver vital information. As Captain Sengka hefts a box containing a message, we are told of "the worthless little necklace that justifies the jewellery box; and beneath that box's velvet padding . . . a heavy disk the size of a large watch": the compass that will guide New Crobuzon to Armada. For a moment, Miéville breaks the illusion that we hear this tale from Bellis. We know more than she; it is a classic moment of recognition, but one that is denied to the "hero."

For at the center of *The Scar* might be, but is not, our protagonist, Bellis Coldwine. Miéville has created a protagonist who is almost entirely marginalized from what is actually happening. Much of this marginalization is achieved by the careful construction of one of the most solipsistic "heroes" since Thomas Covenant. The construction of the lengthy missive—recipient unknown—that punctuates this tale, is a focus of this solipsism. Sent to a reader in New Crobuzon, it would have maintained the internal integrity of the club story. Presented to Carianne, however, to another *witness*, it becomes, in the end, one of many challenges to the impermeable narrative of the quest fantasy.

But before all this, Bellis must rethink her own place in the narrative. As Covenant believed that his own fevered brain generated a world around him, Bellis seems incapable of believing that it is not her story being told. Her anger at Johannes Tearfly when she realizes that her ship was hijacked in order to collect him, is in part a result of her sense of displacement from the center of the narrative (96).

Whether New Crobuzon is invaded, whether the Armada turns around—all are rephrased in her mind in terms of saving *her* city, and how far *she* will be taken away from home. She is incapable of abandoning a map of the universe that places New Crobuzon at the center even while she is capable of admitting its flaws and self-delusions (in a moment that reminds us that at least an element of this world is known to Bellis). We cannot understand "The accounts of the Money Circle and the Week of Dust," because Bellis does not explain it nor does she receive an explanation. For a moment we are estranged twice: once from the world of Armada; second, and more conclusively, from the fantasy in which Bellis is immersed, her personal frame world of New Crobuzon.

Only reluctantly does Bellis ever admit the concerns of others, and she never admits that hers is one of myriad political interests. Miéville is not the first to attempt constructing a quest fantasy from the point of view of a minor character: Robin Hobb, for example, tries this in the *Farseer* trilogy where her protagonist is precluded by birth from ascending the throne. But somehow Fitz contrives to be at the center of the action. The quest is his even if he does not reap the reward.[35]

Bellis's solipsism allows Miéville to undermine the other cardinal rule of the quest fantasy: what one is told, *is*. As Bellis herself acknowledges at various points within the novel—but without notable effect—her understanding of the world causes her to misplace herself within conversations. She is repeatedly manipulated by those who tell her stories. It is not a coincidence that the longest delivered speeches in the book are those of Silas Fennec, the spy (126–128, 164–167), nor that he is one of the few people to actually use the word "trust," to imply that he is grateful that Bellis should trust him. Bellis knows that he is lying; the "maggot of doubt" that Droul plants in her mind wriggles because it is meaningful. But Bellis's understanding of the world makes this nagging doubt of little relevance. She has chosen to believe, "caught up in it" as Doul points out (473), and we, instinctively, believe with her, because the pattern of quest fantasies has taught us to do just that. We too are caught up in the passion and belief of the moment; we insist that there must *be* a quest, a goal, and that those with whom we travel are part of that cozy conspiracy of companionship.

As an (ignored) reminder that such structures are deceptive, what Bellis learns from Shekel is delivered in the past tense, as reported speech: "Shekel told Bellis about Hedrigall the cactae aeronaut. He told her about the cactus-man's notorious past as a pirate merchant for Dreer Samher and described to her the journeys Hedrigall had made to the monstrous islands south of Gnurr Kett, to trade with the mosquito-men" (100). In defiance of the conventions of the quest fantasy, diegesis is both more accurate and more important than anything we are told directly by the candidates for narrative authority, Uther Doul or Silas Fennec—as is the reported tale of the anophelli which Bellis tells to us (284–285).

The epistemology of the quest fantasy is also challenged: as much as in any other quest, knowledge is fixed and sealed either in the mouths of the narrative authority or between the covers of books. The sacredness of book knowledge is a given and here it is duly reverenced. The Lovers steal books, make of them communal property. The errors in their filing are lovingly described. Books are searched for because knowledge can only be re-created from what is already written. Thus Bellis's destruction of the book is all the more shocking, because the convention is that what has been destroyed cannot be re-created, it can only be rediscovered. This convention is reinforced by what the found text says and how it says it. Krüach Aum does not claim invention or originality. Like Gandalf he narrates a history of what was done and discovered in the mists of legend: "I have . . . found a story to tell, of what had not been done since the Ghosthead Empire and was achieved once more, a thousand years ago" (190). At the most, he is a theoretician who has worked out the equations but never tested them. The dynamic of the novel demands not a reworking of the equations, not a pursuit of the physics that made it possible, but a pursuit of the physicist, or at the least, of his books—a dynamic reinforced when Krüach Aum is described as the one who "*fishes for old books in ruins*" (287). For all we know, the book at the center of this section is itself a copy of a copy of a copy, made valuable only by a belief that knowledge does not mutate but sits, waiting to be found. In part this dynamic may have been what Justina Robson meant when she wrote that *The Scar* "has the seeming of subversion but it doesn't really blow up the foundations" (Robson, e-mail 20 May 2003).

I have grouped *The Scar* with quest and portal novels, and I have already identified the moment of portal transition, but the quest is harder to pinpoint in this novel. Miéville, like the other writers in this section, is actively denying us the conventional quest narrative, but this time in a much more direct fashion, and in a way that depends heavily upon the conventions of the quest novel.[36] *The Scar* is an anti-quest novel. We are set up, time and time again, to expect that something will be found, a hero identified, a mission launched. And each time we are denied. Shekel does not turn out to be the predestined orphan; the *magus fin* is precisely that, a maguffin, even though it is perhaps the one moment of undisputed magic (as opposed to alternate science) in the book; and the Scar in the ocean is never reached nor is its power ever quite defined. The Scar may not even exist—we never have a direct view of the chasm.

For many involved, the quest remains opaque, a quest without the power to inspire. As Miéville has argued, the She-Lover is the only character unreservedly inspired by quest-narrative logic, and she is a sociopath, the solipsism of the quest hero taken to the extreme (e-mail 16 January 2003) If there is a true quest narrative in *The Scar*, one that drives a group of characters in a way we identify as the classic quest fantasy—encounters with various peoples, miniadventures, the search for information, and a clear sense of moral justice, which results in success and which allows the protagonists to return home as heroes—it is one we see only intermittently. This is the Grindylow's quest narrative. In the final analysis, Miéville has pulled off the very neat trick of writing an entire quest fantasy from the point of view of those—ignorantly—on the wrong side.

Chapter 2

The Immersive Fantasy

The immersive fantasy is a fantasy set in a world built so that it functions on all levels as a complete world. In order to do this, the world must act as if it is impervious to external influence; this immunity is most essential in its relationship with the reader. The immersive fantasy must take no quarter: it must assume that the reader is as much a part of the world as are those being read about. It should construct an irony of mimesis in which ornamental speech and persuasive speech become inseparable (Frye, *Anatomy of Criticism* 245). The immersive fantasy is both the mirror of mimetic literature and its inner soul. It reveals what is frequently hidden: that all literature builds worlds, but some genres are more honest about it than others. Mimetic literature, that fabulous conjuration of "the real," is the product of a cumulative "bible."[1]

Mimesis is the art of persuading the reader to forget the mediation of language. Irony of mimesis does not necessarily mean that we are assumed to be *in* the world (although this is one technique), but that we must share the assumptions of the world as much as a contemporary reader of Jane Austen shared the assumptions she presented in *Pride and Prejudice*.[2] If we imagine different levels of "reality" as concentric shells around the world, then the reader of the immersive fantasy must be able to sit between the shell that surrounds the narrative and the shell that protects the world as it is built from any suggestion that it is not real—a position Gary Westfahl has termed *double estrangement* (237). In effect, we must sit in the heads of the protagonists, accepting what they know as the world, interpreting it through what they notice, and through what they do not. In this form of fantasy, the positioning of the omniscient narrator (should one exist), is crucial. The immersive fantasy must partake of Irwin's "quiet assertion":

"There are no authorial exclamations about how astonishing all this is . . . [and characters express] straightforward observations, expressing interest rather than amazement" (69). Peter Nicholls, discussing science fiction, describes this strategy as seeking to "domesticate [the world] . . . rather than draw attention to its absolute oddity" (32).

If the above seems prescriptive, let us pause for a moment to consider two fantasies that strive for immersion, but that in their rhetoric make both the protagonists and the readers strange in the land. In the first, *Golden Armour: The Helmet* (Scholastic, 2000) by Richard P. Brown, the children have lived in the castle all their lives and have lived with *themselves* all their lives, but the insistent narration rehearses who and what they are: "When she was a small child, Cassie had discovered that she could heal little creatures that seemed sick" (12), while "Keiron had a gift too—not such a powerful one, but inexplicable nevertheless. From an early age he had learned that he could 'speak' to things in his head, they all had a voice in his head and would answer his questions if they had a mind to" (13). The second example to consider is G. P. Taylor's *Shadowmancer* (2003), a tale in which two children in a northern village strive to defeat the wicked sorcerer-vicar Obadiah Demurral. Again, we have the description of things a child knows about himself: "Thomas Barrick was thirteen years old. He had lived all his life in Thorpe and had never been any further than Whitby. His father had been lost at sea in a great storm when Thomas was seven years old" (17–18). His friend Kate, "always said that she feared nothing. She didn't believe in ghosts, creatures of the night, or God himself. Her father had beaten all the belief from her. To her father she had to be the nearest thing to a son. The son who had died two years before she was born" (39). The list of information—much of it irrelevant and with no impact on the actual novel—processes like a social worker's report across the pages. It is of course a classic example of telling, rather than showing, and as such could simply be dismissed as poor style. But the ability of the writer to show rather than tell depends in part on the assumption of a consensus reality. These writers have made no such assumptions, even though Taylor is writing a deliberately Christian fantasy, and therefore might assume common knowledge. The result in both is to break the consensus reality, to position the readers as ignorant as they might be in a quest fantasy. In a world they are supposed to know, the result is discordant.

The immersive fantasy is a fantasy of thinning (see Clute, *Encyclopedia*). Where the portal-quest fantasies emphasized recognition and healing, the restoration of the grandeur of previous days, the immersive fantasies are overwhelmingly concerned with the entropy of the world. In each of the texts discussed in this chapter (with the possible exception of *Shadowmancer*, whose Wesleyan message demands a rejection of a thinned world), cities and civilizations fall, families follow political systems into moral degradation and decline, absent gods leave men to fend for themselves, worlds once impervious to the external world see their walls breached. Struck by the degree to which thinning was the dominant mood of a set of novels selected relatively arbitrarily, I put the question to John Clute who responded, "Simple. Because in an immersive fantasy, what is storyable is not the discovery of the world (in which we are immersed) but its loss. From within the river flows away" (e-mail 9 September 2004).

Rather than approach this chapter chronologically, I will attempt to show the range of techniques that writers have developed to construct this concentric reality, this irony of mimesis. One disadvantage to this approach is that the sense of historical development that shaped the portal-quest fantasy will haunt, rather than structure this chapter. This lack of a historical narrative is a shame because there are some historical issues that are peculiar to the immersive fantasy.

A commonplace among fantasy critics is that fantasy is the ur-mode of literature. The ideological pressures that marginalize fantasy during the eighteenth century, and leave it the playground of children and poets, are not central to the argument here. Nonetheless, when we think of immersive fantasy in terms of historical development, we tend inadvertently to adopt Whiggish assumptions that may be inappropriate for a genre that is *not* new in the nineteenth and twentieth century. Despite Clute's assertion that "we know fantasy as a literary genre began in subversion and dream around about the beginning of the nineteenth century" (*Scores*, "Taste Iron" 58), it is mimetic literature that emerges as a genre (a fiction in and for itself) in the eighteenth century and that finds new ways to write the real. Clute's assertion that fantasy emerged in opposition to "the Victorian sluggers who make up middle of the batting order of the Great Tradition" (58) is to accept a history written by the literary victors. Ways to write the unreal as fully existing were already established in Bible stories, in myths and legends, and in the traditions of the marvelous (which Christianity never quite quashed). Intrusion, portal-quest and liminal fantasies all need that belief in the dividing line between the real and the not-real to function. Immersive fantasy does not, so that we might want to think of the emergence of modern immersive fantasy as a rediscovery of the reality of the fantastic, and with it a set of ways to express that belief.

I have suggested that the construction of the fully immersive fantasy requires the construction of concentric shells of belief that allow the reader to exist in a space outside the fictional world, but protected from the outer shell of "unreality." The most commonly recognized place to find this concentric construction is in science fiction. Although not all science fiction novels are written this way, the convention that has arisen in that genre is that the world must be both logical and sealed. If a character has to explain to a reader what is happening then the world is not fully real. Early science fiction frequently dodged the issue by keeping the world of the protagonist as like ours as possible. Adventures began with the mimetic shared world and moved out into strangeness into portal-quest rhetorics as they did so ("As you know, Bob . . ." is the popular indicator of the form). Modern sf, even when proceeding into strangeness is much more likely to begin with strangeness also and to force the reader to be a part of that world. Thus, drawing my examples solely from 2004's offerings (the year in which this chapter was first sketched out), Paul McAuley's *White Devils* begins in a world ravaged by disease; Karen Traviss's interplanetary romance *City of Pearl* starts from a world in which the eco-police are the most powerful police force on the planet; Ken MacLeod's *Newton's Wake* leaves until the very end an explanation of how the Earth was destroyed (for much of the book it is simply a given); and Iain M. Banks's *The Algebraist* abandons the world as we know it and sets us down in another culture with assumptions we have to pick up as we go. This opening strangeness leads us rather neatly to Clarke's law of technology.

Rationalized Fantasy

Arthur C. Clarke's Law:

> Any sufficiently advanced technology is indistinguishable from magic. (A. Clarke, 21 n. 1)

To which, perhaps presumptuously, I would like to add a corollary:

> *Any sufficiently immersive fantasy is indistinguishable from science fiction.*

This construction came about as a result of seeing the nomination lists for the Arthur C. Clarke Award in 2001. This is a juried award intended specifically for science fiction. Sir Arthur, however, long ago insisted that "sf is what the jury says it is." In 2001 the nominations included Mary Gentle's *Ash* and China Miéville's *Perdido Street Station*. Both of these books had been heralded as great new fantasy novels. Mary Gentle's *Ash* is less relevant to the immediate discussion, because the magic in her world is regarded with some suspicion by its characters, and there is also a constant concern with the relationship of the world she has written to ours—this is not, in that sense, a sealed world or fully immersive fantasy. *Perdido Street Station*, the eventual winner, was, however, a fully immersive fantasy. It was also a science fiction novel, because the concern of the main characters—Isaac Dan der Grimnebulin and the garuda Yagharek—is with the way the world works and the construction of scientific rules that will allow the world to be worked. Fantasy that is this logical and this concerned with creating a science of the fantastic is usually termed *rationalized fantasy*. Randall Garrett was one of its the preeminent practitioners, and it was popular in the pages of John W. Campbell's magazine *Unknown* (see Wolfe, "Evaporating Genre" 21). If we move away from rationalized fantasy as story, and look at it as technique, we can see how it helps to deepen the immersion and build the world. Viewed in this way, the rationalized fantasy becomes a mode of understanding, shaping the position of the reader vis-à-vis the text. The principal writers I shall consider here are China Miéville, Steph Swainston, and K. J. Parker, each of whom have produced texts that can be read as either sf or fantasy.

There are two aspects to the issue here, the technique of world-building per se, and the relationship of the actors to the built world. As will become obvious, it is actually very hard to separate the two. When I discuss the creation of a logical world of fantasy, what I mean is a coherent world, one that makes sense in its own terms, and within which the actors can predict the consequence of their actions on the world. This coherency, Gary K. Wolfe has suggested in his introductory essay to *Critical Terms* (1996), is the dividing line between fantasy and fancy. Coherency is crucial to creating the ironic mimesis of the immersive fantasy. It is possible to create a world in which anything can and does happen. But if one does this, then it is impossible to make the characters questioning and *extrapolating* beings. In a fully immersive fantasy, the actors must be able to engage with their world; they must be able to scrape its surface and discover something deeper than a stage set. An ongoing example of the problems that can arise is in J. K. Rowling's *Harry Potter* books. Because there is no system of magic, no sense of what each kind of magic can achieve, the choice of potions versus wand spells versus magical objects is frequently arbitrary and prevents planning—Hermione's use of a transformation potion requiring the risky business of securing genetic material is one such occasion. One cannot but wonder why there is no safer, wand-based spell. There may be a reason, but as there are no rules, Hermione cannot make choices or argue her choice.

A vivid manifestation of what a questionable world can produce is demonstrated in China Miéville's *Perdido Street Station*. There are a number of plots in the novel (the immersive fantasy is not a plot-limiting form): there is Lin's painting of Mr. Motley the gang leader, there is the intrusion of the slake moths on the city (for a discussion of whether an immersive fantasy can hold an intrusion fantasy, see chapter 3), there is the political unrest in the city, there is the wing-stripped garuda's search for flight, there is Isaac Dan der Grimnebulin's search for a universal theory, and there is the threat that the city's constructs (robots) have achieved sentience. Five of these six plot elements are dependent for their exploration on the protagonist's sense that the world is arguable. The slake moths prove a *natural* threat in the sense of being part of the natural history of the world. The revolution collapses in the face of realpolitik and the degree to which authority—however unjust—controls the infrastructure of the city. Remaking wings proves impossible and Isaac does not discover the universal theory because he discovers, instead, physics: he makes the transition from alchemist to scientist within the bounds of the novel, even if that science studies forces that do not exist in our world. Similarly, in Miéville's sequel, *The Iron Council* (2004), the making of golems is cast as a science:

> —. . . what we do is an intervention, Pennyhaugh lectures Judah from his notes,—a reorganisation. The living cannot be made a golem—because with the vitality of orgone, flesh and vegetable matter is interaction with its own mechanisms. The unalive, though, is inert because it *happens to lie just so*. We make it meaningful. . . .
>
> Golemetry is an interruption. Golemetry is matter made to view itself anew, given a command that organises it, a task . . .
>
> He buys batteries, switches and wires, he buys timers, he tries to think. (205)

It is as much a science as the making of the new wax cylinders that offers recorded sound for the first time (210). Swanwick uses a similar technique to make the alchemy of *The Iron Dragon's Daughter* (1994) rational but offers an extra twist: alchemy is supported by sex magic, while textbooks contain "mere example-mongering, the establishment of authority by largesse of data" (166). Science in Swanwick's world is made real by its deliberate obfuscation and by the consensus state it demands, as an ancient lecturer (decanted from a jar) explains, "The second state is . . . consensus reality, that set of conventions by which we agree that bread is a meal and wine is camaraderie" (198). The success of science in *The Iron Dragon's Daughter* depends on a shared bible of the world.

In K. J. Parker's *Colours in the Steel* (1998), one of the great ironies is that the most effective weapon we see deployed is made of naphtha, pitch, and sulfur, not magic or the protection of the gods, but "something people can make," even though some would prefer to believe it witchcraft (369–370). This search for the making of the world, the arguing with the way it is to the way one wants it to be, is radically different from the position of portal-quest or intrusion fantasy, both of which search for the morality of the world-system. These forms also argue that knowledge is something to be found, not made, that knowledge is part of the form of the world. The immersive fantasy sees knowledge as argued out of the world, by breaking it open. Miéville's use of "intervention" is particularly interesting: Judah Lowe in *The Iron Council* (2004) *intervenes* in the world. He finds its cracks and twists; to do this, like all scientists, he must stand back and regard the world while remaining fundamentally of it. The attitude to the physics of the world in Miéville's work becomes a metaphor for politics: there is nothing predestined, there is only what we work out. Judah Lowe is an *antagonist*, his stance is one of challenge—the thinned world is a world whose inner works can be seen. This stance will repeat itself, in varying ways throughout the texts considered in this chapter.

Something similar can be found in Steph Swainston's *The Year of Our War* (2004). Here there are at least five stories (I do *not* mean plot): how to save the world from the invading insects; how to organize an economy for war; how a long war will shape a society; how Jant, a street kid, can maintain his position in the inner circle of the castle; the struggles for power within the inner circle. All of these are stories of questioned technology and questioned politics. What makes the book stand out from other fantasies is the emphasis placed on the relationship of people to the world and to their societies, and the way people argue the world into being. One character in particular exemplifies this stance: Lightning, the oldest member of the Circle, a superhero who serves his Emperor loyally, is utterly trapped by his nature and its relationship to the world. In another kind of novel, he would be the man of destiny, the uncrowned prince waiting for justice to win out to grant him a great victory and the throne. In Steph Swainston's world, however, there is no destiny. There is only the logic of decision chains: if this happens, then that happens.

Both Miéville and Swainston are world-builders in the conventional sense in that each of them draw out their worlds in charts and maps and pictures (both are very talented artists, which may or may not be a coincidence). However, the way they draw their worlds emphasizes at each level the interdependence of elements and the sense that no element is coincidental but rather consequential. For both authors, this arguability of the world, the rejection of morality and destiny as driving forces, this *antagonism* becomes essential to the construction of the immersion. For example, Miéville has said in discussion at science fiction conventions that he had to rethink the cactus people when he realized that there was no earthly reason why they had to be good with plants—humans aren't all good with animals after all. Swainston wanted to see how a command economy distorted by the imperatives of war might industrialize, and ended up with a culture in which there are no cars, but the need for military uniforms has produced a basic work outfit not dissimilar to jeans and T-shirts.[3] Similarly Miéville wanted to make revolution real, so his revolutionaries argue and squabble—and in *The Iron Council* spend more time printing newspapers than actually organizing for revolution. Swainston wanted to show how politics meant many things at many levels, and so installed an absolute ruler who relies on the absolute division between military and local power to ensure that the center remains supported by the regions. In addition, she chose a protagonist (Jant), whose every move is politicized: a mixed-breed, a drug user, possessed of a highly desirable skill, and raised so high that his only possible future is a fall. Jant's engagement with the world is not a riding through, but a constant niggling negotiation. Miéville's Lin (a kephri, with insect head and female body) is in a not dissimilar position; her artist status protects her relationship with Isaac, but only at the expense of making that argument every day. Like Jant, her relationship to her world is highly politicized.[4]

Critical Distance: The Protagonist as Antagonist

All of this seems to be drifting away from the argument of this book: that fantasy can be divided in terms of rhetorical strategies. But what Miéville and Swainston have done is to develop a rhetorical strategy in which the characters with whom we ride are *antagonists* within their world. It allows them to question it while staying within the shell of immersion. The characters themselves ironize the world around them; Jant, Isaac, and Ori in *The Iron Council* make their worlds by continually arguing "it doesn't have to be this way" whether they are talking about the nature of politics or about the nature of physics (or in Jant's case longing for the Absurdist world of the Shift, a world to which he can only gain access if he takes illegal drugs). We can see this ironizing best if we make a very brief return to Tolkien.

I placed *The Lord of the Rings* with portal-quest fantasies, because most of the book takes place in a world strange to the protagonists, a condition that makes it very hard for them to question what they see. Tolkien pioneered the argument that to create a coherent fantasy world, one needs to know its history, its archaeology, its geology, and its languages. I would argue, however, that Tolkien, for all his depth and breadth of detail, for all the maps he drew, and his care in the detail in the depiction of Middle Earth, came closest to creating a fully immersive fantasy world only when he wrote of the Shire (and later in *The Silmarillion* which is told "from the inside"). Once out in the great world, his hobbits only ever see the surface of things; they never truly understand the world they move through. In contrast, the Shire has visible depth: perhaps Tolkien's ideal place, it is a locale ruled by a combination of paternalism and anarcho-communalism. Decisions are made in the pub and people band together to carry them out, whether they are decisions to raid Sharkey's den or to plant the harvest. The relationship of the characters to their world is itself depicted as political—although I suspect that Tolkien himself would have denied this; as late as the 1930s, only opponents to the Conservative and Unionist Party (later the Conservative Party) were regarded as political, and introducing "politics" to local government elections was still considered rather un-English. In the Shire, the hobbits know enough of their world to be antagonists, to question the accepted order of things, and Bilbo and Frodo do so. Compare this to the politics of Middle Earth. Essentially high politics, it is the politics of kings and princes, wardens, and stewards, of decisions made and mysteriously carried out. The carrying out is never depicted, the link between decision and action is hidden. This is politics as magic, the will and the word transmuted.

It is this quality of antagonist to the world that allows the writer of the immersive fantasy to write a novel that we all recognize as fantasy but that has no or very little magic. Such a novel is the first book in K. J. Parker's *Fencer* trilogy. The three novels, *Colours in the Steel* (1998), *The Belly of the*

Bow, and *The Proof House* (both 2000), could have been included in the liminal fantasy chapter, in that much of the trilogy is spent waiting for magic to happen, or arguing whether magic really exists—or if it does exist, whether it can be controlled. The same is true of Barbara Hambly's *Stranger at the Wedding* (1994) and Caroline Stevermer's *A College of Magics* (1994). The reason I did not include them there is that in all cases the books are set in worlds in which people know magic does exist and can work. In Hambly's novel it is illegal; in Stevermer's, for the most part, it is available only under controlled conditions in certain places; in Parker's world it is just very difficult and doesn't achieve very much. Even at the end of the trilogy it is unclear whether magic has actually mattered. There is also the factor that in K. J. Parker's world, one of the protagonists is a stranger to the city, which might have suggested a portal-quest fantasy, particularly as a large part of the trilogy involves the delivery of information. My choice to locate all these books in the category of immersive fantasy is related to (1) the degree to which the bare bones of world-building as a *relationship* with the protagonists is central to the rhetorical tone of the novel; and (2) the tactics the authors use to avoid the Pre-Raphaelite landscapes of the portal-quest fantasy. K. J. Parker's is the most exemplary of these texts, so it is the one on which I shall focus.

K. J. Parker's *Fencer* trilogy contains one of the hallmarks of genre sf and fantasy: it wants to tell us a very great deal about things we didn't know. By the end of this book, a careful reader would understand the theories of fencing, sword-making, building a siege engine, holding together a nomadic tribe, the economic geography of a city, and how to work magic. This instruction is a hallmark of China Miéville's work as well, although very often his infodumps are fantastical. How Parker goes about ensuring that such infodump brings you into—rather than repels you from—the immersion, displays very neatly the two elements I have suggested make up the basic rules of this form of fantasy: the concentric shells, and the use of antagonists to describe the world.

Let us take, first, the role of a stranger in the city. *Colours in the Steel* is a story of four strangers: Bardas Loredan who arrived in the city many years ago, a refugee from family catastrophe and now a fencer at law; his brother Gorgas who has come to look for him (but is not terribly important in this novel); the trader woman Vetriz, from the Island; and Temrai, chief of the plains people, who has entered the city of Perimadeia in order to destroy it.

Like the garuda of *Perdido Street Station*, Temrai, a leader of barbarians, is in the city of Perimadeia to gain access to its technological superiority.

Unlike the garuda, however, he is there to learn, not to find. One of the distinctive characteristics of the portal-quest fantasy was the idea of "found" knowledge. Although this idea should not be a necessary characteristic, it is ubiquitous and, as I have already suggested, disempowering, both in terms of the individual as a thinking being and also in terms of the relationship of the individual to the world around him. Those who search for a made item are interested in specifics, rather than the application of general theories. Temrai does not find a new weapon; he learns the principles of engineering, finding order to discover the foundations of the world so that he can pull it down around its inhabitants' ears. Temrai "makes" the world for us. What Temrai "sees" is not a surface vision of the world, transmuted into our terms and described from what we as outsiders (and better informed than he) know. Instead he mediates to us his attempt, as a very intelligent tribesman, to analyze what he *actually* sees. His perspective shapes the world.

> What Temrai saw was a deep pit out of which rose a huge wooden circle with fins radiating from it like the spokes of a wheel. Someone had cut a hole in the city wall seven feet or so from the bottom of the pit; since this was below the level of the estuary on the outside, water poured through the hole, fell onto the sails and pushed the wooden circle round before being fed through into a smaller hole controlled by some sort of mechanism which allowed the millstream out without letting the river in. . . .
>
> . . . The miracle was that although the axle turned slowly, the millwheel went round much faster. . . . (24)

Riding inside Temrai's head, we are positioned as intelligent outsiders, those who can describe a mechanism from the position of what we-as-Temrai might be expected to know and work out. But as Temrai does not know the theory of gears, he cannot make that final leap and it remains a miracle. It also remains arguable.

Immersion and Reader-Protagonist Context

In other hands, Temrai's description of the political geography of the City might become wide-eyed description, that Pre-Raphaelite intensity that has little relevance to what we need to know (described in chapter 1). Parker's work demonstrates that the key to immersion is context and argument: we learn what it makes sense within the context for the protagonist to *want* to know or in this case to puzzle over. Temrai, drunk, rambles, "there's so many things that are different here . . . you have a whole load of people who do nothing but make shirts, and another who do nothing but buy food from one load of people and sell it to another load. . . . And there's people who earn their living owning a house that other people live in" (40). Temrai's descriptions are a puzzling out, not a simple acceptance so that the greater detail we receive, the more we are drawn into *the process that is describing*. It becomes not a repulsion from the immersion, but a way into Temrai's head in which we come to accept as alien what he regards as alien while regarding as normal—because he regards it as normal—that men have more than one wife, "Most people just have one or two. It's because there's more women than men" (39). The shell space we occupy is Temrai's identity. For a brief moment, by accepting it, we can see Perimadeia as strange, not on our terms, but on his.

Making the infodump natural is one of the most difficult problems to solve in science fiction and fantasy. China Miéville mostly uses the method associated with *Dr. Who*: give one's very clever character (Isaac Dan der Grimnebullin or Judah Lowe) a less clever assistant to explain things to. In *The Scar* he pulls a very neat trick by allowing Bellis Coldwine to think she is the Doctor, when she is in fact the assistant. Steph Swainston delivers some of her infodumps as war reports, but also, by casting her main character as a scout (Jant flies above battle scenes), she provides him with a legitimate reason for making lengthy reports, for receiving them, and for having in his head an unfolding narrative of what he has seen. In this case, as with Parker's Temrai, we are contained within the world—rather than excluded by overdescription—so we are drawn into the context in which it is appropriate.

What makes Parker's Temrai tactically interesting, however, is that Parker has also made the *offering* of information by minor characters seem natural. Temrai (that is, Parker) has worked out what phatic discourse is *really* for: "these people who were so puffed up with pride in their city that they preferred to die rather than let it down might very easily tell an enquirer everything he wanted to know, so long as he asked the questions in a way that allowed the Perimadeians an opportunity of showing off in front of ignorant savages" (78–79). And so it proves. Parker succeeds in contextualizing the download and—something that is not entirely relevant to this discussion but is interesting—also uses it to gender his characters: it is always men who provide the downloads, the facts, the figures. Women (Athli, Vetriz), ask awkward questions and see the world as a set of social relationships. Vetriz, in particular, uses this technique to interpret a trading world that her brother Venart can only deal with empirically. Parker can make his downloads a strategy for immersion in part because it is an accurate representation of the masculine-competition interaction observed mostly in pubs (the example described above takes place in a tavern) and functions as a mockery of the infodump. Venart very quickly gets caught up in the competition to know more and more about rope, well past the point where he is capable of making a decision (272), while Vetriz points out that the real issues surrounding the decision were actually political (284). Perhaps more interesting, Parker sometimes uses the feminine approach—characters and their relationships—to render a scene less immediate and, by doing so, make it more real. When Bardas Loredan fences the attorney general he does not relay it to us in terms of the fencing moves, but rather the "feel" of the drama. When her brother Venart comments that Loredan is getting tired, Vetriz "briefly wondered if they were watching the same fight . . . she guessed that what her brother took for exhaustion was actually the short man clearly moving into the center of the floor, making the other fool do all the moving about" (83). Loredan will later make it clear that she was wrong, but the effect is to immerse us for a moment in Vetriz's worldview, and to make of the event an emotional experience, without the direct description of emotion we saw deployed extravagantly in the quest fantasies. We still see only what is observed and understood by our antagonist; we are allowed no privy secrets. Specifically, if we are to remain immersed in their world, we must remain immersed in *them*. The world must be painted from their perspective; it can only have the detail that matters to *them*.

Swainston's Jant, a winged creature, is a master of the overview and this perspective allows Swainston to turn the omniscient distant observation into a moment of immersion: "There was a commotion on the deck as sailors hissed in anxious breaths and scowled at the grey shape. Mist yelled at them. Then he yelled at me. I dropped a little in height, and hung in the air at the level of the railings" (173).

I do not wish to claim that world-building is at its most effective in the immersive fantasy—the Pre-Raphaelite landscapes of the portal-quest fantasies are effective in what they set out to achieve, the sense that one is moving through a world—but in the immersive fantasy, the point of world-building is to create something that can be existed in. If one turns the corner of the street, one will not run off the page of the author's speculation because the coherence of the world is such that out of sight of the author it forms itself. One way to create this sense of an extended world is through perspective. If the portal-quest fantasy paints in the overbright detail of the Pre-Raphaelites (Manlove, *Impulse* 130), then the immersive fantasy is Impressionism: Monet's *Haystacks*, each painted in a specific moment. The immersive fantasy world is frequently constructed from *pointers*, glimpses of a world that hint at something more concrete, so that the world is like Matisse's "fictional truths about shadows and reflections . . . implied by fictional truths about the location of the window, the position and shape of the vase" (Walton 321). The world, like the "real" world, is constructed of fictional clues in which a bare sketch of an object can function as the "sloppy symbol" its edges and colors filled in by the mind of the reader (Walton 318).[5]

Such perspective is person specific. Samuel R. Delany in *About Writing*, suggests that an author should "mention only those aspects that impinge on your character's consciousness" (96).[6] What a person is interested in can and does change; Parker's Temrai can turn and describe his own world as if he were a stranger, because his need to turn the people into a war engine means that "he found himself actually *looking* at his people, as if he was a man from the city come to spy on the clans" (161). The changed perspective legitimates his observation of men's and women's heights, of their clothing, their diet, and their living arrangements. The changed perspective allows him to become our surrogate questioner, to become an antagonist in a familiar world. Jant's wings are what render him a stranger—a mixed breed, he is the only one of the winged Awians who can actually fly—while Isaac's interest in science renders him a stranger in a world he regards as his own.

Where Parker seems to step out of the immersive rhetoric is during the lectures on the Principle (magic), where he directly addresses the audience through the figure of the mage. Some of the techniques he uses are fairly standard for science fiction. The first address is to an audience of undergraduates; later he will have the Patriarch discuss its finer points with a colleague. Two very neat tricks prevent this from becoming the downloads we accept in the portal fantasies. First, these downloads are told from the point of view of the mage. The reader is not positioned as passive audience (as a student) but within the head of the person giving the lecture, so that we learn "Alexius was a cynical man by nature . . . but even he admitted that he had one serious—even sacred—responsibility to each year's intake of novices. He must make them understand, as soon as possible, that they were not going to be taught how to be wizards" (10). The second is that it becomes evident that the Patriarch does not understand everything he says, and knows this. Everything he tells us is an attempt to make metaphor of something for which there is not yet an available vocabulary. Magic/the Principle is made the more real to us because the Patriarch exists in argument with it. He has studied it, considered it, and all he knows is that it works (96). At the same time, he understands that much of what is said is mere handwaving, rhetoric to cover ignorance or to create a sense that more is known than is. So it is that the general conclave can resolve "the synthesis-daithesis debate" by simply reducing the agreed number of elemental principles from seven to six"(171)—although Alexius can point out that this does not change the laws of nature. This incident, small though it is, gets to the heart of the creation of the immersive fantasy. A good immersive fantasy creates the world by writing it in such a way that noncomprehension of what is written and said becomes part of the mortar of the immersion. What is not said is as important as what is.

Casualizing the Fantastic and Making the Ordinary Baroque

The immersive fantasy looks at the world sidelong. The restriction to the worldview of someone who already knows the world has interesting effects: a useful metaphor is to imagine walking down Main Street with someone who is passionate about computers. He points out every computer shop to you and explains who in there are the better salespersons, and the details of what they sell and why. But when you ask what the very large building with the bright windows is, he replies blithely, "Oh yes, that's the Town Hall."[7] Frequently, the casualization of the fantastic depends on the use of the demotic voice. Caroline Stevermer's *A College of Magics* may be the most "perfect" of the immersive fantasies here, because it succeeds in casualizing the fantastic to such an extent that there is no hint that this is not a "mimetic" novel. Faris Nallaneen regards the existence of Greenlaw College and its reputation for magic working as natural. No one ever remarks on it, except to comment that magic cannot be explained or it will stop working. The nearest anyone comes to it is this kind of comment: "Some things can't be taught. Magic is one such. You may or may not learn it. . . . Greenlaw is warded to make magic likelier here than in the world outside. We have one or two traditions which may make learning more likely, too" (47). But no one teaches magic, because magic just is, and will either happen or not. The entire novel functions as a Ruritanian romance—a novel about a place that *might* exist, and certainly never presents any hint that it could not.

The result is that we are alerted to the fantastic not through the awe and amazement characteristic demanded of the reader in either intrusion fantasy (such as horror) or portal fantasy, but because that which is taken for granted by the protagonists is frequently marked by an ordinariness of description. For example, the British Ambassador turning out to be a woman (in the early twentieth century, 374), or Jane, teasing Faris: "Don't even attempt to patronize me. I am a witch of Greenlaw, you lowly undergraduate, and I shall be as lyrical as I please. Now, pay attention. The ward that balances Greenlaw has two anchors. We're very near the lower anchor here. Because there is a difference between the balance within Greenlaw's bounds and the balance beyond, there's a silent spot near the anchors. That's what you don't hear" (103).

But note the assumption that Faris knows what anchors are, that she understands the bounds, and that the significance of "what you don't hear" outweighs that which you do. Buried in this flat-out "exposition" are an awful lot of assumptions. All other descriptions of magic in this book work the same way, a seeming infodump that is still structured around the shared assumptions/shared world of the characters. Hilarion, the warden of the west, explains the consequence of the rift, but he never actually explains what the rift is (168). It is probably significant here that Stevermer does not burden her wardens with capital letters. It is enough that they are wardens, they do not need to be Wardens, with all the additional signaling that would impose.

Stevermer's work relies on a matter-of-fact demotic (an almost stereotyped Englishness, in fact: "It seems I have to save the world." "Oh dear. Do you have the training for that?" [181]) to create immersion. Other writers juxtapose the ordinary with the (to our eyes) absurdity of what is being described. A very simple example is the following description from *Perdido Street Station* (2000) of a cab rank, ordinary in the eyes of the protagonist: "Cabs waited all along the iron fence. A massive variety. Two-wheelers, four-wheelers, pulled by horses, by sneering pterabirds, by steam-wheezing constructs on caterpillar treads . . . here and there by Remade, miserable men and women both cabdriver and cab" (17). This is the first time we meet the Remade. Aware of rickshaw pullers in other countries, it is easy to be diverted by the pterabirds away from what is being described because there is no amazement at the sight, no indulgent description of men and women whose bodies have been forced into the shape of cabs, with metal or flesh extensions. That comes later; here Lin expresses only familiar pity.

Diana Wynne Jones uses similar techniques in *The Dark Lord of Derkholm* (1998).[8] "Elda came galloping up with her wings spread, rowing herself along for extra speed, screaming that Derk was going to be Dark Lord" (21). Only much later do we realize Elda is a sentient griffin. In both Miéville's work and Jones's, the explanations—of the Remade, of Elda—come later, long after we have, metaphorically, walked by. The reversal of the information flow is crucial to the immersive fantasy: an issue is first taken for granted, and only later, in another context, explained. This pattern begins on the opening pages of *The Dark Lord of Derkholm*:

> "Will you all be quiet!" hissed High Chancellor Querida. She pouched up her eyes and glared round the table.
>
> "I was only trying to say—" a king, an emperor and several wizards began.
>
> "At once," said Querida, "or the next person to speak spends the rest of his life as a snake!"
>
> This shut most of the University Emergency Committee up. Querida was the most powerful wizard in the world and she had a special feeling for snakes. (7)

The information we need takes us from detail to general context—precisely the reverse of the way we need to process the information. The result is that even with the direct explanation at the end of the passage, there is an assumed intimacy that frequently clouds the degree to which we have been given only *an impression* of the world. The cognitive technique demanded by the immersive fantasy is syntactic bootstrapping, the construction of a world from pieced-together hints and gradual explanations, the understanding of a world by the *context* of what is told. There are two ways to do this; one is the casualization of the fantastic. Here, Jones is the master. In *Howl's Moving Castle* (1986), she successfully reverses the balance of expectations. In this book, the land of Ingary is "natural," while our world is wondrous and unnerving. When Sophie, the heroine, first encounters Calcifer the fire demon, the description takes place in Sophie's mind in the context of her own thoughts and imaginings. It is an attempt to make sense in her own mind of the space around her:

> She turned back to the fire, which was now flaring up into blue and green flames. "Must be salt in that wood," Sophie murmured. She . . . began dreamily considering what she ought to do in the morning. But she was sidetracked a little by imagining a face in the flames. "It would be a thin blue face," she murmured, "very long and thin, with a thin blue nose. But those curly green flames on top are most definitely your hair. Suppose I didn't go until Howl gets back? Wizards can lift spells, I suppose. And those purple flames near the bottom make the mouth—you have savage teeth, my friend. You have two green tufts of flame for eye-brows. . . ." (28–29)

Sophie moves from rationalizing to "imagining." Indigenous to her world, Sophie is in dialogue with the world around her. Sophie may be surprised to meet Calcifer, but she is not surprised to meet *something like him*. Too often, this kind of meeting in fantasyland would include a statement that, if transferred into the real world, would be the equivalent of remarking to someone of one's own species "My, you're a *human*!" In *Howl's Moving Castle*, Jones remains careful throughout to distinguish the *ways* in which something might be strange to Sophie, rather than to assume that all strangenesses are the same.[9]

Michael Swanwick's *The Iron Dragon's Daughter* offers perhaps the most *classic* construction of the immersive fantasy.[10] Jane, the changeling child, is enslaved in a factory that produces iron dragons. In her dreams, "She was running and skipping through a world of green lawns and enormous spaces, a strangely familiar place she knew must be Home" (2). But awake,

> She bathed slowly, thinking of napalm canons, canisters of elf-blight, and laser-guided ATS missiles.
>
> . . . She fell into a dreamlike trance, the water warm against her naked skin, the dragon's voice almost real, stroking the bar of floral soap slowly up and down her body. (31–32)

The equal normality of dragons and of soap is emphasized in their association, while elsewhere the dragon is normalized in Jane's reactions. Like Sophie and Calcifer, Jane is not in the least surprised either that the dragon exists, or that it is made of metal. The hints have been there for us all along: this is a dragon factory, dragons are war machines, artificial intelligences given sentience through magic. But the *realization* of all this is conducted through Jane's shock and disappointment: "This couldn't be her dragon! 'It's not even alive,' she whispered. 'It's *not*.' But sick with disillusion, she knew she was wrong. It lived, crippled and demented, nursing one last spark of life within its broken carcass and harbouring hallucinations" (38). The machine-magical nature of the dragon is confirmed as Jane accepts it into what she *knows*—and the theme is continued as she proceeds to learn the dragon through its own sense of self:

> . . . she fell, without a shock, into the dragon's memories, and was flying low over Lyonesse on a napalm run. Pink clouds blossomed in her wake, billowing over saturated green rainforests. She felt the shudder of hypersonic acceleration, the laminar flow of air over wing surface as she made a tight roll to avoid the guns of an anti-dragon emplacement. The airwaves were alive with messages,

screams of rage from her cousins and the passionless exchange of positionals by the pilots. (38–39)

And to Jane and the reader is communicated a panorama of information about the world, its climate, its political relations. In this short paragraph, Swanwick uses a sympathy with the world, a law of signatures, to make the unreal real. That which is fantastical is shaped here by what we know. We shall see an extended version of this later when we consider Gregory Maguire's *Wicked* (1995).

As with other *antagonists* in the immersive fantasies we have considered so far, the changes in Jane's life come through the questions she asks, her willingness to interrogate the world she knows, or at least to look inward, to explore secrets. But Swanwick couches this interrogation as intensely natural both to Jane's situation and to her process of growing into adulthood. Where Temrai was a spy, and looked for the levers of the world, Jane discovers the world as she steals from it (clothes from the mall, the Wicker Queen's boyfriend, her own life from the Teind). Jane discovers the world through its loopholes, back entrances, hypocrisy and cracks, learning each time—in the death of the Wicker Queen, or the loss of classmates—the price paid for the survival of society. Frequently she gathers the information the way a child does, by listening to elders who assume she understands: "'This is a Teind year, surely you must know that.' Jane nodded, meaning no" (162). Jane acts simultaneously as a knowing and as an ignorant protagonist as she moves from the acceptance of the world of the child to the negotiation with the world that characterizes the adult, "the sociability of shared guilt" (270). Perhaps one way to characterize the antagonist in the immersive fantasy is that she functions as the adults do in their world.

Creating the sidelong view of the world can also be achieved using the demotic voice to construct a *disengagement*, ironizing the antagonism of the point of view character (a double ironization). An extremely effective example of this is Tanith Lee's *Faces Under Water* (1998), the first book in The Secret Books of Venus. *Faces Under Water* is set in an analogue of Venice. This is the city of Venus, a city that prays to both the Virgin Mary and to pagan gods. It is a city of contrasts, great riches, and great poverty; of piety, jealousy, intrigue, immorality, and generosity. The main character, Furian, is the son of a well-to-do house, his father a merchant and himself marked out to become a gentleman. But Furian has chosen instead to live among the poor, eking out a living scavenging bodies and copying books. Like Jones, Lee releases this information in controlled doses. When we first meet Furian, he is scavenging the canals, but we do not know for what, and when we realize it is for bodies (14–15), we do not realize for some more pages that these bodies are intended for dissection (19). More interesting, however, is the diction of the narrative. The Tolstoyan Furian has chosen to live with the poor but is not of them; he cannot but hold himself aloof and Lee communicates this distancing in the way she uses the narrative voice both as Furian's observations and as Furian's placement within the story. Furian is set as both familiar with the world he moves through—few places are ever explained—and yet an observer. The following paragraph is a good example.

> Steps led up to the high terraces of the Gardens. Here the only horses in Venus were kept luxuriously stabled in a lofty palace with a gilded chariot and four-horse team on its roof. They passed presently the ornate building, and next the wide enclosure where the blue rhinoceros stood, arrogant and forlorn beneath a juniper tree, staring back at those who stared at it. Over its tall railing ran a silver plaque, that proclaimed it a type of unicorn. Shaachen knew better and said so. (42)

Neither here, nor previously, have the Gardens been explained (neither has the mission; only later do we realize we are watching a ritual for the goddess Diana), the whole is described as it might be observed by someone interested in his surroundings, but who already knows what it is he is seeing. The same is true when the world shifts: "Either Shaachen's drug, or the illness, made it seem to Furian as though he walked through thick clouds of liquid. How fitting, here in Venus. Between the dirty stooping shacks and sick tenements, came sudden vistas of the Laguna Silvia, inky green, with pieces of distant buildings seeming afloat on her like tiered ships" (88). Furian, immersed in his world, *naturalizes* his sense of a world awry, fitting it within what he knows. Most impressive perhaps is the degree to which Lee manages to give the impression that the narrative voice is Furian's thoughts, without ever actually saying so:

> Outside he stood and grinned, on the narrow pavement. He did not know why he grinned.
>
> The water wheel churned the water.
>
> Somewhere there was a violin player who distorted the Song of Cloudio del Nero, and perhaps it was he who had aimed at him, from jealousy . . .
>
> A mask was made for friend or lover, either as a gift, or because they were persuaded to take one. And as the artisan worked, he worked out too how to accomplish a death. A very clever death, by madness or suicide . . . (109–110).

Because Furian stands apart from his world he can work it out for us, his casual distance from a world he knows creates the bain-marie of immersive fantasy. This novel, *Faces Under Water*, can be read as a detective story—as fantasy frequently borrows its plot structure from other genres, it would be unwise to make too much of this—but it illuminates again the connection these immersive fantasies seem to make between the character as antagonist and the arguability of the constructed world.

The second means of constructing the cognitive maneuver that is syntactic bootstrapping is through the *baroquing* of the world. This construction relies on the human facility to create meaning out of detail and meaning from sound, and makes use of straight-faced "stylistic clash" to construct the *sound* of ironic mimesis (Booth, *Irony* 68). The result is that a baroqued world is a synesthetic world:

> New Crobuzon was a city unconvinced by gravity.
>
> Aerostats oozed from cloud to cloud above it like slugs on cabbages. Militia-pods streaked through the heart of the city to its outlands, the cables that held them twanging and vibrating like guitar strings hundreds of feet in the air. (*Perdido Street Station* 63)

Or, as in K. J. Parker's *The Proof House*, the continuing references to smell, to an underground world in which the scent of a man's breath—garlic or coriander—is all there is to tell one the difference between friend and enemy, and so becomes a mantra that defines reality (5).

Baroquing constructs the intimate with artifice. Like the artist Gaudí, with his attempt to encode the natural in the innately unnatural of steel and ceramic, Peake, M. John Harrison, Miéville, and a writer I have not yet considered, Jeff VanderMeer—all employ the baroque style to achieve this. Estrangement shapes the mode of description and seems essential to the diction. *Titus Groan* (1946), *Viriconium* (1982), and *City of Saints and Madmen* (2001) share with *Perdido Street Station* the ability to employ the baroque to infuse the everyday with the sense of the fantastic, to enhance the ordinary, filtering the blur of the everyday through the sharp purple distortion of a migraine:

> Inside, Dradin went from sunlight to shadows, his footfalls hollow in the silence. A maze of paths wound through lush green Occidental-style gardens. The gardens centered around rock-lined pools cut through by the curving fins of corpulent carp. Next to the pools lay the eroded ruins of ancient, pagan temples, which had been reclaimed with gaily-colored paper and splashes of red, green, blue, and

white paint. Among the temples and gardens and pools, unobtrusive as lampposts, acolytes in gray habits toiled, removing dirt, planting herbs, and watering flowers. The air had a metallic color and flavor to it and Dradin heard the buzzing of bees at the many poppies, the soft *scull-skithing* as acolytes wielded their scythes against encroaching weeds. (VanderMeer, "Dradin in Love" 42–43)

The baroque functions like the steel rose that Durnik (the man with two lives) constructs at the end of Edding's *Enchanter's Endgame* (1984). Its elaboration is an intensification of attention, a thing made real through focus. Istvan Csicery-Ronay Jr. wrote, "The sexiest category of the grotesque in sf, as in most art, is the excess of the organic" (82), and we can see this excess of the organic in the streets of *Perdido Street Station*, in the marketplace of New Crobuzon, and the cold of Gormenghast (a castle that seems to hibernate but is nonetheless a living character in the tale). Because the detail of the baroque is connected with intimate attention and with the senses, relying on what Albert Wendland has labeled the "*perceptual* method" of "alien-creation" (62), it draws the reader in, narrowing the world to what is being described. It shuts out the distraction of *reality* with the noise of language and with what Csicery-Ronay described as a "recuperative recoil" (81). The fantastic world overwhelms (if only for moments) the ability to distinguish between the real and the unreal; we could borrow a term created by China Miéville and argue that the baroque makes of the immersive fantasy the "ab-real."

This notion helps to explain the construction of K. J. Bishop's *The Etched City* (2003). *The Etched City* begins with two travelers who meet outside in the desert. One (Raule) is a doctor, the other (Gwynne) a soldier. Both are mercenaries who have served together in the past. From the desert they enter the city of Ashamoil and make for themselves new lives. At the end, they both leave the city, again, to make new lives. Given this entering and leaving, the story might have functioned as a portal-quest, but we are not permitted to see their time of transition, their moment of being new. Nor do they plan to leave: they are not tourists but, by the time we meet them again, residents engaged with the world around them. There is no moment where theirs is the flattened landscape of the tourist. Neither of them, however, is indigenous, and Bishop uses this tension to create an antagonism that allows both characters to mediate the world through an intensity of sensation; like Furian they are simultaneously resident and strange. But we do have to consider that first movement, from a place known to a place unknown.

Strictly speaking, neither place is known. The desert where the characters meet is not their home; that is somewhere in the past. But the place known can be the self, and in *The Etched City*, there is a sense that each character begins as someone who does not know herself, and moves into a known personal/self-space. In part this unawareness is because of problems—in terms of creating an immersive fantasy—in the first part of the book (the section set in the desert). When Raule and Gwynn first meet, the immersion is broken by the narrative voice, which rehearses Raule and Gwynn's backstory: neither should need to be reminded that "Their old foe, General Anforth and his Army of Heroes, liked leaving enemies alive no more than Gwynn did" (13). And Raule seems to need to rehearse to herself who Gwynn is: "Raule heard less bravado than self-mockery in his words. Having become famous, or at least infamous, Gwynn had always professed amusement at the disparity between the grandeur that myth demanded of a famous man's life and death, and the bathos and indignities that actual circumstances needed to force upon both" (14). Unlike Furian's thoughts, these do not seem appropriate, because the narrator is quite separate from Raule. The narrator rehearses their history because their history is all they are, and it is related *because* it is a told story, refined into legend. Hence the nostalgic diction of the early sections that describes the failed revolution, the Army of Heroes, and a world that turns revolutionaries into bandits (22).

This tendency for the narrator to recite that which should be known intimately by the characters recurs once they reach the city. The description of the war between the Siba and the war Ikoi as the origin of the Horn Fan gang's prosperity (104) is a good example of how detail should *not* be handled in an immersive fantasy. Having declared that the Horn Fan's role in the war was unknown,

> If a complete and accurate record had been made, it would have included the following facts. . . .
>
> . . . Seeing profits to be made, he [Elm] formed a plan and launched the Horn Fan into international affairs. (103–104)

The omniscient narrator has become the sage, downloading a lengthy (five-paragraph) history. A writer like M. John Harrison might use this technique to deliberately estrange the reader from the world (see the future-planet story within *Light* [2001]); if we consider the technique in that light, Bishop's style can enhance the sense that Raule and Gwynn are strangers to themselves, and that they carry this sense of strangeness with them into the city. In some places in the text, the rehearsing of their history—Marriott's expulsion from his tribe, for example (107)—functions to emphasize their unnaturalness, that this is not *really* their place. Whatever they join, whether it be the hospital (Raule) or the Horn Fan gang (Gwynn), this history is strange to them, it is *not* intimately known. We as readers shelter then in the spaces between their familiarities with, and their alienations from, the city they are in.

Like Furian, Gwynn and Raule make the world around them through their attention to it, but there is a greater sense of the alien and hence the wondrous: "his eyes were entertained by the sight of balls of molten glass being spun on long rods . . . he viewed arrays of beaded and inlaid fans . . . in glass tanks, live tortoises with stones set in patterns on their shells"(122). They do the same with human behavior: Gwynn learns the rules of his society and enacts them meticulously, even to the point of killing his best friend, while Raule makes herself an ersatz conscience to replace the one she lost. *Faces Under Water* used description to emphasize the degree to which Furian was at home in the city. *The Etched City* emphasizes artifice in its narrative technique because it is, in part, about artificial lives.

There is a moment where Gwynn recognizes this artifice and recognizes also the power of his position, both belonging and yet apart; his lover, the artist Beth Constanzin has turned from "scenes of oppressive architecture and elusive life . . . [its inhabitants] . . . only alluded to" (234). Attempting to be a part of what she sees, her new work has the world "now fully exposed. The doors and shutters were opened, to reveal the world beyond the walls" (234), but in "depicting the hidden world, Beth's genius seemed to have deserted her" (234). She has crossed the line from "protean whimsy to one of debased humanity" (234). Beth has lost the antagonism of the scientist/artist, held apart, studying a world that is yet hers; instead, she expresses a "cankerous" madness that, in exposing, she is no longer interrogating. It is Gwynn who retains that position of interrogator.

The position of student-antagonist extends to the omniscient narrator. The narrator emulates the child trying to make sense of the world: "With those looks, was he a passionate libertine or an impassive, merely picturesque dandy? Did the outer appearance explain the inner man, or did it exist in lieu of him?" (55).

But in order for *The Etched City* to be an immersive fantasy, there does need to be a *known* fantasticated world; although these moments are few, they are there, and remind us that the world is strange to Raule and Gwynn because of their position in the city and in society, not because they are strange to its rules. When Raule facilitates the birth of a monster, the girl who bears it speaks, "The river god has the head of a crocodile and the body of a man. . . . I failed. Perhaps the magic went awry in my womb, or perhaps the god tricked me" (149). Raule, although uncomfortable with this talk of gods, accepts the supernatural, as too does the Rev, the defrocked priest, a womanizer and evangelist who can no longer hear God, but "grew cocoons on the palms of his hands" (167) and later "gave up and made the wounds in his hands close, and shoved his knuckles in his mouth to stop himself from howling like a madman" (168). Rev, who is only occasionally our viewpoint character, reminds us that this world is real, as he reminds himself—with a calm acceptance of the fantastic.

The general rule seems to be that the more ordinary the scene, the more elaborate the description. Buried in this is something that takes us back to the issue of perspective: the reader is positioned to a great degree in terms of what is not said, and this sense of the not said, can also be formulated as the not explained. It is this that builds the sense of depth.

Refusal and the Unexplained World

One way to achieve this sense of depth is as indicated above: describing first, explaining later. But a second popular tactic is through the creation of a vocabulary that claims meaning but reveals itself, if at all, only through context, which builds the sense of story and world behind what we actually see. Steph Swainston creates this vocabulary instantly by dropping the reader into the middle of a war; its origins are explained many pages later. In terms of a line-by-line construction, John Brunner's *The Compleat Traveller in Black* (1987) might be considered an exemplar. The opening line of "Imprint of Chaos" (3–55), the story I shall consider in greatest detail here, is typical: "He had many names, but one nature, and this unique nature made him subject to certain laws not binding upon ordinary persons. In a compensatory fashion, he was also free from certain other laws more commonly in force" (3).

Brunner, a supremely confident writer, is willing even to go one stage further than many of the other writers in this chapter and provide information—as above—that he will *never* explain. This withholding of knowledge is relatively unusual in the immersive fantasy. As we have seen, usually the world is explained through accretion, through the syntactic bootstrapping essential to science fiction (hence my first assertion), and through the reversal of the information feed—show first, tell later. But Brunner removes the bootstraps. This is the extreme of ironic mimesis. We shall never learn what "one nature" implies nor what laws he obeys or is exempt from. We do eventually learn that his mission is to drive magic from the world and allow the rational in. His mission is quite contrary to that of the saviors of portal-quest fantasies; he is not there to heal the world's magic but to destroy it, to thin its fabric in ways that will make it more intensely real. Where in other texts the thinning of the world is to be mourned, *The Compleat Traveller in Black* celebrates it.

Elsewhere, part of the first tale in the story concerns Bernard, a man from our world who wanders into the world of the narrative. A number of elements prevent this from becoming a portal-quest fantasy, including that the world we are in is never named. This is at absolute variance with the quest fantasy in which it is *our* world that is nameless. Namelessness, as Brunner implies with his Traveller, is both a definition of reality and an intensifier of it. If the world Bernard enters is to be real, than it can be nothing more or less than "the world." If the world is namelessness, it is also not to be commanded. This world does not unravel at Bernard's need, nor is it shaped by his desire to get home; it does not respond to *him* at all.

Here is no story of hidden princes/gods. Bernard's "recognition" as a god is a mockery of the fantastical in this world, as it indicates its thinning that the people of Ryoval should contemplate it. Further, the story of Bernard's presence in the world is told from the point of view of the world, not of the explorer. It is the watchmen who first see the four-headed god of Acromel, a watchman who sounds the alarm. "One by one the nobles were summoned, and assembled on the ramparts with their retinues. . . . Calmed by an enchantment they spoke in unison, thousand by thousand the common folk acquired makeshift weapons" (43). Although Bernard will find the solution, the disruption—the god of Acromel—remains a disruption resolutely focused on the world, not on the explorer. What we don't have here is the colonialist rhetoric that reduces the reality of the world by heightening the importance of the intruder. At the same time, this is not an intrusion fantasy; although Bernard is an intrusion, he is accepted into the structural order of things, first as a possible god in a world in which gods are real, then as a useful man. Crucially, the insight he brings is one already available to the people of Ryoval. Unlike most intrusions, Bernard is a healer not a disrupter; what he does is to allow the people of Ryoval to return to the rational path they have abandoned and do so within their own paradigm:

> But certain of his [Brim's] fellows who had been lukewarm in their acceptance of Bernard Brown as a ready-made god turned aside to surround Brim in a hostile fashion. "Nonsense!" they said emphatically. "If we had not been lured by fools

like you away from our customary trust in common sense, we would have seen what he saw and done what he advised anyway!" (51)

Bernard as intrusion is not transformative (the people of Ryoval become more what they are, not something else), but neither does the world close up behind him as if he had never been. Here may be the key difference between an intrusion within an immersive fantasy, and intrusion fantasy as a form. Notably absent are the rhetorics of emotion (awe, surprise, negotiation, or repulsion) that are the usual hallmarks of the intrusion fantasy. Bernard's presence is an arguable not an emotional event.

Brunner does something else, a something else that relates to the grammar of thinning in this novel and that connects to the idea running throughout this novel that the thinned world is the fully human world. Brunner's Traveller stands outside of the world through which he moves, but in his "one nature" is more fully of it than is any other participant. He can see more because his nature is denser; a little like Superman, he can see through the makings of the world to its spiritual layers. The result is that the Traveller is the only truly immersed character in the book: all others, although apparently more involved in their world, are subject to greater or lesser surprises as they meet the new. By his very nature, the Traveller cannot meet something new—all is already known. This positioning supports the accretion of the world. As the only real character, there is no one for the Traveller to explain his reasons to; they are as taken for granted as any other aspect of the world.

There is another aspect of *The Compleat Traveller in Black* tales worth noting. The immersion of the world, in particular our sense of what is going on, is created less by the driving narrative (the story) than it is by the vignettes that precede each of the five tales. In classical style, these vignettes embody the rubric to show rather than tell—while only *half* showing—so that the tale of Lorega of Acromel leaves her fate in the transformative waters of Metamorphia rather unclear. The story of the son who wishes to sleep with his sister leaves the fate of the sister unclear, but each follows a ritual that tells us more about the Traveller than any description. In each vignette he watches, waits for a wish, and grants action within the interstices of meaning. These vignettes read like prose poems; their structures emphasize the distance between the Real world of the Traveller and the Shadow world of the frequently unnamed persons who are frequently never more than their stated roles: mother, son, lady, lord.

This reversal of attention, lavish on the ordinary, often sidelong at the fantastical, is essentially a manifestation of the Absurd. The baroquing of the ordinary closes off the fantastic world from external questions. A reverse of the antagonist trajectory I suggested earlier, it creates a world that is fantasticated rather than fantastic, in which belief is constructed through the use of overelaborate language and of the deployment of the Absurd.

The Immersive and the Absurd and the Distillation of the World

In the immersive fantasy, while the baroque functions to focus the reader's attention, the Absurd ironizes the artificial. It invites us to enter into mockery and self-mockery; to recognize the false consciousness of the participants; or, by making absurd the realities of our own world, to recognize this fantastic one as somehow more essentially true. This ironizing can be a matter of plot: in K. J. Parker's *Fencer* trilogy, we discover by the end of the novel that armies have been mobilized, cultures destroyed and individuals beheaded so that one brother can make up a family quarrel with another—and it doesn't even succeed. In Steph Swainston's *The Year of Our War*, an entire religion is structured around an absent god, and the epistle embroidered onto the altar cloth reads, "*Why are we waiting?*" (209).

Alternatively, the Absurd can be encoded in the exaggerated attention to the detail of ritual or place. Either way, the use of the Absurd in the immersive fantasy draws us into conspiracy with the narrator and with the fantastic world itself. In *Titus Groan*, pretense, the pretense that what happens within the castle walls matters, is central to the intensification of belief among the protagonists with whom we have chosen to identify. The use of the Absurd draws attention to the essence of things: the use of the Absurd distils the world.

In the first chapter of *Titus Groan*, we meet the makers of the bright carvings: the objects themselves are unexplained, their purpose unclear because they are understood by both those who make them and those who receive them—and finally so too is the reward that "permitted these men to walk the battlements above their cantonment at the full moon of each alternate month" (10). "Saving this exception of the day of carvings, and the latitude permitted to the most peerless, there was no other opportunity for those who lived within the walls to know of these 'outer' folk, nor in fact were they of any interest to the 'inner' world, being submerged within the shadows of the great walls" (10). For both participants and readers, immersion in the world is a false consciousness. The inhabitants of Gormenghast are themselves caught in the immersive fantasy of a ritual that they cannot question because it is written as if it is unquestionable. It is a clue to the nature of the immersive fantasy: more than any other form, it must be *believed* in. This combination of the Absurd and of intense belief forms a heady mix in Steph Swainston's *The Year of Our War*. Swainston has taken the possibilities of full otherworld fantasy, of the quest, of the grand battles, and made of them something intense, complexly moral, and vibrantly characterized. She has done this by creating an entire world in breadth and depth, and then offering us just one sliver of that history and geography.

The book opens in the middle of the world, and the middle of the war. Swainston has blithely skipped over the traditional first book in which the invader looms, the armies mobilize, the hero grows to manhood. We arrive when the war is two thousand years old. Humans are marginal figures; those of real interest are the winged, but nonflying, Awians. There is an Emperor on the throne who has lived the entire period and who maintains the balance of power by drawing a line between the "religious" (the war against the insects), over which he has complete control, and the "secular" (the rule of the domains), in which he takes little part. Supporting the Emperor is a circle of honest-to-god superheroes, known as the Castle, who win their place by beating one of the fifty incumbents and are rewarded with immortality-until-challenge. Only one of the original circle of heroes is left, and he—Lightning—remains burdened both by what he has achieved and perhaps by the bildungsroman narrative that as an immortal he can never quite complete.

The novel begins with the report of a battle. The Fourlands is involved in a never-ending war against invading insects who are the ultimate enemy, impossible to share land with, impossible to communicate with. Their invasion of the land scorches the earth. They deal death with razor claws and eat their way through vast armies. The natives of the Fourlands—humans, humanoid-winged Awians, and Rhydanne—can hold them back only as long as they stand and fight together in a war of attrition gloomily like World War I. United, the prospects look gloomy; divided, the inhabitants of the Fourlands don't stand a chance. In this context, the death of strong local King and the ascension of his weak brother is the worst of catastrophes. As a chink in the Empire's defenses opens, each of the kingdoms turns to secure its own and the Empire, held by its own code of noninterference in local politics, is powerless. The stage is set for court intrigues, missing heirs, and maybe a prophecy or two. Instead, Swainston takes a long and very hard look at the tensions of a society with four species (maybe more), mortals and immortals living side by side, and an economy that has been subverted both by the needs of the war effort and the political machinations of the Emperor for two thousand years.

The immediate story is of Jant (known as Comet), Awian-Rhydanne mixed-breed messenger of the King, ex-street kid, present junkie, riven with insecurities, and profoundly in awe and in love (in a nonsexual sense, I think) with the oldest of the circle, Lightning, as well as in deepest thrall to Genya, a full-blood Rhydanne, and yet also in love with his Awian wife. In a search for escape, Jant has found the Shift.

Jant's own take on his world is alternately wondering and irreverent. He can describe a bridge made of insect shit with great beauty: "It was grey-white like the cells, with thin, twisted struts. . . . They supported a walkway which curved up for perhaps a kilometre" (115), and later remark of one of his journeys, "There are some advantages to flying over the sea. Unlike the land there are no people below so it is safe to piss from a height if you are desperate, which I was" (237). Irreverence about one's world might be considered an indication that one is secure in its reality.

Within *The Year of Our War* is a portal fantasy. Jant the drug addict uses drugs to move into a possibly real, possibly imaginary other place called the Shift. This place is made real through resonance with older fantasies, other places (an idea that will be explored further later in this chapter) but also through the taking for granted of absurdity. While Miéville's absurd is of the grotesque, Swainston's is whimsical: "Hundreds of creatures looked up as we entered. . . . Long-haired, well-hung Equinnes stood in a group; they bowed muscularly to Delamere. The Equinnes wore little, impossum-fur cloaks trimmed with platimumpus" (215). Elsewhere in the Shift we shall meet whorses who flirt for fares and the vermiform captain of the guard, a "person" who can break down into many little parts, and, most grotesque of all, the Tine gardens where transgressors are *impailed*, not on a spike, but "In a bucket" (188):

> There were rows and rows of canes, irregular against the hot sky. Rows and rows and rows of planted things tied to the canes. Some screamed. . . . (188)
>
> Keziah's peeling face blinked down from a three-metre-high trellis. Cables, ropes and gory tubes held his backbone in place, all covered with strands of dry slime. Keziah's guts were in a bucket, which the Tine drenched liberally with his watering can. (189)

Grotesque though it is, Jant, for the moments he is in the Shift, accepts the standards of possibility of that world.

The Inward Gaze of the Contained Land

One structural theme that emerges as a constant among the many ways to write immersive fantasy is a sense of containment. The immersive fantasy, to make itself real, seems to demand that it is all there is. In *Titus Groan* and *Gormenghast* this containment is part of the Story of the world, and springs in part from the idea (common to the Greeks and the Chinese) that outside of civilization there is nothing *real.* Elsewhere, as in Steve Cockayne's *Legends of the Land* (a book discussed in detail in chapter 5), it is clearly a Conceit, as it is in The City sections of John Crowley's *Little, Big* (1981), sections that are more fully immersive than is the rest of the book. (In both books the lack of names for the cities and the lands intensifies this sense that this is all there is.) There are clearly exceptions to this idea—Diana Wynne Jones's *Chrestomanci* sequence is very clear that there are many worlds—but there remains this sense that the microscopic obsessive gaze of the immersive fantasy is directed *inward.* There are at least three aspects or forms of this that I can find played out in the immersive fantasy: the tendency of immersive fantasies to be set in cities; the creation of pocket universes; and the use of genre referentialism to direct the gaze inward. These three aspects are not wholly separated.

It may be merely a coincidence (they were certainly not selected for this reason), but of the immersive fantasies discussed in this chapter, almost all are set within cities or within citadels—places that imagine themselves the center of the world. In contrast, the portal-quest fantasy is mostly identified with the rural landscape. As we shall see in chapter 3, intrusion fantasies seem fond of the suburban—perhaps because of the blandness needed to heighten the emotional impact of the disruption.

One possible reason for the domination of the city in the immersive fantasy might simply be what we think of as the urban mind-set, popularly summarized in Saul Steinberg's 1976 cover for the *New Yorker,* "View of the World from 9th Avenue," which shows Manhattan dominating the world map, with Europe, Asia, and the Atlantic and Pacific Oceans mere specks. Clute has written, "A city may be seen from afar, and is generally seen clear; the U[rban] F[antasy] is told from within, and from the perspective of characters acting out their roles" (*Encyclopedia* 975). The inward-facing gaze of the urban resident, combined with the belief that there is *so much there* that there is no reason to search outward, and the constant belief that there is more and more to discover within the environs of the city, helps to create an emotional trajectory that spirals inward, toward a core. It may also help to explain why the stranger in the city seems to own a different gaze to the stranger who passes through the city on a quest. For the former, the city becomes the world, and one can only ever go deeper into the urban labyrinth. For the latter, the cities are nodes in the world, beginnings and ends of journeys.

Of the books discussed so far, *Perdido Street Station*, *The Etched City*, and *Titus Groan* all clearly demonstrate the blinkered gaze of the urban inhabitant. In each of these three books, the secrets of the fantasy are at the heart of the city. Miéville's slake moths are hatched in the dark locus of central government; the brigands of *The Etched City* are its economic underbelly; the castle of Gormenghast looks only toward its rituals, and the external seasons have become irrelevant. The utter destruction of Isaac Dan der Grimnebulin's life is summed up in his need to *leave* the city. In the sequel, *The Scar*, Bellis Coldwine will find herself forced out also; much of the subversion of that novel comes from a protagonist used to looking in and deep, being forced to look out and wide.

A mind such as Peake's Steerpike's, whose rise to power comes about through his close study of the way the city works, its deep place and dark crevices, is typical of the immersive fantasy. But if we consider other heroes of immersive fantasies, we can see the ways in which that close study is celebrated and rewarded while constantly reiterating a trajectory that is always *farther up and farther in*, so that Furian peers into the canals of Venus; Jane heads from the dragon factory and the wilderness to the city, to the place of knowledge; Faris Nallaneen in *A College of Magics* must go to the city of Aravis to find the secrets of her own magic; and Captain Vimes investigates the gutters of Pratchett's Ankh-Morpork.

We have already considered Temrai: his joy in discovering the city, its secrets, its enfoldings, is marred by the fact that he wants to destroy it. A much more loving version of the same character can be found in the work of Terry Pratchett.

It is now customary to divide Pratchett's Discworld series into four groups: the Rincewind novels, the Death novels, the Witches novels (with the Tiffany Aching stories as a spur), and the City Watch. In terms of the types of fantasies outlined here, the Witches novels are (with the exception perhaps of *Witches Abroad* [1991]) mostly intrusion fantasies, the Death novels are also intrusion fantasies, and the Rincewind novels are screwball comedies for the most part, which might be defined generally as farcical quests. For the purposes of this chapter, however, it is the City Watch novels that are the most interesting. Their development and that of their characters supports this idea that the city as edifice contributes to the inward focus of the immersive fantasy.

The first of the Watch books, *Guards! Guards!* (1989), is the most straightforward; it wears an exoskeleton of intention. It is a pastiche; Vimes's drunken declaration, "The city wasa, wasa, wasa wossname. Thing. *Woman*" (7) is drawn directly from the work of U.S. hard-boiled detectives. The opening of Ed McBain's *The Mugger* (1963) is almost identical.

As in most urban crime novels, this book is about the relationship between a detective and his city. In later Watch novels this relationship will become a refrain. By *Nightwatch* (2002), Vimes can do the Elm Street beat without thinking, and knows the city through his boots (27, 94, 107–108). But in this first book, two characters display their love for the city: Vimes in his drunken, angry defensiveness, and Carrot, the human-adopted-by-dwarfs who has come to serve in the City Watch.

Guards! Guards! is essentially a book concerned with the secrets at the heart of the city. The dragon that terrorizes the city is brought to life by a conspiracy of small-minded men, concerned with petty quarrels held close to home. The city is ruled in the dark rooms of the palace, by a Patrician appointed by yet another conspiracy, who rules by ensuring the conspirators spend more time conspiring against each other than him—a theme that will be played out further in *Feet of Clay* (1996) and *Jingo* (1997). Solutions are found in the city. In *Guards! Guards!* the hero brought from the countryside to fight the dragon first defeats it, then, when it returns, is promptly eaten. But Vimes, the antagonist, knows his city and his world enough to question what happens. His relationship is loving but critical, and as the series extends, he adds to a world-weary resignation, an increasing cynicism. Pratchett uses this cynicism to tell us about the city, to tell us about its bones. Where Temrai watched fascinated at the interlocking sections of the economy, Vimes's despair at the idiocy and complacency of the masses is expressed in comments about the willingness of the poor to accept their poverty in the name of respectability (*Feet of Clay*), and sarcastic comments about the nature of racism (*Jingo*). Both characters express a *loving* antagonism with their cities that opens them up to the reader and allows us to forget that there is a world outside. At the same time, Captain Carrot (as he becomes) is in a way the archetypal *reader* of the fantasy, accepting what the city tells him it is, while simultaneously accepting Vimes's interpretation and setting upon it yet another: the literal-mindedness of the dwarf. Captain Carrot becomes immersed not just in Ankh-Morpork, but in the Story of the city.

As the Watch books develop, and Ankh-Morpork grows and enters a rapid scientific revolution (by 2004 Ankh-Morpork is oscillating between the seventeenth and nineteenth centuries), we move from an isolated city whose landscape somehow retreats into myth, to a place with a genuine hinterland and a relationship to it much like Washington or Manhattan to the rest of the world. Pratchett being Pratchett, the growing "urban mind-set" is mocked and made fun of. In *Jingo*, Lord Rust has to be reminded that Ankh-Morpork is *not* the world and not everyone will assume that its interests are their interests. But *The Fifth Elephant* (1999), *The Truth* (2000), and *Monstrous Regiment* (2003) demonstrate the degree to which a metropolis cannot but see itself in terms of its ecological and political footprint on the map of the world. The dwarf population in Ankh-Morpork is now so large that the expatriate votes of its dwarves can swing an election in the far regions of Uberwald. The city's economy is so strong that other cities need the news provided by the printing press and the clacks (a telegraph system). Even a war in far-off Borogravia becomes of concern to Ankh-Morpork as its efforts to look to its own concerns force it to be concerned with others. The increasingly outward vision of this immersive fantasy is brilliantly illusory: even in *Monstrous Regiment*, the story always looks back to tells us something about the primacy of the city. Just as K. J. Parker's city of Peremedia never really regarded the plains tribes as "real," so too, the citizens of Ankh-Morpork cast the people of Borogravia as actors in an interesting drama. When Ankh-Morpork deals with the world, it wants to know how many of its citizens perished in the earthquake.

This "city mind-set" can be formulated as a version of the pocket universe: in order to create the place of the city, the author creates a no-space outside of it. Within the city/pocket universe there is reality around every corner, outside of it, there is uncharted territory (in the quest fantasy the charted space is the road, once off the road we again run into the blanks). This might be linked to the Ruritanian tradition that seems to be one taproot of the immersive fantasy: the ability to construct a place that exists in a shadow liminal space between known worlds; this place is quite different from the Utopia that is discovered elsewhere, this is somewhere that already exists if we only wanted to look at the map carefully enough. Caroline Stevermer encapsulates this attitude neatly; the English Jane Brailsford tells her Galazon companion, the Duchess Faris Nallaneen, "If it isn't the Empire, it's all the same to me; Galazon, Aravill, Graustark, or Ruritania. You really can't expect me to keep all those little countries straight?" (43).

Two books that illustrate extremely effectively the ways in which an immersive world can be created or intensified by isolation are Diana Wynne Jones's *Black Maria* (1991) and Martine Leavitt's *The Dollmage* (2002). *The Dollmage* is a genuine pocket universe novel; *Black Maria* demonstrates the metaphorical resonances between the construction of the immersive fantasy and the construction of the pocket universe. Both of these novels have as one of their elements the construction of a world no one will wish to leave.

In Diana Wynne Jones's *Black Maria*, Aunt Maria rules the small seaside village of Cranbury with a fist of iron, but it is a fist clothed in a velvet glove. To all intents and purposes—as Aunt Maria's niece and nephew, Mig and Chris, discover—the people of Cranbury appear to desire the emotional imprisonment imposed. The pocket universe is here a sensibility. Men do leave the village to go to work each day, but the impression is that this is a ritual. It is Cranbury that is the real world.

Interesting for this discussion are the rhetorical tricks by which Jones creates the sense of a pocket universe. Not unusually for Jones's characters, words are at the heart of magic. The first device is the use of Mig's diary; *Black Maria* is a tale told mostly as a diary. Our view is restricted entirely to Mig's experiences and interpretations: "Now I'm writing it down, I can see Chris was lying to make me feel better" (48).

The first person is an intensely immersive device. It demands that the readers subsume their points of view to what the narrator as authorial voice is willing to reveal (there are tricks an author can play of course, but they are tricks dependent on this expectation). In *Black Maria*, there is a struggle over who will dominate the "narration" of the story, whose "first person" will write the fantastic world of Cranbury: Aunt Maria or Mig. Mig writes of Aunt Maria's powers, "On and on. You end up feeling you are in sort of bubble filled with that getting-a-cold smell, and inside that bubble is Cranbury and Aunt Maria, and that is the entire world. It is hard to remember there is any land inside Cranbury" (23). And when Aunt Maria attempts to bring Mig into the compass of her storing of Cranbury—to immerse Mig and to transform her from first-person narrator to second-person character—it is done entirely through talk, and as a lecture on the power of language to create a world: "So this is really your first lesson, dear. . . . The main spell is just talk, and that's quite easy, but of course you are working away underneath the talk, putting all sorts of things into people's minds" (183).

Combining a direct discussion of the construction of the world with a first-person narrative is a particularly powerful mode of constructing the immersive fantasy. The first person provides one of the layers of the shell—burying the reader in what is known by the narrator—but the actual discursive creation of what the world will be takes us further in. This approach is quite different from that of the omniscient first-person narrator; these narrators tend to spoil the immersion because they know too much. A fine example of this is in Robert Swindell's *Brother in the Land* (1984), in which chapters frequently end with this sentence, or a variant, "If I had only known then, what I know now" (see the end of chapters 2, 11, 20, and 26). In contrast, Mig is arguing with Aunt Maria over the fate of the village to the end.

This idea of a world argued for and created in the immersive fantasy can be traced through all the books discussed so far—Miéville's Judah Lowe and Pratchett's Vimes are all struggling for their version of the world—but the most direct version of this I have found is in a children's novel, Martine Leavitt's *The Dollmage.*

The Dollmage is the story of Annakey and Renoa, two girls born on a day on which it is prophesied that the new Dollmage will be born. It is also the story of the old Dollmage, Mother Hobblefoot, of her unwillingness to die, of her resentments and rivalries. It is about the life of a small village, protected from the outside world by the powers of the Dollmage. And it is, finally, about the making of story, for this is what the Dollmage does.

The Dollmage is unusual in a number of ways, The most significant for this chapter is that it is told from the first person but directed in the interrogative ("you" is used throughout, but it clearly addresses the audience, it is not an externalized internal narrative). The main character, Mother Hobblefoot, stands in front of a crowd of which we become a part *telling* us what has happened, interpreting the past, and leading us to the present. It is a revision of the nineteenth-century club story, and one is struck by the fact that it *should not be possible* to write this book—or, at least, it should not be possible to write it in this way, without producing something to which the reader is utterly external. Instead, Leavitt has constructed a fully immersive fantasy. Before I explain the rhetorical strategies Leavitt deploys, however, we need to consider the story itself, because the story has implications for the construction of the immersive fantasy.

We might consider *The Dollmage*, like *Black Maria*, to be a pocket universe story. Also like *Black Maria*, this is not the true state of affairs—there is a world out there—but the story is in part about whether that world really exists. *The Dollmage* is a fictional construction around the old philosophers' conundrum: If a tree falls in an empty forest, is there any real "sound"? In *The Dollmage* the question is, Can a world exist that we have not imagined and built in our minds? In its construction of a pocket universe, one way in which *The Dollmage* makes itself "real" or immersive, is by denying the reality of everything else.

Seekvalley is a small village hidden in a valley away from the "robber people." The mundane explanation is that these are refugees from somewhere else caught up in the strains between hunters and agriculturalists. The more fantastical explanation lies in the metaphorical understanding that *The Dollmage* is a creation myth: "There are no more valleys. . . . The valley where my great-grandmother lived was taken over and infested by robber people. . . . We came here to the only other valley that could be found in the endless range of mountains that make up our world" (18). Within the founding stories of Seekvalley lies the classic construction of a fall from Paradise. Once there were only the People of Seekvalley, with their utopian culture of promise-keeping; then came the hunters and the People had to withdraw into hiding, protected by God and by promises made and kept. The world of the valley exists because of a compact between God and the People. In return for keeping their promises, God gives to them a Dollmage, a person who can make the story of their world through the construction of representational figurines—dolls. This sympathetic magic extends to the whole village. The Dollmage keeps in her house a model of the village. A house built without first being modeled will fall. A figure that is broken, will presage an accident to the person or animal it represents. In effect, therefore, within the story as it is told, there are narrators and there are characters. The Dollmage, Annakey, and Renoa are all narrators. Other people in the story function as characters. The three storytellers struggle to be the ones to shape the narrative—this story could be rewritten as three gamers or three gods. That it is not, is because part of the narrative is the difficulty Mother Hobblefoot has in remembering that, to God, she too is just a character.

The problem at the heart of *The Dollmage* is that Mother Hobblefoot has avoided naming a successor; as tradition says that there can be only one Dollmage, to do so would be to announce her death. Even when her husband dies, a man she has promised to follow into death, Mother Hobblefoot avoids naming a child. If we follow the insistent lessons Mother Hobblefoot tells, it is this broken promise that is the beginning of The Fall or the thinning of Seekvalley. The private promise becomes a highly politicized event: the thinning of the fantastic will presage the thinning of civil order.

When Mother Hobblefoot finally asks God for direction to the new Dollmage, she is told that the child will be born on a given day. Instead of one child, there are two: Renoa, daughter of a large family of daughters, and Annakey, only child of Vilsa and Fedr. Mother Hobblefoot is secretly furious. Apart from the problem of what to do, Mother Hobblefoot dislikes Vilsa and Fedr. Fedr has gone to seek a new valley to take the overflow of population, against her wishes. Because she did not believe in the project, the "doll" of the sought valley was made poorly and discarded. Believing as she does in her powers, Mother Hobblefoot believes she has doomed the expedition and resents Fedr bitterly for her own guilt. Partly in consequence, she resents Vilsa, who persuades her to make the valley doll, and who refuses to believe Fedr is dead. But Mother Hobblefoot also resents her because Vilsa clearly has the powers of a Dollmage: she can will her own happiness. These hidden feelings deafen Mother Hobblefoot to God's message.

In order to decide the succession Mother Hobblefoot makes two promise dolls (all children are given promise dolls on their naming day that in their shape and materials hold promise to a child's future). Both dolls have the slanted eyes of the Dollmage but one is beautiful and the other frowns. Annakey reaches for the smiling doll but Renoa demands it, and the little Annakey settles for the frowning doll. Mother Hobblefoot, resentful of Vilsa, declares that this means Renoa will be the Dollmage. Over the next few years, she will encourage Renoa while putting obstacle after obstacle in the way of Annakey. The more wild and spirited and mean Renoa becomes, the more Mother Hobblefoot loves her. The more gentle, creative, and generous Annakey becomes, the more she is resented. Her everyday contentment becomes a constant proof that Mother Hobblefoot is not in control of Annakey's story. By the last third of the novel she is not even in control of the village's story; the robbers have found the village.

At the end, Renoa lies dead. Mother Hobblefoot has come to realize that one girl (Renoa) was intended to lead a party to the new valley—hence the child's belief that her powers became stronger the further away she went—while the other girl (Annakey) was meant to stay behind. And Annakey, who has broken a forced promise to marry her rapist, is standing in front of a crowd who wish to stone her, while her lover (Manal) stands in front of her, and Mother Hobblefoot relates the story I have just summarized.

The skills of the Dollmage are the skills of the world-builder. When Annakey emerges into her powers, she does so through the skill of the things she makes: "The blanket was sky blue, with a yellow sun and pink and white clouds. Charming, but nothing that could not be done by another girl her age. What was startling was that there were birds embroidered into the sky. They were so cleverly sewn that one could distinguish what kind of bird each was. . . . On the other side of the blanket was a worn, gray flannel lining" (49). For Annakey, the world is a matter of detail. It can be made "real" through a physical replication as intense and detailed as the baroque language of China Miéville. Renoa's making skills are more generalized, less intense. If we made the mistake of assuming that there is only one way to describe the world, we might make the mistake—as the resentful Hobblefoot does—of wondering if Annakey is the more talented of the two. But the immersive fantasy is a fantasy of perspective and while Annakey, close to the village she loves, builds the detailed foreground in the microdots of pointillism, Renoa, who loves the hills, sketches her village from a distance, producing something essentially more impressionistic. It is not that each will make a different world, but that they make the world together.

So far, I have discussed the tale in which Mother Hobblefoot is herself a character, but in the telling of the tale, she is the storyteller. When the story that Mother Hobblefoot tells (as opposed to the one she is actually in) opens, her powers are fading: her skill at making is diminishing, her power to link what is made with what is—to make the story of Seekvalley—is weakening. But the last tale she tells is one that still has power.

The Dollmage is, as I have suggested, a club story. It tells a story that the audience is not expected to question. There is something intensely cozy about the club story. But there is nothing cozy about *The Dollmage*, nor do the audience sit passively. From the opening lines Leavitt makes it clear that she is challenging this configuration:

> My people, lay down your stones.
>
> Before you stone this Annakey Rainsayer, you know it is the law and her right to have her story told. It is my duty as Dollmage to tell it. Each villager has the right to one stone, and no one will forbid you to throw it. But listen to me, and each of you will decide for yourselves if this Annakey is worthy of execution. (9)

Let us consider the challenges: "My people, lay down your stones" is a direct breach of the formula "Are you sitting comfortably?" that presages, in some form or other, the club story. The audience are not settling back, they are leaning forward. They seek for a chink in the tale, rather than accepting its impermeability. "Each villager has the right to one stone, and no one will forbid you to throw it" (9). The audience for the tale has been drawn into it. The tale will not just be about them; it will demand they are participants in it. And finally the permeability of the tale is insisted upon. Although the Dollmage will with her words seek to make the world, "each of you will decide for yourselves" (9).

The power of this opening lies with what it does to the reader position. Most first-person narratives either imagine an inner audience that becomes the reader, or are written for posterity (real or imaginary). In the first, we are essentially lied to, given the illusion that we have the narrator's inner thoughts and therefore a "reliable" vision of the world; even where the narrator is unreliable, the mimesis they build is impermeable. In the second, we the reader have no part in the shaping of the tale, and we are rarely gifted with the documents that might allow us to question it. (Christopher Priest's *The Separation* [2002], discussed in chapter 4, is a rare experiment in this direction.) This narrative is directed *at us*. The imagined reader becomes part of the angry crowd—the link to the biblical Woman Taken in Adultery is presumably not accidental.

Our role in the crowd is to be shaken out of crowdlike mentality, in effect, to be taught to resist the power of a Dollmage. If we doubt this, we should consider its chapter 8. In this chapter Annakey tries to make friends with Renoa at a party, but by this time Renoa has come to resent Annakey's talent and life-pleasure, and most of all to resent the love Manal, the best boy in the village, has for Annakey. When Annakey gives Renoa a cake: "Renoa did not smile, and because she did not, neither did her friends. Renoa's storymaker was so powerful that others submitted to it and allowed themselves to be mere characters in her world. Once they were in her story, it was difficult to escape, for if they did they might disappear" (102). In contrast, Manal "had a self-promise of which he was deeply aware and which he honoured above all other promises" (103). That the subject of this promise was to have a great love is not in itself relevant here; the issue is that Renoa's domination of story is counterbalanced here with the belief that one must honor one's promises to oneself. Annakey too, with her promise to herself (and her mother) that she will be happy, is defended against Renoa and the Dollmage. If we turn this into a reader-response theory, Leavitt seems to be creating an immersive fantasy by protesting that we must *not* become too immersed in it. Using the repulsion qualities of the direct narration, that by nature create both distance and the false intimacy of the tale told just to *you*, only to *you*, Leavitt strengthens the intimacy, bizarrely, by telling us over and over again: hold to the inner truth of yourself as reader, question the tale told, do not become a victim to someone else's narrative.

The political implications of this narrative strategy are complex. The Dollmage's narrative, although apparently omniscient, is a finding out: what she relates of Annakey's life is what she has learned. The contextualization of this omniscience transforms it: the intimate but distorted perspective used to project into the mind of a character becomes here a deliberate character study. The Dollmage becomes the writer and interpreter and in this honesty draws us closer into the immersion.

Leavitt demands that each reader write her own tale while simultaneously accepting that of the Dollmage. Unlike the other novels considered in this chapter, we are told the nature of the world directly. But we are continuously told it as if we know it already: we know to break a promise is to break our compact with god; we know Manal to be the best boy because second-best at everything; we know Annakey to be untrustworthy because we have heard Renoa say so every day of our lives. Leavitt has created immersion by presumption (rather than assumption) within a story in which the reader of the tale is acknowledged. By confronting rather than ignoring, she absorbs.

Knowing: Worlds within Worlds

Knowing has been a continual thread in the immersive fantasy: how can a writer force the reader to accept as normal things that are fantastical? One way is to create a universe within the worlds and stories the reader already knows. In one sense, this is almost the definition of genre, the building up of that common bible of expectations (and why both "mainstream" fiction and literary criticism are also genres). In fantasy, reworking old stories in ways that leave those stories visible is common: Robin McKinley has made a career of it with books such as *Deerskin* (1993) and *Spindle's End* (2000). Collections of reworked fairy tales are very common; some of the best have been edited by Ellen Datlow and Terry Windling. All of these fairy tales, because they are fairy tales and we mostly know the ending, or can predict how they will end differently, frequently do not function as immersive fantasies.

But an author can use the *knowing* of the reader to imprison the reader within her immersion, to use the sense of expectation to seal off the fantastic world and make it real. These authors use the legacy texts of fantasy to create endoskeletons around which both the story and the world are draped.

Even if one knows the shape of the skeleton one does not know the story per se, but one might know how the story works. Pratchett has used this technique in some, although not all of his Discworld novels. *Wyrd Sisters* is one of the earliest examples: the reader who knows *Macbeth* knows the trajectory of the novel, although here *Macbeth* is perhaps worn a bit too obviously on the story's sleeve. A better example is *Guards! Guards!* already mentioned. A reader of crime novels will recognize the structures, but anyone who has read hard-boiled detective novels, and perhaps particularly those by Ed McBain, will also know that all trouble comes via women. *Of course* the dragon is female. In terms of the creation of immersion, Pratchett has constructed multiple shells within which we sit: we see the city through Vimes's eyes. And if we step further out we still see it through the eyes of the genre reader. We are held in this immersion at least in part through our expectation of what should happen.

Guards! Guards! is a rather crude example of this technique. In later Pratchett books, the subversion of expectation forms yet another of the concentric shells around the reader: *Carpe Jugulum*, in which Granny Weatherwax uses what vampires (and we) know about vampires to defeat them, is a superb example. Pratchett has constructed nodes of recognizability that keep us within what is, after all, a rather silly world, But these might still seem merely variations on an ur-text. To see what I mean about the weight of expectation functioning as a tool of immersion, we shall find it worth turning to the work of Gregory Maguire and particularly his first book for adults, *Wicked: The Life and Times of the Wicked Witch of the West* (1995).[11]

Wicked is not a simple retelling; in fact, the tale of *The Wizard of Oz* emerges only in the very last chapters of the book. But the story is weighted with knowledge of what is to come and our curiosity to see how Maguire will bring the known ending together with the unknown backstory. And he does, with verve and with honesty. *Wicked* shows many of the traits of the immersive fantasy I have already outlined. It is told as if the world is known to us: the plates of saffron cream at wakes are *of course* what one does, just as social hierarchies are racial, and Animals are not the same as animals. Where Maguire cannot avoid the direct provision of information, it is contextualized. When Galinda (later to be Glinda) travels to boarding school, she receives a lecture on Animal Rights from a disgruntled Goat—a biology lecturer and campaigner for civil liberties.

The choice of point of view characters aids the immersion also: much of the book is told not from the point of view of green Elphaba (later to be Wicked Witch of the West), but from the perspective of her friends. This is a biography constructed through the glimpses we get of Elphaba as she grows up, through the memories of Frex her father, the self-centered

Galinda, the warm and generous Boq, and through the eyes of her lover, Fiyero. The result is a 360° view of Elphaba, who becomes a metaphorical edifice. This perspective keeps us looking inward, toward Elphaba and into the fantastic world; later, when the book switches decisively to Elphaba's narration of her own life in part 4, the author also signals that we are now in "the present." Throughout, as the various characters grow up, the knowledge they accrue confirms the world: " 'Underground' said Glinda, thinking of legendary menaces like the Nome King and his subterranean colony, or dwarves in their mines in Glikkus, or the Time Dragon of the old myths, dreaming the world of Oz from his airless tomb" (170).

The world of Oz is arguable. In contrast to the original book, in which social relations are taken for granted (the assumption that both the Tinman and the Lion can be appointed kings over groups of people comes to mind), in *Wicked* the argument about what is and about meanings *is* the story of the book. Elphaba, the Goat, the Wizard of Oz, and the professors at the University—all argue about the nature of the world, about whether Animals are people with souls, about the nature of leadership, and the desirability of order.

The arguable world is the revealed world. Glinda is not amazed by her first sight of the Emerald City; she hates it, a "brash upstart of a city" (169). Elphaba does not don emerald-glass spectacles when she enters it. She sees its "high self-regard" expressed "in public spaces, ceremonial squares, parks and facades" but sees as well "branched alleys, where shelves of tin and cardboard served as roofs for the flood of indigents. . . . Rag merchants with pushcarts. Kiosk keepers whose goods lay locked beneath safety grilles. And a sort of civil army . . . strolling in foursomes on every second or third street, brandishing clubs, angular with swords" (170). Some of these are images we can recognize; the neat parades of soldiers rendered sinister, the bars everywhere made futuristic in the movie. Maguire has made his world three-dimensional or "real" by pointing to the two-dimensionality or falsity of its MGM depiction. Later Maguire will remind us what Glinda the Good *really* looked like in the movie, "a huge Glindaberry bush. . . . There were sequins and furbelows" and in her face "beneath the powdered skin" could be seen "the wrinkles at eyelid and mouth" (340).

Part of what makes *Wicked* special is the degree to which Maguire keeps to the original text, but by a shift in context and perspective, continues this process of removing the veils of reader infatuation. Elphaba and Glinda's meeting with the Wizard is very similar to Dorothy's years later. The Wizard blusters and patronizes:

> "I do not listen when anyone uses the word *immoral*," said the Wizard. "In the young it is ridiculous, in the old it is sententious and reactionary and an early warning sign of apoplexy. In the middle-aged, who love and fear the idea of moral life the most, it is hypocritical." (175)

The structure of the speech, as with so many of the Wizard's speeches in Baum's original novel, is homiletic, cod philosophy standing in for great insight, a perversion of rational thinking. But Elphaba is *not* Dorothy. She knows her world and knows the context that the Wizard dismisses. Elphaba can see through the snake-oil salesman that the Wizard clearly is, can see the trickery in his fantastical appearances and the shallow maliciousness at the heart of his deep thought. Throughout, Maguire makes metaphorical Dorothy's later physical pulling back of the curtain at the end of *The Wizard of Oz*.

The politicization of Oz in Maguire's *Wicked* reaches out tendrils into the built world of Baum himself. Some of the threads of memory play not to our knowledge of Oz, but to our memories of Baum's Kansas. Oz is struck by drought in the early years of the novel, and Glinda travels through "overgrazed fields . . . dotted with cows, their withers shrivelled and papery, their lowing desperate. An emptiness settled in the farmyards. The farms gave way to deserted mills and abandoned granges" (169). This is Baum's Kansas of the dust bowl, not MGM's prosperous vision of a well-kept farm with three farmhands. Elsewhere, Maguire reminds us of what Baum wanted to do: to create fairy tales for America's children. Oatsie, the guide across the Vinkus, considers the purpose of evil within the *Märchen* (German for fairy tale, a form of which Baum was fond): "To the grim poor there need be no *pour quoi* tale about where evil arises; it just arises, it always is. One never learns how the witch became wicked, or whether that was the right choice for her" (131). For all the political metaphors that can be found in *The Wizard of Oz*, the tale simplifies good and evil, makes evil something that just *is*. Baum wrote a *Märchen*; Maguire is writing a full fantasy. Within the tale, he continually reminds us, are the simplicities of story that we somehow keep letting into our lives, as Elphaba herself becomes immersed in the old tales of the Kumbric Witch. However much she tries to write her own story, it is being written by the older tales and by her context. Maguire keeps this dichotomy spinning; the immersion is continually deepened by the resonance with older, simpler tales, and newer, more polished ideologies. The superficiality of fairy tales and racism in turn is rendered more important and more immersive through the effect of moral and intellectual challenge.

Pratchett and Maguire's nodes of recognizability are taken from modern fiction although Maguire has also used the tales of Cinderella, Beauty, and Snow White in his work,[12] and Pratchett's *Witches Abroad* (1991) has much to say about fairy tales. The models of Greer Gilman, of Nalo Hopkinson, and Alan Garner are frequently much older. All three use the idea that the same tales are played out endlessly, the actors performing only variations on the notes. This idea seems at first to run contrary to what I have argued about the antagonistic relationship of the characters to the world. But as a reading of Garner's *Thursbitch* (2003), Greer Gilman's "A Crowd of Bone" (2003), and Nalo Hopkinson's "Riding the Red" (1997) indicates, the variations appear in the tales because of the tendency of people to resist the power of story.

My reason for drawing attention to these writers in particular is that they are in effect writing about the *process* of immersion in which the trapping of the character within the tale pulls in the reader. Reader and actors share the knowledge of the way in which the story should go, *wants* to go. Greer Gilman's "Jack Daw's Pack" (2000) for example, is a Persephone tale of a goddess who births then eats herself, whose cycles are those of the seasons, transformed into a ritual that feeds the land and feeds on the ritual players. Alan Garner's *Thursbitch* tells of the remnants of bull worship in the Cheshire Pennines, counterbalanced with a story of a woman looking for a place to die. Nalo Hopkinson's "Riding the Red" refigures Little Red Riding Hood as a tale of menarche. And the undercurrent of story allows each of these writers to play with the possibilities of language.

In none of these cases is this play an exercise of the baroque. Rather, each of these writers relies on the solid tune of a story recognized and resisted to draw the readers into a world sung in a language not quite their own. Garner's *Thursbitch* is written in the heavy dialect of mid–nineteenth-century Cheshire, "that lot, once them preachifiers, once them lot gets hold, there's neither end nor side to 'em. They must have it as how first was their roaring chap, and he was, like, borsant with being by himself" (3). "Riding the Red" is written in a colloquial rich Cheshire English, the language of fairy tales (Hopkinson, personal communication):[13] "Pretty soon now, you're going to be riding the red, and if you don't look smart, next stop is wolfie's house, and wolfie, doesn't he just love the smell of that blood, oh yes." "Jack Daw's Pack" and its sequel. "A Crowd of Bone" is written in a fantastic dialect with echoes of the North Country: "Me mam and her gran—they'd ta'en him and slain him. For an Ashes child. And sown his blood wi' t'corn."[14] But if this language play were all that each of these writers did, then their worlds would be no different from the unexplained and imaginary ones of Brunner or Miéville. Where the baroque writers tend to reserve the baroque for the ordinary, the demotic for the truly fantastic, Garner, Gilman, and Hopkinson each conjure magic from the sheer possibility of language. Each of these writers demands that their palate be as rich as the world they seek to describe, aiming to write synesthesia, to write the textures of the world. It is here that *antagonism* reappears as they break down the world into fragments of feeling:

> The whitehaired child had slipped its lead; he whirled and jangled as he ran. His hair was flakes of light. He whirled unheeding on the moor. And childlike fell away from him, like clouds before the moon, the moon is a hare, the hare a child. He lowped and whirled and ranted. Whin caught him; he was light, and turning her blood to sun. She bore it. . . . The child was burning in her hands, becoming and becoming fire. And she herself was changing. She was stone; within her, seed on seed of crystal rimed, refracted. (Gilman, "Jack Daw's Pack" 91–92)

Garner can use similar language to describe someone struggling with his world and his illness and in the language's complex dissection of the world create the same kind of magic: "She slipped as far down onto the floor as the seat would let her, and pulled at the grab handle and the steering wheel to get herself up. His head was resting on the wheel, tears of laughter running down his cheeks, and when the wheel turned he fell across her lap. They lay until he could sit straight. His neck bounced in the headrest" (*Thursbitch* 64). Again the visceral description, the sense that what is to be described is the feeling, the sense of something in its most physical form.

This visceral quality is most overwhelming in Nalo Hopkinson's "Riding the Red." Whether the grandmother is talking about a woman's cunt or the inside of a wolf's stomach is sometimes in doubt, but that doubt buries us in the hot redness of the story: "First slip past the old mother, so slick, and then, oh then, isn't wolfie a joy to see! His dance is all hot breath and leaping flank, piercing eyes to see with and strong hands to hold. And the teeth, ah yes. The biting and the tearing and the slipping down into the hot and wet. That measure we dance together, wolfie and I."[15]

But Hopkinson has also rewritten this story as a monologue, "Red Rider" in Jamaican vernacular. And the move into language that demands we understand and accept intensifies the experience (although that statement colonializes the story. This story will work differently for the audience for which it was written, a point discussed later when we get to magical realism).

(Steupps) Old woman story? After is old woman who tell the story best! That story is fe-we life, and some of we survive to pass on the tale. She think I forget I was young girl once too? She think I forget how I did sweet, how I did drunken 'pon the smell of me own young girl blood flowing through me veins? She think I ain't know how the scent make Master Puss Tiger nosehole flare open wide to smell me better? Lawd, it make me body just a-tremble and feel nice to see that. I could make Puss Tiger mouth spring water, you see? Him would beg me, Lawd, Sweetness, just one more dance, nuh? Make I stay near your body heat little longer. Me did too love that, leading Master Puss by him nose!

The rhythm of this language builds the world, turns us inward to accept the world of the story on its own terms. The first version was a hybrid, a European tale worked into a Caribbean tale-telling tradition. This second version demands far more attention from the audience, turns us further away from the external world.

Hopkinson, Gilman, and Garner use names very sparingly. Garner allows his characters to address each other by name, but keeps them mostly as "he" and "she" in the narration. Gilman, although using names a little more often, is similarly sparing. The absence of names reinforces the sense that we know these people, as the story itself demands we recognize their patterns, and the feeling of the world they move through. The process of immersion is itself the subject of living. By the end of Gilman's "Crowd of Bone," Thea has been immersed within the network of the world, "My mother fed me to her crows, she burned my bones and scatted them. . . . Six weeks she watched me naked, travailing from Hallows until Lightfast eve; then Morag's knife did let thee crying from my side, and I was light" (48). She is no longer a character through whom we see the world: "In winder do I bear the misselbough, the Nine, entangled in my crown" (51). Instead Gilman has turned her into the world itself and we (and her lover) walk through her.

Magic Realism and the Immersive Fantasy

Before concluding this discussion of the immersive fantasy, there is one category of books yet to consider. This book is essentially about English-language fantasy; it has to be because it is about rhetoric and language. It would require a real expert in the alternative languages to assess accurately whether the arguments I have made here have validity—and to make use of translations would, however good the translation, essentially perform as a study of the translator not the author. (The problems that this limitation can create can be seen in an article by Alecena Madelaine Davis Rogan, which relies on David Le Vay's translation of Monique Wittig's *Les Guérillères* [1969] to discuss *the language* with which Wittig delineates her sexual politics).[16] A frequent question posed by audiences, however, has been where to fit works of magic realism into this taxonomy. Although some people have suggested that they are intrusion fantasies, the commonest proposition is that they belong with liminal fantasy, those texts in which the fantastic is both accepted and in doubt. Both these suggestions wrench magical realism from its context and force it to exist within a genre text in which the Anglo-American world, with its sense of magic as foreign, is the primary world of the story.[17] The "taking magic for granted" is thus refigured as a rhetoric or device, where in reality it is the representation of a "once world" similar to the "once world" of classical mythology.

Regarding the role of magic in magical realism as a device does work for some of the fiction of Jorge Luis Borges. His story "The Library of Babel" (1941) constructs an Absurdist, baroque, and sealed world, in which metaphor is taken to its rigorous conclusion, in which books prove themselves true, argue against other books, are unique from one another as commas slip and periods are omitted. "The Library of Babel," in which the library is the universe, in which men hunt for meaning or for prophecy, is a classic immersive fantasy bearing all its signatures: it looks inward, there is no world beyond the world, all that is to be known is within these walls—there can be no outside—the extravagant language bears witness to entropy. Jeff VanderMeer, whose work has been linked to magic realism (and some of whose writing is certainly Borgesian), wrote a short story, "Secret Life" (2002), that although it acknowledges an external world, bounds its characters' lives within in an office block. The story is built through the relentless drive of the Absurd; takeovers become bloody battles, the seemingly innocent becomes threatening, the pen taken by mistake looms large as a symbol of territorial challenge, tradition is invested in the faulty air conditioning and in the "breathed air that their predecessors had breathed years ago" (7). Like Borges's library, VanderMeer's office block moves from glory to decay. Of the two, Borges's library is more fully immersive because there is no world out there; in "Secret Life" there is, at the end, only the sense that nothing will ever again be as *real* as the world inside. Comparing the two stories allows us to place the Borges story as recognizably within the fantastic genre; work like this was clearly *meant* to conjure the fantastic.

The same is not true, however, of many novels that have come to be regarded as magic realist. These are set in a much clearer facsimile of the "real" world. They are not meant to act as genre text. Instead, the world from which the text was written is the primary world. It only becomes fantastical because we Anglo-American readers are outsiders. I think that the critic Richard Gullon is correct, when he argues that Márquez "is a realist in the presentation of both the real and the unreal" (27), because what I have come to believe is that the magic realist novels of the kind written (for example) by Gabriel García Márquez or Isabelle Allende, take the Anglo-American reader into an *other* world, which is to an immersive fantasy world (nineteenth-century Latin America) in the sense that it is told by a narrative voice that absolutely believes what is told, and in which the ghosts and gods fit fully into that structure. We need to recognize the full alienness of this, and the alienness of ourselves to this picture. Seeing these books as either intrusion or liminal fantasies of any sort is to say to the culture in which these novels are born: *this is not real* in the sense that we mean real; that is, to colonize them with our expectations. John Clute has written, "fantasy can only exist if the ground-rules of reality are being broken" (IAFA mailing list, 4 September 2002). As is made clear at the beginning of *One Hundred Years of Solitude*, the marvelous takes place within the ground rules as they are understood at that place and time. When the rules change, the magic fades away. It cannot continue existing once its context has thinned. The consequences of arguing that a magic realist text can be read in the context of the Western Enlightenment can be found in Smadar Schiffman's 2003 article "Someone Else's Dream." Schiffman insists that "the narrator cannot possibly intend this to be taken literally" (360) and that "the implied readers in all these works are presumably products of the Western Enlightenment (i.e. rationalistic) worldview." But this is manifestly not the case. Toni Morrison is writing for Americans of the southern United States, Márquez for Latin American readers; both are steeped in a religious sensibility that regards the supernatural as an ever-present companion on the daily rounds of life. If we accept these worlds as fully real and fully alien, then the books function as immersive fantasies for the Anglo-American reader in two senses: (1) in their insistence that the supernatural is real; and (2) in their trajectory, which is firmly aligned with all the other immersive fantasies I have considered so far, in that they emphasize a thinning and thinned world. In these works the decline of magic is accompanied both by the rise of rationalism, but also the decline of a civilized world—even if that civilized world is not always approved of in total.

Given that I cannot cover the totality of magical realism to prove this point, I shall concentrate on two of the best-known magical realist novels, Gabriel García Márquez's *One Hundred Years of Solitude* and Isabel Allende's *The House of the Spirits*. And because I cannot consider the language itself, it is worth focusing on the trajectory of these novels, which in themselves seem to confirm the trajectory of thinning that has been such a hallmark of the immersive fantasies discussed in this chapter.

Both *One Hundred Years of Solitude* and *The House of the Spirits* concern the lives of one family through the generations, their rise to prominence and their subsequent fall under the pressure of political and economic changes that spoil the balance of the world. In each case, we are left with only one heir, one possible savior of the family—a trope we saw in *Titus Groan*, in *The Dollmage*, in *Colours in the Steel*. I am not claiming that fantasy owns this structure, but there is a resonance.

The first point is that each of these novels is narrated as a history. The very distance of the past, the sense that the narrator is looking back, allows the externalized position of the reader to be embedded in the telling of the tale. The second point is the way in which the fantastic is depicted. As in other works we have considered here, the fantastic is casualized. In *One Hundred Years of Solitude*, the gypsy's magic carpet really flies and gives the villagers rides around the village. When little Aureliano Buendia, at the age of three, predicts that a pot will be spilled, Ursula is alarmed because this means he has special, inconvenient gifts, not that the idea of the gift (the pot itself seems to respond to his prediction) is unbelievable (*Solitude* 15). Clara, the youngest child of the del Valles, can also make objects move: "The other children had organized a system so that in case of visitors, whoever was closest would reach out and stop whatever might be moving on the table before the guests noticed and were startled" (*House* 8–9). Rosa the Beautiful has green hair and, apart from her nurse's initial scream, it is admired for its beauty. When Jose Arcadio Buendia kills a man, the dead man is seen by both himself and his wife strolling around the courtyard (*Solitude* 23).

But the world is thinning around these characters. As science moves in, magic fades away, and scrutiny makes it leave faster. Jose Arcadio Buendia learns that the world is magical from the scientific imports of Mequiades the gypsy—but a later group of gypsies, who specialize in entertainment, convince Buendia of the world's ordinariness. The vermin expert fails to expel the ants that torment the Treuba estate, and rages when the elderly Pedro Garcia tells the ants to go. His explanation—just talk to them—falls on deaf ears. This action is not sufficiently vulnerable to reason. The family home of Esteban Treuba decays like Gormenghast (*Solitude*); Fernanda's house is mired in insistent ritual (*House*). In a thinned world in which men are absorbed in reason, magic becomes increasingly a feminine affair: Clara and Blanca are left uneducated (*House* 117), both because education is for men, and to make them suitable vessels for the supernatural. But Blanca is too practical, too worldly, "and her modern pragmatic character was a serious obstacle to telepathy" (187).

In this world, the power of technology is still indistinguishable from magic: the banana company is "endowed with means that had been reserved for Divine Providence in former times, they changed the pattern of the rains, accelerated the cycle of the harvests, and moved the river from where it had always been" (233); eventually they call down rains that last for four years and eleven months. Over in Márquez's world, magic ceases to impress: "Father Nicanor tried to impress the military authorities with the miracle of levitation and had his head split open by the butt of a soldier's rifle. The Liberal exaltation had been extinguished in a silent terror" (104). The crosses placed on the foreheads of Aureliano Segundo's children leave an indelible stain, long after they are washed from the foreheads of others: but the crosses have lost their power: they can identify but no longer protect. On one night, sixteen of the seventeen boys are assassinated. The thinning of the fantastic plays alongside the thinning of the political and civil world. Like *Titus Groan*, each of these novels takes place in a polder sheltered from the world. When the world breaks through, it does so with soldiers.

As the world alters, it leaves no room for magic. Clara's magic was intimately connected to her uselessness. After the earthquake, she becomes practical; on her return to her city house, not a single mystic arrives to greet her. The power that sent out messages to the world has diffused—or perhaps the world has refused it? "'It's not me who's changed.' Her mother replied. 'It's the world'" (14).

Alba, a much later child, is sent to an English school: "Senator Treuba . . . was convinced of the superiority of English over Spanish, which in his view was a second-rate language, appropriate for domestic matters and magic, for unbridled passions and useless undertakings, but thoroughly inadequate for the world of science and technology in which he hoped to see Alba triumph" (256). When Senator Treuba's house is raided by the soldiers of the new order, "The books from Jaime's den were piled in the courtyard, doused with gasoline and set on fire in an infamous pyre that was fed with the magic books from the enchanted trunks of Great-Uncle Marcos" (340–341) And in *One Hundred Years of Solitude* a young Amarante Ursula will not wait for soldiers: "With a sweep of her broom she did away with the funeral mementos and piles of useless trash and articles of superstition. . . . 'My, such luxury,' she would shout, dying with laughter. 'A fourteen-year-old grandmother!'" (383). But with the loss of magic is perhaps the loss of virtue: Amarante Ursula will die in a rush of blood in childbirth.

By the end of these books, the inheritors of the houses and lands no longer believe in magic. Neither do they believe in good patrons who supported their peons and made a good world for all. All of this is swept away in a tide of repression and revolution, of fascism and communism. Both books end in a thinned world: once there were fairies, but now there are iron and bullets. Restoration (Healing) remains out of sight.

One question that is frequently asked in fantasy circles is whether there is an English-language version of magic realism. In discussion and in reviews, many critics point to the works of Jeff VanderMeer but this feels wrong to me: his worlds are elaborate contrivances, their alienness signposted, wrapped in a baroque very similar to that of China Miéville. Similarly, there is none of the irony or equipoise in the works of the magic realists, which might suggest that they do not have anything in common with the writers of the liminal fantasies (discussed in chapter 4). Magic realism is written precisely without irony; it is written with the sense of fading belief. If we are looking for some form of it, we need the literature of a similar culture, one in which the presence of other powers is a real and vibrant thing, even if it must exist alongside scientific rationalism. In her book *The Dream of Arcady*, Lucinda Hardwick MacKethan provides one very strong candidate: the pastoral literature of the Old South, a literature written in "oppositions," "town versus wilderness, Old South versus New South, past versus progress, man in nature versus man in science" (215), and that crucially shares with magic realism the sense of a thinned or faded world. It is hard to read the magic realist novels—particularly *The House of the Spirits*—without being reminded of postbellum Southern culture, with its mourning for the memory of "good slave owners" and its constant insistence on antebellum grace in the face of the Northern world of industry and capitalism.[18] If the American South grieves for a lost war (a civil religion of nostalgia) or for, as Walker Percy noted, a South now "almost as broken a world as the North," the fatalism that informs it resonates with the construction of the magical realist novels (MacKethan 217; Olsen 88–90).

In *Queen of the Turtle Derby and Other Southern Phenomena* (2004), Mississippi journalist Julia Reed writes of the tendency of Southerners to see God and the Devil in everything:

> Southerners tend to think that pretty much everything is an act of God. It's easier than trying to figure out why we lost the war, why we remain generally impoverished and infested with mosquitoes and flying termites, why there is in fact "brokenness" in our world as well as plenty of tornadoes and floods and hurricanes and ice storms and hundred-percent humidity levels. Hell, it's easier than trying to figure out what made the battery go dead. (5)

This acceptance of the supernatural extends to illness, life, and death.

> Another friend of mine once called me to tell me about a mutual acquaintance of ours who had almost died because "his blood just backed up on him and he liked to choke to death." That is, sort of, what went on, but what had led up to that event was that the fellow in question drank a super-human amount of whiskey for almost thirty years until his liver simply ceased to do what my dictionary says your liver is supposed to do. . . . However, my friend rather touchingly related the story to me—and indeed perceived it—as something that just up and happened. (6)

This sense of the imminent supernatural runs through the work of Southern writers. Lucinda Hardwick MacKethan observes, for example, the way in which Eudora Welty imbues her work with an awareness of the supernatural. In *The Golden Apples* (1949) the character Virgie's "perception of the things in time . . . allows her to open Morgana's windows to the world" (MacKethan 202): "Then she and the old beggar woman, the old black thief, were there alone and together in the shelter of the big public tree, listening to the magical percussion, the world beating in their ears. They heard through falling rain the running of the horse and bear, the stroke of the leopard, the dragon's crusty slither, and the glimmer and trumpet of the swan" (*The Golden Apples* 277).

That last line can be read as metaphor, but it is more properly read, as with magic realism, as mimesis and the awareness of a more intense and spiritual world. In both *One Hundred Years of Solitude* and *The House of the Spirits*, both of these elements are played out: the rain that falls on Macondo is the final revenge of the banana company, an act of God brought about willfully in response to successful union action. People die of fright in these books, or are decapitated in dangerous cars, but it is always fate. A man shrinks in response to a curse, and not because of osteoporosis.

Overeating on one night causes apoplexy, but the sense of long-term care of the body is absent.

The likeness is even stronger in the handling of madness. Both Allende and Márquez present madness as a part of the spiritual spectrum. Remedios the Beautiful, who sends people mad, is always regarded as some kind of saint in her inability to communicate with the rest of the world. Clara's spirituality positively precludes practicality. And of course when Remedios ascends to heaven, it is only to be expected. As Reed notes of the South, people

> do not question unexplained phenomena or the mysteries of nature, human or otherwise. This is a place, after all, where a great many livelihoods are literally at the mercy of the weather, where thousands of people still speak in tongues every Sunday. Stuff happens. So, if somebody simply loses it one day and is back to normal the next, or indeed, in sixty days [the portion of a life sentence one woman served] , we take it at face value. (44–45)

Although we do not, therefore, think of Faulkner and Welty as part of the fantasy tradition, it is perhaps to Southern literature of the United States we should look if we want to find an English-language equivalent to magical realism, and not to the shelves of genre fantasy.

Perhaps the most interesting issue to emerge from this chapter is that there are many ways to write immersive fantasy. Of the four modes, it seems to be the one that is most about the direction of gaze. Although the emphasis on thinning, on a lost world, is important, it is the least determined by emotional response (unless we are to regard as an emotional stance, "taking everything for granted"). So to conclude, let me quickly run down the means by which it seems possible to construct the immersive fantasy.

First, the fantastic should be dealt with casually, while the ordinary is made strange through the application of a synesthetic baroque or the eye of the Absurd. As a corollary to this, the world should be described, not explained, and the vision should come first, elaboration later, forcing the readers to construct the world from hints and glimpses. The harder they work, the more they will be a part of the world.

The perspective of the protagonist must mediate any information delivered: what he understands is all that can be described to us, even if we can add in additional detail. To grant the reader more information than the protagonist has is to unseat the reader from her perch.

A protagonist must be engaged with the world, and must critique it in terms of his needs—must be, in fact, an antagonist. The character must be able to challenge the world in some way, to step aside from it, and judge it. To return very briefly to *Shadowmancer* (a book I suggested did immersive fantasy poorly), we can see here how essential the role of the antagonist may be. One of the flaws in the book is that the trajectory Tom and Kate follow is *away* from antagonism and challenge, toward frequently irrational acceptance: "Thomas looked into his eyes, and he realized they were the eyes of the cross . . . all-seeing, all-knowing" (52). Thomas's complaint that God never listened to him, receives the response: "He has more love for you than you have ever realized, but faith starts with an acceptance" (197). Each time we or the children are told something directly, the possibility of challenging the world is closed down. In chapter 1, I suggested that the portal-quest fantasy was oddly Christian. *Shadowmancer* appears to suggest that evangelical Christianity (or any faith position), with its requirement of unquestioning belief, might be at odds with the rhetorics of the immersive fantasies.

An immersive fantasy is oriented inward, shielding our vision, creating itself by obscuring the external. It can use an edifice, a language, or a story to build the external world. What matters is that author create the sense of a place understood.

Finally, immersive fantasies are mostly fantasies of thinning. In their intense focus on the world, they watch that river that Clute mentioned flowing past them. They rarely tell of building, because building is a venture into the unknown. Instead they start with what is and watch it crumble.

Chapter 3

The Intrusion Fantasy

This chapter was originally planned as chapter 2, immediately succeeding the discussion of the portal-quest, of which it seemed a mirror image. It has been moved because I disagree with Brian Stableford's comment that an intrusive fantasy ipso facto begins in a simulacrum of the real world (2005, liii). Granted, the intrusion rhetoric seems best hosted in the primary world—perhaps because in this mode the contrast between the mundane and the intruding fantastic can be heightened—but in practice, immersive fantasies can host an intrusion (see the Slake Moths of *Perdido Street Station* or the alternative worlds of Laurell K. Hamilton's *Anita Blake* sequence [1993–2000], or Robin McKinley's *Sunshine* [2003]) and I might argue that almost every Dark Lord of the portal-quest fantasy is an intruder. They never seem to be natives to the Land: one of the early models for the form, the White Queen of *The Lion, the Witch and the Wardrobe*, is descended from an intruder from another world; while in J. K. Rowling's Harry Potter sequence, both the evil intrusion and the disruptive humor are located with half-breeds (Lord Voldemort and Hagrid respectively). It is quite possible, as we shall see when we consider intrusions within immersive fantasies, that one rhetorical function of the intruder in an otherworld fantasy, is to render that otherworld more "real" by virtue of the juxtaposition. It consequently makes sense to place this chapter after the two chapters within which it can work, and before the chapter that Stableford argues is simply a subspecies of intrusion (but that, I am more inclined to argue, is perhaps the most antagonistic to it). There is also an argument that runs through this discussion, that the intrusion fantasy, in normalizing the "other," can actually function as an immersive fantasy in that it (sometimes) demands that the protagonist, if not the other characters, accept the fantastic as normal. We shall see this use of immersion in the discussion of *Jonathan Strange and Mr. Norrell*, in which the fantastic is the norm, but the specifics of the fantastic intrusion are not. This approach of course ties in with the idea of the club story, the idea that belief, not reason, reigns supreme that I have discussed in chapter 1 and shall discuss again here.

The trajectory of the intrusion fantasy is straightforward: the world is ruptured by the intrusion, which disrupts normality and has to be negotiated with or defeated, sent back whence it came, or controlled. In a few cases the intrusion wins but there is always a return of some kind (see Clute and Grant for an explanation of return). Edward Eager saw this trajectory as the basic shape of his comic urban fantasies, elaborating on the formula in the chapter titles of *Seven-Day Magic*: "Finding It, Using It, Taming It, Losing It, Thwarting It, Being Thwarted, Keeping It?, and Giving It Back." (Attebery, *Tradition* 142). Eager of course took this structure from E. Nesbit's fantasies. In *Five Children and It* (1902), the screwball comedy structure always begins with the intrusive consequences of an inappropriate wish and the tale of each chapter is the children's attempt to cope with the consequences. Each day, however, is begun anew. As Eve Kosofsky Sedgwick understood in her discussion of the Gothic, once you know a novel is intrusion fantasy, its structure is unnervingly transparent (8).

As a rhetoric, the form appears to depend both on the naïveté of the protagonist and her awareness of the permeability of the world—a distrust of what is known in favor of what is sensed. This lack of trust sets up an interesting dynamic around the issue of what is known. As Stephanie Moss (2005) has pointed out, the role of the skeptic is frequently crucial to generating the push/pull rhythm of the fantasy. The trajectory of the intrusion fantasy is from *denial* to *acceptance*: from taking a meal with a vampire and ignoring his lack of reflection, to the point where the protagonist reaches for the stake. For all that the intrusion fantasy appears—usually—to be a "this world" fantasy, the narrative leads always toward the acceptance of the fantastic, by the reader if not the protagonist.[1] At least one of the necessary considerations for writers constructing intrusion fantasies is how to negotiate this acceptance.

The rhythm of the intrusion fantasy is a cycle of suspension and release, latency and escalation, hesitation and remorselessness. It can be constructed within the plot, within the description of the text, or—as Kathleen Spencer in her discussion of Charles Williams's novels has pointed out (68–70)—in the alternation between direct and indirect speech. The suspension of the intrusion fantasy does not seem to be constructed in the same way as the estrangement or knowingness of the liminal fantastic (see chapter 4). Where the liminal fantasy is about doubt, the intrusion fantasy constructs its suspension through escalation. The intrusion fantasies are remorseless. As with the crime novel (which may be a form of the intrusion fantasy), there is no escape—or, if there is, it is hidden or encapsulated within this trajectory. One of the themes that came to the surface of the novels as I read them, was a sense of encroaching intimacy. Peter Straub once wrote, "Most fiction alluded to death in a respectful way, and in a few superior novels you walked past the (closed) coffin, but horror opened the lid and climbed right in there with the main attraction" (8). The direction in which horror moves in Straub's blithe summary is not coincidental. In the intrusion fantasy, the fantastic likes to breathe down the reader/protagonist's neck (it may be for this reason that lacy nightgowns have become an indicative trope of horror, even while they are actually rare).

The intrusion fantasy uses the form of the club story—the unquestioned tale—to construct consensus reality, then renders the walls of the world-story translucent. Like the portal-quest fantasy, the intrusion fantasy demands belief, but whereas the portal-quest fantasy demands belief in the surface of the world, the intrusion fantasy requires faith in the *sub*-surface, the sense that there is always something lurking. We might call this latency: the withholding, not of information, but of visuals or events. Many horrors take place offstage, or are first represented onstage with hints and warnings: for example, *The Strange Case of Dr Jekyll and Mr. Hyde* (1886), where the narrative is constructed through evidentiary clues; or in Shirley Jackson's *The Haunting of Hill House* (1957), where latency is interwoven into point and counterpoint of event and emotional reaction. It is in constructing the awareness of the latent (Yvonne Leffler's "anticipatory reading" [177]) that many authors of intrusion fantasy expend their greatest creativity, which in turn shapes the often prosaic tones with which they describe the mundane. If the portal-quest fantasy emphasizes recognition then the intrusion fantasy plays one prolonged note of thinning. Recognition (or perhaps *revelation*) is frequently a late, and hurried note in this form, and this is connected to the importance of *escalation*.

If latency is one of the most powerful techniques of the intrusion fantasy, the form also relies heavily on the *escalation* of effect. Intrusions begin small and often quite distant. They increase in magnitude, in scope, or in the number of victims. Yet what strikes me most about the intrusion fantasy is the extent to which each is "concluded." However mysterious the ending, there is the sense that there can be no *next*. We are left suspended on the edge of the void. Any *next* would be an anticlimax. There are, of course, ways to mitigate this abeyance; there *have* to be because of the propensity of genre fiction to spawn sequels. And the sequels divide neatly into two strands: the re-creation of naïveté and the escalation of threat, both of which are essentially about the re-creation of the naive response, and both of which are steadily exhausted strategies.[2]

What all of the above points to is that, if the portal-quest fantasy was a fantasy of the *visual*, I am increasingly convinced that the intrusion fantasy is a fantasy of the aural. Guy Barker, speaking of Jazz, observed, "Music is always based on tension . . . release, tension . . . release."[3] As the intrusion fantasy develops from the baroque Gothic styles to the more demotic language of the urban fantasies of writers like Nesbit, and on to Stephen King and his heirs, this rhythm of tension and release remains a constant.

Having set out what I think are the basic shapes of the intrusion fantasy, and before I move on to the variations that authors have played on these notes, I want to start with a short discussion of an exemplary text, Neil Gaiman and Dave McKean's *The Wolves in the Walls* (2003). Although I have suggested that the intrusion fantasy may be primarily an aural mode, visual cues do matter, and nowhere more than in the sense of initial setting. As we shall see, authors expend a great deal of energy in the intrusion fantasy in creating the sense of the setting as "spooky," places that harbor the latent. Peter Straub's *In the Night Room* (2004) begins with two chapters that are entirely about constructing latency in *place* through a complex mirroring of spatial cues. In each case there has to be—simultaneously—the construction of a sense of a protected space, one that cannot be ruptured, and a sense that such a rupture is imminent. Almost all crime novels are novels of place; the most obvious subgenre to fit this rubric is the English domestic mystery novel. *The Wolves in the Walls* constructs this duality through pictures. The first two pages of *The Wolves In The Walls* contain all the indicators of the domestic (a staircase, pictures, flowers, a young girl) set at uncomfortable angles, with distorted perspective or, in the case of the pictures that hang on the walls (mere sketches of open mouthed canines), harboring hints of the intrusion.

We turn over the page to a domestic scene.

- Inside the house everything was quiet. Her mother was putting homemade jam into pots.
- Her father was out at his job, playing the tuba.
- Her brother was in the living room playing video games.

The accoutrements of domesticity are there, but the pictures belie the comfort: they are oddly angled, their colors subtly threatening (dark reds and beiges). By the next page, when Lucy begins to hear voices, we have already been set on edge. The construction of the uneasy space is essential to prime us for the use of "reason" rather than a scientific explanation; that is, the construction of an explanation from the first principles, from Baconian observation rather than accumulated scientific hypothesis. This insistence on *what one can see and observe*, rather than what one actually knows of the world, seems to me to be fundamental to the construction of faith in the fantastic of the intrusion fantasy. The insistence on observation stands in opposition to, but is no less distorting than, the portal-quest system where what is encoded in books frequently supersedes the evidence of the senses.

Because *The Wolves in the Walls* is a picture book for children in which onomatopoeia is taken for granted, we can miss the degree to which it is also exemplary to the intrusion text. The *sound* of the fantastic—from the Gothic onward—drives the escalation of latency.

- Lucy heard noises.
- The noises were coming from inside the walls.
- They were hustling noises and bustling noises.
- They were crinkling noises and crackling noises.
- They were sneaking, creeping, crumpling noises.

Reading this section with children it is noticeable that as they join in (after several repetitions of course), they escalate the sound. This is even more the case as we move onto the "refrain," "If the wolves come out of the walls, then it's all over." The intrusion fantasy, to state the obvious, is about the *approach* rather than the arrival of the fantastic: all too often, as we shall see repeatedly in this chapter, the actual arrival is a bit of a letdown; it marks the end of the adventure rather than the beginning.

But before we get to the moment of intrusion, the rhythm of tension and release needs to be established. In *The Wolves in the Walls*, Gaiman constructs his pattern in the A/B structure of a child's misprisions about the world.

- "There are wolves in the walls," she told him [her father].
- "I don't think there are, poppet," he told her. "You have an overactive imagination. Perhaps the noises you heard from rats. Sometimes you get rats in big old houses like this.
- "It's wolves," said Lucy. "I can feel them in my tummy. And pig-puppet thinks it's wolves as well."

Although Lucy does not talk in questions, she is questioning. In some of the other fiction I shall consider, this questioning will be less immediately obvious, but in the intrusion fantasy the role of the *question* is vital. I've already suggested that the intrusion fantasy is a form of the club story (structured around a consensual suspicion of the world's boundaries); in contrast, however, to the portal-quest fantasy, which depends on the preservation of the club story's impermeability, here its purpose *is* to be challenged. The protagonist is frequently the sole person outside the club story of consensus reality. In *The Wolves in the Walls*, the club story of "adulthood"—rational, based on what is known, what "everyone knows," or what authority asserts (Mr. Wilson who knows there "are no wolves in this part of the world . . . wolves don't live in walls, only mice and rats and bats and things" says Lucy's brother)—is questioned by the "Reason" of the child working from the first principles of what she observes.[4]

All of this is conducted in a chant, emphasizing that point and counterpoint to which I shall repeatedly be drawing attention: Lucy stating the reality of the fantastic, her family underscoring the stability of the "real" world. Lucy is the advocate for a belief in the substructures of the world, the lurking other beneath the surface.

In *The Wolves in the Walls*, the wolves come out of the walls in the middle of the night. The illustrations shift from the uneasy reds and browns, to black-and-white drawings enhanced with touches of color—the yellow of the wolves' eyes intruding into the picture-text. The shift to another mode of drawing—from block prints to line drawings—emphasizes their fantastic nature: as the lines are imposed over the block prints, so the fantastic rides over the mundane. As we shall see later in this chapter, one of the strategies that marks the intrusion fantasy is that the fantastic in the intrusion fantasy is frequently delivered in a demotic voice; it is the latency that is elaborate and Dave McKean has encoded this latency in his visualizations.

The family flee and move to the garden, pictured in blues and greens, a cool, safe space. While they are there, they imagine what the wolves might be doing: "watching their television and eating food from the family's pantry and dancing wolfish dances up the stairs and down again." After the rhetorical escalation of Lucy's insistence, the wolves are almost fanciful. Not a letdown, but a breathing space. The intrusion of the other is almost a relief after the creation of tension. There is a pause as the family work out where they could live.

Lucy's decision to go back into the house reverses the trajectory. For a moment, she is the intrusion, she becomes the latent other:

- Quick as the flick of the wing of a bat,
- Lucy slipped into the wall.
- She crept through the house on the inside.

- through the downstairs,
- up the middle
- and into the wall of her bedroom.

As with Pinter, the pauses matter. They *sound.*

Lucy finds a wolf wearing her socks, snoring. The fantastical once it has emerged becomes less threatening because it is now manifest. In the intrusion fantasy it is the unmanifested fantastic that is most threatening (as I shall discuss later, showing the unshown can be a real problem for writers of horror).

Lucy convinces her family that the walls are quite nice and that they should go and live there. In a neat reversal they peek through the eyeholes in the paintings, this time sketches of the family. (The other pictures were of the wolves. The implication is clear: we like to live with the possibility of what scares us.) What they see is the wolves creating mayhem, wearing the family's clothes, sliding down the banisters, having a party. The images that Dave McKean creates again combine the block prints of the household accoutrements (the video game, Dad's tuba) with the sketches of the wolves; the result is to emphasize two world-layers interacting. But also with ritual. The intrusion fantasy is structured less around a known plot, than a known *response.* Like Toad and his fellows in *The Wind in the Willows*, the family decides to launch a raid; the wolves react in horror:

- "Arrgh!" howled the wolves. "The people have come out of the walls!"
- "And when the people come out of the walls," shouted the biggest, fattest wolf, flinging aside the tuba, "it's all over!"

Gathering up their favorite possessions, they flee. Order is restored, the intruder has been repelled, and normality is signaled with a party feast, in bright reds and yellows, vivid enhancements of the dark reds and beiges of the threatened place at the beginning of the book.

But then, just as we think the world is restored: "Lucy noticed something funny . . . she heard a noise that sounded exactly like an elephant trying not to sneeze." Gaiman and McKean capture the way in which the ending of the intrusion fantasy seems to be caught in a cleft stick. It can of course indicate the permanent reinstatement of the mundane. But if there is to be any kind of opening, its only available trajectory appears to be in escalation.

Gaiman and McKean's *The Wolves in the Walls* seems to encapsulate the tropes of the intrusion fantasy: the belief in what cannot be seen but is sensed, the preference for what the senses tell one over "knowledge" (Van Belkom 12); the unreasoning nature of the threat; the feeling that the real pleasure is in the latency of the threat; and that "feeling" (I deliberately eschew "emotion" here; that is not quite what is happening) is the heart of experience; the remorselessness and escalation of the horrors, and the need for the audience to respond to all of these with sensibility not intellect (for the form to be, as critics have frequently described it "sensationalist" literature). Finally, there is the aurality of the text, to which I shall keep returning. The intrusion fantasy creates response directly through the sound of the world, the sound of horror, of fear, or of surprise.

Unlike the portal-quest fantasies, which I suggested had their origins in Greek quest myths and later Christian grace texts such as *The Pilgrim's Progress*, it is harder to trace historical antecedents for the intrusion fantasy. Clearly any story into which magic intrudes fits this category. Fairy tales in which the supernatural disrupts an individual's life are intrusion fantasies, but as they are handed down orally, it is hard to judge their rhetoric; when they do begin to be written down in the eighteenth and nineteenth centuries, it is with a sense that there is a way to tell a fairy or folk tale that overrides alternative modes. We can see hints of the intrusion mode, however, in some of the Grimms' tales. In "The Story of a Boy Who Went Forth to Learn Fear," although it is the boy who goes to the haunted house, we can see his fear as it grows described in onomatopoeic language that links sound and sensation to conduct the shivers. As with most intrusion fantasy the tale ends with a finality, a feeling that a sequel of any kind could be only escalation or anticlimax. We can look elsewhere—for example, to the plays of Shakespeare—in which the interjection of a disruptive influence is a common device, but here the poetry of the language makes it hard to distinguish the rhetorical structure from the dramatic. Nonetheless, in those plays in which he wished to induce horror—*Titus Andronicus*, for example—we can observe in action the philosophy that escalation of atrocity is the way to go. The intrusion fantasies as we know them get going with the arrival of the Gothic mode, specifically with *The Castle of Otranto*.

Horace Walpole's *The Castle of Otranto* (1764) is the first novel to fully fit the pattern we can overlay on *The Wolves in the Walls*. It relies on a conflict between that which is known in a formal sense, and that which is believed, felt, or intuited by the characters. Its trajectory moves from stability, through disruption, to a new mode of stability (one that rights the "wrongs" encapsulated in the old order), and it is written with a note of deliberate, ever-growing hysteria in which both the plot and the language escalate the sense of what is at stake.

The Castle of Otranto functions as a club story on three levels. The first is well known: that it was published initially masquerading as a text that had been translated from an earlier original. For the purposes of this book, it is worth considering this claim as more than just a hoax. What Walpole did was to mock a scholasticism that was already on the wane, that prized the found knowledge of the ancients over the scientific understandings being generated by the new natural philosophers. It is an irony Tolkien would have recognized: Walpole spawned a genre that valorized that which he mocked.

The second level of club story is that *The Castle of Otranto* is in part about the making of history. Manfred, prince of Otranto, has constructed a story of his inheritance to which the world around him must accede; and the fracturing of this story is one of the horrors of the novel. The third and final level is the classic club story of the intrusion fantasy in which, as events unravel, the club story constructed of horrors and portents will acquire increasing veracity and seize the belief of the participants in the tale. The subsurface of the world comes to be less open to question than the surface. The way to understand this traject is to compare the transition that takes place in the portal-quest fantasy. In the portal-quest fantasy, the prophecy, the lost heir, the hidden treasure are each secured for the club story by "evidence." This evidence may be flimsy: the prophecy is laid down in a codex; lost heirs produce nurses who remember them; the treasure is indicated by a map, its bestowal decided by the law of finders-keepers, but it is harnessed to the world by the accoutrements of the real world. What marks out the intrusion fantasy is the way in which "revelations" are harnessed to the world by markers of the unreal or the subconscious, by a "sense" of kinship, of fear, of intuition.

We can see this pattern of links in the very opening of *The Castle of Otranto*. Hippolita's reasons for not marrying off her son early are earthly (or earthy). He is too young, he is frail. Yet the real danger will turn out to be from the nebulous prophecy, "*That the castle and lordship of Otranto should pass from the present family whenever the real owner should be grown too large to inhabit it*" (17). We are told: "It was difficult to make any sense of this prophecy; and still less easy to conceive what it had to do with the marriage in question. Yet these mysteries, or contradictions, did not make the populace adhere the less to their opinion" (17). There is no "paralleling" here; the second statement does not answer the first, it provides a substructure to it. It also immediately introduces the idea that in the presence of stability, disruption is latent, entropy inevitable.

This inevitability, however, creates a problem: entropy or the process of disaster is fascinating; the actual disaster rarely is. In his introduction to the Penguin edition, Michael Gamer observes that many critics "noted that Walpole's ghosts often undermined the very effects they were supposed to produce. They appeared too often, or else were too large, too substantial, too *corporeal*" (xxix). This materiality is a factor from the very first scene of horror. That large helmet, fallen from nowhere on the young heir, is a huge anticlimax. It is just too concrete and cannot be supported by the rhetorical scaffold Walpole has erected.

But let us turn to the rhetoric. The description begins in the second paragraph with a static moment. Conrad's espousals have been fixed, and the company is assembled in the chapel—a secure place, one that resists disruption. When Conrad is missing, Manfred sends a servant for him, and the servant returns, "breathless, in a frantic manner, his eyes staring, and foaming at the mouth" (18). The company are "struck with terror and amazement" (18). His mother "without knowing what was the matter, but anxious for her son, swooned away" (18). There has been a shocking escalation and a rapid transfer of focus from what is said, to behavior that is displayed; from reason, to intuition, and a sense of something wrong. By the next page, we have added to this the idea that what is to be known must be experienced through physical sensation: "[Manfred] touched, he examined the fatal casque; nor could even the bleeding mangled remains of the young prince divert the eyes of Manfred from the portent before him" (19). What is to be experienced is not the "reality" of the dead prince, but the authority of the intervention.

There is also, as many people have noted, the escalation of the speech indicator. "Said" is replaced by "cried . . . wrathfully" and similar epithets. The hyperbole ratchets up the *matter* of the text: Manfred's response clarifies immediately that this will not be a drama of accident but one of import. Beneath arbitrary occurrence will lie meaning, yet the absence of meaning becomes itself a testimony to meaning. When "nobody could give him the least information" (20), Manfred (or Walpole) invents the conspiracy theory. This creation of conspiracy, structured around the conceit that what is felt is meaningful, makes sense of otherwise meaningless outbreaks, such as Manfred's declaration that Hippolita has "cursed me by her unfruitfulness." The choice of words render Hippolita's action deliberate and again, escalate the sense of a world disrupted from the outside. Manfred sees himself as the only one outside the club story of consensuality. Isabella cries: "Look, my lord! See heaven itself declares against your impious intentions!" The response: "'Heaven nor hell shall impede my designs,' said Manfred, advancing again to seize the princess" (24).

Manfred increasingly places himself outside of society, a trend we shall see in both heroes and villains in the intrusion fantasy. In turn, society gives increasing evidence for conspiracy, something hidden beneath the surface of rational meaning. As the source of Manfred's doom approaches, "the trampling of a horse was heard, and a brazen trumpet, which hung without the gate of the castle, was suddenly sounded. At the same instant the sable plumes on the enchanted helmet, which still remained at the other end of the court, were tempestuously agitated, and nodded thrice, as if bowed by some invisible wearer" (53). Two "normal" events—that herald a visitor—are coupled by an unusual one to create the inexplicable, the secret mystery. And, as in an earlier incident, when a portrait, "uttered a deep sigh and heaved its breast" (24), sound, not sight, emphasizes yet another round of escalation.

Where sight does become important is in the cadences of the visual. Walpole sets up what will become one of the rhetorical hallmarks of the intrusion fantasy, the counterpointing of adjectives and nouns. So that Isabella experiences "momentary joy," an "imperfect ray of clouded moonshine," each of which creates latency or pause around the object; elsewhere in the fantastic, adjectives activate the object (27). The apparent overwriting supports this sense of latency, of impending action that is so much more effective than the actual horrors Walpole does show. Descriptions of emotional response (I hesitate to call them actual emotions) work similarly—although note again that adjective-noun pairing as a mode of intensification: "Alone in so dismal a place, her mind imprinted with all the terrible events of the day, hopeless of escaping, expecting every moment the arrival of Manfred, and far from tranquil on knowing she was within reach of somebody, she knew not whom, who for some cause seemed concealed thereabouts, all these thoughts crowded on her distracted mind, and she was ready to sink under her apprehensions" (27).

When the book enters the realms of true magic, it is almost disappointing. Three drops of blood fall from the nose of a statue, "A clap of thunder at that instant shook the castle to its foundations . . . the walls of the castle behind Manfred were thrown down with a mighty force" (85), and a vision appears. All are described relatively baldly. Walpole clearly wants to introduce a difference in rhetoric but the result is that the excitement of this novel lies very much in the time we have spent waiting for explanation. When it does come, it is—as with the portal-quest fantasy—delivered by those with the right to interpret on behalf of others, a priest, and eventually the vision himself. What is interesting about this exposition, however, is that, as well as reinforcing the idea that under the world lurks an entire new level of meaning, it also underscores passivity in the face of the intrusion. The most active participant in this tragedy is Manfred. The others run, faint, or scream. Cutting across the much-discussed political implications therefore (punishment for sexual activity, the role of the colonizer and colonized) is an argument that while the inquisitive and active may be punished for these traits, *they will learn more about the world.* The passive may survive, but they will live forever on the world's surface, never seeing behind the wainscot. The intensity of language is in part (I think) about the intensity with which protagonists are expected to engage with the hidden world. But it is also, as David Punter argues, about linking language with sentiment and the moral: "The angelic beauty, the fading languor, the excess of thankfulness have nothing to do with the reasonable, and very little to do with the real: they are designed to angle the scene towards the demonstration of the moral and aesthetic lesson which it so obviously preaches" (29).

We can see Punter's argument rather well in Ann Radcliffe's *The Mysteries of Udolpho* (1794), an intrusion fantasy that—unusually—proceeds as a travel narrative. What sets *The Mysteries of Udolpho* apart from quest fantasies is the way in which new places and situations are handled. In chapter 1, I pointed out that in the quest fantasy, as the protagonists traverse the landscape they learn about it in such a way as to acquire intellectual and cultural ownership. Questions about the landscape are handled by the guide figure with guidebook detail. In Radcliffe's work, the guide intends to teach not just about the land, but the appropriate sensibility that should be brought to the appreciation of the landscape. As James Watt observes, descriptions of landscape in Radcliffe's work are carefully constructed in ways that "acknowledged the current theories and conventions of the picturesque. . . . Radcliffe attempted to form her readers, and shape the way they read her work, by enhancing descriptive passages with references to the landscapes of artists like Claude Lorrain and Salvator Rosa" (112).

The land in this construction is barren, its shape is to be "made" not by those who live there but by those who travel into it and depict it, in words or pictures, frequently in the face of the intransigence of locals who resist the process of definition. The artist of the picturesque, William Gilpin, complained of landscape as it existed: "We had hills but they were tame and uniform, following each other in quick succession, that we rarely found either a foreground or a distance. . . . It is not sufficiently divided into portions adapted to the pencil" (Howard 57). This desire to refigure the landscape, to make it other, runs through the relationship between intruder and intrusion in Gothic and its successors. But note that what frustrates Gilpin is that the land is not wild *enough.* For it to become wild, what is impressed upon it, or dug up, is a belief that the civilized exterior is merely a mask. In scenes that will be imitated and refined by many horror writers (and later parodied, as in Terry Pratchett's *Carpe Jugulum* [1998]), questions are answered in ways that tantalize with hidden knowledge.[5] The club story of the narrative is constructed by placing the protagonists outside the contextual knowledge system. An example:

> "Which is the way to the chateau in the woods?" cried Michael.
>
> "The chateau in the woods!" exclaimed the peasant, "Do you mean that, with the turret, yonder?"
>
> "I don't know as for the turret, as you call it," said Michael, "I mean that white piece of a building, that we see at a distance, there, among the trees."
>
> "Yes, that is the turret; why, who are you, that you are going thither?" said the man with surprise.
>
> St. Aubert, hearing this odd question, and observing the peculiar tone in which it was delivered [note the emphasis on the aural again], looked out from the carriage. "We are travellers," said he, "who are in search of a house of accommodation for the night; is there any hereabout?"
>
> "None, Monsieur, unless you have a mind to try your luck yonder," replied the peasant, pointing to the woods, "but I would not advise you to go there."
>
> "To whom does the chateau belong?"
>
> "I scarcely know myself, Monsieur."
>
> "It is uninhabited then?" "No, not uninhabited; the steward and housekeeper are there, I believe."
>
> On hearing this St. Aubert determined to proceed to the chateau, and risque the refusal of being accommodated for the night. (61–62)

There are two devices and one trajectory encapsulated in the above. Latency here is created simply by holding onto St. Aubert's metaphorical shirtsleeves as the peasant acts dumb and withholds information. The way in which this is done is the second device: the peasant exists within the club story of his world. He is puzzled that St. Aubert knows nothing: as we shall see in other intrusion fantasies (Elizabeth Hand's *Mortal Love*, 2004, is a very good example), there is a tension over who or what is the "intrusion." Thus within this scene is a short intrusion story in which the peasant negates the intrusion by sending it on its way. But most interesting is the trajectory of the scene, which moves St. Aubert into the fantasy by upping the stakes. The same scene presented in a demotic voice would hold no threat even with the same absence of usable information from the peasant. It is the apparent *withholding* that serves to wind the spring tight.

Nowhere is this withholding more evident than in the "letdown" over the figure underneath the veil. It has been pointed out by almost every modern commentator that the discovery that the figure is merely wax wrecks *The Mysteries of Udolpho* for the fantasticated Gothic. The entire novel appears to have been wound up to discover mystery and the supernatural; instead, it resolves into complicated bloodlines and a wax figure. Its trajectory is less toward negotiation with the intrusion of mysterious strangers and portents than toward their negation; in this it is the taproot text for the rationalized Gothic, the common ancestor between the crime novel and the intrusion fantasy. *The Mysteries of Udolpho* is a forebear of *Scooby Doo* and *The X-Files* in that it secures its victory at the expense of belief in the intrusion around which it is focused. Its return is overcomplete. However, that sounds like a dismissal, which would be inappropriate when considering a text that did not aim to construct the fantastic.

Ann Radcliffe, if she found she could not accept the present of the fantastic into her world, was fascinated by the intrusion of class, the depiction of which takes us back to the intrusion fantasy as a fantasy of felt emotion: Emily's role as a heroine is to *feel* and to feel deeply. Reprimanded (wrongly) for her behavior, she remembers, "the delicacy and tenderness of St. Aubert" (in contrast to the "coarse and unfeeling behaviour of Madame Cheron" (108) and later "sat lost in melancholy reflection." My point here is less that the upper classes are meant to have greater sensibility than the idea that *sensibility* is the right and proper way to understand the world. Nowhere is this idea more obvious than in the language used to clear up that matter of the wax figure at the end of the book:

> What added to the horror of the spectacle, was, that the face appeared partly decayed and disfigured by worms, which were visible on the features and hands. On such an object, it will readily be believed, that no person could endure to look twice. Emily, it may be recollected, had, after the first glance, let the veil drop, and her terror had prevented her from ever after provoking such a renewal of suffering, as she had then experienced. Had she dared to look again, her delusion and her fears would have vanished together, and she would have perceived that the figure before her was not human, but formed of wax. *The history of it is somewhat extraordinary. . . . A member of the house of Udolpho, having committed some offence against the prerogative of the church, had been condemned to the penance of contemplating, during certain hours of the day, a waxen image, made to resemble a human body in the state, to which it is reduced after death.* (my italics, 622)

There are two points made here. First, that sudden shift in tone to the demotic that exposes the world or rips the mask off the villain, reduces the fantastic to the mundane. Second, and perhaps more important, that Emily's mode of sensing the world is *correct*: "On such an object, it will readily be believed, that no person could endure to look twice." The world that Emily perceives is richer by far than the world of reason that the second half of the paragraph outlines. As Gothic it is, as Punter points out, dependent on an "habit of distortion, as if looking through a badly made window" (229), the substructure is here more attractive than the surface—a philosophy relentlessly mocked by Jane Austen in *Northanger Abbey* (1817) and *Sense and Sensibility* (1811). Yet this is the thread that Radcliffe offers to the intrusion fantasy and that will shape the later Gothic novels of the nineteenth century.

Which leads us, inevitably, to *Dracula*. Dracula is too long a novel to consider in detail so I am going to concentrate on one passage. In the final chapter of the novel the company approach the lair of the vampires. Mina Harker's journal is pregnant with meaning: there is too much garlic in her food, "I can't abide garlic" (464); and the air is "heavy" and "oppressive"—adjectives that conjure up an intimacy with the atmosphere. One of the new elements Bram Stoker adds to the intensity of the intrusion fantasy is the sense of the opening chasm between the protagonist and his social circle. This division becomes a motif of the intrusion fantasy that we shall see best explored in de Lint's Jack of Kinrowan stories, and in the experience of the once slave, now servant, Stephen, in Clarke's *Jonathan Strange and Mr. Norrell* (2004). The threat of the fantastic draws the victim away from his own world: as Lucy is drawn physically first to the graveyard and later to the slums of London, so the gallant company are extracted from the club story, the consensual world, into something darker. We begin to see the pull effect of the intrusion, which seeks not just to enter and disrupt, but to drag the innocent across borders (or contaminate). At the end of the novel, as the country gets wider, the company draws together and the threat draws closer. The tension is drawn from this constant balancing act: a movement away from the safety of the consensual world is toward intimacy with the intrusion.

But the kind of melancholy latency with which Mina Harker writes needs to be set within a dynamic rhythm and here it is counterpointed with the excited anticipation of Van Helsing's memorandum. Here too there is an emphasis on the intimate: Van Helsing focuses on the detail of Mina Harker's behavior, on her bodily response. He records her loss of appetite, that she sleeps all day, that she wakes refreshed. His examination of her mirrors that of the vampire's careful ministry to Lucy. The rhetoric is of the close-up, of *scrutiny.* Van Helsing, in turn, notes Mina Harker's growing intimacy with the vampire; Mina knows the way, and Van Helsing does not think it is because she has read Jonathan's journals. As with the reference to the garlic in the food, the undercurrent of meaning is left unspoken. This close observation—crucial to Van Helsing's characterization as a scientist, but a scientist who believes the "scientific method" exemplified by the skeptical Seward to be inadequate—also reinforces the sense of intimacy as *process*. Descriptions of landscape, far from emphasizing the newness, the foreignness, the sense of displacement, instead draw us into an intimate relation with the surroundings. Van Helsing's notes ensure that the landscape becomes a character in the novel with moods and emotions of its own so that the precipices frown; when "the snow came in flying sweeps . . . the wreaths of mist took shape as of women with trailing garments" (471), humans and animals respond to this viscerally: "the horses cowered lower and lower, and moaned in terror as men do in pain" (471). Animals, less inclined to think, are frequently first and worse affected by the intimacy of the threat, and equally respond best to the physical intimacy of protection. "When they did feel my hands on them, they whinnied low as in joy, and licked at my hands and were quiet for a time" (470–471). Dr. Seward's entry builds tension entirely through the consideration of the emotion of landscape:

> The snow is falling lightly and there is a strange excitement in the air. It may be our own excited feeling but the depression is strange. Far off I hear the howling of wolves; the snow brings them down from the mountains, and there are dangers to all of us, and from all sides. . . . We ride to the death of someone. (474)

The intimacy of the relationship between people and their surroundings is repeatedly emphasized: "the mist began to wheel and circle round, till I could get as though a shadowy glimpse of this women that would have kissed him [Jonathan Harker]" (471). With this intimacy comes the sense that evil can be conducted in the air—which it *can*, as Van Helsing remonstrates with Mina, the mist coalesces into the three female vampires. But even here, the horror is in their approach, in the holding off. The ring that Van Helsing has drawn around himself and Mina cannot be breached and the rest is a case of waiting:

> And so we remained till the red of the dawn began to fall through the snow-gloom. I was desolate and afraid, and full of woe and terror; but when that beautiful sun

began to climb the horizon life was to me again. At the first coming of the dawn the horrid figures melted in the whirling mist and snow; the wreaths of transparent gloom moved away towards the castle, and were lost. (472–473)

Of particular interest here are not only the intense adjectives of feeling but something that is quite noticeable and, I think, particular to the intrusion fantasy. In this one paragraph is the entire trajectory of the intrusion fantasy; the sense of threat, of waiting, and of repulsion of the horror. The further we go into classic horror fiction, the more evident it is that the primary method of escalation is connected to an episodic structure in which the whole is made up of many *identical* parts. No matter which way you slice the text, you receive not one element of the intrusion trajectory, but all of it at once. The intrusion text is hologrammatic in form.

The denouement—the finding of the graves, the execution of the vampires—is masterly. Stoker escapes the sense of anticlimax because he builds delay and the *possibility* of delay into the event and again uses the *escalation* to create a moment at which the characters and the readers reach a precipice of emotion. Van Helsing simultaneously describes both the event and the metarhetorical structure of the event:

many a man who set forth to do such a task as mine, found at last his heart fail him, and then his nerve. So he delay, and delay, and delay, till the mere beauty and the fascination of the wanton Un-Dead have hypnotise him; and he remain on, and on, till the sunset come, and the Vampire sleep over. Then the beautiful eyes of the fair woman open and look love, and the voluptuous mouth present to a kiss. (475)

All of this is up close and intimate; consider, in contrast, the description of the death of the vampires. Where landscape and feelings were reported in the present tense, this latter description is immediately relegated to a past, not quite offstage, but certainly held at a distance. This distancing enables Stoker to focus less on the deed, than the reaction to the deed: "it was but butcher work . . . I tremble and tremble even yet." His peace of mind is kept by the feelings he sees in the faces of his victims as they die, the transformation from "the horrid screeching as the stake drove home" to them "placid each in her full sleep of death" (477). And yet still there is more to wait for because, in the tradition of escalation, there is still the biggest monster to deal with: Dracula himself. The trajectory of intimacy is reversed: where Dracula once approached the Harkers through friends and family, now they have approached him through his. The mirroring of threat is part of the moral rhetoric of this kind of fantasy. In other texts—in Laurell K. Hamilton's work, in Charles de Lint's, or in Susanna Clarke's—we shall see how retaliation also escalates, also becomes more intimate, and draws closer to the center through the threats to friends, allies, and family.

At the very last minute, we have a segue into the language of adventure fiction, with "the sweep and flash of Jonathan's great knife." The pace speeds up, the latency breaks—but Stoker allows this move into action to last only three lines; from there we move to the gradual dissolution of mood and, with it, the body of Quincey Morris. His death allows Stoker to preserve an intimate attachment to the consequence of the tale, to retain emotional consequence to the end.

Before we leave *Dracula* we should return to that comment I made about the hologrammatic form of the intrusion novel. In *Dracula* this hologrammatic form and its rhetorical structure of the intrusion fantasy are encoded in the epistolatory structure of the novel. Correspondence—the exchange of letters—encodes delay and waiting into a ritual. Letters each begin with a statement and *escalate* to discussion. And the letter, written from one to another, is the most intimate of forms. The entire structure of this novel plays with the reader: the epistolatory mode is a control tap on the emotional stream.

Robert Louis Stevenson's *Dr. Jekyll and Mr. Hyde* rings different changes on the patterns of club story, on escalation and intimacy. Its latency is less in its rhetoric than its structure. More obviously than the texts considered earlier, it moves from the outside in, from the external narrative of an acquaintance, to a report from a friend, into the intimate ministrations and reports of a valet, and finally to the first-person narrative of Jekyll. The only part of the story that is actually acted out in the narration is the most extreme perimeter; all the rest of the tale is related to us. The closer we get to the actual *events* of the transmogrification of Jekyll, the further we are distanced via the narrative strategy, until the details are finally provided for us posthumously. It is as if the story is constructed around the first law of thermodynamics: the energy invested in the events is inversely proportional to the energy invested in the intensity of the narrative.

The increasing tendency of Jekyll to be dominated by Hyde is a continual spiral inward. One can read this spiral in the construction of the language. If one opens the book at different stages, one can track a distinct intensification of voice matched with a growing attention to what is felt. The story opens with a description of the desiccated Mr. Utterson, "never lighted by a smile . . . backward in sentiment . . . when the wine was to his taste, something eminently human beaconed from his eye" (5). But when Mr. Utterson and Mr. Enfield meet in the chapter "Incident at the Window," Utterson remarks, "Did I ever tell you once that I saw him, and shared your feeling of repulsion?" (35). On witnessing, toward the end of the scene, Dr. Jekyll haggard at the window, they are struck by "an expression of such abject horror and despair, as froze the very blood of the two gentlemen below. . . . They were both pale; and there was an answering horror in their eyes" (36).

There is shift both to sentiment and to the unrestrained body, which, of course, parallels the overall theme of the tale and is encoded in Jekyll's final, posthumous statement in which the body, and the experience of the body, is constantly referenced: "I felt younger, lighter, happier in body; within I was conscious of a heady recklessness, a current of disordered sensual images running like a mill race in my fancy, a solution of the bonds of obligation, an unknown but not an innocent freedom of the soul. I knew myself, at the first breath of this new life, to be more wicked, tenfold more wicked, sold a slave to my original evil; and the thought, in that moment, braced and delighted me like wine. I stretched out my hands, exulting in the freshness of these sensations; and in the act, I was suddenly aware that I had lost in stature" (57).

As we rush towards the denouement the restraint of body encoded in restraint of language gives way to "recklessness" and a "disordered" mill race of language in which idea is piled up on idea in sharp contrast to the final testament of calm, analytical consideration of waking in the morning: "shaken, weakened, but refreshed. I still hated and feared the thought of the brute that slept within me, and I had not of course forgotten the appalling dangers of before; but I was once more in my own house and close to my drugs; and gratitude for my escape shone so strong in my soul that it almost rivalled the brightness of hope" (68). Instead of the accumulation of words and imagery, Jekyll, when in his senses, is all qualification and hesitation. Link words pull him (and the reader) back from the brink over which his fantastic self would plummet. In the final paragraph, when he accepts that he has lost his fight, that his restrained self cannot hold back this most intimate intrusion he lapses into melancholy in which the language of sentiment is itself presented as the symbol of a lost battle: "Half an hour from now, when I shall sit shuddering and weeping in my chair, or continue, with the most strained and fearstruck ecstasy of listening, to pace up and down this room . . . and give ear to every sound of menace" (70). With a last moment of analysis, Jekyll seeks to hold back the overwhelming fantastic of emotional release.

What Edgar Allan Poe brings to the construction of the intrusion fantasy, and the pattern of club story, latency, and escalation, is the visceral of the obsessive. "The Pit and the Pendulum" (1842) ratchets up both latency and escalation, not through the events themselves, nor even precisely the language used—although there is a constant hyperbole of the visceral in which horror is "delirious" (251), a hand "suffered" to remain (253), an idea is "fearful" (254)—but through the intimacy that is constructed through the intensity of obsession. Where *Dracula* presented a story in which the threat drew ever closer and *Dr. Jekyll and Mr. Hyde* presented a threat from the inside, in "The Pit and the Pendulum," the threat is absolutely external—but the threat of intrusion is a breach of the body. What is markedly different to these other tales is the way in which Poe, in this and other stories, forces the reader to *pay attention*. The sense of threat is created by the intense scrutiny of the prisoner's surroundings, the intense study of the prisoner's senses and feelings, and the focus upon study of the threat. The prisoner focuses on the walls, the sliminess of the floor, the nature of his bonds, the food, the rats, and eventually the pendulum. Each of these is described not so much in detail as "up close." They become the sole focus of vision:

> In feeling my way I had found many angles, and thus deduced a feeling of great irregularity; so potent is the effect of total darkness upon one arousing from lethargy or sleep! The angles were simply those of a few slight depressions, or niches, at odd intervals. . . . What I had taken for masonry seemed now to be iron, or some other metal, in huge plates, whose sutures or joints occasioned the depression. The entire surface of this metallic enclosure was daubed in all the hideous and repulsive devices to which the charnel superstition of the monks has given rise. (258)

But this kind of description is very different from the same scene as set, perhaps, in a science fiction novel. The exploration is obsessive, but its point is to intensify the sense of imprisonment, not to seek out freedom. Until very late in the tale, this type of study is an accumulation of evidence without analysis. Latency is held by a refusal to analyze anything other than visceral response, and by the embedding of practical evidence within an experiential context. For example, the first exploration of the dungeon describes what is found; "a wall, seemingly of stone masonry—very smooth, slimy and cold" (255), but reserves analysis for "My excessive fatigue [which] induced me to lay prostrate." All this is encapsulated in the notion that the exploration of the dungeon is of little object and "certainly no hope" (256). So the majority of the tale is an intense study of the process of resigning oneself to fate and the "thrill" of dwelling on the mechanisms of death. In this case, escalation is also linked to this notion of obsessive study of the surroundings. Earlier, the protagonist had noticed the iron of the walls: whereas in a thriller, anything noticed must be a route to escape, in the intrusion story anything noticed must eventually intrude on the personal space of the actor. The *intimate* relationship between threat and threatened is underscored by the protagonist's exclamation: "Fool! Might I not have known that *into the pit* it was the object of the burning iron to urge me? Could I resist its glow? Or if even that, could I withstand its pressure?"(266). Although the threat is but a tool, inanimate, it acquires here intention, and that acquisition supports a reverse of the personal focus that is the story's trajectory: if the protagonist has focused obsessively on the world in relation to itself, the story in turn is told by him as to indicate that *the world* is focused on him. While on one level the torture is arbitrary, the story relies for its effect on the protagonist's belief that it is personal and tailored just for him. There is a really interesting tension here that I am not sure I can explore within the remits of this chapter: does horror work best when impersonal or apparently crafted to the protagonist? James Herbert's impersonal rats, or Laurell K. Hamilton's joyfully sadistic, haute couture vampires?[6]

As we move from Poe to Lovecraft, we become increasingly aware of the degree to which the language of the intrusion fantasy, in its search for the contrast between the mundane and the intrusion, is parting company with other forms of fiction and developing its characteristic dual mode: an outer, "real" world depicted in a demotic, often faux-analytic voice, and an intruding "inner world" that must acquire a grandeur in order to communicate a sense of the otherness.

In John P. McWilliams's *The American Epic: Transforming a Genre, 1770–1860* (1989), he writes of the search for a language for the American epic:

> [Nathanial] Tucker stopped before he had to select a language suitable to describing American nature. Nouns like "Vale," "Pile," "Deep," or "Flood." Verbs like "glister," "heave," or "round," adjectives like "vasty," "redounding" or "darksome" comprised the accepted diction for the sublime. (33–34)

Considering both the work of Poe and the later writing of H. P. Lovecraft, one wonders if—when the American epic poem finally collapsed under the weight of its expectations of self[7]—its language wasn't taken up wholesale into the new weird fiction, a link McWilliams himself suggests, although he does not expand upon it.[8] Consider this extract from "The Call of Cthulhu" (1928): "The Thing cannot be described—there is no language or such abysms of shrieking and immemorial lunacy, such eldritch contradictions of all matter, force and cosmic order" (177). Or, one of my favorites, "In this phantasy of prismatic distortion it moves anomalously in a diagonal way. So that all the rules of matter and perspective seemed upset" (177). Or, "It lumbered slobberingly into sight and gropingly squeezed Its gelatinous green immensity through the black doorway into the tainted outside air of that poison city of madness" (177). Along with the peculiarity of the "gibbous sky" (177), the division between the outer story and the inner one is almost absolute: "The Call of Cthulhu" begins as a scientific report into an event that has happened. As the "author" moves closer into the secret, he sees the permeability of the world and the latent god (the actual intrusion in this tale are the god's minions, who intrude both their vile religion and their vile race and racial miscegenation); the language shifts to this intense conjuring-of-the-fantastic through faux scientific, scrupulous hyperbole.

One of the characteristics McWilliams identifies of early American epic poetry is its tendency not to celebrate great events, but to herald great events that will take place in some long-term, but assured, future.[9] Comparing Lovecraft to Poe or to the earlier Gothics, this sense of things that happen off the edge of the page, horrors that are to come, rather than horrors that happen within the purview of the tale, is noticeably stronger in Lovecraft. "The Call of Cthulhu" resolves with the threat drawing nearer; the "greatness" of Cthulhu is heralded as the American poets of the epic heralded the future "great American epic" poem. This sense is even stronger in "The Shadow Over Innsmouth" (1942). McWilliams argues that the problem the writers of American epic faced was that farmers and tradesmen—the two groups valorized in the American republic—aren't really material for the epic. Lovecraft deals with this problem by appropriating the notion of the leisured gentleman who has the freedom to investigate the world—and the world of Lovecraft's gentleman comprises those very places that should be *exemplary* in the American tradition. In "The Shadow over Innsmouth," this is the American small town. Our gentleman investigator is there to open the chink in consensus reality: the result in "The Shadow Over Innsmouth" is that the corruption of the town intrudes into the hinterlands, the life of farmers and tradesmen disrupted in the name of a greater glory. Seen as a whole, it is as if Lovecraft, accepting everything he had read in the attempts to write American epic poetry of the future Golden Republic, sought to write its mirror image, the epic poetry of the age of corruption. The story shows all of the issues outlined so far, but the one I want to focus on is how the escalation of fear is constructed in the escalation of descriptive detail, an approach I have previously associated with the portal-quest fantasy (a category for which this story—with its protagonist newly arrived in town—might actually be a contender).

One of the striking issues about the intrusion fantasy is the degree to which many of them closely follow the portal-quest narratives in their intense description of landscape. I don't think this similarity is either coincidental or precisely an overlap of form. We can consider this passage from "The Shadow Over Innsmouth":

> Re-crossing the gorge on Main Street bridge, I struck a region of utter desertion which somehow made me shudder. Collapsing huddles of gambrel roofs formed a jagged and fantastic skyline, above which rose the ghoulish, decapitated steeple of an ancient church. (14–15)

My contention with regard to the portal fantasies was that this unrolling of landscape actually shut the protagonist out of real engagement with the world, sealed the protagonist into the club story with the superficial factoids of tourism and a sense of wonder. In the intrusion fantasy, this rolling out of landscape, rendered in epic emotional intensities, does not seal the protagonist into the club story, but opens the scene out to him as a privileged observer with an inherently more sensitive awareness of the true landscape than its desensitized citizens have. And it does so precisely by moving the descriptive element from *sense of wonder* to *sense of fear*, from the intellectual-emotional nexus to a visceral-emotional nexus.[10] The protagonist, if he becomes sealed into anything, becomes sealed into his own belief that he is *outside* the story—which is why the denouement to many intrusion/fear stories is the discovery that the protagonist is merely the final victim. This sense of being outside also helps to explain the continual switch between the coolly analytic "voice" and the hyperbole with which the fantastic is described. The switch in voice not only represents the difference between the present and the intruding worlds; it represents the protagonist's relationship to the structuring club story / consensus worlds. As "our world"—or, in the case of "The Shadow Over Innsmouth," the world of "ordinary Americans"—is disrupted, the protagonist can no longer see himself as external to it. A common theme of modern horror is the person unhappy in suburbia who comes to accept that he belongs through his defense of it against intrusion.

There is an existential angst to many intrusion fantasies. The protagonist "must make himself a lack of Being in order that Being may be there is to say that man must recognize—not in a single flash of inspiration but continually—that he alone determines the values by which he lives that he is not endowed with a ready-made self or nature but rather must be constantly making himself" (Barnes 42).

The intrusion of the fantastic is matched by a dragging of the protagonist into its range, or into the "true story" of the world. In most intrusion fantasies, even though the primary trajectory is that of the intrusion breaking through, there is also a secondary trajectory of the protagonist moving into this secret world (we shall see this even more clearly in the modern intrusion fantasies of Laurel K. Hamilton, Graham Joyce, Charles de Lint, Susanna Clarke, and others).

In "The Shadow Over Innsmouth," these two trajectories are generated by two rhetorics directly transferred over from the portal-quest fantasy. First, the download of secret information from the elderly Zadok Allen (but unlike the mage in the portal-quest fantasy, Allen is considered by the protagonist to be unreliable or mad). Second, the discovery that the protagonist is the "uncrowned prince," the "secret heir." In each case, however, the protagonist's relationship to these tropes is the reverse of that of the portal-quest fantasy. Allen's tale breaks the club story of the world, rather than confirming it, and the protagonist himself refuses to accept it until it is proved by events—destinarianism is denied even as it proves true. And the destiny, when it arrives, is unwelcome not just because it is nasty, but because what it does is to *deny* the protagonist the exceptionalism that portal-quest destinarianism usually grants.

The route to modern horror is not particularly straightforward (there is no Whiggish theory of intrusion fantasy offered here) but one of the wayposts is a novel that has clearly influenced later writers, William Hope Hodgson's *House on the Borderlands* (1907), although its influence is diffuse. The novel's second two-thirds anticipate the elegiac astronomical romances of Olaf Stapledon and Don A. Stuart (pseudonym of John W. Campbell Jr.), but the first third of the novel is redolent of the later formal ghost stories, and of the modern intrusion fantasies with their surprising refusal of the kind of story arcs found elsewhere in the fantastic. Robert Holdstock's *Mythago Wood* (a novel I shall consider later in this chapter) might be read as an expansion, commentary, and celebration of the slight but distinctly eerie tale Hodgson constructed.

The House on the Borderland, like *The Castle of Otranto*, is a twice-found text, introduced by a note from the author describing the "account . . . as it was handed to me" (Ace, frontispiece), and continuing with a lengthy subtitle that describes the text as "From the Manuscript, discovered in 1877 by Messrs. Tonnison and Berreggnog. . . ." It then proceeds in the voice of Mr. Berreggnog who tells first the tale leading up to the discovery, and then in the voice of the reader of the tale. The book closes with Mr. Tonnison's reflection on the found narrative, one feature of which is the refusal of Mr. Berreggnog to return to the ruin in which the manuscript was found. A second feature is the "discovery" of confirmation of the contents of the manuscript, with the unearthing of a story that "in the ancient man's youth" (156) a great house had once stood in the ruins, visited only by the supplier, and that one day the man had returned from his regular trip to discover the house gone and in its place a "stupendous pit" (156). The story retains its duality, however; despite this apparent closure: "Of the author of the MS, who he was, and whence he came, we shall never know" (157).

The main frame tale (of Tonnison and Berreggnog) is related with all the hallmarks of the rationalized Gothic: they seek information from the locals as to their surroundings (they are on a fishing trip) and receive no answer (6–7). Although their refusal to answer turns out to be because the locals speak only Irish, it is a tactic that aids the construction of isolation from the consensual story of the world. The world itself is intuited rather than observed:

> Presently, I looked up and across to the further side of the chasm. There, I saw something towering up among the spray: it looked like a fragment of a great ruin. . . .
>
> "Come along." He [Tonnison] shouted above the uproar. "We'll have a look at it. There's something queer about this place; I feel it in my bones." (11)

Although sentiment is often appropriate (dizzying terror over a chasm), it is at the expense of a sense of wonder and analysis of the protagonists' surroundings. Thus when a "a strange wail noise [came] out of the wood on our left" (14), it is no surprise that they leave rather than investigate. There is an assumption here that the visceral response is meaningful in itself.

Hence it is rather surprising that in the tale told in the heart of the book, the unnamed protagonist moves forward to meet the intrusion. This unforced maneuver is not the trajectory we have come to expect: in the Gothics, force of circumstance moved the protagonist toward the intrusion. The latency of the tale is, in effect, constructed by beginning with a rather mysterious portal fantasy in which the description is pregnant with significance but not with the kind of directed or interpreted meaning (or Story) we might associate with the portal fantasy. There are some similarities here with David Lindsay, except that in *Voyage to Arcturus* interpretation is intended, if forever out of reach.

The tale is told in the past tense, to begin with. It is a tale that has happened. All of the previous stories discussed here were told through the proscenium arch of the present tense in which we watched them unfold. Hodgson uses this past tense to intensify the sense that we are waiting for the tale, as the narrator has waited "some ten years" for the tale to unravel. Yet undercutting this is the narrator's assertion that he had seen puzzling things and had perhaps felt others. So we meet early the characteristic seesawing between the belief that nothing is there and the *feeling* that something other lurks. The feeling is the qualification, but it is also the truth.

The primacy of feelings is reinforced by what happens next: the candles gutter, then shine "with a ghastly green effulgence," the lights sink into a "dull, ruddy, tint," so that the room glows in a way that is strange. And unlike the portal fantasies, corroboration of the strange comes not from further description or from explanation, but from Pepper, the dog "cowering under my dressing gown. Pepper, usually as brave as a lion!" (18). The intimacy of the intrusion is doubled, by coming first into the domestic sphere and then upon the dog who is both best friend and extension of Man's dulled senses (but is *not* the all-knowing teacher).

Hodgson's protagonist can "think of nothing better to do than wait," and while he waits the intrusion comes to him: a light, approaching from the end wall (the visual effects sound rather like those in Terry Gilliam's movie *Time Bandits*), that lifts him (let us call him Mr. X for ease) above his chair and moves him out into the night, and then into the universe, past the earth, "an enduring globule of radiant blue" (19), and beyond the stars. Until now, Mr. X has experienced little other than the cold—no sense of wonder—but inexplicably, "the atrocious darkness seemed to creep into my soul, and I became filled with fear and despair" (19). Eventually, he is brought back to earth, to a "great waste of loneliness" (20), to a world that may be lit by a different star. Through all of this, Mr. X's response has been singularly untouched by his surroundings, and he never participates in them. Rather than the message of the portal fantasy—that the world is created for his exploration—his position as an outsider is maintained absolutely. This is not a world he is moving through so much as a chance to observe the mythological wolves that lurk under the walls of his world.

This positioning of the protagonist, as neutral observer rather than as a tourist, is reinforced when Hodgson moves to specifics, when the desolate plain is invaded by "a vast shape of blackness, giant-like," "The thing was black, and had four grotesque arms" (24). Eventually, Mr. X realizes he is looking at the incarnation of Kali, goddess of death, but the image is more frightening the vaguer it is kept. When it *is* identified, Mr. X does not seek to decorate the image: "Now, I saw that there were other things up among the mountains. Further off, reclining on a lofty ledge, I made out a livid mass, irregular and ghoulish. It seemed without form, save for an unclean, half-animal face, that looked out, vilely, from somewhere about its middle. . . . Several, I recognised, almost immediately, as mythological deities; others were strange to me" (24). If we consider these passages, it becomes clear that the baroque style that had dominated much fear fiction is not to be found in *The House on the Borderlands.* Instead there is a descriptive *vagueness* rhythmically alternated with clear identifications.

Eventually Mr. X gathers his conclusions (based, naturally, on gut instinct not evidence): "I grew to wondering if this might be the immortality of the gods" (25). What he is seeing is the threat that lurks, the promise of the intrusion. This promise comes to a point when he sees the swine thing—the body of a man, the head of a pig—loping around the Jade House. This animal is searching for an entrance to the House, but instead sees Mr. X and turns toward him: "Only a hundred yards, and the brutish ferocity of the giant face numbed me with a feeling of unmitigated horror" (26). But Mr. X is again lifted into the air leaving the swine thing snuffling where he stood. As Mr. X glances down again, the Plain has disappeared: "I was wrapped in an unpalpable, lightless gloom" (27).

All of this, this vision, has been the latency prepared for the intrusion. Mr. X, a distant observer of the threat that lurks behind the wall, finds in chapter V ("The Thing in the Pit") a creature that reminds him of the Thing that haunted the Arena on the plain. This thing comes calling. As Mr. X stood on the edge of the world, so this thing leans in over the edge of the windowsill, arousing in Mr. X a visceral disgust. The action of the scene, however, is concerned mostly with the delaying of the swine thing's arrival, the locking of the door. The thing seems no threat—approached, it quickly flees—but Mr. X lovingly relates the making secure of the house. The intrusion, when it arrives, is one of sound; "Gradually, imperceptibly almost, something stole on my ear—a sound, that resolved itself into a faint murmur. Quickly, it developed, and grew into a muffled, but hideous, chorus of bestial shrieks" (36). When, in the following chapter, the swine thing appears in the pit, while its visage is merely "hideous," the sounds it makes are described in great detail. Again, instead of trying to conjure the horrific through detail, Hodgson does so through absence of description and a focus instead on sensitivity, "a gust of horror and fear took me," "I had a return of the horrible sensation of fear, that had assailed me on that night . . . the same feeling of helpless, shuddering fright" (43). Unlike the portal fantasy we live not through the protagonist's eyes—these are oddly cloudy—but through the sharp response of gut and blood. The swine things are described in the vaguest terms, and mostly in plain terms (white-faced, swinelike), while the escalation of language and imagination are reserved primarily for the emotions, which churn ever more frantically.

The defeat of the creatures, their fall into the pit to drown, is something of an anticlimax. Yet it is also indicative of where Hodgson's real interests lie: at the moment the swine fall into the pit, the response is not relief but awe at the realization that the pit lies far down into the earth, reaches right under the house. The conclusion is an opening up into the secret/hidden world that will lead Hodgson into the ecstatic mood of the rest of the novel, which is not an intrusion fantasy at all. This note of elation that concludes Hodgson's novel will be repeated in the fuller instantiations offered by Elizabeth Hand's *Mortal Love* and Susanna Clarke's *Jonathan Strange and Mr. Norrell.*

Perhaps the classic form of the intrusion fantasy, the kind that truly is the club story, the peering into another world, the insistence on the impermeability of the tale (nudge it and it will collapse), is the classic ghost story. What is particularly interesting about these stories is the degree to which (1) they rely on the combination of factual improbability and straight-faced, plainspoken prose, and (2) the degree to which the intrusion frequently moves into the lives of very ordinary people. Washington Irving's "The Legend of Sleepy Hollow" (1819–20) is perhaps one of the taproots of the genre, encapsulating both these plot devices and a rhetorical structure in which almost all of the tale is devoted to the period of latency. In Irving's story, nine thousand of the total eleven thousand words are the buildup to the story, an endless litany of landscape and character and circumstance that is narrated so intensely as to give the impression that it is important. It *is* important, but in terms of function, not content.

What the ghost stories bring to the intrusion fantasy is the powerful latency of melancholy and nostalgia. Take just two examples, Robert Aickman's "Ringing the Changes" and Cynthia Asquith's "Who is Sylvia?" from *The Third Ghost Book* (1957), which I selected because it was the most typical collection I could find. Both are written from a distance, as stories that have happened. Robert Aikman's "Ringing the Changes" begins as a recollection of what happened on a honeymoon; although it moves quickly to a more direct narration from within the story, throughout the past tense is used: these are events that have retreated. The note of melancholy is then thickened by the setting: an apparently almost deserted village, and triply thickened by peopling it with characters whose lives have essentially been lived: the hotel owners; the Pascoes, once respectable (even impressive) people, who now exist mired in drink and depression; and the Commandant, whose past is apparently unspeakable and who chooses to stay in this haunted town for no discernible reason. When the dead arise, it seems appropriate to this story, which is in part about a man seeking to recapture his youth by marriage to a younger woman. This plot and structure builds a nostalgic latency. Cynthia Asquith's "Who is Sylvia?" is even more indicative of this trajectory: a woman opens a letter from her best friend to discover that she (the woman) has lost her one chance at marriage to a young newcomer who has stolen her male friend's love without actually appearing to want it. Told primarily through letters that turn out to be old and outdated, the story also turns out to be older than the victim (Susan) believes. Sylvia is not a young innocent, but a practiced manipulator, one who delights in undermining the happiness of others: this she does less by destroying someone's life than by tying that person to the site of their own destruction, by leaving them in love with their destroyer (Sylvia) and nostalgically attached to the ruins.

It is important to recognize that while much of modern horror fits in the very center of the intrusion fantasy subset, horror is not ipso facto intrusion fantasy. Anne Rice's novel *Interview With a Vampire* (1976), for example, is (in my schema) a portal-quest fantasy, as we are guided by the vampire in his process of *becoming*. At the other end of the spectrum, outside of the supernatural field, horror segues without break into crime fiction; hence my contention made casually on a number of occasions that crime fiction is essentially intrusion fantasy. Much modern horror, however—particularly of the supernatural sort—is *quintessential* intrusion fantasy. This is the one chapter where I seriously considered using film and television texts because of the degree to which they conform to the rhetorical and structural outlines I have sketched. I was convinced by Gary K. Wolfe's argument[11] that this would be as much a transgression as conflating sf literature and sf cinema; nonetheless, I point the reader in the direction of the *Buffy* episodes "Hush" and "Once More With Feeling," which are each brilliantly original plays on escalation. *Friday the 13th* and its sequels are the best illustrations of the peculiar susceptibility of horror to iterations of the same text: each has followed the formula of introducing new innocent victims to recapitulate the normality against which the horror will be tested; or, alternatively, of re-creating a victim who is now traumatized or recovered from trauma, but essentially complacent that the world is healed. And, of course, each maintains a continual need to escalate the horror.

Horror novels from the 1950s, through the 1970s and onward construct their worlds in a cozy vernacular (although where that vernacular is located shifts from the drawing room to the high school, to the dark street of the big city) that is threatened by the occupants of the wainscot (skirting board) (Clute, *Encyclopedia of Fantasy* 991–992). These occupants of a hidden fantasy world in turn eventually break through, escalates, and are defeated.

This construction and commonality can be seen vividly if we group the following three novels: Shirley Jackson's *The Haunting of Hill House* (1959), Stephen King's *Carrie* (1974), and James Herbert's *The Rats* (1974). Superficially, these novels could not be more different: a haunted house seeking to replenish its ghosts; a marginalized child wreaking revenge on her schoolmates; vicious rats that appear with very little explanation. (Explanation is relatively unimportant, one of the features that distinguishes sf from this kind of "scientific thriller.")

The tones of the three are also very different. Jackson's novel is genteel, its latency encoded in the politeness of the northeastern middle classes that itself becomes a metaphor for the tightly constructed "real" world. Middle-class manners *pretend* the wainscot of the world is simply not there, or can be kept under control by rigid *self*-control, and this is true whether the wainscot world is supernatural or natural. Sexuality and class—both elements in this book—hide in these metaphorical wainscots. In *The Haunting of Hill House*, these lurking wainscot mores become the flaws and cracks that the house finds out. Much of the latency of *The Haunting of Hill House* is established through reverie, the self-contemplation of Eleanor, and one way to "read" the book is to note that it is the figure who indulges in reverie—who, though always told through the third person, is the character whose internal narrative we have access to—who is vulnerable to the supernatural. Eleanor's continual contemplation of her actions sets us up for the "fright," but also intensifies our intimacy with her—and specifically indicates the house's intimacy (or intended intimacy) with her. It is quite possible to read this book as if it is the house that is figured as the invisible narrator. Indeed, much of the latency of the novel is structured around the "romance" between the house and Eleanor. To make use of Roz Kaveney's comments that there is an intimacy of seduction and an intimacy of disgust,[12] *The Haunting of Hill House* is a narrative of seduction. As Eleanor becomes a greater part of the house, her introspection becomes increasingly a stream of consciousness that distances her from her colleagues by rendering her as *atmosphere*. From chapter 9:

> "Coming? Coming?" she heard far away, somewhere else in the house, and she heard the stairs shake under their feet and a cricket stir on the lawn. Daring, gay, she ran down the corridor again to the hall and peeked out at them from the doorway. They were moving purposely, all together, straining to stay near one another, and the doctor's flashlight swept the hall and stopped at the great front door, which was standing open wide. Then, in a rush, calling "Eleanor, *Eleanor*," they all ran together across the hall and out the front door, looking and calling, the flashlight moving busily. Eleanor clung to the door and laughed until tears came into her eyes; what fools they are, she thought; we trick them so easily. They are so slow, and so deaf and so *heavy*; they trample over the house, poking and peering and rough. (163)

By the end of the quotation, Eleanor has conflated herself with the house, in an interestingly understated moment of recognition. This is why the true moment of "horror" in this novel is the moment when she is being sent away. The crash, the space in which Eleanor deliberately drives her car into a tree, is a consummation of the relationship between her and the house, a moment of intense *sexual* intimacy. The final lines reposition the house in postsexual terms: "Within, its walls continued upright, bricks met neatly, floors were firm, and doors sensibly shut" (174). You can almost see the tweed and sensible shoes in which the house is now garbed.

For an example of Kaveney's intimacy of disgust then we can turn to Stephen King's *Carrie.* Set in the heated and high octane environment of a high school, The novel is one of intensely physical escalation. The horrors inflicted at the prom, from the bucket of blood on Carrie's head to the wild vengeance she wreaks—all are horrors of the body and horrors of disgust. Water "hits" the basketball court. There are sizzling flashes. People are burned, crushed, drowned, but King extends the horror of the narrative by circling around it.

Here the latency is laid down in two distinct ways: (1) the controlled hysteria of manners and propriety exhibited by Carrie's mother; and (2) the encoded chatter of high school children, the meaningless yet simultaneously meaningful white noise of adolescent jostling for status. In King's world, this white noise disguises herd instincts. It keeps at bay the intimacy of hatred and revulsion that breaks through in that iconic shower scene. Here the stream of consciousness becomes the stream of accusations, of isolation, the list of indignities visited on Carrie. When Carrie indulges in introspection, it is to draw herself closer to this white noise, to embrace it: "And if he didn't come, if she drew back and gave up? High school would be over in a month. Then what? A creeping, subterranean existence in this house" (101). When she considers her powers, it is an intimate, exploratory process: "It was like being another's body and forcing her to run and run and run. You would not pay the cost yourself; the other body would" (102). But the denial of ownership is an extension of the body hatred she has acquired from her mother. Carrie's tragedy is that she misses her moment of recognition. She rejects the details of her mother's madness, but not the actual construction. The structure of *Carrie* moves in and out from the center: the more tormented Carrie is, the more introspective. Those moments when she considers what her body can do and that it does not feel like her body, chimes with a Cartesian dualism that argues that rationality is not embodied. It is because Carrie refuses to trust her sensibility, refuses to allow her feelings their due that she is fated. Belief in the rational world condemns her.

Stephen King's *Carrie* cuts from character to character, from personal account, to third-person narration, to newspaper clippings. At the very moment Carrie is destroying her peers, the book shifts to an investigative interview with a distant observer, a nonparticipant. When it shifts back to Carrie, it takes us back, back to the trigger moment (the falling bucket), and back further, into her head, and into an ultimate moment of revulsion from self: "In a flickering kaleidoscope of images she saw the blood running thickly down her naked thighs . . . tasted the plump, fulsome bitterness of horror" (149). The trajectory is an alternating current of latency and escalation, distance and intimacy. In the horror novel, cross-cutting brilliantly enhances latency's intimacy-creating properties. The further afield we travel—as in the national newspaper reports on the "Carrie incident"—the more the author forces us to regard the incident as somehow the center of the emotional universe, so that the horror novel becomes a fiction of *focus*, of emotional solipsism. Shirley Jackson's *The Haunting of Hill House* similarly mixes third-person *dissection* of character (particularly of the lesbian, Theodora) with third-person *introspection* (in which the narrator tells us what is going on in the character's mind, as if the mind is a window), with little lectures from Dr. Montague, and short conversation pieces designed, once again, to get into the minds of characters.

James Herbert's latency is constructed in perhaps the most traditional context, the cozy world of London suburbs. Unlike the two American novels, his is not a novel of social anxiety in quite the same way. Although I don't want to go too far down the route of political analysis, generally U.S. horror fiction is about the outsider in our midst, the one who does not conform or threatens the system from within. U.K. horror is much more fixated on the invader from without. It doesn't take too much effort to match this latter approach to current social concerns. Herbert's novel, therefore, constructs its latency on the backs of generations of cozy English catastrophe and cozy drawing room murder novels. Of these three authors, he is the most situated in genre knowingness of many kinds. Take this comment about the effect of the rats on London:

> People living in the East London boroughs demanded immediate evacuation. The government urged them to remain calm—the situation was firmly under control. Parents refused to send their children to school. The wartime measure of child evacuation came into being once more and the children were shunted off to all parts of the country. Poisons were laid in cellars, gardens and dustbins. . . . Restaurants were mistrusted and not used. Butchers decided to close up shop for a while—the thought of being amongst all that raw meat proved to be too uncomfortable. Any job that involved working beneath ground was turned down. (12)

Here the latency is contextualized within the notion of people *not panicking*, of wartime Britain and the Blitz, of knowing what to do. But note it is also encoded in a cross-cut, an aside. In his escalation in chapter 11, Herbert uses cross-cutting to emphasize both the horror of the humans, but also of the repelled intruder: as the rats die in the basement of the school, they scurry, climb, swim, gnaw, jump, and climb. The intensification of verbs, often several in a sentence, hurries the pace. Furthermore Herbert ensures that the written experience of the rats mirrors that of the humans. Where King constructed an alternating current of point and response, Herbert's horror is made of a series of parallels. Even at the end, it is the fate of "the rat" that is related with poignancy. In the final line, Herbert writes, "Patiently, they waited for the people to return," flipping the intrusion fantasy on its back.

Although much of this chapter has so far been devoted to horror and its ancestors, the intrusion fantasy also has strong connections with the fairy tale. I shall not discuss fairy tales here, because they take place in the realm of fancy, rather than fantasy; their magic is part of the background context of the world, even though they disrupt the lives of the protagonists, but their influence as intrusion in modern fantasy is seen in the work of George MacDonald, in C. S. Lewis's *The Magician's Nephew*, and, of course, in the work of E. Nesbit. In these early figures, however, part of what is at stake in creating the fantastical is the dissonance between the real and the unreal intrusion and the way in which fairy or fantasy makes the real world look absurd. In the modern intrusion fantasies that emerged in the 1980s, this sense of the absurd was a muted quality (we see it much more in the fantasies of the liminal). Instead, these new fantasies—most often referred to with Attebery's label, *indigenous* fantasies—brought the fantastic into the cities as a way (1) of providing the cities of the modern Americas (and they are almost all American)[13] with complex historical layers; and (2) of saying, "the modern world is boring, there must be something more than this." Although not strictly relevant to this discussion, these types of fantasy seem as much a denial of history as a creation of it. Repeatedly we can see that the American indigenous fantasy draws on European folklore, not the legends of the indigenes (Alex Irvine's *A Scattering of Jades* [2002] is a rare exception). This tendency may help to explain that, whereas the intimacy of the horror novel is an intimacy of repulsion, the intimacy we see in these novels is loving. Even where these intrusions are horrific or frightening, what divides the modern intrusion fantasy from the horror novel is the sensibility. Scott Westerfield's *The Midnighters: The Secret Hour* (2004) offers a good example. The intrusion of the dark things into the suburb, while it still constitutes the revelation of a wainscot world, is approached by the protagonists not with wariness, but with *enthusiasm* (something that we shall see repeatedly in the next section of this chapter). It marks the difference from the tense horror of Hodgson's *House on the Borderlands* to the unrestrained curiosity of Robert Holdstock's *Mythago Wood* (1984). In these fantasies, the trajectory the protagonists follow may resist intimacy with the intruder, but never for very long. Quite often the reader finds oneself feeling almost sorry for the unwary intrusion.

I shall begin my examination of nonhorror intrusion fantasy with two of the most oft-cited intrusion fantasies: Emma Bull's 1987 novel, *War for the Oaks*[14] and Charles de Lint's *Jack the Giant Killer* (1987). (The latter's sequel, *Drink Down the Moon* [1990] will also be briefly considered.) *War for the Oaks* provides us, if we need one, with a classic model for the modern (nonhorror) intrusion fantasy. In *War for the Oaks* Emma Bull picks up on all the ideological positionings that emerged from the Gothic, through authors such as Poe and Lovecraft, and uses them to construct a world in which the intrusion fantasy itself constructs an immersive fantastic.

The classic plot of these fantasies is for the intrusion to be met by a naive outsider, one who, like Lovecraft's protagonists, is aware of the underside of the world by virtue of standing slightly to one side. In this case she is a musician. The prevalence of musicians and artists in these fantasies is not, I think, coincidental but positional: it allows the protagonist to be hyperaware, to go anywhere and to be both of and outside of society. Whereas in the horror novels, however, the intrusion is beaten back, leaving a world disturbed but fundamentally intact, the modern intrusion fantasy is by its nature a novel of instantiation: the intrusion wins, not so much in terms of the individual story line—the fantastic is frequently sent back to its own world, if only temporarily—but by fundamentally remaking the world into one that can be sited within the immersive fantasy. One effect of this structure is that in the event of sequels, the author is frequently forced into a cycle of retreat and advancement. For example, in Charles de Lint's *Drink Down the Moon* (the sequel to *Jack the Giant Killer*), a new naive protagonist in the form of Johnny Faw must be introduced to represent the shock and confusion necessary to the tone of the intrusion fantasy.

The modern intrusion fantasy is a narrative of convincement: by the end of the novel the protagonist has usually ceded to the fantastic its right to exist within her world. Like the portal-quest fantasy, much of what is accepted is what is *told.* Information is downloaded from the representative of the intruding world (in the case of *Jack the Giant Killer* from a hob)—and, again as in the portal fantasy, there appears to be very little challenge of these downloads. The difference is that the emotion felt in the reception of the information is frequently "confusion." Although this confusion can seem formulaic, it serves two rhetorical purposes. First, it allows naïveté to be preserved longer (contributing to the construction of a sense of latency even while, as in these two books, the fantastic is already in our and the protagonist's face). Second, and perhaps more important, it will breach the club story of any inevitability that the inhabitants of the fantastic world have constructed. By this I mean that while the protagonist of portal-quest fantasies seem destined to succeed by following the rules, in many intrusion fantasies (and certainly in both *War of the Oaks* and *Jack the Giant Killer*) the protagonists succeed by challenging the rules or changing them—usually in the face of the pessimism of their colleagues from the fantastical lands. This is of course the colonialist fantasy of rescuing the natives from themselves, whatever I say later about the seduction narrative of the modern intrusion fantasy. Nalo Hopkinson confirmed this reaction, writing in response,

From my perspective as a black and "Third World" reader, . . . the fantasy land is the colonised land, and the fantasy is of the coloniser being helplessly apprehended and seduced/kidnapped into the colonised land, rather than being a marauder. It's the old rape justification of "it made me do it! It seduced me! It was asking for it!"[15]

This trajectory contributes to the instability of this version of the fantastic (and I mean that as a rhetorical strategy, not as a pejorative), manifested as the tendency for both the escalation of intrusions within texts or across series and the diminishing returns of the sequels. At each moment, the sense of the fantastic taking over must be re-created. Alternatively, the law of diminishing returns is so great that the sense of wonder is lost altogether, or displaced elsewhere, as in Laurell K. Hamilton's Anita Blake novels. These novels, although intrusion fantasies, are intrusion fantasies based in an immersive world in which vampires are normal (and in which in the first book, Anita Blake has already met Jean Claude, the master vampire, which negates his role as intrusion). In these novels the intrusion is always the crime, not the fantastic element itself. The most vivid example is the recent novel *Obsidian Butterfly* (2000), which re-creates the sense of intrusion by removing us to an area that is fantastic in another way (the South), and making of both Anita and Ted, and the hunters, intrusions into the magical realism of southern culture.

Latency, in the modern intrusion fantasy, is about this process of falling into immersion: how long can the author hold the fantastic at bay? One way is to begin with a protagonist who is hyperaware of her own environment, who does not behave as we might expect someone sited fully in her own world to behave, who does *not* take the presence of any particular building or greensward for granted. Here is the opening of *War for the Oaks*:

By day, the Nicollet Mall winds through Minneapolis like a paved canal. People flow between its banks, eddying at the doors of office towers and department stores. The big red-and-white city buses roar at every corner. On the many-globed lampposts, banners advertising a museum exhibit flap in the wind that the tallest buildings snatch out of the sky. The skyway system vaults the mall with its covered bridges of steel and glass, and they, too are full of people, color, motion. (1)

The intensity of description is quite different from the surface description of the portal-quest fantasy: this is not a description for tourists as such because it is not a description tourists can follow. As with the Gothic horror, the emphasis is on feel and sound, on *sensation* rather than the visual mapping. Later, every description Eddie will provide us, will be a description meant not to introduce us to her world, but to site herself within it:

> Eddie hung over the back of her seat watching the Minneapolis skyline rise up and unroll behind them. White light banded the top of the IDS building, rebounded off the darkened geometry of a blue glass tower nearby. The clock on the old courthouse added the angular red of its hands. (9)

With each iteration, Bull contrives to use landscape to fix Eddie in place, to make it clear that this is a stable world of which she is the center (even as, later, she will be marked out as on the periphery, able to see through its walls).

The rest of the novel is balanced between two strategies: the effect of the intrusion in changing the way Eddie sees the world and, *crucially* to this form (and it may be what separates it from the classic horror novel), the degree to which Eddie functions as the guide to her world for the intruders. This guidance is quite different from the unintentional guidance offered by protagonists of immersive fantasies. When Eddie meets the fantastic, she offers her knowledge of her world to the visitors; she folds them in, shapes them, gives them the tools they need to slide through the world. So for example there are the constant intrusions of her attackers, which escalate in horror and in effect in much the same way as in the classic horror novel. But there is also her relationship with the Phouka: Eddie does not retreat, but offers instead morality (why fairy gold may punish more than the victim), practicalities (the use of a motorbike to escape the confining effects of iron), or information on how to blend in with humans (be outrageous and they will see only outrage). In terms of reader position, here we stand with the intruder, invited by Eddie (and later Jack) into her world.

Rather than—as in the horror novel—being drawn toward the fantastic world, by having it breathe down her neck, Eddie draws the two worlds (three, if you count the world of the reader) closer together. She breaks down the wall between them, not by permitting an invasion from either side, but by making that wall translucent and permeable.

The trajectory is even stronger in Charles de Lint's work, perhaps because Jacky Rowan, far from being hyperaware of her own world, is dissociated from it. The novel opens with the exit of her boyfriend, hurling epithets about her refusal to connect with the world. The crucial thing is that Jacky regards this as correct. At least at first, Jacky Rowan is open to accepting the world as it presents itself to her because she is the *ultra*-naive protagonist. Where Eddie takes the intrusion and molds it on her own terms, Jacky is much more amenable to being absorbed by the intrusion; it becomes the domineering boyfriend who tells her to understand the world his/its way. This allows de Lint to construct concentric circles of intrusion, where Jacky accepts the intrusion of the fantastic to the degree that she herself becomes a traveler in a portal world, and then in turn accepts her hosts' definition of a hostile intrusion—the invasion of the Unseelie court into Ottawa. This concentric series of intrusions may be a hallmark of the subset of indigenous fantasy, constructing their worlds as they do as colored filters across the landscape. In *Drink Down the Moon* the faerie of Kinrowan keep court below the Parliament buildings. In Neil Gaiman's *Neverwhere* (1996) or China Miéville's *King Rat* (1998)—both of which are portal, rather than intrusion fantasies[16]—a fantastic London underlies the London we know. What prevents these from being wainscot stories, is that (1) access to them is intermittent and privileged, a function always of someone leaving and intruding into the mundane world; and (2) the worlds can exist in the same spaces at one and the same time, so that the scenes in *Neverwhere* in the underground stations do not take place in the nooks and crannies but in a parallel world that overlays the mundane world.

But to return to the emotional tenor of *Jack the Giant Killer*, de Lint encodes the instability of the relationship between the worlds in Jack's insecurity, an insecurity that leads her continually to question. When she stumbles, Finn's anxious smile does nothing to comfort her, and she queries who has marked her (20), but when Finn explains something, unlike in the portal-quest fantasies, the explanation clarifies nothing: "In peaceful times . . . the Gruagagh sees to the welfare of Kinrowan itself. He sits in his Tower, weaving and braiding the lines of luck that flow through the earth by the will of the Moon" (22). The vagueness draws Jacky in, but it also demands a very different response from that of the questor in the portal fantasy. Jacky is being treated not as a tourist, but as a child who must be educated in the ways of the world, bootstrapping the world from clues given by its inhabitants living their everyday lives. This education results in a protagonist much more functional than that of the portal fantasy. Although below I shall suggest that there are political problems with this trajectory, by the end of these modern intrusion fantasies, there is a very strong sense that the protagonists have genuinely learned to function in these worlds by applying lessons they have learned to more general problems. By the end, they have supplanted their guides (frequently by offering an unorthodox solution) not made them Merlins.

For all that it might seem that Jacky is moving into the fantastic world, a better image (and one we shall see in a scarier form in *Mythago Wood*) is that the intrusion is tempting her to a greater intimacy, so that it might absorb and take her over. The relationship between the fantastic and Jacky Rowan is essentially the same as between Eleanor and the house in Shirley Jackson's novel. In *Jack the Giant Killer* latency becomes a tool of temptation, while threat entices intimacy. Finn tells her, "in a few years time, it'll be only the Unseelie Court that walks the twilight shades of your world" (25); at the same time, Finn disguises, or deflects attention from, the intrusion-threat that he represents (this deflection and doubling technique is one we shall see in *Mortal Love* as well but used for a different purpose). What the deflection specifically entices her to do is to overstretch, to go beyond what is asked—to rescue the Laird's daughter as well as the Horn—and so to let the fantastic take her over further. The intrusion of the magical on Ottawa is complete almost from the start; the real story is the intrusion of the magical on Jacky and her absorption into it. If the intrusion fantasy is essentially about the threat, fear, or embrace of the intruder, then in this, and many intrusion fantasies, the colonized land is the body and mind of the protagonist. Sometimes this embodying is expressed directly: "For a long time after the creatures had stopped pawing at her, Jacky lay still, hardly daring to breathe. The sheer horror of her predicament had unnerved her to the point where it was all she could do to keep herself from fainting dead away again. The touch of the hag's tongue, all those hands and fingers, squeezing and prodding" (95).

This very sexual language imposed on the actions of the hostile intruder is counterbalanced by the prevalence of romance in these fantasies, which functions as a metaphor for the romance between the mundane and the fantastic, but also renders palatable what is unpalatable when originating from the hostile: At the same time these novels function as imperialist fantasies, if you consider the enthusiasm with which the protagonists embrace the aims of the invader—"Jacky wasn't sure why she was so caught up with the fate of the Laird's daughter. She just knew it was important" (30)—and frequently the representative of the invasion, a fairy prince or a handsome vampire. That many of these fantasies are essentially willing slave-girl fantasies is a very uncomfortable thought, but one that Elizabeth Hand and Susanna Clarke both make manifest in their counternarratives of fairy invasion. In *Jack the Giant Killer*, Jacky is told that each time she gazes into fairy it becomes easier. But if we reverse this, what is actually said is that she is losing her ability to exist in her own world on her own terms (118). By the following book, it is clear that Jacky has been "seduced," that she now identifies with her conquerors. De Lint makes clear that this is an imposition. Finn describes it this way: "Think of it as a painting that you've had for years. A nice landscape, perhaps. One day someone comes in and says, 'Look at that face in the side of the hill,' and from then on you'll always be aware of that face. Because you'll *know* it's there" (118). Jacky's vision and judgment have been colonized.

If latency pulls the protagonist toward the intrusion, escalation pushes her: in these indigenous fantasies, it is necessary (as in the portal-quest fantasies) to emphasize continually the need to ally with the "good" intrusion. But whereas in the portal-quest fantasies this conviction is usually constructed through the layering of word, the intrusion fantasies in the tradition of horror do it through the escalation of deed. What is unnerving is the degree to which this escalation is done by the numbers. In *Jack the Giant Killer*, *War of the Oaks*, the Anita Blake novels, and others, threats arrive in ones or twos in the first chapters, but by the end of the book (where the portal-quest fantasy frequently reduces the final conflict to a two-person standoff), the protagonist is overwhelmed by villains. In order to make the conflict fair, the accompanying trajectory has seen the accumulation of companions so that the whole is rendered like a team game, an inherently individual-absorbing structure.

Escalation is also found here in volume and in sound effects. Intrusions in the classic modern intrusion fantasy mostly begin quietly: the man in the audience, the vampire at the door, the girl at the party, the watcher in the wood. As the intrusions escalate, as well as becoming more numerous, they seem to get louder. By chapter 17, the hags in *Jack the Giant Killer* screech, the giants boom. Monsters that at the start of Anita Blake novels exist offscreen, their only sounds the weeping of victims, by the end are accompanied by the crash of furniture, and bodies flying everywhere.

When we considered the portal-quest fantasies, one very important question was the extent to which the formula could be subverted. Among the intrusion fantasies, the regularity of the formula is almost overwhelming. As we turn to the "subversions," what we shall see is less a reworking of the form, than a naked honesty in the work of writers who have traced this counterpoint of latency and escalation, of intimacy and seduction, and made it manifest. One of the most impressive is Robert Holdstock's *Mythago Wood.*

Although *Mythago Wood* can be understood as a portal fantasy, in which travelers explore a strange land, there is a crucial ideological difference. In the portal fantasy the protagonist retains the upper hand over the otherworld. Even when beaten, shot, and nearly killed, there remains the sense that the protagonist is the most important element. In this novel, all the power is with the wood. It reaches out, disrupts; when it does draw the characters in, it is for purposes of its own.

Superficially, *Mythago Wood* reads as a reworking of William Hope Hodgson's *The House on the Borderlands.* It begins when Stephen comes home to find his father disappeared and his brother Christian obsessed with the disappearance of his lover, a red-haired woman who came from the wood. When Christian disappears, Stephen finds her body, and becomes in turn obsessed. As he reads his father's notes, he discovers that the wood is a mystical place that generates mythagos, manifestations of the Jungian subconscious. He discovers his own red-haired woman and, what his father discovered before him, that there is one ur-tale, one source for the tales of the wood, endlessly retold, endlessly mutated.

Holdstock takes the iterations of the intrusion fantasy and makes them central to the plot, the diminishing returns of the generic conventions here manifest as the thinning of the Land, the gradual fall away from the ur-myth. Similarly, the notion of the intrusion as seducer is made manifest as the wood in the form of Guiwenneth, who pulls first George Huxley and then his two sons within its embrace. At the same time Holdstock (unlike the other writers we have considered so far) also recognizes the fundamental dishonesty of this characterization. Throughout the novel Holdstock demonstrates the degree to which George, Christian, and Stephen in turn both wish to be taken by the wood (while denying this intent) and view the wood as something upon which they can impose their wishes, a place that they can *fix* (as in C. S. Lewis's *The Voyage of the Dawn Treader*, daydreams are confused with the true intensity of dreams).[17] Christian, the brother who becomes the monstrous Outsider, fulfills Nalo Hopkinson's contention (in reply to my own thoughts) that it is the person who characterizes himself as the seduced who is the rapist, who comes to defend his actions in the language of helplessness and victimhood. Stephen inadvertently reveals this to Keaton and himself when he says, "The wood turns you around. It defends itself. . . . My father found a way in" (104), and later when he finds the notes from his father concerned "with the way to penetrate the outer defences of the primal woodland" (115).

In tone, *Mythago Wood* is very like *The House on the Borderlands*. Its latency is coded in the careful, formal, and reflective narrative of Stephen, the younger brother. Much of the "action" takes place in Stephen's head: "I stared at the arrow for several seconds, reliving the man's agony, and the tears that Christian and I had wept for him as we had helped him back from the woodlands that cold autumn afternoon, convinced that he would die" (24). Latency in this novel is built through sentiment, a revival of the Gothic life of the mind in which significance is found in everything, in which the landscape is part of the emotion of the land, and through which the highly significant, the magical, can thus step through as a matter of course: "I went out into the yard; it was after dusk, but still quite bright, although the oakwoods were melded together into a grey-green blur. I called for Christian, but there was no response. I was about to return to my paper when a man stepped towards me. He was holding on a short, leather leash, the most enormous hound I have ever seen" (27).

Yet the response Stephen offers is of helplessness in the face of the foreign, not fear or excitement. This helplessness (or confusion) that Stephen repeatedly displays, the sense of someone waiting for someone or something else to take control, runs through the novel, as Stephen is placed in the position of a watcher, first as someone who watches his brother, then as he watches the wood. This positioning enables Holdstock to construct for Stephen an intimacy of seduction, doubled by the occasional intervention of George Huxley's notes. Intimacy of analysis, the anthropologist's tool, both allows the hard stare and distracts from the reality of subjectivity. It allows the protagonist to construct himself both as "in charge" and as detached.

The dynamic tension of the novel, the push-pull rhythm discussed earlier, is encoded in *Mythago Wood* as a call-and-response of bafflement followed by "explanation." Where other authors of the intrusion fantasy allow their protagonists to be correct in their hypotheses, Holdstock uses all of the Huxleys' belief in their abstract objectivity to increase their vulnerability to the wood. George Huxley's diary is particularly telling: he wraps up the phenomena of the wood in pseudoscientific language, believing as he does so that ever more complex descriptions are in themselves explanations.[18] This same tactic is used by Stephen to explain to himself the vulnerability of George's Guiwenneth, and the greater strength his own possesses. Again, Holdstock has taken a common trope of the intrusion fantasy—that which is described is understood—and revealed it for what it is, an attempt to assert ownership over the intrusion.[19]

One thing to consider is why *Mythago Wood* is not a portal fantasy. For much of the novel the wood's field reaches out into the world, encompassing the farm, and extending toward, but not into the village. The field allows the wood's inhabitants/manifestations to burst through into modern life. The disruption we see is the wood's physical and emotional effect on the farm's inhabitants, and the rhetorical strategies are geared to have us not admiring the landscape or seeking a purpose, but wondering what comes next. The protagonists and the reader are nakedly at the mercy of the intrusion, not in notional command of the adventure.

Landscape or surroundings in this novel are always expressed in terms of movement and emotion. Their relationship to the protagonist is the center of the focus: "Shapes darted about the fence. They seemed to pour from the woodland edge, spiralling and leaping, grey, shadowy forms that vanished as quickly as they came, like tongues of grey smoke from a gorse fire" (64). Later, "The elementals came in force . . . rising about me, hovering, probing, and making strange sounds very like laughter. . . . My hair was touched, my skin stroked. Invisible fingers prodded my back" (65). These descriptions are so often of things that "seem," their nebulousness a contrast to the solid landscapes of the portal fantasy. In the intrusion the world is something constructed by porous perception.

Later, however, in the travels into the wood, and in the explanation by the tale tellers, the novel as a whole toys with the portal, and could be thought of as resolving into a portal fantasy in the last third, when Stephen and his friend Keeton finally enter the wood. For Keeton, anxious to find the world he lost in the ghost wood of France, it may indeed be a portal fantasy. This last section is told with the classic description of landscape passed that we associate with the form. In portal fantasies, however, the travelers are important to the story that is told within the portal, and in this novel, Stephen is never important. Even Christian, who becomes the Outsider, a figure who ravages the landscape, never becomes more than an intrusion in the Land; he is not a part of it. When Stephen defeats him, and restores the Land, the problem he resolves is one he helped create, not one that is intrinsic to the wood. We are told this; only the Kinsman can kill the Outsider (242). The Cain and Abel story is alien to this land (whose own story is of a kidnapped child rescued by a martyred father) so that Stephen and Christian have imported their own narrative. They remain extrinsic to the Land. When at the end Stephen finally loses Guiwenneth to death, it is an act of repulsion: the fantasy finally both rejects him and lets him go. The "seduction" is over. Of course, the above is exactly the classic tale of the portal fantasy: the "good" intruder repels the "bad" intruder. Holdstock revisions the ur-text by providing a host culture that recognizes that *it* is the landscape over which an outside quarrel is being fought. Like the peasants in Lloyd Alexander's *Taran Wanderer*, the host inhabitants aren't interested in who claims to be their champion, but only in their lives, distorted by the imposition of someone else's story (which, as Diana Wynne Jones has pointed out in *Tough Guide to Fantasyland*, is what most quest narratives are).

One of the most impressive recent subversions of the intrusion fantasy is to be found in Elizabeth Hand's 2004 novel, *Mortal Love*. Unlike the modern fantasies considered so far, fairy in *Mortal Love* is foreign to the Land, an accidental invader that must survive in the interstices and feed where it can. Creativity is its coprolites and we can examine the results—the art, the music, the literature, the strange folk movements, and the mystical neoreligions of late nineteenth- and late twentieth-century intelligentsia—to track its path. Fairy in *Mortal Love* produces behavior that is essentially *un*-English.

The novel begins when Daniel (an American journalist) arrives in London to write a book on love and is introduced to Larkin, the ex-lover of a rather damaged friend. He is seduced by Larkin, left with physical and mental scars, and then watches as he loses her to Val, a rather mysterious young American with mental health problems. Running parallel to this is the story of another American, Radborne Comstock, an artist and medical student in the nineteenth century who has been offered a position in a mental asylum caring for those who have been damaged by the ferocity of their creativity (and also, incidentally, caring for the young lady who is the flame).

In Hand's work, fairy is an intrusion into the calm English world, an invader, but one that has its own counterpart in English culture, in the "maze of paths and stalls around Camden . . . stray items of clothing—boot, jockstrap, sequined scarf, a turquoise sock" (259). Like the Gothic that only barely haunts the tale, there is a "topography of parallelisms" (Sedgwick 49). Englishness here is constructed of materials, of rich silks and velvets, the spilling of emotional restraint into material excess. Hand's fairy appeals to the artifice of aestheticism and the vibrancy of commerce and industry. Even the nature images are brighter than bright, a "vale of apple trees in bloom . . . white blossoms and pale leaves, light the colour of tourmaline and shallow water, greenstone and beryl and new-grown ivy" (347).

As usual in a Hand novel, the central characters—Daniel Rowlands and Radborne Comstock—are the poor saps drawn into uncaring magic.

Unlike those in the fantasies discussed earlier, these protagonists are precisely *not* the special, the predestined, the potential imperial rulers of fantasy. Hand's magicians and fairies never deliberately harm humans, any more than humans deliberately tread on ants, and it is within this tale of careless, thoughtless damage, that Hand's particular take on the lies told in many intrusion fantasies is constructed. The modern intrusion fantasies we have discussed so far each cleave to three crucial notions: that the intrusion can be repelled, that we are fascinating to the intruder, and that consorting with the enemy can be of benefit to the protagonist. In *Mortal Love*, Hand dismantles these ideas. Larkin, the fairy queen, is in our world partly by accident. Until she finds her prince, she cannot return to her own world. Hand has reversed the portal fantasy and told the quest from the point of view of that unrolling landscape destroyed by the contending armies. Radbourne Comstock, Angust Swinburne, Jacobus Candell, Daniel Rowlands—all are "episodes" in Larkin's quest narrative, momentarily important for the information they provide, for the growth she may experience, but in essence, only stage sets and redshirts in her *real* adventure, which has nothing to do with them:

> "Mortal love," repeated Juda softly. "That's what draws us. Your taste, how fast you move and how soon you die . . . we see how with every moment you quicken with your own death and it is so beautiful—it moves us, it captivates us." (336)

In each of these episodes, the human protagonist makes the mistake of believing that he or she is important and fascinating to Larkin. The artists Larkin entraps mistake her *general* fascination with the human world for a specific love. When at the end of the novel Larkin finds in Valentine Comstock her missing prince, it is not that she abandons Daniel, but that he barely exists for her.

This reversed portal structure is doubled within the novel: both Daniel and Radbourne Comstock are themselves intruders in London. As tourists (writer and artist respectively), they have personal missions of artistic development. The pain that Larkin causes is so intense in part because Larkin does to them what they (unintentionally) wished to do to London, to create of London an "episode" from which they would construct memory and art. Hand uses the doubling to remind us that art both takes from and imposes upon the world. It is not a neutral commentary and it is from this realization that we begin to perceive that Hand selects her language around color and texture. She constructs her intrusion in the nexus of pain and beauty. In the opening pages of *Mortal Love*, Learmont, a nineteenth-century doctor, places his wrist in a flame: "Learmont turned his hand back and forth, gently tugging at the sleeve of his cotton shirt to reveal an arm latticed with older scars, red and pale blue, ice-white, petal-shaped scars like the one that bloomed upon his palm" (8).

Later, Radborne Comstock is tempted by Swinburne to look into a peephole: "Within a green world, prismatic things flickered and flew and spun, rubescent, azure, luminous yellow, the pulsing indigo of a heart's hidden valves" (14). The intensity of color that Hand uses to represent the intrusion becomes the petals tempting an insect. When the very young Valentine Comstock first encounters his grandfather's painting, he is drawn by the wild weirdness of it, of the "man, or a sort of man . . . kneeling between her legs, grasping each of her calves and pulling them apart so that he could peer between them" (24), drawn in until he sees the silvery green "spilled from the cleft between her legs" (24) which opens out into another world where figures can just about be seen. In both of these moments Hand offers to the reader the challenge of who is the colonized and who is the colonizer. Both Comstock and Valentine see themselves as entering into other worlds. Both are entered/infected by fairy in these moments. Comstock has found his muse, while Valentine is more obviously taken over, and more willing to acknowledge that this is what has happened as his life is increasingly absorbed by the notebooks he fills with world-drawings.

As the book develops, it creates a world in which there is real, and then there is *more real*, in which the everyday mundanities of the world are constantly at risk of the intrusion of creativity, in which creativity is "the endlessly replicating honeycombs traced across your eyelids during an acid trip" (22). For Valentine Comstock, this reality is reduced to a diagnosis of bipolar disorder, hypomania in spring, depression in winter, which itself transparently registers the intrusion on the landscape that is spring (spring may be the archetype of intrusion fantasies). For Daniel, this sense that there are levels to the real are encapsulated in "barrows full of oranges and figs from Israel, greengage plums, grapes so round and golden they looked like champagne bubbles in an old Merrie Melodies cartoon" (39) against the rather grimy surroundings of Inverness Street. Camden itself exists on a tide of cultural intrusion of tourists and markets. The permeability of the world is expressed in small gestures as Larkin coughs up an acorn (itself is a motif of the intrusion that is growth).

This multileveled reality leads us to consider the conflicting dynamic of the intrusion/portal-quest doubled structure. Over and over again, the intrusion is expressed by Larkin in the motifs of spring and growth and art, and reworked by the humans around her into sexual desire and obsession. Hand takes the conventional "the intrusion is sex" structure of the horror novel and asks who imposes that interpretation, leading us back to Nalo Hopkinson's insight that the intruded upon is himself an aspirant colonist. Larkin's victims, particularly those of the earlier nineteenth-century sections, seek to impose on Larkin their interpretation of the world as codified/embedded in the construction of psychiatric explanations around the threat presented by Larkin/Evelyn Upstone, where her ability to attract men becomes a symptom of her sickness, not theirs.

Here life is the intrusion. As Radborne gazes at a man in the street: "When once again he opened his mouth to sing, vapor poured from it, and tiny black things. Radborne turned and fled, filled with a horror he could not explain or obviate" (93). In Victorian London, that which is filled with life—sex, the earth—is uncontrolled horror. Radborne and the Pre-Raphaelites are caught in their own repression. Swinburne tells him, "He lures them to his lair and shows them Beauty, and She devours them—but, oh, how they love to burn!" (121). The embracing of the intrusion and the chaos it brings is expressed over and over in images of fire and earth. When Juda tries to warn Daniel, every word she or Nick speaks ignites a flame:

> He reached for the door, was arrested by the crackle of flame and something that blurred his visions: a bright arabesque coiling and uncoiling in the air before him. He cringed, watched in horror as the shining arabesque became a rainbow-finned tail. The pressure in his mouth exploded into the taste of burned fish and honey. . . .
>
> Around him the room shuddered, the way the image thrown by a jammed projector shifts, then changes. Then the room was gone. In front of him, a fire burned; he could feel the heat, near scorching, of something in his hands. (146)

The language of intrusion here is less about an embracing intimacy than it is a rape. Daniel (and Nick and Radborne Comstock before him) are taken over by the intrusion, robbed of breath to breathe or thoughts to think. There is none of the euphemism of earlier intrusion fantasies. The "intimacy" is total and truly violent, Hand's choice of words expressing the rawness of the attack:

> He remembered everything. That there had been a green world within a woman's eyes; that he had lain with her and heard her cry out at the touch of his

mouth; that an owl had called in the night. That order and meaning could be tasted; that desire had a color and the void a sound. That his skin bore the marks of claws; that there were hazelnuts everywhere about him. That they contained each of them a world. That the world beneath him was not earth but water. That everything he knew was wrong. That this world, his world, bounded by steel and grass and poured concrete and bread, a buzzing mobile phone, dried blood, semen, sugar—*that*—world was a lie, a scrim, a veil . . . (254)

As Daniel's thoughts spiral, they escalate from poetry to panic. The intimacy of the intrusion becomes the intimacy of flayed skin as he is ripped from his own sense of the world. He is, as Juda later tells him, poisoned by contact with the other. He can never be fully a part of his own world again because he has seen it through the eyes of someone who does not truly believe it real. Radborne Comstock, without ever actually lying with Evelyn Upstone, is drawn into her sexual world; he masturbates and donates semen, to become the father, in another time, of Valentine, his seduction drawn in the sound and scent, "skirts moved slowly across the floor, not silk or linen but a swirl of underwater green. . . . He smelled vetiver, vervein, veridigris; tasted bice metallic as scorched pennies" (289).

Elsewhere the language of intrusion is more moderate, specifically with regard to Valentine Comstock: twenty-four hours without medication is "enough time to open a crack in my skull and let the light seep back in" (273). This moderation creates the latency that shapes his meeting with Larkin. Rereading the book, we see the hints and links between Larkin and Val resolve; on our first reading, however, the characters seem utterly separated. Only Val's artwork, in some ways the typical comic art of an adolescent boy, points to deeper connection.

The moment, when it comes, is a moment of *interruption*. It is crucial to the shaping of the intrusion rhetoric that although the moment is told from the third person, Daniel is the viewpoint character:

On the other side of the kitchen, Val Comstock was staring at Larkin, but she hadn't really registered him yet. She was looking at Nick, her lips parted and her face tilted to one side, as though she were trying to figure out what was going on here, what she had wandered into. A surprise party? An argument?

"Um . . . ?" she said, turning.

And she saw Val. (315)

The point of this scene is the way in which it swivels both Larkin and Val and reconfigures the relationship of the reader to the text. This is not just "and then suddenly." To return to the point made earlier, for Larkin this is a portal-quest fantasy, and this is the moment at which *Daniel* realizes this, realizes that he is irrelevant, that he is merely part of the stage set, that there is another world out there that is the Primary world, and that he is merely part of the secondary. All is encoded in a moment of deliberate hesitation:

> A shimmering instant, the moment between when a crystal glass is struck and when it cracks. Daniel's hand grasped the corner of the kitchen table; Nick stood with his beer, mouth open to speak. Separated by the table, Larkin and Valentine Comstock stared at each other, Larkin in her outdated Gypsy glory, Val with his dirty red bandanna and sweat-stained jeans and T-shirt. In the back of his throat, Daniel tasted bile, bitter green suddenly flooded by the taste of scorched fish. There was a scent of apple blossom and the sea. Somewhere a dog barked. Very slowly and without looking away from Larkin, Val reached to set his beer on the table, his hazel eyes wide and wondering as a sleepwalker's.
>
> *Enchantment.*
>
> Daniel saw the pen-and-ink figures of conjoined lovers in a field of endless green and white, felt Larkin's hand upon his face and taloned fingers clawing at his breast.
>
> *Discovery.*
>
> "I know you," murmured Val. Gazing at him Larkin nodded silently.
>
> "Yes," she said, and Daniel felt a door close upon him forever.
>
> *Recognition.*

Recognition is, of course, one of the four quarters of John Clute's "Full Fantasy," and the full fantasy is played out most fully in the portal-quest subgenre. That moment of recognition is both about the recognition that Larkin has found what she sought, and Daniel's recognition of the type of story he is in.

We end the novel with the leaving of the Land, so typical of portal-quest fantasies but seen, once more, from the point of view of the people left behind. Larkin gives to Daniel an acorn: "It belongs here. It is just that I always found them so beautiful and strange. Like everything here. That they are so small and so quickly grown" (352). And at the end,

> The world turned to gold. There was no line of demarcation between land's end and sky and sea. Before him hung a city in the air, spires and pennons and a whirl of birds, blue and gold and silver, green leaves and the endless flash of things that flew and dove and sang. The world he knew rolled back like a wave

from sand, the world was revealed: one blazing instant like a flash of flame, and he could see it all, both of them, all.

"Larkin!" he shouted. "*Larkin!*"

And it was gone. Before him the sun rose from the dark roil that was the Atlantic, bands of green and yellow striping the sea cliffs. He stood upon a small rise, alone. Behind him was the ruins of a cottage, the wreckage of a manor house. It was morning. The air felt cool and sweet . . . (352)

The melancholy air of this parting, and of the final chapter, clues us into something that was apparently missing from this fantasy. There has been little latency, little sense of waiting—once more because we were not actually seeing the book from the true protagonist's viewpoint. Larkin was the one caught up in latency. But in her departure, she leaves behind expectation, metaphorised in that unexpectedly meaningful acorn that Daniel continues to hold "so tightly in his hand that he bore its mark for many days, a brown-and-green weight like a living jewel" (353).

At the end of *Mortal Love*, Larkin leaves behind localized devastation, changed people, but not truly a changed world. The promise of instantiation is a doorway opening, not a flood encompassing. From the images of fire, and pain, and spring, and growth, we have expected instantiation. The instantiation is denied, however, because this adventure was never really about us. We were only ever the stage set and our fate is to be consumed not remade.

For the full instantiation of the intrusion fantasy we can do no better than to turn to Susanna Clarke's *Jonathan Strange and Mr. Norrell* (2004), and specifically to the concluding sections when magic rolls out across England:

"And now for the magic itself," said Strange. He picked up the book and began to recite the spell. He addressed the trees of England; the hills of England; the sunlight, water, birds, earth and stones. He addressed them all, one after the other, and exhorted them to place themselves in the hands of the nameless slave. . . .

The gentleman was already on the packhorse bridge. Stephen followed him and . . .

. . . and everything changed. The sun came out from behind a cloud; it shone through the winter trees; hundreds of small, bright patches of sunlight appeared. The world became a kind of puzzle or labyrinth. It was like the superstition which says that one must not walk upon lines between flagstones—or the strange magic called Doncaster Squares which is performed upon a board like a chessboard. Suddenly everything had meaning: Stephen hardly dared take another step. If he did so—if, for example, he stepped into *that* shadow or *that* spot of light, then the world might be forever altered.

"Wait!" he thought, wildly: "I am not ready for this! I have not considered. I do not know what to do!"

But it was too late. He looked up.

The bare branches against the sky were a writing, and though he did not want to, he could read it. He saw that it was a question put to him by the trees.

"Yes," he answered them. (762–763)

The magic sweeps over Stephen, its transformation a lighting up of the world. Magic in Clarke's book is not in opposition to the mundanity of everyday life, but an enhancement, it makes the world *more* alive in much the same way that Larkin made her lovers more alive. But where Larkin's magic was a scorching fire, Clarke's is sunlight through stained glass. The world it shines on is more colorful and less *proper*. In *Jonathan Strange and Mr. Norrell*, the aspect of the world that is fundamentally transformed is the world of *manners*: women are magicians and a black man is king of Fairy.

If we return to the start of Clarke's novel, we can see that this is first and foremost an immersive fantasy and that it, for the most part, takes advantage of the asset the immersive fantasy possesses: the ability to construct a complete world in which much that is different is taken for granted. Within this context, magic is presented as both utterly normal and an intrusion. John Holbo writes, "the renaissance of English practical magic is astonishing to these Christian Gentlemen yet—being magic Christians from the start, merely lapsed ones—they are not astonished in the *way* we are (19). Clarke encompasses this ironic intrusion by encoding it as a comedy of manners.

Jonathan Strange and Mr. Norrell begins as a history of the revival of English magic. Clarke's Englishness is one in which magic as a gentlemanly occupation is a branch of antiquarianism; one studies books, one writes learned papers, one presents to one's friends. The first "intrusion/disruption" (a link I shall use without quotes for the rest of this section) is John Segundus, a man apparently younger and poorer than the other magicians of the York society. He brings into their colloquium an unhealthy interest in "why," specifically why no practical magic is done. Inadvertently he uncovers class prejudice, a sense that the possibility of practical magic allows the talented but ill-born to supplant the mediocre but well-educated: "Magic (in the practical sense) was much fallen off. It had low connexions.

It was the bosom companion of unshaven faces. . . . Oh no! a gentleman could not do magic. A gentleman might study the history of magic (nothing could be nobler) but he could not do any" (4).

This fear of the "unfit" doing magic is the dominant note in the magician Mr. Norrell's understanding of the world, but it works as both metonym and metaphor. Although Norrell is a knowledge miser, he is also genuinely afraid of the wrong people being magicians because he is afraid of the potential of magic itself to disrupt the social order. Knowledge and ways of knowing are the fuel of the text. Whether knowledge itself can be good or evil, whether it is possible to control the flow of information—all underpin the struggles between these two. The magicians fight essentially over the democratization of knowledge and therefore of society. Mr. Norrell has no allies, only servants. Strange has no servants but many allies and friends, including John Segundus, the theoretical magician who showed the rare mettle to stand up to Mr. Norrell's intimidation.

Mr. Norrell is reclusive, selfish, a book miser, and a Scholastic, who wants English magic vested in him only, and sees it as a careful gleaning of material from the revived ancients. Jonathan Strange is young, enthusiastic, openhanded with knowledge and improvisational; a scientist. They argue over what scholarship is and how to write. Norrell waits for his work to be perfect, Strange uses writing and publishing to argue with himself, to see what can be done. Norrell's magic is codified and written down, while Strange's magic is a matter of working the process through as he goes, taking a principle and riffing on it. After swapping a book with its reflection, he says of the experience. "I have only the haziest notion of what I did. I dare say it is just the same with you, sir, one has a sensation like music playing at the back of one's head—one simply knows what the next note will be" (233).

To extend the metaphor of the aural, Mr. Norrell plays the classics, Strange plays jazz: he improvises, often (as we hear later) using Norrell's spells as the basic tune on which he spins his variations. The result is that he works brilliantly with Wellington, whose response to any setback is "find another way." But Strange also invites in disruption; he visualizes it as a surfer might see a wave, something to ride and to know.

All the magic in *Jonathan Strange and Mr. Norrell* is intrusion/disruption. Magic is always portrayed as being brought into the controlled and mannered world of society. Greer Gilman has written of Clarke's work that it is "very cool and dry, like dry white wine and a biscuit: it's all in the Englishness of understatement. Plainfaced and unbedizened" (LiveJournal 23

August 2005).[20] This coolness is true even in the terms of the magic of architecture. Take this description of a Cathedral town:

When going about one's business in the muddle of narrow streets one is sure to lose sight of the Cathedral, but then the town will open out and suddenly it is there, may times taller and many times larger than any other building, and one realises that one has reached the heart of the town and that all streets and lanes have in some way led here, to a place of mysteries. . . . (25)

Clarke writes of wildness with tight control, and it is in this control, this English understatement, that Clarke introduces the latency of the intrusion fantasy. Englishness *becomes* a riff on latency (Farrell 33–37).

Where in other intrusion fantasies, intrusion is linked intimately with sexuality, in *Jonathan Strange and Mr. Norrell*, it appears to be linked primarily with *bad manners*, which is why the most disturbing intrusion—at least until Strange calls the Land—is not magical, but Strange's review of Lord Portishead's *Essay on the Extraordinary Revival of English Magic* with its capitalized words and forceful attack on the status quo. Also the sign that fairy is creeping into England is found in the appearance of establishments selling magical items such as philters and mirrors (which are, however, quite fraudulent). The breakthrough of magic is first expressed by children (who cause the ears of their tormentors to fly into the bushes [692]), and Lord Sidmouth's objection to magic in England is that it is somehow not proper, or English: "It is one thing to change Spain by magic . . . but this is England!" (693).

The magicians of York and their snobbery are small players, but from the moment Mr. Norrell rejects the assistance of fairy (with the exception of his revival of the dead Lady Pole), he is engaged in a struggle to uphold the dike that prevents magic from flooding the world. His precision in casting spells is in part an attempt to create the least crack in the dike possible for what he wants to achieve. For Mr. Norrell, magic is about the creation of lists and tables that stall both the creativity of the magician and the flood of magic. Childermass realizes in his glimpse into fairy (when Lady Pole shoots him) that "if what he had seen was true, then everything that Strange and Norrell had ever done was child's play. . . . Strange and Norrell had been merely throwing paper darts about a parlour, while Magic soared and swooped and twisted on great wings in a limitless sky" (512). One of the rhetorical strategies we can see here is that Clarke constructs her intrusions in *movement*, linking the stasis of Norrell to his mean magics, and tracing an arc through the greater energy and movement and grander magics of Strange, into the wildness of the real thing, until finally, Strange will call on nature to send messages to England and nature will respond. *Jonathan Strange and Mr. Norrell* can (although probably should not) be read entirely as a challenge to the belief in English identity as constructed through English reserve.

When magic does intrude, it is (as we now know, customary in the intrusion fantasy) expressed through the senses, not the intellect. When Norrell calls a fairy, the spell "took effect almost immediately because suddenly there was something green where nothing green had been there before and a fresh, sweet smell as of woods and fields" (83), and this magic happens *suddenly* in an atmosphere in which every movement is mannered. The clearest description of this interaction is at the dinner party for Sir Walter Pole, managed by Stephen (the Negro butler). Into this carefully ordered precision, the footmen see a "queer figure," hear the music of a pipe and fiddle (143–144). As the month wears on, the house in Harley Street becomes haunted by an invisible wood growing around the house and by the sound of music; the neat precision of its servants is undermined. Sensibility, prized in the Gothic, is here feared for the way it renders people vulnerable to the fantastic.

One cannot write about *Jonathan Strange and Mr. Norrell* without considering the footnotes. The experienced reader is conditioned to see footnotes as dry, as a way of grounding the text in reality. But footnotes are also an intervention, or intrusion into the flow of the text, and Clarke takes advantage of this figuring. In *Jonathan Strange and Mr. Norrell*, it is in the footnotes that the world of the fantastic slips through to disrupt the meaning or common understanding of the tale told in the main text. The "explanation" they offer is of worlds slipping between each other, of uncontrolled contact with fairy. The best example is the story of the magician Absalom's house. When he died, his daughter Maria refused to repair the house: "In her fiftieth year the ivy was grown so vigorous and had so far extended itself that it grew inside all the closets" (211). Within the main text, the tone is dry and disapproving. Maria is guilty of releasing self-control and control over her domestic environment. The footnote, however, argues that Maria was consciously allowing the house to die, "in accordance with the commonly held belief that all ruined buildings belong to the Raven King" (211 n. 1). Here the intrusion is not the decay, but the rejection of society's rules, while maintaining society's refusal to discuss such transgression. The counter of balance and intrusion is exchanged within a culture of mannered silence. Similarly, when John Segundus is told to try Pale's Restoration on Lady Pole, it is described in the text as simply "So Mr. Segundus did the magic" (728). In the footnote, however, we are told that "Mr. Segundus used a spoon and a bodkin from Lady Pole's dressing-case which Lady Pole's maid tied together with a ribbon" (728 n. 3). The grand manner of writing grand deeds is replaced by the feminine vernacular of materials.

Yet despite this insistence by the society Clarke presents, and by the understanding and practices of both Norrell and Strange, the truth of her world is that magic is not an intrusion, but part of a palimpsest. Here is the account of Segundus's first encounter with Norrell:

> No candles had been lit: two fine windows gave plenty of light to see by—although it was a grey sort of light and not at all cheerful. Yet the idea of a second fire or candles, burning somewhere in the room, kept occurring to Mr. Segundus, so that he continually turned in his chair and looked about him to discover where they might be. But there was never anything—only perhaps a mirror or an antique clock. (8–9)

Much later, when Strange and Norrell have reactivated the interaction with fairy, Norrell's servant Childermass will follow Segundus in requiring the lead of a servant to negotiate the palimpsest of worlds:

> Behind the stone-and-oak passages of Starecross Hall,[21] a vision of another house leapt up. Childermass saw high corridors that stretched away into unthinkable distances. It was as if two transparencies had been put into a magic lantern at the same time, so that one picture overlaid another. (725)

When Childermass meets the enchanted Lady Pole, he sees two ladies, and when she speaks of the curse upon her, he hears both the enchanted words and those Lady Pole wishes to express. But for Childermass, there is an interaction of talent and choice. When Stephen walks through a Piccadilly transformed into the wooded path to Lost-hope, the underlying scene of the palimpsest threatens to overwhelm him. This six-page section is one of the most illuminating in any consideration of how Clarke writes her intrusion. In this scene, Stephen is being presented with the symbols of Kingship.

> "I am sorry, sir," said Stephen, "that I could not hold him [the thief] for you. But, as you see, I have your property." Stephen offered the man the rod of silver and the red velvet cloth, but the man did not take them.

"It was my mother's fault!" said the gentleman, angrily. "Oh! How could she be so negligent? I have told her a thousand times that if she left the drawing-room window open, sooner or later a thief would come by it. Have I not said so a hundred times Edward? Have I not said so, John?" . . .

The gentleman reached out to take the sceptre, but suddenly drew back his hand. "No!" he cried. "I will not! I vow I will not. If I were to return this treasure to my mother's keeping, then she would never learn the evil consequence of her negligence!" (252–253)

In place of emotion on the part of Stephen, who stands at the center of the chaos, Clarke substitutes his calm, polite helplessness. The emotional outbursts are reserved for those who inadvertently serve the purposes of fairy. Throughout the novel, instead of the growing intimacy between the invader and the invaded, we have Stephen's dry-as-dust courteous passivity. Part of the dynamic here is Clarke's re-creation of Victorian romanticism, which regarded kingship as inherent and romantic, but which was also rather uncomfortable with the emotionalism of romance. Stephen, in his efforts to be accepted (or at least invisible) has become more English than the English, and his primary reaction to the intrusion is discomfort—which in turn becomes a mode of narrating throughout the text, so that the intrusion of magic in *Jonathan Strange* might be likened for much of the time to an itchy collar, characterized by Norrell's fear of competition, and Strange's sense that there are others performing magic in his attendance.[22]

Through the figure of Stephen—brought to England as a tiny baby—Clarke reminds us that the palimpsest of the world is constructed through perspective. If the magicians see a different world than do the rest of us, so do servants from their masters, and the black man from the white men around him. These disjunctures provide openings for magic: the gentleman with the thistle-down hair reads the mundane world *literally* (the way fantasy readers demand the fantastic is read). The refusal of metaphor in the world becomes a dramatic response to Stephen's situation: in each case where Stephen is humiliated (or where there is potential for humiliation) the gentleman intervenes. In those situations where Stephen is both desperate to pass unnoticed and aware that this is impossible, the gentleman with the thistle-down hair executes on Stephen's behalf some maneuver that renders him *more* noticeable (presentation with a mace, an orb and a crown for example). Where Stephen is kingly, the gentleman sees a king and makes it so. But Stephen himself is an interesting character in these terms: a servant but not a slave, he is enslaved by his color (there are few other places he can go) and by his own perception of his color (he will not associate with other black men, yet cannot bring himself to recognize the love of the white Mrs. Brandy). The gentleman with the thistle-down hair can enslave Stephen because Stephen does not know that he can resist. His experience of the changing shape of the house, of his own odd familiarity with places such as the Disemboweller's Tower—all become a metaphor for his doubled familiarity and dislocation within London. Stephen is figured as both intruder and intruded upon. When he is abandoned by the magic, he is emptied, a hollow shell, and chooses to cast off not only his past, but his name. Confused again by his refusal to accept what is happening, he leaves England forever, a place he fears would hang him for the death of two people the law does not recognize (the gentleman with the thistle-down hair and Vinculus, the tramp), and becomes the intruder in the fairy court and the new king.

As Stephen moves through the portal to become a permanent resident of fairy, the old fairy of rust and dust and cobwebs dissolves. The language is slow and beautiful and emphasizes the landscape; the truly important piece of information and rhetoric, however, is not in the main text but in the footnote: "A surprising number of kings and princes of Faerie have been human. . . . Fairies are, by and large, irredeemably indolent. Though they are fond of high rank, honours and riches, they detest the hard work of government" (769 n. 1). In the instantiation of the world, it has truly been turned upside down; the words said of Africans are now applied to Fairy: Stephen the "African Prince" becomes the ruler of a "dark land," providing Englishness to the indigenes. The scene emulates Conrad's *Heart of Darkness* (1899) and Stephen's fate is to be the intruder. "This house," he told them at last, "is disordered and dirty. Its inhabitants have idled away their days in pointless pleasure and in celebration of past cruelties. . . . All these faults, I shall in time set right" (769). There is no greater intrusion than the new broom sweeping clean. And with Stephen's ascension comes the instantiation of the magical world of England: we learn that Mr. Taylor, a respectable clergyman, comes to York to meet the reconstituted society of magicians, not on his own behalf, but as escort to *his daughter*.

The trajectory of this chapter has been to move from the margins (the early Gothic) into the center of genre through horror and modern intrusion fantasies. At this point it is time to start moving outward again, through texts that are popularly categorized by genre critics as "slipstream." Slipstream is not really a category: its books are almost all defined through the Damon Knight method of "it's slipstream if I point at it." But all these are books written by authors accepted in the mainstream whose allegiance to fantasy is various. They all walk on that dividing line where one has to consider whether the fantastic is being presented as metonymic or metaphorical. Many of these books fall into the category of the intrusion fantasy because they are all, to some extent, about the disruption of the world, that being the default position from which what China Miéville calls "Lit Fic" and other critics call "the modern novel" begins.

Given that I cannot explore the whole of slipstream, I am going to pair two novels that seem to sit on either side of the line: Graham Joyce's *The Tooth Fairy* (1996), a novel that embraces the fantastic from the beginning in both the tale and its telling; and Jonathan Carroll's *The Marriage of Sticks* (1999), which begins as a tale of a disruptive woman, and mutates to metaphorize said disruptive woman as a vampire in a piece of almost classic Gothic misogyny.

The Tooth Fairy is structured around the coming of age of three boys from one village: Sam, the cosseted child of loving parents; Clive the super-achiever in a bemused working-class family; and Terry, who loses two toes to a pike, escapes his father's murder of his mother, and eventually blows off his own hand. As is traditional in this kind of novel, there is a girl (Alice) for whom they all compete; and an older girl, Linda, whom they all lust after impotently. And there are issues of friendship that need to be worked out. There is also the Tooth Fairy.

When Sam loses a tooth in a boyish brawl, he and his friends debate whether the Tooth Fairy exists. They decide Sam should test this out by placing the tooth under his pillow but not telling his parents. This he does, but he is accidentally woken by the Tooth Fairy, who freaks when it realizes that it can be seen (the use of *it* for the rest of this discussion is deliberate, as the Tooth Fairy's sex is apparent, not real, a reification of Sam's desires). For the rest of the novel, Sam struggles with his desire first for Tooth Fairy intervention (in the way children *do* desire deus ex machina in the service of their sense of justice) and then, as he grows older, with his horror at the way the Tooth Fairy acts upon his petty resentments and damages those he loves.

The novel is a masterpiece of doubling; as is common in the horror novel, desire for Alice and Linda is confused and metaphorized with Sam's desire for the Tooth Fairy and intimacy with horror and danger. Running alongside this, Sam's solipsistic view of the world structures his relations with Clive and Terry and again the Tooth Fairy. One reason why this book is so firmly within genre, however, is that it is the "real" world that provides the lessons Sam needs to deal with the fantastic. The *direction of metaphor* ensures that the mundane is metaphor for the "real" of the fantastic: in *The Tooth Fairy* Sam's relationships with "real" people form the metaphor for his dealings with the Tooth Fairy, and not the other way around.

The rhetorical structure of *The Tooth Fairy* has most in common—perhaps ironically—with *Jonathan Strange and Mr. Norrell.* Joyce constructs his fantastic within a very matter-of-fact sphere. Because Sam is very young when the Tooth Fairy first appears, although frightened, he is able to accept it within the compass of his world. The fantastic is simultaneously an intrusion and part of what Sam understands as the mimetic world. The confusion between the two in the understanding of the young (for whom the entire world is equally fantastic) is delivered neatly when Terry's father dies. There are journalists hanging around:

> Sam knew they were ghouls because that's what his father had called them. They looked like ordinary people, with overcoats and polished shoes, but Sam knew that beneath the human disguise these ghouls leaked luminous grey slime from ear and nostril. He didn't want to become a ghoul, but the caravan summoned him. (55)

Sam's understanding has been shaped and is contextualized by the appearance of the pike at the beginning of the novel and the manner of its telling:

> It hung inches below the surface, utterly still, like something suspended in ice. Green and gold, it was a phantom, a spirit from another world. Sam tried to utter a warning, but the apparition of the pike had him mesmerized. It flashed at the surface of the water as it came up to take away, in a single bite, the two smallest toes of Terry's left foot. . . .
>
> Sam followed behind her, understanding that Terry was only five and life had already taken away two of his toes, presumably forever, He hoped for better luck for himself. (4, 5)

This incident is the defining moment of Sam's life (and of Terry's, but Sam holds the trauma to himself as he will with all the other things that afflict Terry). It encapsulates two key movements: paralysis in the face of expectation, and suddenness. Sam will continue to see the world and its events in those terms for the rest of the book. When the Tooth Fairy first appears, there is the "shocking stillness" of the room that "wanted to blister and peel back like a skin." Again there is both paralysis and the desire for movement (16). In chapter 4, when the Fairy returns, "Whenever he tried to speak to the Tooth Fairy his heart swelled up and his tongue stuck to the roof his mouth" (24). What Sam does not do is to *react*: he absorbs the presence of the Tooth Fairy into his world. It is the Tooth Fairy who reacts: "Calm down. I was only pretending to be mad. . . . I've got to think of a way out of this for both of us. I meant what I said when I told you we were both in trouble. Bad things are going to happen if we're not careful" (25).

All the clues to the end of the book are here if we remember the trajectory of surprise/horror/anger followed by negotiation/repulsion/defeat of the intrusion fantasy. For all that we shall see Sam discussing the problem of the Tooth Fairy with his shrink, Sam remains accepting of and paralyzed by the Tooth Fairy throughout the book. As with China Miéville's *The Scar*, we have to resolve *The Tooth Fairy* as a figure and ground puzzle: everything the Tooth Fairy does can be seen in this way as its attempt to deal with the disturbance in its life. Thus, the Tooth Fairy's language is intimate, passionate, inherently of the emotions. Sam's language will always be descriptive of the world to which he is accustomed. A nice example of this is the mass hysteria Sam inadvertently induces in the playground. The Tooth Fairy has taught Sam to hyperventilate. To him it is part of his growing immersion in his own world, nothing unnatural. Joyce relates it this way: "Then the other two boys each had a go, followed by Terry, and within moments they had an audience of ten or fifteen kids, all wanting to take a turn at the new game" (40). The fantastic element is delivered in the consequence of the meme that the Tooth Fairy has fed into the group: "Then a strange thing happened. Sandra Porter from Sam's class suddenly fainted without even hyperventilating. The same thing happened to Janet Burrows and to Wendy Cooper, followed by Mick Carpenter, and then three other girls, and four more boys, until they were all fainting clean away" (40).

In contrast, when the Tooth Fairy meets Sam over the struggle to get at the Nightmare Interrupter, it yells at him, "You want to know what pisses me off about you? You're always *looking at things*. Always looking at *things you shouldn't be looking at!*" (59). Apart from the intensity of its reaction, the Tooth Fairy is describing the intimacy of the intrusion, the threat it feels at the focus the intrusion brings with it. The Tooth Fairy can feel the vampire [Sam] staring at its neck. Although much of the sexual activity within the book is about Sam's growth, it is also about this intimacy of the intrusion, as the Tooth Fairy seeks to deflect one kind of intimacy—an intimacy in which Sam imposes definition[23]—into physical intimacy. This is why Sam's sexuality is so often written with the emotive intensity, with all the weight of expectation and latency of the intrusion:

> Did she touch? Did the outstretched fingernail make contact? He never knew. The moment was blotted out by a booming thunderclap of the heart. Some exquisitely fine elasticity linking brain and bowel snapped and a canal opened, flooding like the slow-fast, fast-slow lava flow of some primeval subterranean pool, pumping from the agonized cock still squeezed in his fist. The explosion blew the Tooth Fairy clean out of the window, shattering the glass and the window frame together. (81)

In this passage, sex and sexual intimacy damage the Tooth Fairy. Most of its other sexual encounters with Sam are framed in ways that can be read as the Tooth Fairy attempting to tame, or negotiate with Sam's sexuality; hence the final sex scene in which Sam does finally "give" in a reciprocal encounter in which the Tooth Fairy is more than a sex object, and the very final scene in which Sam simply wants the Tooth Fairy asleep in his arms, a moment in which acceptance overwhelms the intrusion of [his] desire. Each of these scenes is depicted casually. It is important that the most baroque of these encounters (chapter 16 "Blood Dream") is also the least "real."

The absence of an apparent mode of expectation or latency in the writing is a pointer to the truth of the story, which is that it is the Tooth Fairy who expects, and Sam's presence in its life that is the latent threat. And, because we have identified with Sam, we too are the threat, the scrutinizer rather than the scrutinized.

What Joyce does in *The Tooth Fairy* is to write the trajectory of escalation in the Tooth Fairy's attempts to disentangle itself from Sam, encoding what Yvonne Leffler has called the "anticipatory function of repetition" (189). It goes from childish tricks in the night, to bringing friends along to scare the Churchgoers, to (possibly) causing the death of Linda's boyfriend, Derek. But what becomes ever more apparent is that the Tooth Fairy's threats cannot actually "defeat" Sam. When he creates a blood-and-skin bond between himself and Alice, the Tooth Fairy can only menace, predatory, teeth gleaming (188). In actuality, it is Sam's resistance to the Tooth Fairy as his level of belief in its powers diminishes, that is the real "escalation" in the story, so that even as he sees the Tooth Fairy reach out to touch Linda (216), he is resisting the negotiation with the Tooth Fairy, resisting what it is telling him, even when it tells him flat out, "This is not a one-way thing. . . . You may think I'm your nightmare, but you in turn are my nightmare" (223). Hence he still does not understand that when he resents Terry, he is the one who escalates the Tooth Fairy's actions. This is why the scene in which Terry loses his hand is related as pure mimesis; it is part of Sam's trajectory of escalation, not the Tooth Fairy's.

Midway through the book, the Tooth Fairy is disintegrating under the pressure of Sam's demanding scrutiny. Toward the end of the book, the Tooth Fairy is begging to be allowed to go, begging to be freed from Sam's gaze. Here there is a reversal, and we are reminded that from the Tooth Fairy's point of view, this is also a portal fantasy. It is being dragged into Sam's world. That is the nature of his intrusion on its life, as it drags Sam, just for a few moments, long enough for Sam to see how the Tooth Fairy understands itself, long enough for a true consummation, one in which Sam finally grants the Tooth Fairy something of himself (304–307). And this is the moment at which Sam begins to grow enough to tell Terry that he regards his life as a tragedy because of the things that have happened to his friends, and to finally have it forced back on him what a solipsistic little shit he is—and as M. John Harrison commented, as we have accepted the world as seen through Sam's point of view, we also have to accept what solipsistic little shits we are, absorbed as we are in the importance of the Reader, an issue that might also shape our reading of *Mortal Love* and *Mythago Wood*.[24] The novel ends with Sam delicately placing the Nightmare Interceptor on the nose of the Tooth Fairy and falling asleep with it in his arms. When he wakes, it is gone.

In his book, *Horror Fiction in the Protestant Tradition* (1988), Victor Sage writes, "de Sade, Breton and Freud were originally right, to this extent: that horror is not a literary genre, in the narrow sense, at all. It is a cultural response, which implies a broad series of relationships with the whole of the culture in which it is produced. The narrower the conception of genre, the more one is moving away from the possibility of explaining it" (xiii). Yet what I am interested in is precisely horror and intrusion fantasy as genre, because what I am concerned with is their rhetorics. What has been surprising so far is the degree to which the rhetorical structures and strategies of intrusion fantasies have supported/facilitated the "cultural response" we associate with horror. Intrusion fantasy—like portal-quest fantasy—seems an inherently politicized genre. The metaphorization of seduction, rape, and colonization mimics the tempo of latency and breakthrough, pause and escalation. As we move into the work of Hand, Clarke, and Joyce, we can see the subtleties that can be brought to bear within this outline. One might expect that as we move out into the slipstream the rhetorical structures of the intrusion fantasy might become yet more subtle. However, this is not always the case: in the discussion of both immersive and liminal fantasy, part of my contention (and that of other critics) was that the successful conjuration of the fantastic relies in part on metaphors being read metonymically. In the intrusion fantasy, however, this reading strategy rests a very fine dividing line of consensual disavowal. Over and over we have seen how important sexuality and intimacy is to the intrusion fantasy, but we have also seen the way that latency is constructed in part through a holding back, a denial of sexuality—and of the truth of relationships between the protagonists.

Without this structure of denial, the tension of the intrusion fantasy falls, and with the loss of the tension one can see through to the fetid corpse of *manipulation* that exists at the heart of this kind of fantasy. Jonathan Carroll's *The Marriage of Sticks* is a good example. The book lacks tension in part because the split between the first and second parts of the book is too extreme. In the first part, Miranda (a rare-book dealer) discovers her high school sweetheart (James Stillman) is dead; has fuck-buddy sex with an old college boyfriend (Doug Auerbach); is hit by a man who decides to end their relationship after four dates; and falls in love with a married man (Hugh Oakley) who, against her expectations, leaves his wife (without prompting from her, this is crucial), moves into a new house with her, and then dies in his sleep. Throughout this first half there are occasional hints of the fantastic. Before Miranda is told James Stillman is dead, "Hadn't the ballroom been billiard-chalk-blue before I'd gone into the bathroom? . . . yet now it was a weak ochre, the color of young carrots" (41). Later she sees his ghost in the street (94), and a child she presumes to be hers and Hugh's in the house they have chosen for themselves (124). All of this is told in a reflective tone, because it is told in the past tense. The narrator is Miranda, writing as an old woman.

> . . . What was that smell? I took a few steps into the house, looked around, and closed my eyes.
>
> When I opened them a moment later, the hallway was full of people. Full of children . . .
>
> One little boy in a crooked party hat stood in the middle of the hall watching the party whirl around him. . . . He looked like a miniature Hugh Oakley. . . . This had to be Hugh's boy. (123–124)

This past-tense reflective defuses any tension from the actual intrusions of the fantastic by imbuing it with acceptance; it moves the emphasis instead to *watchfulness*, an awareness on the reader's part that all of this must, according to literary rules, prove significant. The only exceptions to this delivery are when Miranda discovers a slimy chewed bone, and a warm door handle. Then analytic wonder replaces acceptance, and bangs with it a sense of threat. It is at this point that Miranda prays that everything will be all right, but there is still no real sense of the fantastic lurking (133).

Carroll's choice of the reflective past tense also renders Miranda an unreliable narrator. When she reminisces that Hugh never derided his wife, and comments, "We have affairs because we are greedy. People are brilliant at justifying their motives. It's one of our ugliest talents" (107), we cannot know whether she thought this at the time, or considers it the truth now. This uncertainty is a very real problem because Miranda's honesty and reasonableness undermines what happens in the second half of the book.

At the very end of part 1, the fantastic shows itself when Frances Hatch (a famous mistress of many famous men) tells Miranda she is pregnant and that she can tell from colors on the tips of her fingers. From here on, this story of love and betrayal flips into a story of Roumanian mystics. The unsubtlety of Carroll's choice of origin for his mysticism—which is clearly meant to be humorous—is unfortunately extended into the rest of the text. Whereas in the other texts we have considered so far, the fantastic is usually something shown, Carroll prefers to tell us what is fantastical and he does this, by—in the second half—having the ghost of James Stillman berate Miranda.

Carroll likes to lecture his protagonists. In the later *Glass Soup* (2005), none of the male protagonists are very bright, and they have to be told what to think. This in itself is not a fault: in *Glass Soup* in which the plot turns around, enabling someone to negotiate his way through the afterlife, the portal-quest structure absorbs the downloads. In *The Marriage of Sticks*, however, it renders Miranda ignorant in the face of her own life, and curiously passive. This passivity rather suits what happens next: as she discovers that she might be magical, as her house turns on her, and, as she realizes that she is the focus of someone else's hatred, the independent woman we have seen in the first half of the book disappears. We have been forewarned about this: when Charlotte (Hugh's wife) called her to try to break up the relationship, Charlotte asserts that Hugh is only interested in her because she is weak, and Miranda agrees. There has only been one indication that this might be true, when she cries because someone has hit her—shortly before a meeting with Hugh. If Miranda *is* weak then the evidence is that it is because she believes it when she is told it, that she can be shaped by those around her.

This discussion slightly takes us offtrack, because it is a criticism of the plot Carroll constructs and its politics, but it is very hard to separate this plot from the rhetoric of the book. Having told us that Miranda is weak, and having had her admit it, Carroll first forces Miranda to see what would have happened had Hugh not left Charlotte—another thirteen more years, a boy child (the one she had seen)—and then to hear from James Stillman what would have happened had she slept with him the night she refused to break into a house with him (he would have been caught and sent to prison and become a sober person who wouldn't have crashed his car at the age of thirty). All of this is delivered as accusation. The intrusion is not of the fantastic (by this point the fantastic is so absorbed into the whole as to produce an immersive fantasy in the terms discussed here) but of hatred and blame. A bewildered Miranda stares at the man she loves and hears, "Stop whining and asking questions. You're here because someone *wants* you here, Miranda. Figure it out! Stop playing the poor little puppy. You waste so much time crying *why me*" (193)—which could be turned around and said to James Stillman, who screwed his own life up after all.

But Miranda takes this onboard. Stillman forces her to experience all the lives she has lived: the mistress of an artist who persuades him to fund her art, the life of a child who died in a stage performance, herself. Ultimately she realizes "the only thing they thought about was themselves. They were all total egotists" (204). The problem is that Carroll's straightforward misogyny, in which Miranda is continually blamed for others' choices and by which she is eventually convinced to give up her immortality so that Hugh's and Charlotte's child might live, rips the shroud from the intrusion fantasy (which as we have seen, repeatedly looks for someone to blame). Carroll has people simply tell Miranda that she is to blame, actually assembles thousands of them in a stadium from her life and from her past lives, and has her "Recognize": "Some of them had asked for something back, some of them for a lot back, Each time I gave only what I wanted or had a surplus of and wouldn't miss. They gave what they cherished or what kept them alive" (217). By the time Hugh's son walks out and tells her, "You're a vampire" (218), any tension has been drained from the scene and all that is left is to walk away. Carroll completes the novel by having Miranda decide to sacrifice her immortality in favor of Hugh's child (this too has to be explained to her), lead an ordinary life, and at the end be collected so that she can be put in a wheelchair to die at the side of a motorway. At the last moment she is rescued by Hugh's son—which ironically, undercuts the *effective* anticlimax that Carroll has created and replaces it with something much limper.

By removing the latency of the intrusion fantasy, the sense of waiting and the sense of intimacy through what is implied and threatened and promised, Carroll inverts the power of the intrusion fantasy. That *The Marriage of Sticks* is a powerful novel is in part because Carroll defuses the expectations of this structure and replaces it with a downward trajectory of entropy, reinforced by the content of the novel, which rips the illusion of courtship from the dance of victim and attacker.

Joyce and Carroll have each moved us across the borderland, ever closer to seeing the intrusion fantasy from the point of view of the intruder. Patrice Kindl, in her winsome children's book *The Woman in the Wall* (1997) takes us right into the wainscot to explore the intimacy of the watcher for the watched, and to narrow our identification until we stand absolutely with the intruder and her sensibility. In *The Woman in the Wall*, Anna, the middle of three daughters, is a very quiet child, shy and reserved and almost invisible. When Anna was a baby, her mother had difficulty finding her; as she approaches seven, she has rendered herself almost unseeable. When school threatens, Anna retreats into the walls of her house. A practical girl, she has built an inner lining to the house, creating between it and the original walls, rooms and corridors, access points into the back of cupboards, and peepholes so that she can continue to watch and care for her family. Fearful of others' gaze but curious about the world, Anna becomes the lurking presence. In portraying this, and in writing it entirely from Anna's point of view, Kindl emphasizes the intimacy of the relationship between the intrusion and its focus:

> These holes gave me a disjointed, fragmentary view of my mother and sisters. Only occasionally did I see them in their entirety; more often they were represented by a hand, an elbow, the back of a head, sometimes a knee or a foot. I learned to read emotion from the lift of a wrist, the angle of a spine, the nervous twitch of an ankle. (34)

Escalation in this novel is the escalation of the intimacy Anna seeks with those on the other side of the wall. Sometimes, one is aware that the object of intimacy might have a more complex response than the one Anna discerns:

> Every once in a while I let Kirsty see me. It pleased her and did me no harm. I'd creep up behind her as she brushed her brown hair in the full-length mirror in the bathroom, and then slip away when she turned around. If she was sad, I would reach out and tough her hand. Kirsty hardly frightened me at all. (40)

Kirsty comes to construct her sister as an imaginary friend whom she talks to; in return Anna leaves little gifts of beautifully sewn clothes, or cookies. Anna's mother—who has pushed Anna to the back of her mind—accepts without question the way that the house gets fixed up, and presses her hand to the wall at night to say "goodnight, Anna." As Kindl constructs Anna as a latent presence, Anna becomes the house. This changes only when Anna receives a communication from F., a boy who thinks he is writing a note, never to be found, for Anna's elder sister Andrea. F. (Francis) discovers that Anna is real, and lives in the walls and intrudes on *her* space, but it is Anna, forced out of latency, who remains the intrusion even as she figures Francis as the intrusion. When she attends Andrea's party, she inadvertently becomes a competitor for one of Andrea's beaux. Kindl's construction of the party, of Anna's hesitation to become involved emphasizes the sense that something is being waited for—and what is waited for is the moment that comes in all intrusion fantasies, the moment when the intruder is turned up, becomes the focus of mass attention, of mobs with flaming torches and pitchforks:

> I wrenched my arm away from Kirsty and ran away; up the stairs.
> They ran after me. (172)

With the entire party chasing after her, Anna retreats to the attic, only to be stopped by a couple kissing on the stairs. As the number of people looking increases, Anna's panic escalates and Kindl shows us the world from the point of view of "the monster." Because Anna turns, and accepts the gaze, Anna as intrusion is finally negated by being incorporated, and (as the Tooth Fairy feared) cut off from her own world: "Very well then, I thought, I will be my own house. I will build myself a house of my own flesh and bones where my frightened child self can shelter" (182). There is a tenderness here that runs through the book and which emphasizes the vulnerability of the intrusion in a way that reminds me strongly of Joyce, but also of Gaiman and McKean. Anna's responses, her fear of the very people she intrudes upon, can be seen in the eyes of the wolves in McKean's artwork.

So what conclusions can we draw? More than any other form described here, the intrusion fantasy holds true to the unreasoning delights of *fancy* eschewing the rules and rigors of fantasy. This disregard for the rules is one reason why the protagonist/reader position can be summarized as "confused." The generically irrational fantastic keeps the protagonist/reader off balance, and without control of the situation (even when such control is posited as part of his eventual destiny). This approach clearly departs from the control structures of the portal-quest fantasies, which are *precisely* about being in charge of the adventure.

The intrusion fantasy is Baconian in its worldview, dependent on the evidence of the senses. Unlike the portal-quest fantasies, it distrusts what is written down or what is told. Unlike the immersive fantasies, its fundamental irrationality and fanciful nature means that what is "known to the inhabitants" is necessarily wrong. The intrusion fantasy constructs a rhetoric in which the shiver up the spine is more trustworthy than scientific discourse; when it adopts apparent scientific rigor, it is always a pseudoscience that clothes feelings in faux analysis.

The intrusion fantasy separates or slices the protagonist and the reader from the world. Frequently (although not always), the reader/protagonist stands observing the effect of the intrusion upon the world—which is why so many of the protagonists seem passive. They do not regard themselves as wholly of the world (or of the common herd). The form's political stance repudiates responsibility, while positing the importance of the protagonist. It is tied up in a dance of intimacy and repulsion, in which we do not always know who is the ravisher and who the ravished. That very lack of clarity creates a mask for an often vicious colonialist attitude to the Other.

The intrusion fantasy is aural and musical. As the closest descendant from the ghost story or fairy tale told around the fire, the intrusion fantasy depends for its effect on the tempo of the tale, the constant seesawing between latency and escalation. As with the oral tale, it is the degree to which latency is achieved that secures the impact of the escalation; thus any baroque language is generally reserved for the pause, for the holding back. The intrusion itself may be rendered more frightening by the sudden shift to the prosaic.

The intrusion fantasy is hologrammatic. Each scene (often each paragraph), contains within it the tempo of the intrusion fantasy. Where the portal-quest fantasy is a fantasy of the world Re-made or of Healing, the intrusion fantasy is a fantasy of entropy and resistance to entropy.

Chapter 4

The Liminal Fantasy

Liminal fantasy as I originally conceived it, was *that form of fantasy which estranges the reader from the fantastic as seen and described by the protagonist* (hence the original designation of "estranged" fantasy" in the original article). A vivid example is to be found in Joan Aiken's "Yes, But Today is Tuesday," a text I shall discuss in greater detail later in this chapter, but for now: there is a unicorn on the Armitage family's lawn. When, we, the reader, mentally express surprise, the family tell us, "Yes, and it's Tuesday, magical things only happen on Mondays." But although there is an element of what McHale calls the "rhetoric of contrastive banality" (76), in which our amazement is reinforced by the naturalization of the fantastic, it is not the simple relationship we see in the immersive fantasy. There is dissonance: both we and the family see fantasy, but we see it in different contexts and interpret it differently. We place the absurd in different moments, but doubt because the family seems to question whether anything truly fantastical has happened at all. We could even see this as an immersive fantasy because the protagonists take it all for granted. Except that they do not.

The liminal fantasy is one that relies on Wayne C. Booth's construction of stable irony, "a reconstructing of implied authors and implied readers [that] relies on inferences about intentions . . . [that] often depend on our knowing facts from outside the poem" (*Irony* 133). Or it relies on "equipoise," the term Clute suggests in his essay in *Conjunctions 39* and that is essentially a more positivist construction of Todorov's concept of hesitation (*The Fantastic* 25). Or it relies on both, to create a moment of doubt, sometimes in the protagonist, but also in the reader. The two elements, although related, are distinguished here for a reason. While irony is one element in the construction of equipoise—it relies, after all on a *knowingness*—equipoise is not intrinsic to the construction of irony. The liminal fantasy can be balanced between dichotomies or, as Bernadette Bosky suggested when we were discussing my choice of terminology, it can be truly liminal, "what it's like to have fallen into the crack" (e-mail 10 March 2005). However, rather than being (as Bosky suggests) "anti-structural," this fiction is striking for just how how tightly structured it is. A story like Kelly Link's "Lull" (*Conjunctions 39*), for example, may spiral away from the starting point, but does so in carefully choreographed swirls.

Crucial to the construction of liminal fantasy is that it is a two-way process. It depends on *knowingness*, or what Barthes described as a shared code: "The code is a perspective of quotations, a mirage of structures . . . so many fragments of something that has always been *already* read, seen, done . . . the code is the wake of that *already*" (20). Scott Maisano terms this "fluency" (76). Although the dialectic between reader and author is always central to the process of interpretation, in the liminal fantasy, it is central to the *construction* of the fantastic. Brian McHale writes, "Granted that somebody must experience epistemological hesitation, otherwise there is no fantastic effect at all in Todorov's sense, then why not say that, in the absence of a character to do the hesitating, the reader himself or herself does it" (75). The construction of the category *liminal* fantasy builds on Jameson's argument that genres are social contracts "between a writer and a specific public" (106). Consequently, one term I considered for this category was the "possible fantasy," after the possible sword in Miéville's *The Scar* (2002). In *The Scar*, the sword creates possibilities from which one can choose. Liminal fantasy creates possible readings. In Roz Kaveney's phrase, it "makes readings available." In this, it is the direct opposite of the quest fantasy, which, as I argued in chapter 1 of this book, shuts down such readings.

The difficulty with this form of fantasy, however, was that it had no obvious boundaries. It seemed to come into the classic category of "I know it when I see it," which is simply not good enough. More than any other category in this book, liminal fantasy was my category most susceptible to, and perhaps most in need of, Attebery's argument for the fuzzy set. One possible route in was to create a network of the writers I felt fitted this category and consider their influences. Even a cursory glance revealed that the authors I had in mind (Crowley, Hand, Harrison, for example) all referred back to certain authors as inspiration. This referencing provided a positioning point for a potential fuzzy set, a center from which I could work outward, from things that were "like" to things that were not. One of the outward links was to Anglo-American slipstream writers such as Jeanette Winterson and Andrew Greig. However, one of the arguments I shall be making toward the end of this chapter is that it is that element of *knowingness* essential to the construction of equipoise that, in the final analysis, distinguishes between liminal fantasies and the fantasies of the slipstream.

At the center of my fuzzy set lurks an unusual and not well known novel, one that is cited as an influence by a number of the writers I shall be discussing in this chapter and that has recently come back into the frame with the reprint in Gollancz's Fantasy Masterworks sequence. Hope Mirrlees was the most common name cited in conversation by the writers discussed here. Her 1926 novel, *Lud-in-the-Mist*, is structured around the complementary elements of irony and equipoise: its setting is presented through the ironic positioning of reader to protagonist; it depends on a resistance to the fantastic that is encoded within the continued denial of magic by the people of Dorimar, and in the construction of the conclusion that denies the fixed understandings of both portal and intrusion fantasies. *Lud-in-the-Mist* rests the supernatural on the knowingness of the reader.

Lud-in-the-Mist exists at the very edge of the turn from fancy to fantasy. It is a novel of fairies, not of elven Lords; of burghers and farmers, not of kings and princesses. Its setting is early modern rather than medieval, and it is written with a down-to-earthness that never departs, even at the height of its whimsy. It offers a quite different model for fantasy than the grandeur of Tolkien. The fantastic here lurks at the bottom of the garden, with an intimacy more common to intrusion fantasy. And superficially, *Lud-in-the-Mist* is the fantasist's challenge to Mr. Gradgrind. The country of Dorimar and the town of Lud-in-the-Mist overthrew the capricious Duke Aubrey many years before and with him banished the court and influence of neighboring Fairyland. This is a practical world in which whimsy should have no place. But with the reappearance of fairy fruit and the sightings of Duke Aubrey, the materialist values of Dorimar are under threat.

There is some argument for placing this novel in one of two other categories. We can see an intrusion novel in the fairy fruit that is smuggled into Dorimar; the fruit is the bringer of chaos and catastrophe which must at first be defeated, and later negotiated. But Lud-in-the-Mist is written without awe or wonder or horror, and most especially without naïveté. Perhaps the novel could be considered an immersive fantasy. Nathaniel Chanticleer knows his world fully; his learning process is much more one of recognition and remembering. And we learn much of Dorimar and of Lud-in-the-Mist through what he does *not* tell us. But the reader is not presumed to share this competence and although we see Lud-in-the-Mist as Nathaniel accepts it, Mirrlees does not allow us to take it for granted. We do not see Lud-in-the-Mist through Nathaniel's casual eyes; nor do we see its beauty as he understands it. From the beginning, Mirrlees sets us on an interpretive path at variance to that of Nathaniel. It is not that we see more (although there are moments when that is permitted) but rather that we see different dissonances to the ones he perceives. We are positioned ironically.

Some of Mirrlees's sense of irony, her insistence that we stand to one side of the proceedings, is communicated in the placement of sentences. We can see this in a configuration that repeats frequently in *Lud-in-the-Mist*:

> It had, indeed, more than its share of pleasant things: for, as we have seen, it had two rivers.
>
> Also, it was plentifully planted with trees. (2)

In this configuration, that last "and another thing" line that seems to signal a matter of import is almost always utterly irrelevant. Its significance is that it prevents us from achieving synchronicity with the matter of the text and distracts our gaze. And once the reader is used to it, it can be and is deployed to slide in information that *is* important. (In this case, it is the rivers that are important, not the trees.) Although Mirrlees does not extend this technique to the structure of the novel as a whole—mysterious strangers *always* turn out to be significant—as we shall see in the work of others in this chapter, the technique is a core constructor of ironic liminality and frames the narrative of the novel. The flippant proverb "the Dapple flows into the Dawl" proves predictive, should we listen to it closely enough.

Elsewhere, irony is built into an interpretive template. Mirrlees constructs her landscape as instructional:

> Outside this kitchen-garden there was no need of flowers, for they had many substitutes. Let a thing be but a sort of punctual surprise, like the first *cache* of violets in March, let it be delicate, painted and gratuitous, hinting that the Creator is solely preoccupied with *aesthetic* considerations, and combines disparate objects simply because they *look* so well together, and that thing will admirably fill the role of a flower.

In early summer it was the doves, with the bloom of plums on their breasts, waddling on their coral legs over the wide expanse of lawn, to which their propinquity gave an almost startling greenness, that were the flowers in the Chanticleers' garden . . . (2)

We should heed the warning encoded in this passage: what we see we may interpret less in terms of what it is, than how it functions as a foil for something else. Embedded in this description, in fact, is a description of the paradigm that Dorimar has constructed. Since Duke Aubrey was overthrown, the townsfolk of Lud-in-the-Mist have come to define themselves in terms of what they are not, positing themselves as a foil to fairyland.

The problem with seeing oneself in terms of what one is not, is that this is a fundamentally negative set of virtues, an attitude that leads to a draining of soul and sensibility. Mirrlees, in her depiction of the stout burghers of Lud-in-the-Mist, uses three levels of irony to demonstrate this abnegation: the first is in the townsfolk themselves who deal with the dilemma by denying its existence or rendering it an obscenity. In this land, the very word "fairy" is taboo, and to call someone "son of a fairy" the worst of offences. The consequence is that the hero, Nathaniel Chanticleer, is a conflicted man; having heard the Note of fairy in his youth, he cannot acknowledge what it is he is searching for. Equally significant is that in this tale of drug dealing and seduction, "fairy fruit" cannot so be named, because it and fairy are not permitted to exist (17).

Mirrlees mocks this denial and the convoluted means adopted to support it when she creates a legal fiction that describes fairy fruit as contraband silk.[1] Mirrlees is clear: the delusion of law is no more or less fanciful than the illusion of fairy. The law itself is part of the construction of irony within the text: "Master Josiah Chanticleer . . . had drawn in one of his treatises a curious parallel between fairy things and the law. The men of the revolution, he said, had substituted law for fairy fruit. . . . But, whereas fairy magic and delusion were for the cozening and robbing of man, the magic of the law was to his intention and for his welfare" (13). And if we believe this, we have already allowed our attention to lapse. "as Master Josiah had pointed out, the law plays fast and loose with reality—and no one really believes it" (13–14). In this configuration Mirrlees creates a crucial element of the ironic fantasy: the insistence that what is fantastic to the protagonist is at variance to what is fantastic to the reader. To the inhabitants of Dorimar, the supernatural is real enough to be denied. The law, on the other hand, they know to be a creation of the mind.

If the law plays fast and loose with reality, so too do the names of the characters in *Lud-in-the-Mist*. Mirrlees's pragmatic burgers, who have eschewed fairy, have "names like Dreamsweet, Ambrose, Moonlove, wedded to such grotesque surnames as Baldbreech, Fliperarde, or Pyepowders" (15). The names of dishes, "*The Bitter Sweet Mystery* . . . *The Lottery of Dreams*" (27) similarly betrays the longing for fantasy—a trope that seems to operate as a base layer of this category—and the hidden nature of its existence. The attempt to expunge the supernatural from the world has met with moderate success. The sense that fairy is out there, waiting, permeates the fantasy in this way, among others.

A second element in Mirrlees's construction of irony is in her placement of Nathaniel Chanticleer. Nathaniel is central both to the narrative (he is the protagonist) and to his world, for he is the mayor. Nathaniel should be our competent protagonist and most of the time, he is. But Mirrlees subverts Nathaniel's depiction of his own town. He introduces it to us neither unconscious of our presence and through the doings of his everyday existence, nor through the self-conscious tourism inflicted on the reader of the portal fantasy. Instead, Nathaniel introduces *himself* to his own world, and we are privy to this internalized process of estrangement: "Though he did not realise it, he was masquerading to himself as a stranger in Lud-in-the-Mist—a stranger whom nobody knew, and who was thus almost as safe as if he were invisible. And one always takes a pride in knowing one's way about a strange town" (7). It is thus a shock to Nathaniel when he realizes that his son Ranulph is also longing for fairy. As with all things hidden and held in common, it makes Ranulph real to Nathaniel (31), but also positions him as a threat: he may inadvertently uncover Nathaniel's realness. Instead, it is Ranulph who sees what is and isn't real around him. When he hears Dr. Endymion Leer talking to the widow Gibberty about trout fishing, he idly comments, "That isn't *real* talk. . . . That isn't the way you really talk to each other. That's only pretence talk" (61). The phatic communication of the portal/quest is punctured.

If the irony is encoded in names, and positionings, the equipoise emerges in the sense of expectation that Mirrlees constructs. The use of additional lines to distract attention from what is really relevant is one device used extensively, but Mirrlees expands on this to use landscape in the same way:

> There was also a pleached valley of hornbeams.
>
> To the imaginative, it is always something of an adventure to walk down a pleached alley. You enter boldly enough, but very soon you find yourself wishing

> you had stayed outside—it is not air that you are breathing, but silence, the almost palpable silence of trees. And is the only exit that small round hole in the distance? Why, you will never be able to squeeze through *that!* You must turn back . . . too late! The spacious portal by which you entered has in its turn shrunk to a small round hole. (3)

It is that process of being caught that shapes the novel: the paragraph ends by reminding us that we have stepped into liminal space, the tunnel between portal and portal, between world and world. Much of *Lud-in-the-Mist* is constructed to remind us continually of this position. To use landscape to create atmosphere is usual, to create metaphor quite common. But here Mirrlees does something a little different: there is no one in this landscape but ourselves; it can therefore be meaningful mostly to us, the reader. Although it belongs to the Chanticleers, we are not experiencing it with Nathaniel but separately from him. As we have to understand the land of Dorimar as a comment on its citizens, so to we are given to understand the character of Nathaniel through his garden. Nathaniel's character is one of hesitation, keen to adventure but torn by the desire to stay home, one caught in the liminal moment between the mundane and the magical: "it had generated in him what one can only call a wistful yearning after the prosaic things he already possessed" (6). Nathaniel, like so many of the characters we will consider, embodies latency.

Also caught in the liminality of understanding is the plot: *Lud-in-the Mist* is constructed to elicit our sympathies in one direction. For Nathaniel, anxious to protect his family and his town from the corrupting influence of fairy fruit, and against Dr. Endymion Leer, doctor, fruit smuggler, and murderer. Leer is an unpleasant character. Mirrlees ensures we do not trust him, and that mistrust is correctly placed; there is no irony within the actual depiction of Leer. But Leer is there to misdirect our gaze from the true consequences of the fantastic. Because it is he who is in league with Duke Aubrey, we are convinced that we know the pattern of the novel: Nathaniel will discover who is smuggling the fruit, put an end to the trade and the status quo will return. Healing, as Clute describes it, will be assured. Instead, two things happen. Nathaniel crosses the portal, and Leer turns out to be correct.

The presence of Fairyland in *Lud-in-the-Mist* has been held at bay for most of the length of the novel. Unlike the other worlds in *The Iron Dragon's Daughter* or *Vurt*, however, it has not been positioned as desirable: it is a place to avoid. The tension in the novel is in part about refusing fairy, and refusing to cross the portal is a vital part of this tension.

Thus Mirrlees creates equipoise (1) by having her characters denying the very existence of magic, while we the readers continually mark its influence, and (2) by this secondary technique of making the portal undesirable to the characters, while again we the readers, still desperate for our dose of the fantastic, wish to cross it.

When Nathaniel eventually does cross the portal we are "disappointed" in two ways: Fairyland is described very diffusely. Dissonance, rather than detail creates Fairyland, "instead of the cheerful variegated din that is part of the every-day fair, over this one there reigned complete silence" (244); "Round and round whirled the tarnished horses and chariots with their one pathetic little rider; round and round trudged the pony—the little, dusty, prosaic pony" (246). Here there is none of the description and detail, the attempt to paint full landscape that we can see in the quest and portal fantasies. We have crossed a border, but there is a sense that we are not fully "in" Fairyland. Encounters have the air of dreams, not reality.

When Nathaniel finds the girls who have run to Fairyland, they are being sold at auction: "Suddenly Master Nathaniel felt convinced that this was not merely a story he was inventing himself, but, as well, it was a dream—a grotesque, illogical, synthesis of scraps of reality, to which he could add what elements he chose" (248). And what he chooses is the law: as Mirrlees has continually reminded us, the law is the figment of men's imaginations, and it enters Fairyland with the power that imagination gifts. Nathaniel Chanticleer wins his daughter and her friends back from fairy by an exercise, not of magic, but of illusion. The boundaries of magic and illusion remain vague, their landscapes indeterminate: "Now they were dancing, some slow old-fashioned dance . . . in and out, in and out. Why, they were only figures on a piece of tapestry flapping in the wind!" (250).

The delay and tension that surrounds the portal, the vagueness of the other world once entered—all contribute to the sense that the magic is not quite where we thought it was, that our understanding of events is disoriented. This bewilderment is confirmed by the final outcome of the tale: when Nathaniel returns to Dorimar he does so at the head of a troop of fairies. Endymion Leer, that villain, proves to have been right. The message of the anonymous book he had published many years before—that Dorimarites should embrace their connections to Fairyland—is reiterated by the staid and staunch Ambrose Honeysuckle: the gifts of the Dapple, of fairy fruit and of imagination, should be accepted with as good grace as the Dawl's gift of gold (266).

In the final irony, Lud-in-the-Mist experiences instantiation, it is remade, a remaking that takes us to the ethereal language with which Fairyland was described:

> The accounts of what took place immediately after the entry of the fairy army read more like legends than history.
>
> It would seem that the trees broke into leaf and the masts of all the ships in the bay into blossom; that day and night the cocks crowed without ceasing; that violets and anemones sprang up through the snow in the streets, and that mothers embraced their dead sons, and maids their sweethearts drowned at sea. (268)

For the first time perhaps, our perception of what is and what is not supernatural and fantastical in this land is synchronous with that of the protagonists, but we are distanced from it. We are not permitted to be fully part of the fantasy. In the end, we are held in tension at a distance from this world.

Although I have discussed *Titus Groan* (1946) already in the chapter on immersive fantasy, it is to *Titus Groan* (and to the Gormenghast trilogy generally) that we must turn to see an early extension of Mirrlees's techniques. There are ironies in *Titus Groan*. The rituals that confine the lives of the castles' inhabitants are fabulous in our eyes but not theirs. But this is mere context. Although we are amused by these absurdities, they offer little in the way of the supernatural or the marvelous. The means by which the fantastic enters this text is in the degree to which equipoise comes to form an element of the construction of the supernatural in and of itself. Because the immersive fantasy is not directive of plot, we must wait for that something, and it is on the waiting that the latency of this novel hangs.

Titus Groan is an edifice fantasy. The "protagonist," such as it exists, is less Steerpike, the ambitious kitchen boy, than the castle Gormenghast itself. We know this from the beginning. The opening lines of *Titus Groan* describe the castle as if it were a person: "Gormenghast, that is, the main massing of the original stone, taken by itself would have displayed a certain ponderous architectural quality were it possible to have ignored the circumfusion of those mean dwellings that swarmed like an epidemic around its outer walls" (9). Throughout the text, there are constant hints of the "life" of the castle. It moves and breathes, amidst the stifling ritual that is imposed upon and embraced by the House of Groan. The castle resonates to the rhythm of life within its walls. Peake emphasizes the importance of the castle in the ironies he builds into the text: that the great grey slabs of stone are the concern of eighteen men whose "privilege on reaching adolescence" was to discover they had inherited the mantle of stone scrubbers may be a comment on class and exploitation; nonetheless, it simultaneously confers upon the stone of the castle awe and majesty. When the Birthday breakfast is over, "An indescribable atmosphere of expectancy filled Gormenghast" (354). Titus is born with violet eyes (40), which prove significant of nothing; the Countess calls her cats who appear "through the narrow opening of the door and moved into the fumid atmosphere of the room an undulation of whiteness, so that, within a breath, there was no shadow in all the room that was not blanched with cats" (50). But the cats have no supernatural powers, although they do lead to the downfall of Flay; Fuschia experiences a love "that equals in its power the love of man for woman and reaches inwards as deeply" (64)—but there are no catastrophic consequences of this love. Peake studs the novel with warnings and prophecies that appear to have no meaning. Each time Peake raises the stakes with intense, Gothic language, yet denies us the supernatural, the stone of the castle becomes imbued with these qualities of the fantastic. We accept this novel as fantastical because we are encouraged to see the supernatural lurking, ever around the corner.

But where to go from Peake and Mirrlees? Unlike other categories of fantasy, there is no unbroken or well-attested lineage. In this chapter, my handful of texts are, as I have pointed out, essentially personal but not arbitrary. They have been selected to focus on the two elements I named as essential to the liminal fantasy, irony and equipoise. To begin with, I want to consider the short story form.

Of the liminal fantasies, the form that I recognize most easily as fantastical are the fantasies of irony. In these, we are presented with the obviously fantastical, and watch while the protagonists ignore it or respond in ways that feel dissonant. The fantasies of irony here read much like the setup for the immersive fantasy; they may even *be* a form of immersive fantasy. But where it appears to subvert the immersion is that in some way or other, the fantastic within the text should be as alien to the protagonist as it is to us.[2] The moment of doubt is triggered by our sense that there should be some reaction to the fantastic. The acknowledged master of the fantasy of irony must be Joan Aiken, whose short story collections use irony to construct cryptic riddles and English comedies of manners.

The example to which I want to return, and the one that I have used most often to explain liminal fantasy, is Joan Aiken's short story "Yes, But

Today is Tuesday." There is a unicorn on the Armitage family's lawn. When, we, the reader, mentally express surprise, the family tell us, "Yes, and it's Tuesday, magical things only happen on Mondays." There is dissonance: we do not see as fantastic what the family see as fantastic; and doubt, because the family seem to question whether anything truly fantastical has happened at all. We could even see this as an immersive fantasy because the protagonists take it all for granted. Except that they do not; instead they conceive the events as both fantastical in their specificity but normal in their occurrence.

So let us consider how Aiken creates this situation, because her format—the juxtaposition of the intrusion with *acceptance* instead of surprise—underpins the work of most of the authors discussed in this chapter. In an immersive fantasy, what we see is what we get. To a very great extent, we are required to accept the assessment of what is and what is not fantastical, what is normal to this world, as it is provided by the protagonists. We work out the nature of that fantasy and its rules through the eyes of the protagonist. Most usually, if a fantasy is fully immersive, all that appears supernatural or magical is accepted as normal, a part of the everyday. However, in "Yes, But Today is Tuesday," there remains a sense that the fantastic is *improper*. Although Mondays may be the rightful place of magic, there remains an understanding that the magic or adventures that happen on Mondays are strange to that world. From the beginning of the story, Aiken puts her finger on a key facet of a certain kind of fantasy: it takes place while parents are absent. So that "Monday was the day on which unusual things were allowed, and even expected to happen at the Armitages. For on Mondays Papa Armitage went to London to see that the office was managing all right without him, and Mamma, of course, was out most of the time doing the National Savings" (17). But the parental reaction to what is happening behind their back is utterly recognizable. The Armitage parents fortify themselves with sherry before hearing of the doings of the day.

These doings are intrusions. We might describe this story as an "anticipatory intrusion fantasy" and the degree to which intrusions seem to form an element of the liminal fantasy supports Brian Stableford's arguments that liminal fantasy may be only a subcategory (*Dictionary* 218). Fantasy becomes a part of the everyday at the same time as there is a clear indication that some participants (the parents) are trying desperately to preserve the mundane habits of everyday life in the face of evident chaos.[3] People do expect strange things to happen (hence the blacksmith has a list of animals that includes unicorns), but they still mark them as strange. Should the fantastic appear on any other day, it is a breach in the order of things. When, therefore, a unicorn is reported on the lawn on Tuesday morning, "Mamma was firm. 'Finish your shredded wheat first, Harriet. After all, today *is* Tuesday' " (18).

The consequence of this dissonance for the text is that unlike in the classic immersive fantasy, the fantastic element is formally recognized as out of place, but unlike in the classic intrusion fantasy, its very existence, its "reality" is taken for granted. The result is ironic fantasy in which Aiken is able to make the ordinary things in life—policemen, breakfast, and farmers—seem themselves to be the more fantastical elements of the tale because they end up feeling more out of place than the unicorn.

The unicorn, when it is met, turns out to be beautiful, as unicorns are, and hungry, which is less common and somehow very mundane (if feeding it turned out to have magical significance that would be different, but here the only effect of feeding the unicorn is that it is less hungry). The children feed it on milk and honey and begin to discuss riding it. Just as it looks as if things may become exciting, however, as if they may be off on a magical adventure, life becomes prosaic once more. A policeman arrives, although this, too, is something that doesn't usually happen on a Tuesday, so it is not just magical disruption that is banished to Mondays, but all forms of intrusion. Mrs. Epis, for example, has also arrived on this particular Tuesday and her place too is on a Monday. It is as if Monday itself is a "full fantasy," an otherworld. The very fact of the policeman is made to seem as if it is magical even before he makes his demand. Aiken emphasizes that this is not a policeman whom Harriet has ever seen before. He must, therefore, be significant in some way.

The policeman, because this is the fantasy of irony conducted through the intrusion of the *prosaic* into the fantastical, demands a unicorn license. The money for this is provided by the brushing of the unicorn's tail, which yields gold; having dispensed with that problem, they take the unicorn to be shod. Mr. Ellis, the blacksmith, regards the unicorn with a comical lack of surprise. After a dromedary, a unicorn at least has " 'ooves of a normal shape" (21). His only reaction is to the possibility that he might become impaled on the unicorn spike. For the rest, unicorns appear on his list of prices, so unicorns can be shod. It is unusual that it be a unicorn, but not actually impossible.

The next stage of the story, as with the moment when we think Mark and Harriet will ride the unicorn, uses our sense of expectation. A magician appears and claims the unicorn, who shows no desire to return. The magician curses them and disappears. Mark and Harriet clutch the unicorn as they are whisked away in the language of transition and transformation: "A great wind whistled through the trees. Candleberry stamped and shivered. Then the gale caught up all three of them and they were whisked away through the air" (23), and the adventure begins. . . .

Except that we stay at home. We do not transfer with them, we do not ride by their side in the fantasy. Instead, we are left behind with Mamma and Papa to deal with the mundane consequences and concerns left behind by the impact of the fantastic: the spoiled garden; the missing children; the now one hundred unicorns on the lawn. And all these are then dealt with as if they were the same, mundane problems. The garden is put to rights, the children are waited for, and the unicorns are advertised: "Unicorns given away. Quiet to ride or drive" (24), and sent off to various farms and to an artist to carry his paints. And this despite the fact that *unicorns* are not a part of the everyday world of the Armitages. Yet they are spoken of and dealt with as if they were horses.

The conclusion of the story maintains the tone. When Harriet and Mark return they must relate the story—we have not been with them, we are estranged from their experience of fantasy (a technique that both Peter Straub and M. John Harrison extend)—and they themselves have lived through ironies. The magic took them only to Brighton. The people of Brighton would not take unicorn gold so they organized a show on the beach to earn bus fare. For them, the fantastic is less the unicorn than the adventure of Brighton and returning to home. For Harriet, Mark, and their parents, the true fantastic seems to be centered on the mundane events that supernatural events create. The unicorn is somehow understandable, a trip home from Brighton on a bus, a strange marvel.

My other examples of form in the short story are taken from issue 39 of the journal *Conjunctions*, edited by Peter Straub and published in 2003. The stories in *Conjunctions* return me to my three initial questions.

- How does the fantastic enter the text?
- What are the consequences for the position of the reader within the text?
- What are the consequences for the structure of language as it is used to create this mode?

If Aiken uses the demotic voice to construct irony, Patrick O'Leary in his story, "The Bearing of the Light" turns it around and uses irony to construct awe. This fantasy is constructed from the point of view of the intruder. The intruder is "just" a man. His encounter with a young boy is quite normal. He has met the boy's father. Later we discover he introduced the father to crack. He enters a store where he sees pardons for sale. He purchases one, and is taken through a ritual. He leaves in awe of the woman he had believed a faker, relieved of his burden and capable of release. That is one, metaphorical, understanding of the text and one that is not discouraged. But the story, like so many tales in this category, is a figure-ground puzzle. The man is the devil. He buys absolution from a woman who turns out to be the godhead.

But consider the way the story is told. The Lightbearer enters the life of a young boy. The boy sees nothing, only a man searching for a witch, and the boy rejects contact with the fantastic. As the Lightbearer muses, if only he knew. By moving us into this position we are denied the awe and horror usual with the presence of evil. Although writing from the devil's point of view is a commonplace in fantasy, by taking us into the devil's mind, O'Leary allows us to ride inside his head, we see not a defense of evil, or a gleeful chuckle, but the awe and amazement at the real world, the sense of beauty in the smallest dandelion, the wondrousness of taking a piss after long years without relief.

The irony revels in the reversal of the sublime. We are amazed not at the sublime, but at the more than mundane, the minute. And alongside this there is a moment of doubt: Is this the devil? We are shown no proof. His serpent stays between his legs. His sole moment of magic is to remain unseen by a woman self-absorbed in her own tasks. He does not need to be the devil to have performed the deeds he claims. Neither does the witch need to be either magical or the godhead. The pardons she sells may be just what they look like, gaudy souvenirs. The magic she performs may be metaphorical, the tanning salon to burn the sin, the dragon brooch to remember the beast, the pager that he be within reach. But this is the heart of the liminal fantasy, that moment where metaphor and magic become indistinguishable, where the reader is expected to suspend faith, not in reality, but in metaphor, to allow metaphor to become concrete.

O'Leary's tale works in part because it is in collusion with the reader. It utterly depends on our knowingness. While this collusion is not uncommon in other forms of fantasy, it is intrinsic to the creation of the irony of the fantastic.

The fantasies of equipoise are, like those of irony, dependent on recognition. In this case, however, it is the recognition of the significance of the doubled world, both mundane and simultaneously a fantasy. In the archetypal fantasy of equipoise, the protagonist may have the moment of recognition of his own role, but not a moment of recognition of fantasy. Such stories hold in their hands the possibility of both fantasy and of metaphor. They are almost inevitably melancholy. They mourn for possibility. Three examples from the special issue of *Conjunctions* showcase this technique: M. John Harrison's "Entertaining Angels Unawares," John Crowley's "The Girlhood of Shakespeare's Heroines," and Elizabeth Hand's "The Least Trumps."

M. John Harrison's "Entertaining Angels Unawares" plays with a sense that metaphor and magic are indivisible, that the universes are not parallel so much as a helix, crossing and recrossing, permeating the boundaries of the mundane as the mundane permeates the boundaries of the fantastic. As with all fantasies of extreme equipoise, it can be read as nonfantastical. We wait, paused, for the fantastic to break through. Instead it becomes difficult to locate where that fantastic element is. Both church and graveyard are promising. There are young bodies in the graveyard. The buttresses of the church are false; they can no longer support the edifice. From the tower, stone louvers plummet. The church is held together with gobbo, a material made from that satanic animal, the goat. The *possibility* of fantasy lurks at every corner. The story (as with Crowley and Hand) is told in the first person, as if only then the point of equipoise can be held. The protagonist lives in a desert kingdom; purple and green carpets are coated in decades of dust. In one reading it could be Kansas, the place where nothing grows, all is gray, there is no life. The man he envies bestrides the world, is perhaps a traveler, a man who bestrides *two* worlds. We are asked to contemplate, as the representative of extremes, the confusion of a loving man, a father, whose dreams are those of a psychotic, who each night finds himself stalking through a city, the Angel of Death. The difficulty is whether we are to take this as any kind of otherworld. The hesitation, or latency, is that while *we* might not, are given no encouragement to do so, the protagonist clearly *does*. He sees fantasy. What do we see? The Angel of Death? Characteristically of Harrison's work, the protagonist's last actions, to write on the back of a child's picture, to begin smearing the gravestones with gobbo, seem unrelated. One possibility is that these last actions consist of incantation and ritual, the story ends in the moment before the portal opens.

Elizabeth Hand's story continues constructs liminality as a tease. What is it about this story that intrigues? We begin with a place of familiarity and discomposure. A children's writer whom we all "know," who is not the woman we thought. We are allowed a peep into her life, but quickly taken in another direction: the life of her daughter. We are told that the enchanted isle is merely a metaphor, but Ivy is physically sick when she crosses the boundary. The isle is a place of safety, a polder, but also a borderland. Texts can be held on the island, preserving a moment or kind of reality, but held in a space in which changes that fold and ripple the world can be made.

Blakie and Katherine (Ivy's aunts) are the twin queens, and the magicians, and the imprisoned princesses. Katherine is Penelope, but a Penelope who searches for her lover. And just when we think it is all metaphorical, when the language that has held us in tension reaches breaking point, the transformation of tarot card to tattoo ruptures the order of the world. The heart of "The Least Trumps" is a summoning spell. Ivy has been told she will never have to go into the world; the world will come to her. This is a Rapunzel story, but the witch is kind and caring, Rapunzel a reluctant entrant to the world. When her prince is summoned it is through scar magic; a representation tattooed from tarot card to leg. He traverses the thorns and roses of previous relationships, of the keloids left by his own sister. The witch looks on benignly. Tattooing becomes a metaphor for internal scarring: by making scars visible can they be healed? But the tattoo breaks more than one enchantment. When the thorns that surround the castle are pulled down, the world is changed. Transformation cannot take place only for the individual; it must ripple outward. But whether the tattoo is magic or metaphor is never ultimately resolved. Our narrator, after all, is not the most stable of people. It is quite possible that there is no magic here, that the narrator has fictionalized her world.

John Crowley's "The Girlhood of Shakespeare's Heroines" is on an even more extreme point of balance than Harrison or Hand. A crucial question to ask is, Where is the fantasy? Is there an alternative world lurking here? It is liminal in the sense that it pauses on many borders. Several perhaps, in the desire that Shakespeare not be the bard? In the possibility of a summer without polio?

We begin with self-referentialism, the acknowledgment that this tale takes place in a liminal place, a Brigadoon, a locus of the momentary possible. The stating of this placement both acknowledges and denies its meaning. It cannot be a real Brigadoon, because it is *real*, but the dreamlike qualities, the portal that is polio (that provides the before and after) casts doubt on which is the frame, which the other world.

Both Harriet and the narrator have already passed through one portal of the mundane, from ill-health or isolation into the Real of communal "ordinary" life. It strikes me that the period of time spent in the summer camp *must* be the fantasy, because to each side of it is bitter or mundane reality. Harriet's plunge down the stage trap is perhaps almost too obviously representational: on the other side is the mad world of theater. Perhaps this is our world, perhaps it is not. The narrator himself is aware of the dissonance: the theater he dreamed of was not the theater he was able to see—that form had long passed away. The protagonist himself *never* explains this as fantastical yet seems to recognize the moments of equipoise. We, on the other hand, are left wondering in which direction we should be looking: "Somehow without my even asking it had been passed through the membrane of common reality into another space, where things were not as they were where I came from, where Shakespeare was important and everything else less so" (16).

The liminality is doubled and redoubled as the portal passes us from many Frames to many Fantasies. The most liminal of these metaphors is Harriet's photography, images made on panchromatic printing paper, "The resulting image is exact and exquisitely detailed but softened and abstracted—both warmed and cooled-by the light's passing through a textured paper negative rather than a transparent plastic one. The very first photographic negatives were made on paper" (12–13). The old-method photograph mutates reality as does sickness and time (unlike modern photographs, which we come to see as a substitute for memory).

There is a moment of recognition, not of the fantastical, but of the possibility of the fantastical, when the protagonist "caught her looking at me in the rearview mirror of the bus. . . . But I looked frankly back at her in that mirror, and not away, and maybe that was enough" (17). But enough for what? On one level it is the enough of desire. On another it is the shared experience of the looking-glass world. What each will have seen is not the other, but the other's reflection.[4]

As the man, the stranger, tells them of Bacon, and the Baconian heresy, the protagonist recognizes that there is another possible fantasy narration here, the one in which "a trick or trap were being constructed," within which the protagonist, divorced from his frame world, his frame of reference, would be trapped. But this is not the closed world of the quest fantasy: it rests entirely on the willingness of the protagonist and the reader to question, *not* to accept, so the trap cannot close, the old man does not become the omniscient guide, and meaning is left unfixed. The liminal fantasy is *not* a club story.

And this structure is acknowledged: "the man's self effacement and reasonableness and sweetness were part of it" (20). All of which inclines me to the belief that "The Girlhood of Shakespeare's Heroines" functions to punish the club-story narrative common to the fantastic (and discussed by John Clute in his essay in *Conjunctions*) by laying everything open to doubt and to pause. When Harriet and the protagonist visit a library, they find the scholarship (the scholasticism) to make true the guide's narrative, and *still* they do not believe. Even his own line, "that nothing needs to be the way you've always thought it has to be" serves to move them further into their nonacceptance, not into the trap of closure and trust he seeks to create. The theme of the tale is multiplicity. The multiplicity of meanings buried in the text of "Shakespeare's" *Henry V.* The layered possibilities of Bacon. The layers of meaning of the summer and of love all build to create an extended moment of waiting.

What all of these fantasies share—whether constructed through irony, equipoise, or both—is that they rest on the firm belief that the reader will recognize that which is merely hinted at. They rest on knowingness or genre expectation, without which neither of the two dynamics of liminal fantasy is possible.

With the exception of *Lud-in-the-Mist*, all the examples discussed so far are short stories. Maintaining irony and equipoise (liminality) in the short form is unexceptionable, but an obvious question is whether it can be retained at novel length. How long can an author continue to resist resolution into the fantastic? *Wizard of the Pigeons* (1986), by Megan Lindholm, extends Aiken's idea that it is the *idea* of the ordinary that can be estranged. Lindholm uses a number of techniques; in particular we see the emergence of very plain descriptions of the fantastic juxtaposed with baroque descriptions of the real that challenge our understanding of which is which. Furthermore, it is around this literary device that Lindholm constructs her plot.

Wizard of the Pigeons is set in Seattle. The protagonist, Wizard, feeds pigeons, and tells those who ask him the Truth. His powers depend on his willingness to scavenge, to leave the world behind, and on looking after his pigeons. At night he lives in a squat; his only friends are Cassie and Rasputin, also urban wizards. All this is threatened by an evil power called MIR, which channels itself through the waitress, Lynda. This is one Truth.

In the other Truth, Wizard is Mitchell Ignatius Reilly, a very disturbed Vietnam veteran, listed missing in action, who, in his saner moments, is trying to prove his identity. Lynda promises rescue from this maelstrom.

Wizard of the Pigeons challenges us to choose a Truth, and to work out which of the worlds depicted is the illusion. It does this by encasing the ordinary in the language and expectations of fantasy and magic at its most traditional. *Wizard of the Pigeons*, unlike the other tales considered so far, is about the rules from which fantasy is constructed, but also the rules from which "real" life is created. The ironizing of both sets of rules creates the fluidity that makes this book work and denies us the chance to simply assume metaphor or automatically assume that Wizard is insane. Similarly, the novel depends on the ironizing of destiny. The liminality of *Wizard of the Pigeons* depends intensely on the reader's familiarity with the codes of fantasy. Its conclusion plays with our desire to suspend disbelief.

Wizard of the Pigeons opens in a manner instantly familiar to the reader of fairy tale: "On the far western shore of a northern continent there was once a harbour city called Seattle" (1). As with *Little, Big* (which I shall consider later), the reality of the locale is held in doubt. In this opening chapter it is *storied*. The same is true of Wizard. The conventions that the protagonist be described is twisted; instead he is made legend of. "Some said he had been an engineer and a warrior who had returned from some far battle with memories too fearsome to tolerate. And some said no, that he had been a scholar and among those who had refused to go to that far strife" (1). The insistence of the fluidity and arguability of legend runs absolutely counter to the fixed interpretations of characters in the portal fantasy. Wizard cannot be delineated, he can only be narrated. At least part of the story will be the struggle for control of Wizard's narrative.

The sense of a legend—and a legendary struggle—being told is intensified by the language of destiny and boundedness that surrounds Wizard and that is built into the telling of the tale that begins "On such a day the cries of the gulls seem to drown out the traffic noises. . . . It was a day when no one was immune to magic, and a wizard might revel in its glories. The possibilities tugged at Wizard's mind like a kite tugs on a string" (2). Conscious archaism inducts Wizard into the world of fantasy.

Wizard's movements, and the movement of the world around him, are delivered with import: "With a flash of light and a roar of wind, he appeared in the door of the restaurant" (7). His travels around the town have the air of duty and destiny, so that the bus that takes him North seems sent entirely for him, and the market, when he arrives, is a place on the map of fantasyland: "It never showed him the same face twice. Depending on how he approached, it was a bower of flowers, or a banquet of fresh fish, or a tower of shining oranges. From Alaskan Way at the bottom of the Hillclimb, it was the magic castle rising up at the top of the stairs" (45).

Wizard of the Pigeons is structured around the commonplace of the portal fantasy that the world revolves around the protagonist, that he has the power to move the world. For Wizard, that power is restricted to Seattle, and specifically the free-ride areas. But Wizard is not the hero of the fantasy, he is the guide. He engages in many adventures and many tales that are not his own, and delivers Prophesy to individual after individual he never sees. Most frequently, Wizard receives problems from individuals who never look at him, never really consider his presence. His advice, his Knowings, are never commented upon, but the audience always leaves newly impelled.

Elsewhere other structures of the portal fantasy are acknowledged by Wizard; he lives in a thinned world. "He paused at the pay phone on the way out, to put the receiver to his ear, then hit the coin return and check the chute. Nothing. Well, he could not complain. Magic was not what it once had been. It was spread thinner these days" (13).

Wizard of the Pigeons is a book about illusion and reality. Lindholm builds uncertainty not only through the apparent dilemma over Wizard's sanity, but also in the way Wizard lives his life. Wizard is a tramp, but one who can "pass," who constructs his life from little props: cologne, a good overcoat, a newspaper rolled up and visible in a neat plastic bag. One issue in the book is the preservation of the delicate balance of the day-to-day world; one slip and Wizard's magic begins to unravel.

The unavoidable question at the heart of this book is whether Wizard's magic is real. Is his bag of popcorn really inexhaustible? Does Wizard do magic with candle flames when he dissuades a father from bullying his son? (11). Note the way moments of magic are written in this early chapter; "The woman's face flushed with embarrassment, but Ted was too focused on his dominance to care if he caused a scene. The stranger was oblivious anyway" (11). The switch away from Wizard's point of view takes us outside the frameworld of the story and makes Wizard an intrusion into another tale (which he is in the most literal sense as well; he has forced himself onto their table). So which is the intrusion fantasy? MIR intruding on Wizard's life? Or Wizard's wandering into the "real" world? Can this be an intrusion fantasy from the point of view of the intruder?

In Wizard's world, words count. Cassie collects songs and skipping rhymes and defuses them, tapping the power they release (19). Cassie's power, like Wizard's, lies in telling the truth. Her curse is that she will not be believed, and cannot give without being asked. Cassie's narrations provide some of Wizard's "real" background, but in story vein, they are distanced. He does not have to embrace them and chooses not to.

At the start of chapter 3, as the intrusion in Wizard's life begins to make itself manifest, Lindholm depicts it through sense: "A subtle wrongness pervaded his room. To his nostrils came the familiar mustiness of the dank walls, the city cat stink like damp wool, and beyond that the cheesy odour of pigeon droppings. . . . all of this was absolutely and totally as it should be. The very rightness of it stiffened his spine with dread. Whatever it was, it was very clever" (24, 26) Reading this passage out of context, we must accept that this is a description of classic clinical paranoia. It gets worse. When he finally opens his eyes, "Horror clutched at his throat" (26). "His cardboard had been wrenched clear of his window to lie atop the clotting puddle of blanket on the floor" (26). Nothing in the on-page descriptions of the scene suggests the fantastic. Lindholm has switched styles: from the ironized exaggeration of the mundane that has made Seattle fantastical, to the emotional intensity of the intrusion fantasy. Lindholm creates the fantastic from Wizard's reactions. He "kept his breathing steady, from the skin in he trembled. His heart longed to gallop, his lungs screamed for more oxygen, faster. He smothered them, choking on fear, and tried to think" (27). This contrast of the careful description of the cardboard and blanket against the window, the practical yet ritual construction of the polder against the sensing of magic, the physical against the ethereal, intensifies the impact of the latter.

The sense of the fantastic is deepened by moving inward, not outward: "at least it thought he was sleeping. He reined his power back, risking no contact. It wanted him. . . . If he trembled, if he flinched, if his power just brushed it, it would suck at him" (27). If we choose the mundane, metaphorical understanding of this book, this is a description of trauma, of the literal haunting of memory. But it can be read as a fantastical threat. When the glass of the window finally breaks, the cat is injured, and Lindholm piles on the ambiguity; Wizard reaches out, seals off the pumping veins in the cat's stump, and "the winds of eternity screamed past his soul." At the very moment where we might choose the mundane explanation, we are steered once more back to the fantastical: Wizard drops into reverie and the memories of three boys ordered to slaughter chickens (one reluctantly, one joyously, and one in fear and trembling of the birds' vengeful ghosts) and from there into a tunnel, too small for a man of his height.

The presence of ordinary objects is imbued with threat: "The footlocker seemed to swell to fill his room" (35). The emphasis is continually on distortion, the reordering of perspective. This reordering is crucial to understanding the disintegration of Wizard's magic. His magic depends on the maintenance of a perspective on the world in which he is not one of the "bizarre patrons" (37) attracted by the Amtrak washrooms, and in which his own status is above that of most inhabitants of the street. His self is constructed to question what his own reality is. So that he muses, "The one thing an expert scavenger could not look like was a scavenger.

Leave that for the dreary men in overcoats perched on their benches. Strange, how they looked like scavengers, but were not. They were not even survivors" (38).

As his perspective is disoriented by the intrusion of MIR, so the perspective in which he is seen—the confidence that allows him to pass—breaks down, and he becomes "visible." The first "rupture" is when he is seen by Lynda stealing her ex-boyfriend's coffee. The sighting is not the rupture; it happens, but Lynda offers him charity, knowing what she is doing, and "there was nothing of power or magic in her gesture toward him; only pity" (42). Previously, Wizard has received contingency gifts: he has been in the right time at the right place, the wizard cloak will be found in a dumpster truck to which he has been directed. But Lynda's gift of food is direct; it fixes him in the world, a hint that this is what Lynda will try to do.

Contingency is the narrative hook in the novel: the sense that things happen when the right moment occurs. A donut appears just in time, a magic cloak must not be worn until Wizard is ready to claim his power. The assertion that coincidence is more than coincidence is in itself powerful, so that the moment at which Lynda takes Wizard's empty popcorn bag is devastating. It is a moment of recognition, if not *the* moment of recognition: "it was gone, his gift taken as abruptly as it was bestowed. He had never known how he could feed the pigeons, and now he would never understand how he could not" (85). Up until this moment, we had not known that this was so crucial. This is the moment of rupture, when Wizard accepts Lynda's narration of his story.

Once the perspective is broken and Wizard becomes visible (in chapter 7), things no longer just happen; people do not sit by him on the bus, and the waitress reappears. Her very reappearance is a failure of the contingency—which asserts that everything happens just as it ought and then passes on—that Wizard *not* be a part of the world but a partaker. This change in perspective is signaled in the language: metaphor (as used to describe the market) is replaced by explanation, the Klondike Gold Rush Memorial Park is a "designation [that] meant a storefront building on South Main where a bored man in a ranger suit presided over memorabilia of the Gold Rush" (78), and the enjoyment of the landscape and the sense of owning the city is replaced by furtiveness, the seeking of safety.

And Wizard's musings change; they go into retreat. Instead of interpreting the world, commenting on it to the persons delivering their monologues, he retreats, stiffens, and loses control of the story. The first sign of this is his rescue of an old man from muggers. Not the rescue, but the ease with which he almost kills them (stopped only by the old man). Retreating to his den, he can see "it" watching him. "It had nearly had him tonight; it knew it, too" (92).

It is because of the importance of perspective and semblance that so much of this book is delivered as a relation of internal musings. Our distance from Wizard is imperative; if the story were told in the first person, we would see the world entirely as he sees it. Instead, we are asked continually to test our understanding against his, and against what we know of fantasy. Throughout, it is easy to lose sight of the fact that Wizard does Know. As far as we can tell, he does tell the Truth (although even this is based on trust). We never see the outcome of his Knowings, so it is his power as the narrator of his tale that we accept this.

The issue of *maybe* is raised again in Cassie's initial rescue of Wizard. Finding him crouching behind a dumpster, she takes him back to her apartment, through "no Seattle he knew . . . all alive and watching . . . no place of dead stones and bare pavements. . . . This was an ecosystem, vital and aware" (56). A place that is another Seattle, the Seattle that would have existed if the great fire had not happened. Wizard has stepped through a portal, but there is none of the intense description of the portal fantasy, and Wizard resists Cassie's guidance. In the classic dream rupture (long rejected by the writers of fantasy), "he had awakened shivering in the melting snow behind a blue dumpster in an alley" (64).

Faced with the intrusion of MIR, Wizard does what all protagonists of intrusion fantasies do: he seeks refuge in rules. Waking the day after meeting Lynda on the bench, he determines to be conscientious and part of this is being an element of the city. As in the first chapter, Lindholm does not move her protagonist through the city but allows the city to move through him: "When Wizard stood in this small triangular plot of history, he felt as if the spirit of Seattle flowed through him, backwards and forwards in time, with him as a sort of intelligent filter" (95–96). The knowledge, acquired by drifting along with city tours, is no less a part of him for that. But the collapse of his powers entails the collapse in knowledge and in camouflage: suddenly he is hidden in the wrong sense, his power negated. A bus driver challenges him: "As he stared out the window, he mentally reviewed his appearance. He was shaven, washed and tidily, if casually attired. So why had the driver been able to pick him out as a resident of the streets?" (96). As his external image is penetrated, so his internal construction begins to fragment, "He closed his eyes to let it pass. A blacker darkness closed on him and MIR laughed. His mind was flooded with images, stark, terrifying, and disgusting. . . . They were real.

Each slashed face, each savaged body had led a life and been part of a whole" (96). Yet at the moment we assume this is Wizard's past breaking through, he relocates the images. They belong to a knife, a knife carried by another passenger, and Wizard is back within the magic, if only for a short while. MIR is using the magic of the knife to draw Wizard in, offering, then withholding it, teasing Wizard: "Bereft of his magic, the edges of the world dimmed and the colours all ran together in muddiness. He groped after the magic and the knife, but it was like trying to reach without arms" (97).

And in the space that is left by magic, something else intrudes, a piece of information, waves of giddiness washing over him, Wizard wonders if he has taken fewer pills that day (101). Never referred to again, they are a leakage in his world, an indication that he is falling further from his reality. Almost immediately he is escorted from a restaurant, despite the coins in his pocket. And by the next page the intrusion is becoming more vivid, the "illusion" that is homelessness is taking over. He carries more money than he has ever had before but cannot get anyone to sell him coffee: the illusion of capitalism exposed, the illusion of Michael Ignatius Reilly emerges as he moves through the streets clutching the money: "Money. He had withdrawn from the major economic system of this country a long time ago. He didn't need their official federal confetti, or their Social Security, or their welfare, or their lousy Veterans Administration" (102). The chant in his head takes over; Wizard loses his train of thought and his sense of the city. The city is no longer emerald but seedy; "He could hear the gulls crying on the bay like abandoned babies in bombed out places" (104). By the end of the chapter, tired, hungry and with a hacking cough, he can brush his hair back to feel "the tenderness of old scar tissue just back of his hairline" (108). Michael Ignatius Reilly has intruded physically into Wizard's body.

When Lynda reappears, her words "pattered and splashed against him like the rain" (113). She takes him for food, and when he tries to escape into the warm air, she takes him for coffee and alcohol, dragging at him "like a riptide" (118). Wizard abandons himself to her, allowing himself to be taken into a bar that sets his hackles up, in a way depicted as both magical and mundane: "Danger was screaming in here, pressing in all around him like a million tiny needles trying to pierce his flesh with their warnings. Danger and trap and an exposed back and idiot on point and a coward on drag" (118). By this time Wizard is sufficiently estranged from "reality" that he cannot recognize Cassie when she comes into the bar, "a stout woman, dressed all in black" (120).

Lynda, meanwhile, adds one more layer to the illusion as she reverts to baby voice to seduce Wizard. "He looked at her very carefully. She sounded like a different woman than the Lynda who had fed him earlier. He wondered which question he was supposed to answer" (121). "Lynda had something she wanted to say, but she said everything except what she was trying to tell him" (121). He begins to realize that the bar itself has a message, of disregard and insult, a place one does not bring someone one cares about. Inevitably, Lynda's ex-boyfriend turns up. Also inevitably, Lynda steps back to watch the outcome of the fight, her options left open. Wizard's Knowing works differently this time, supplying him with the lines and the moves to get them out of the bar, and to tackle Booth (123–125). By the end of the chapter, he has escaped from Lynda and got home, aware that the alcohol has poisoned him, made it impossible to see Cassie. And then Lynda arrives, having followed him home and lifted herself onto the fire escape. She has fully entered his narrative.

Lynda's vision reorients the perspective on Wizard's life and living. Where he sees security and magic, she sees a slum. Even the candle she lights is fundamentally different from the light of his world, "Hers burned white and harsh. It was searching and merciless as an illumination flare" (134). And before he can stop her, it is too late. She has forced upon him an unwanted moment of recognition: "The scene remained forever fixed on his memory, like a tinted illustration from an old book. The light from the candle flame limned Lynda in gold, setting off her silhouette from the darkness that crouched before her. She knelt in the maw of the closet, her hands curled in front of her breasts, her mouth slightly ajar with intent interest. The lid of the footlocker gaped open before her" (134). Finding the service records of Michael Ignatius Reilly, she forces the identity upon him as she later forces marijuana and sex, all the while insisting that she is there to look after him. In the dim recesses of his mind he retains awareness that she is dangerous, but the passivity that allowed him to listen and Know here undoes him. And as he is undone, as he is forced into sex he does not want, "all the forbidden and dangerous things came pressing out from the corners of his mind, to leer and snicker at him" (140).

When he wakes the next day, it is as Michael Ignatius Reilly, disoriented as to his location, convinced that a call home will resolve his problems—while unclear what his problems are. Chapter 11, in other words, tells the story of the transportee in the other world, in a dream world in which scenes segue so that the "temporal continuity" (141) moves from the room to the phone booth to the man at the veterans agency—all without Mitch actually moving. The world is depicted as spinning around him, stopping to let him interact with different stations. The ethereal nature of his interaction—"The electronic winds blew his words back to him" (143)—mirroring the world that blows back his existence, tells him he isn't really there, he is missing in action (144). The parent who tells him to stick with it, that he will get it all straightened out, with little comprehension what "it" is. A looking-glass world of incomprehensible rules.

And then the next day he is back in the world, back as Wizard, back in reality. And as ever, when in reality, he comforts himself with facts, this time the nature of the park he sits in, the original headquarters of the United Parcel Service (148–149). This comforting with facts is interesting because it is facts that anchor Wizard throughout. Mitchell is discomfited and disoriented by what passes for the factual in his life.

Lynda's presence at the den is too easy to surrender to. It is easier to have his life be taken over, to have Lynda force him into his wizard's robes, and thereby rob them of meaning and magic (158); to turn him into Mitchell Ignatius Reilly, to allow the interloper to take over the body, to play the games of romance and sex. Eventually he retreats into impotence: "He kept himself divorced from it, holding back the touching and feeling that could unleash the pain. It was a fair trade. If he let himself be reached, she would hurt him, would drive him with agony until he destroyed the source of the pain. No touch of pleasure, no touch of pain. Being numb was the key to it all. He found the balancing point again and felt a certain bitter satisfaction from it" (168). Wizard, at least, believes that his magic exists purely in that liminal space.

The conclusion (chapter 15), writes magic through the intensity of feeling, and of cityscape. Very little that is fantastic is actually done, but the scene, in which Wizard confronts a man with a knife, rescues a girl, is confronted by MIR, and rescued by Cassie and his pigeons, is dark and wet and written to estrange. When he drags himself from Lynda, he "fled through the night, a hunted thing. MIR had stalked him well, from a perfect blind" (198). His confrontation with the knife-man is written as heroic, prophetic fantasy:

> The robe was cut full and loose, but not loose enough to allow for the full swing of the kick. It snapped tight, jerking the balance from Wizard's other leg. He staggered sideways and the hungry knife went slipping past his ear. He caught himself and spun to face it, but the knife was already before him, weaving a song

of blood as it hovered before his face. . . . The magic limned it for him, setting it glowing with a toadstool light in the blackness of the alley. (201–202)

The language moves us through metaphor into the fantastic so that we are forced to question whether any of it was metaphor. We accept at the same time as Wizard accepts, that the real enemy is the knife, not the man. The knife is imbued with MIR. The knife, anthromorphized, is shamed, "a joyous tool perverted to butchery" (202). In this passage we can see the shift between the mundane and the magical: "Was he supposed to grab the damned thing! He imagined a sudden, successful clutch and the fingers slipping silently from his hand. . . . The knife flickered and flashed, burning before his eyes. He reached and felt for it with magic" (202). Wizard needs to recognize the visual indicators of the magical world in order to cross into it and be activated. The portal is no less there because the two worlds exist in the same physical space.

So when the confrontation is over, it is not surprising that Wizard, for the first time in the book, declaims prophecy: "If ever thou takest up a knife in thy hands again, be it even for so innocent a thing as the buttering of bread, the metal of the knife shall find revulsion in thy touch, and break again into a thousand splinters. But those splinters will pierce thy eyes and thy heart" (203). Nor is it surprising that MIR is not a metaphor, it "fell on him with the weight of the earth itself. . . . A talon or tooth or blade penetrated Wizard's guard" (208). It is real enough that Cassie—who was the victim, used by MIR to draw Wizard—returns with Wizard's pigeons, "they came, hungry always. . . . They dived to his feet, squabbling and crowding one another as they fought for the writhing threads and juicy gobs of greyness" (208). Filling themselves to capacity until there is nothing left but a small grey document box in which something scrabbles. Wizard kills it. He and Cassie take the box and drop it in the river. Anything in there that was a threat, is now gone. And so too has Cassie. In giving without being asked she has broken her own rules. The tale ends with the princess once more out of reach, but with Wizard, resplendent in his robes, sitting with Rasputin in a park, both secure in their invisibility.

Thence to M. John Harrison's *The Course of the Heart* (1992) which turns the matter of fantasy and the liminality that can be encoded in language a few more degrees. Harrison's work is frequently constructed of short stories and vignettes that have appeared elsewhere as stand-alone pieces. But these are no fix up novels. Consider instead a sculpture. Turn it this way, stand it in one place, and we see a couple, kissing. Turn it almost halfway around, tilt it, create a new base and adjust the lighting and suddenly it is something else. The light and perspective shift as new pieces are affixed.

The Course of the Heart makes latency *storyable*. It opens with a small boy waiting: "When I was a tiny boy I often sat motionless in the garden, bathed in sunshine, hands flat on the rough brick of the garden path, waiting with a prolonged, almost painful expectation for whatever would happen, whatever event was contained by that moment, whatever revelation lay dormant in it" (13). The reader and the protagonist are in this moment of expectation, but manipulated by those not so content: Pam, Lucas, and the maybe magician, Yaxley.

Sometime in the past Lucas, Pam, and the protagonist have performed magic with Yaxley, with the intention of entering or breaching the Pleroma. Pam and Lucas have been damaged by the experience. Quite late we discover that each has been haunted: Pam by two figures who writhe and fuck in her vision, Lucas by an apparent dwarf (although the later implication is that it is a child). But we also learn that the narrator also has been haunted, by the green lady. The difference, as we eventually work out, is that the narrator's ability to *wait* has enabled him simply to accept these manifestations as moments of wonder. Pam and Lucas—waiting for what they think they want—can only see them as *a consequence*, or a punishment, and so are incapable of realizing that they are the manifestation of the Pleroma, precisely as promised.

The Pleroma is less a place—although this is how Yaxley implies it—than a borderland. It segues into and out of the world. But this liminality makes it indescribable, and Pam and Lucas need the concrete. Unable to find this detail in the Pleroma, they substitute the tale of the Coeur, a fantasy of both an earlier and otherworld. It is the interrelationship of the Pleroma, the world, and this tale of the Coeur around which liminality is constructed. The layering of one over the other, the juxtaposition of the apparently unrelated, creates the space within which the Pleroma exists.

The past and the present are almost interchangeable. In *The Course of the Heart*, the past is something that we are led to think we understand and know, that we have visited. Harrison uses the techniques of the flashback to create a cozy internal knowingness that actually leaves us none the wiser. Take this from early in the book:

> 'Pam,' I said, 'all that was over and done with twenty years ago.'
>
> The fact is that even at the time I wasn't at all sure what we had done. This will seem odd to you, I suppose, but all I remember now is a June evening drenched

with the half-confectionery, half-corrupt smell of hawthorn blossoms. . . . But what the three of us did under his guidance escapes me, as does its significance. (24)

We have been brought into collusion. The narrator's confusion and forgetfulness becomes ours too. It is only much later that we begin to wonder how genuine such forgetfulness might be. Do Lucas and Pam share this supernatural amnesia?

We begin the story with Pam sick with depression and drugs, and the narrator trying to intervene on Lucas's behalf, from whom she is now divorced. Pam is sick. Having been a frail child with epilepsy, she later develops migraines and eventually also breast cancer. Liminality is created in part by misdirection encoded in the detail. If we consider most mimetic fiction as the creation of perspective, in which the point of perspective is to replicate the illusion of bifocality, Harrison's work resembles far more the use of perspective in medieval paintings. Perspective is used to manipulate what we see, to force us to pay attention to the background, sometimes at the expense of the figure:

'Go home Lucas. Go home now.'

He turned away miserably, walked off, and disappeared into that unredeemed maze between Piccadilly and Victoria—alleys full of wet cardboard boxes, failing pornography and pet shops, weed-grown car parks, everything which lies in the shadow of the yellow-tiled hulk of the Arndale Center. I meant to leave him there, but in the end I went after to him to apologise. The streets were empty and quiet: by now it was almost dark. Although I couldn't see him, I could sense Lucas ahead of me. He would be walking very quickly, head thrust forward, hands in pockets. I had almost caught up with him near the Tib Street fruit market when I heard a terrific clattering noise, like an old zinc dustbin rolling about in the middle of the road.

'Lucas!' I called.

When I rounded the corner, the street was full of smashed fruit boxes and crates. Rotten vegetables were scattered everywhere. A barrow lay as it if had been thrown along the pavement. There was such a sense of violence and disorder and idiocy that I couldn't express it to myself. But Lucas Medlar wasn't there; and though I walked about for an hour afterwards, looking down alleys and into doorways and I saw nobody at all.

I had lied to him about Yaxley, of course. For what motives I wasn't sure, though they had less to do with guilt than a kind of shyness. Even after so many years I had no idea how to proceed. Nothing would have been achieved by telling Pam and Lucas the truth, which was that my dealing with Yaxley began again at their wedding— (46–47)

So we have three elements brought to our attention. The first, in the "foreground," is Lucas's disappearance. The other two are in the background: the disturbance in the street, and (almost as an aside) the lies told about Yaxley. Of the three, the disturbance of the street, painted as landscape, is the most significant "figure."

Liminality in Harrison's work is also encoded in unexpected juxtapositions: sentences end to be completed by other sentences, unrelated yet somehow leading. Sometimes this liminality is figured in the events. Yaxley's face appears under the marquee at Pam and Lucas's wedding, uttering gnomically "The Upper World empties itself of everything which has previously choked it" (50).

But the wedding itself is composed of "inane or incompetent speeches—which gave me feelings of nightmare, disorder, the certain failure of everything the ceremony was supposed to represent—the children laughed at every pause, as if they were trying to understand less what to laugh at than when, so that in later life they could measure their responses as accurately by the rhythms of an occasion as by its content" (49–50). The ordinary becomes uneasy and characterized by wrongness, but it relies almost entirely on our own recognition of the familiar within this structure. Interestingly, it is Pam and Lucas who create their own understanding that this wrongness exists.

In Pam and Lucas's life, this wrongness of the ordinary becomes the dominant motif, accompanying their housekeeping and Lucas's work, shaping their interactions. In order to escape this wrongness of the ordinary, they begin to develop skills of avoidance, both of the everyday and of each other. This avoidance is expressed in the story they create of the Coeur, which they use to communicate. It begins with Lucas reading to Pam the biography of Michael Ashman, a travel writer who begins exploring Europe in the 1930s and later segues into his "discovery" of the history of the Empress Gallica XII Hierodule and the end of her principality. Pam and Lucas become embroiled in the discovery or re-creation of her line, which eventually they "establish" as ending with Pam. It is unclear whether Pam knows that the story is wholly invented—the narrator imagines this scene. In itself, the story they narrate, although held in tension at first with our uncertainty as to whether Michael Ashman exists, is the least important part of the whole. The narrator discovers it only after Pam has died. He has his own story through which he communicates and his involvement with Yaxley, which is sporadic and never understood. If we are to take involvement metaphorically, he does not wish it to be understood. The narrator's take on life is surface. If his wife and daughter express love for him, it is enough. If Yaxley requires his assistance, it is enough. Unlike Pam and Lucas, he does not need to go below the surface because he knows it is *all* surface.

The story is important to the conversation here. First, the narrator imagines much of the process of its construction. We are persuaded to believe that this imagining is true, but as neither Pam nor Lucas are very forthcoming, in reality, the generative process is hidden from us and its retelling as fictive as the story is itself. Also, insofar as that narrative is about the Heart, it is about the presence and absence of something within the world that can be both and yet neither: "that somehow, and in special circumstances, the Pleroma breaks into ordinary existence, into political, social and religious life, and becomes a country of its own, a country of the heart" (61).

The meaning of the story of the Heart lies in part in the acknowledgment of its fictionality. It is both pieced together and created. As Pam insists, "We know nothing" (62), and as Lucas points out, "When we talk about the Fall of the Heart . . . we are actually using a figure of speech. Further, this 'fall' has two opposing trajectories: even as we watch the City recoil from the world and back into the Pleroma—a swooning away from us 'into the mirror to die in root and flower'—we interpret this movement as its precise opposite, as a fall into experience of the world, which we read as the loss of ontological purity" (69). At moments like these, when Lucas appears to most be talking whimsy—that fantasy which *demands* sly complicity—what he is actually describing is the trajectory that the novel follows. The entire fantasy of the Coeur can be read as the loss of youth and expectation. The narrator can only see it as whimsy because he has chosen to exist in the moment of expectation.

The narrator's involvement with Yaxley begins again as he assists in the procurement of Lawson's daughter/daughter substitute. It is never clear what Yaxley wants from this, nor is it clear why the narrator is involved. He is somehow dissociated, and when it all goes wrong, it is this dissociation that enables him to survive psychically. But it is also this dissociation that creates the narrative structure of belief in the fantastic. The narrator does not know what is intended, but *still* believes that there is magic. This means that he sees something we don't see: "For Yaxley, everything had to be clouded, discerned with difficulty, operated at several removes" (80). For the narrator, while skeptical of this, the cloudiness of Yaxley seems to authenticate the fantastic. The visions are the confirmation of Yaxley's hints and allusions, when, driving back with Lawson's daughter, he sees a rose garden "blooming . . . on top of the Polytechnic of North London" (91). Pam and Lucas's dissociation in some ways shields us from that of the narrator, which is much greater for all that it is less vivid. Lucas's denial of Pam's final illness, in its creativity, is more real than the narrator's acceptance of death.

The Course of the Heart uses its intense involvement with language to hold both fantasy and mimetic reality suspended. Harrison's work is a contrivance, beautiful in its deliberation. We are made intimately aware that we walk along the hell mouth. Liminal fantasy does not have to be so audacious in its ambiguity and tension.

My next two books would very rarely be considered fantasy, but they *feel* like fantasy (a nebulous but not uncommon statement in the field that I think this chapter may help to explain, but that I hope to distinguish from "slipstream" by the conclusion). One of the things I have tried to demonstrate is that liminality can be constructed through irony, manifested in the text by the often straightforward and nonelaborate description of the fantastic juxtaposed with baroque descriptions of the "real." *Holes* (1998), by Louis Sachar, and to an even greater extent *Tiger's Railway* (1987), by William Mayne, combine the straightforward, almost "flat" style of Joan Aiken with juxtapositions of events and perceptions similar to those developed in the work of Harrison and Lindholm that move the ironic to the full-fledged Absurd. While *Tiger's Railway* is the most developed of this model of liminal fantasy, Louis Sachar's very spare, minimalist book is rather useful to demonstrate the technique I am trying to describe. The irony in this book is, in part, in the language; it is also in the way a classic quest fantasy is "disguised" within a "realistic" boy's adventure story.

Stanley Yelnats is hit over the head by a pair of sneakers that he is then accused of stealing, and is sent to a boot camp in the Texan desert where the inmates are made to dig holes. It eventually turns out that the holes are dug in order to find a treasure buried by Kissing Kate Barlow, whose black lover was lynched by the townsfolk, led by the ancestors of the Warden. Stanley—with the help of Zero, a boy apparently without family—finds the treasure and discovers that it is the lost fortune of his ancestor. From this moment on, Stanley's family becomes successful.

It is too easy to claim that a quest fantasy hides in a boy's adventure. The quest narrative and the bildungsroman are intimately related but *Holes* contains curses, prophecy, and destinarianism. Stanley Yelnats and his whole family (which is small, in accordance with the conventions of quest fantasies) is *possibly* under a curse. The insistence of the blurb on the Yearling edition notwithstanding, this curse is not absolutely definite.

After all, this is the modern world and curses aren't real. The family jokes about it. But meanwhile, Stanley follows the path of the quest hero: he is ignorant and is educated in the way of the fantasy world (the camp) by the leader of the gang. Stanley assists someone weaker, and this assistance turns out to be "predestined," and the clue to breaking the curse and fulfilling the prophecy. At the end he helps Zero up a hill and finds him water, the very act that the great-great-great-grandmother of Zero had asked Stanley's great-great-grandfather to perform. What Sachar achieves is something that has eluded many writers of quest fantasy: the depiction of a quest narrative in which the questor genuinely has no idea that he is on, or at the center, of a quest and in which his haplessness does not seem a fabrication but a genuine consequence of the backstory. Every small, apparently meaningless event or person carries the kind of significance we are used to finding in the excessively "mapped" form that is quest fantasy. Whomever you meet will *matter*. And by page 187, Stanley has a moment of recognition that what is important to the tale is not the treasure sought, but the meeting between himself and Zero. But *Holes* is not narrated in the mode I have described in chapter 1: it lacks the sense of naïveté and discovery that I have associated with the quest. Because Stanley seems accepting and almost blasé about the world he enters, we do not have that same sense of a world mapped for us by the protagonist in portal fantasies. Sachar may have succeeded in constructing that rare thing, a liminal quest fantasy, which elsewhere in this chapter we have seen only in the progenitive work, *Lud-in-the-Mist*.

The insistence on relating the story almost as reportage is one facet of this achievement. *Holes* is told through two points of view. One is the omniscient narrator who relates the "history" of Stanley's ancestor and Kate Barlow. These sections are less written than *told*, in that they read as if they were spoken aloud. Although none of Sachar's sentences are long, in these sections they are staccato, punctuated for aural impact. Take this example from the opening of chapter 28:

> After twenty years, Kate Barlow returned to Green Lake. It was a place where nobody would ever find her—a ghost town on a ghost lake.
>
> The peach trees had all died, but there were a couple of small oak trees still growing by an old abandoned lake. Now the edge of the lake was over five miles away, and it was little more than a small pond full of dirty water.
>
> She lived in the cabin. Sometimes she could hear Sam's voice echoing across the emptiness. "Onions! Sweet fresh onions."
>
> She knew she was crazy. She knew she'd been crazy for the last twenty years.

"Oh Sam," she would say, speaking into the vast emptiness. "I know it is hot, but I feel so very cold. My hands are cold. My feet are cold. My face is cold. My heart is cold."

And sometimes she would hear him say, "I can fix that," and she'd feel his warm arm across her shoulder. (120–121)

It may seem indulgent to quote so much from one chapter, but let us take this section bit by bit to see how the sense of the fantastic is steadily built up. That staccato start in the first paragraph is repeated in the fourth "She knew she was crazy." There is a Pinteresque element to the structure. We can hear the pauses. Reinforcing the sense of something slightly awry is the use of not-quite non sequiturs, in which each sentence is connected to another that moves slightly at a tangent rather than in a direct line of plot, and that reveals something important about the landscape that Kate is moving within, both externally and internally. There is the bald statement that she knew she was crazy, which classically belies her craziness, and this is then juxtaposed with an illustration of her craziness *if* this is not a fantasy. If, however, it were a fantasy, if we were to accept the reality of the curses imposed by the gypsy and by Kate, then as with other tales I have considered in this chapter, the perspective shifts and Kate is not crazy, but living with an awareness of the supernatural. What supports this reading—in addition to the prologue and epilogue of the novel, which emphasize the fantastic framing of the text—is that this feels written as if it is to be *told*, and the most powerful form of the *told* fantastic is the ghost story.

Ghost stories are told around campfires, and Stanley is at a camp, although Stanley is never told the story. But Kate's story is never actually corroborated, leaving instead a sense that this is folk legend of a very immediate sort, a fantasy that is being spun to explain the conditions of the present—a creation-of-the-land story as it is emerging.[5]

Those sections of the story that concern Stanley directly are written in a complex but bald, self-reflective mode (which can be seen elsewhere in the work of Daniel Pinkwater and Tim Wynne Jones). Description in this form is simultaneously intensely detailed but intensely *spare*: "As Stanley tried to turn over on his cot, he was afraid it was going to collapse under all his weight. He barely fit in it. When he finally managed to roll over on his stomach, the smell was so bad that he had to turn over again and try sleeping on his back. The cot smelled like sour milk" (23). There are "ands" and "becauses" missing here. Information begins from the general and moves to the particular. Detail always feels a bit more than seems quite normal *because* it moves in this direction. The description feels as if taken by a camera, the initial image taken at a distance, then later zooming in, or shifting angle to create not a more detailed picture, but an *additional* picture. The technique is repeated throughout, but here is one more example, from the opening of chapter 29:

> There was a change in the weather.
>
> For the worse.
>
> The air became unbearably humid. Stanley was drenched in sweat. Beads of moisture ran down the handle of his shovel. It was almost as if the temperature had gotten so hot that the air itself was sweating. (127)

The technique is intensely and essentially cinematic; one can see it as a series of clear-cut shots. And in that last sentence, the only one that breaks from this technique, we are provided with that classic twist that repeats itself in liminal fantasy: the "real" providing the metaphor for the fantastic, so that instead of "it was almost as if the air was sweating, it was so hot," it is the increasing heat that seems fantastical. The thing that is real is made into a simile. The description that is actual metaphor reads as if mimetic.

When this cinematic structure is transferred to individual perception, it creates the impression of ennui. Stanley, like many of Daniel Pinkwater's characters, like Tiger Malik in *Tiger's Railway*, has learned to accept the world exactly as it is and *as it appears at any given moment*. So it is that Stanley accepts that if he is assigned to dig holes, then his concern is to do it properly (preferably without annoying anyone else). There is no hint of resentment, just a concern that "as he dug, he was careful to dump the dirt far away from the hole" (48), in order that he not have to move the dirt later. The experience is reduced to the event, not the feeling about the event. In consequence, the surprise, the injustice, the supernatural, is as utterly normal and to be expected—perhaps even more to be accepted than most of what *we* consider to be normal, because the very act of considering requires *us* to look forward and anticipate. In contrast, all of these characters have, for one reason or another, discovered that living in the moment, acting only on the situation and the landscape here and now, is safer. The way we see the world—the way in *Holes* the Warden sees the world—as a long-term game to be planned and plotted, is utterly fantastic to these characters. In *Tiger's Railway*, Tiger Malik, superintendent of the railway, is the master of this kind of immediatism, while Slivon, the stationmaster, the man who thinks long-term, and who *should* be representative of sanity in the text, is the most estranged from his world. *Tiger's Railway* is the fantasy of the Absurd.

The central fantasy in *Tiger's Railway* is Tiger's stealing of engines, one that Malik refuses to see as fantasy but instead repositions as the "real world":

> When Tiger Malik was a boy he used to eat apples that did not belong to him, taking them from orchards. . . . He used to fill his hat with cherries, too, and knew that was wrong. But when he was grown up and made Railway Superintendent of Bessar District, and wore the Superintendent's cap with the real gold embroidery, he stole a railway engine, and felt quite happy about it. (9)

Mayne proceeds from this intriguing beginning to ignore the conventional ideas of explanation and motivation. We segue into a lecture given to his son, Pauli, and Pauli's friend Katrina (niece of the stationmaster Slivon), who have also been stealing apples. When Malik later takes Pauli out to steal the engine, his explanation for his hypocrisy is blunt: "There is a time and place for everything. . . . This is the right place and the right time, and I have given myself permission" (11).

This first engine, when stolen, is just an engine. Abandoned and neglected, it is still a simple piece of machinery. But as the novel moves on, these engines become increasingly anthropomorphized. By chapter 4, "Hiffle Hiffle and Humpy Dump," a small steam engine is a "little cockled-up thing," "sweet, and handicapped" (61). It turns out, as it happens, to be a mountain train, oddly shaped to manage the incline. In its own way, it is as much magical mountain folk as is its driver, Gonsk. In chapter 5, "The Load of Bamboo," the Chinese train is even more magical, an oriental dragon visiting the "real world." By the time Tiger fails to steal the Vindabona express he has come to see himself as a wizard, creating the magic that aids these trains personally. It is the process of anthropomorphizing the trains, accepted by Tiger, his wife and son, and by Katerina, that creates in part the air of fantasy. *Tiger's Railway* never spills over into the full immersive fantasy of *Thomas the Tank Engine*, but Mayne seems to play deliberately on our residual memories of this text.

Tiger's Railway is a satire on the absurdities of bureaucracy. Although it is set in the Soviet Union it is instantly recognizable to readers of the comic strip *Dilbert*. Tiger Malik is the superintendent of Bessar District railway in Eastern Europe. It is his role to ensure that the railways run to the standard expected in a culture in which the correct paperwork is more important than the actual servicing of the line. Malik becomes involved in a complex dance in which he creates mutually existing fantasy worlds, the simplest of which is the fantasy of the perfect record he creates for central headquarters.

In the absence of a line from Insk to Onsk, Tiger writes a timetable, calculated to meet the desires of headquarters. It is regular, it has exceptions for Sundays. It is "how timetables ought to look" (29). The central headquarters, like the Warden, have a view of the universe that is oughts and shoulds, ironizing the "fiction of desire" that Gary K. Wolfe has suggested is at the heart of fantasy—or, in my terms, the insistence within fantasy that *justice* is the storyable argument. The stationmaster Slivon's insistence that the truth be told, is, therefore, doomed; while Tiger Malik commits the sin of accepting that this is fantasy and choosing to humor the fantasists, Slivon commits the much greater one of *taking it seriously* and attempting to take as "real" what is the fantasy of desire.

Early on, while Tiger still has some grip on reality, we can see this fantasy of desire in the dissonance of humor. After Tiger puts together the fantasy timetable between Insk and Onsk, headquarters rewards him with some equipment. There is talk also of a tunnel, but this, it is suggested by the engineer Aleksy, would be awkward. There is nowhere to put a tunnel. " 'We'd have to bury it,' said Pauli. 'They keep quite well underground' " (30). The humor passes unnoticed by Slivon who can only write in his notebook that the trains are leaving on time, and that this must be stopped (30). For lies once begun, spiral, and Malik quickly finds that he must invent engines, with a full history of their own. Tiger ends up sending in coal bills for engines that he does not have because without the bills, he will reveal his duplicity (33). Slivon, the "sane" one, understands what is happening: "They are successfully running a railway line that does not exist. The money is going into their own pockets, and the coal into their own stove" (33).

Reality is beginning to slip and Headquarters—who presumably have targets of their own to meet, and paper trails to create—begin to connive with the fiction that Tiger has created. This awareness that they *are* creating fiction is sporadically reinforced by Andri, another engineer with a penchant for writing heroic poetry. At each engine theft, he threatens epic, hesitating only because "it is not always wise to say exactly how you are helping your District, your Area, your Headquarters, and your country" (57). But elsewhere Tiger and his coconspirators create their fictions as if they are a mimetic representation of reality. It is Slivon's notebook, ostensibly a record of actual events, that begins to seem like the fantasy world as Tiger talks into being his world of perfect schedules and beautiful trains.

As lies accumulate they often make it impossible to tell the truth. Secret messages cannot be passed on because they are secret (147). History—the invention of the steam engine and of powered flight—may be rewritten (154). Even more fantastical is the work of the heavy gang, girder-twirling women come to lay line (136). Thoroughly efficient, they construct the line from Insk to Onsk until they come face-to-face with a unbridged gorge (139–140). At which point Tiger, intending to turn around, discovers: "The fact was, that the work gang had only enough rail for about four miles of track, so as they went forward they picked it up from behind themselves and laid it in front" (141). All this has been disguised in the cheerleading, in the apparent *efficiency* of the gang, and in the assurance that despite appearances the state knows what it is doing. When Tiger goes on holiday, his most significant fear is that Slivon will try to put things right: conforming to *reality* would bring the entire artifice down.

But it is the conclusion to this novel that pushes it into the fantastic. In a high note of absurdity, headquarters acts on Slivon's reports. It promotes Tiger for his diligence, and Slivon for the quality of his reports, and then challenges the "superintendent" (now Slivon) to account for the missing trains, the invisible railways, and other discrepancies. Slivon finds himself demoted to stationmaster—the post he prefers—while Tiger keeps his promotion and Bessar the missing engines. With Malik's thefts absorbed and validated by the bureaucracy, we see his "fantasy" absorbed into the "real world" or frame world.

Because this novel is manifestly part of the tradition of the Absurd, it could be argued that I have incorrectly appropriated it. And given that I shall attempt to draw a line between liminal fantasy and "slipstream," the danger is that my choices at this borderland may seem arbitrary. But there is one—and, as far as I can tell, *only* one—indication that adjudging this text a fantasy is correct, and that my suggestion that Tiger has created a fantasy world that is later rejoined to the "real one" is a useful reading. In chapter 10, "Bessar the First," Slivon burns two pages of "coiled writing, crumpled them in his hands (he could feel the barbs sticking in because he hated to destroy what he had written) and dropped them into the stove. The paper burnt up, but the writing stayed twisted up in the ashes, just like wire" (146). We can see here the same twisting of metaphor that we saw in *Holes*: the barbs are metaphor written as if they were mimesis and through this construction are "realized."

What all the texts discussed so far share is an element of *knowingness*, in effect, a conspiracy between author and reader. One of the most extreme expressions of this technique is to be found in John Crowley's *Little, Big*

(1981), in which the intersection between the magical and the mundane is the center of the story. Of all the texts so far considered, this is the one that most seeks to make the fact of liminality storyable.

Little, Big is constructed around a conspiracy of knowingness, the sense that author and reader share a set of common values and cultural currency around which can be spun new stories. It is a true *mise-en-abyme*. But the reader is left to work this out for himself, based on what he *knows* of the fantastic, which is the primary world. The most visible and acknowledged elements of this *knowingness* are (1) the continual presence of Lewis Carroll's *Alice*, as manifested in Daily Alice Drinkwater; (2) some of the technical aspects of the world Crowley constructs; and (3) the construction of "in jokes" in the language, verbal exchanges, and structural metaphors of the novel, as William H. Ansley has mapped (2003). Where Carroll is not himself the referent, the world in which he lived—in which it was possible to believe that children had captured fairies—is the stage for the players.[6] The result reads somewhat like a Richard Dadd picture, not merely complex, but dense: the further in one delves, the greater the detail. The structure of the novel reinforces its central conceit: the world is constructed of concentric rings and the further in one moves the greater the level of Realness, manifested in that attention to detail, to the familiar and the intimate. This conceit helps to explain the main character Smoky's position within the novel (inasmuch as there *is* a main character once one leaves the first book): outside of Edgewood he is vague. On meeting Alice, he gains density, and within Edgewood he becomes a core.

In many of the other novels I have discussed in this chapter, the position of the reader vis-à-vis the protagonist is central to the construction of liminality. It is the disjunction between the interpretation and understanding of this protagonist and that of the reader that has created the moment of hesitation: we frequently wish to believe, but we are not sure in what. In *Little, Big*, however, Smoky Barnable is himself a figure of doubt and hesitation. He is positioned as the reader of the Tale told by the Drinkwaters and it is he who strives to believe without being terribly sure what it is he is expected to accept. This alteration has implications both for our perspective and for our own levels of belief. Smoky's skepticism provides an outlet for ours; it siphons it off, and leaves behind belief.

The construction of this relationship is complex. It begins with distancing us from Smoky as he himself is distanced from the world. Smoky's entrance onto the stage of the Tale is *announced*: "On a certain day in June 19——, a young man was making his way on foot northward from the great City to a town or place called Edgewood, that he had been told of but never visited" (3). Crowley delays our identification with Smoky Barnable. His name is introduced only in the second sentence. We shall not ride with Smoky as we would in the quest fantasy but instead shall be granted a form of omniscience, expressed in part by the maintenance of Smoky's distance from the Tale. Repeatedly, Smoky looks down upon both the landscape and the story:

> You could see a long way south from this height, he noticed. You could see the steeple at Meadowbrook, the roofs of Plainfield. Amid them the greening clumps of woods were misty; beyond the towns the woods thickened into the great Wild Wood on which Edgewood stood, which went on growing always deeper and thicker toward the South far father than the eye could see. (518)

Perspective here is a tool with which to construct the sense of the fantastic as potential: we (with Smoky) are placed at the center of a panorama. Yet all this tells us is what we *cannot* see: the fantasy grows densest at the edge of vision.

Smoky's position as the stranger entering the strange world implies that it is through him that we will understand the Tale. We follow his transition within an extended portal that includes a bench "where people could catch buses from Somewhere to Elsewhere" (3). Only toward the end of the novel do we realize that we have been traversing the portal itself, that we have not stepped through, and that this may be a portal constructed from multiple portals, interlocking and embedded. Graham Sleight, considering the hidden clues within *Little, Big* has suggested that "every instance of the capitalised *Somehow* in L.B. (and there are lots of them) marks or finesses a fantastic transition of some kind" (IAFA mailing list, 21 October 2003).

Smoky himself is a fantastical figure created out of the discards of the modern world. John Clute has described him as surrounded by a "nimbus of longing" (in discussion, 11 October 2003). His understanding of the modern world is not so much limited as filtered through wavy glass, so that his descriptions of the world make of us strangers within the familiar:

> [Smoky] worked in a wide, white room where the little sounds he and the others made would rise to the ceiling and descend again strangely altered . . . the names that looked up at him through the glass bar began to grow faces, ages, attitudes; the people he saw in buses and trains and candy stores . . . began to mingle through his flimsy pages; the Book began to seem like a great epic of the City's life. (7–8)

And further, in those last two lines, his understanding makes concrete fantasy out of metaphor.

Smoky's position within his own world is oblique and this obliqueness defamiliarizes us from our starting point. In quest and portal fantasies, the protagonist is usually very clear where she comes from and this shapes her consequent interpretations. Smoky, who accepts Alice's gift of a childhood because his is so indeterminate, is a liminal figure, and brings with him not contrast but diffusion. He is a place through which information passes, but it is not processed. When he unfolds the endpapers of the final edition of *The Architecture of Country Houses* (the great work with which the original generation were concerned and that is at once both a guide to country houses and to fairyland), "He lifted its edge, it rose up lightly like a moth's wing so old and fine it was, a shaft of sunlight pierced it and he glimpsed complex shapes studded with notions; he laid it down to look at it" (36). And the passage ends there. We do not find out what Smoky sees. At the very moment when the close attention to Smoky's thoughts and experiences are most revelatory, we are denied them.

Toward the end of the book, we comprehend Smoky's (and therefore our own) incomprehension. This accepting incomprehension is centered around the issue of "the Tale": a phrase repeated as chant, as silencer, and as mystifier throughout the novel. In a revealing moment, Smoky regards his love and prospective marriage as, "a collective act of will, which at the same time they concealed from each other: like make-believe, but different" (16). If this is not how the book functions, it describes in part our own conspiracy as readers and Smoky's position. He is engaged in making believe that the game played around him is as true as the other participants assert.

> "But why?" he said, delighted, in torment: why are you so sure?
> Because it's a Tale. And Tales Work Out.
> People in Tales *don't* know, always. But there they are. (17)

When Smoky, much later, acknowledges to Auberon that he has conducted his entire life pretending he believed, it leaves both of them wondering what would have happened had he ever confronted Violet with her belief. Smoky's doubt, his position outside the fantasy, confirms the duality of Auberon's doubt and simultaneous belief—and performs the same function for the reader. Once the doubt is expressed, once we can acknowledge that we, like Smoky, are not terribly sure where the fantasy is (or whether it is there at all), we can relax into the fantastic. The manifestations of the fantastic become more overt in the last one hundred and fifty pages of the novel, after Smoky and Auberon have had this moment of recognition.

In *Little, Big*, we have a novel that takes place entirely within the liminal space of the portal. Edgewood, the house that is five houses, has exits and entrances to other worlds. Some of its people—the sleeping Sophie for example—live entirely on the edge of these worlds. John Crowley suggests (in a 2003 interview with Alice Turner) that if correspondences are to be drawn with the Alice books, it is not Daily Alice who is *the* Alice, but Smoky: "Alice would not be Alice. It would be Smoky, because he doesn't make it to the other side of the mirror" (Ansley, no page numbers). Doorways are at once the subject matter, the nature of the people (Mrs. Underhill), and the place. But the mirror, the portal, is Edgewood itself. In *Little, Big*, Violet tries to summarize this:

no two doors to them are the same*
And beneath that she wrote:
*but the house is a door.

And with this she realizes that "what she had was a sort of precis of several chapters of the last edition of the Architecture, deprived of the billowing draperies of explanation" (107–108). Violet may find this summary no more help than ever, but the realization that the house is built to tell the Tale of the Architecture is one of the moments of recognition that Crowley deftly slips under our nose.

If Edgewood is the Architecture and the portal both, action comes from leaving Edgewood or from what is brought to Edgewood. Auberon and George, neither of whom truly believe, are both able to move through the boundaries of Edgewood and the mundane world. Auberon walks to the heart of the city park and from there into the forest that surrounds Edgewood. As the Tale concludes, Auberon finds he can see "from the gate the street stretched out, townhouse-lined for a block, then marching into the brown uptown distance between vague castles, old power, that scraped the sky" (521). It is as if there are certain positions vis-à-vis liminality that each character is permitted to take up. The less one believes, the more it is possible to navigate the borders. Those who believe most firmly are the ones most bound to place. The "proof" of this structure lies with Sylvie, Auberon's sometime girlfriend. It is only once she abandons her Destiny that she too can pass through the walls of the world.

The place itself and most of its permanent inhabitants—Daily Alice, Sophie, Violet, or Aunt Cloud—are curiously still. Edgewood is a place of magic rather than one in which magic is performed. Daily Alice in particular is forced to accept that her role is as an element of the magic rather than an actor within the Tale. Alice has a connection to the Powers but it is symbiotic, not interactive:

> she saw that she knew what advice she would get if she went to get it; it would only be made clear to her again what she already knew, what only grew dim or clouded now and again by daily life . . . if this were indeed a Tale, and she in it, then no gesture she or any of them could make was not part of it . . . if they fled the tale or struggled against it, well, that too was part of the Tale. (145)

Alice's acceptance of her destiny is curiously like that of the narrative of the quest fantasy. The difference is that Alice acknowledges her helplessness and embraces her passivity: "those tellers couldn't be blamed for anything told of in it, because in fact they neither spun nor told it really, but only knew how it would unfold in some way she never would; and that should satisfy her" (145). Alice believes the primary participants, those who *believe* in the narrative, are the least dynamic, a narrative that runs counter to the discourse of the quest. Instead of looking for the fantastic and for the end of the Tale, the central figures sit and wait for it. They may even conspire in creating the disbelief of the younger generation. As Aunt Cloud is dying, she considers that perhaps,

> they thought it had all Somehow slipped out of their reach. each generation slipping further from it as the inexorable slow fall of time was consumed to embers, the embers to ashes, the ashes to cold clinkers, each generation losing something of the last's close connection, and yet (Cloud knew it to be so) each generation in fact grew closer to it, and only ceased to search or bother themselves about it because they felt fewer and fewer distinctions between themselves and it. And, upon a time, there would be no searching at all for a way in, Because there they would be. (257)

Aunt Cloud sums up the difficulties of both Auberon and August. Their lack of closeness to the mysteries is what keeps them from vision. George and Sylvie, who come to simply accept their existence, are barely aware when they cross the portals. And the portal, as Graham Sleight has pointed out, is encapsulated in that capitalized Somehow. The Somehow is concrete, a moment and a transition (IAFA list, 21 October 2003).

It is those who are entirely magical (August, now Grandfather Trout) or the *apparently* entirely mundane (Smoky) who, by forming the links between fairy and the world respectively, balance the liminal position of Edgewood. Which is why neither Smoky nor Trout cross into the next circle and why, despite his desire to search for Auberon, Smoky never leaves Edgewood. Bosky argues that Smoky might indeed be *the* most liminal of characters "because he always travels and never arrives, and he likes it that way" (e-mail 10 March 2005). The resolution of liminality for the inhabitants of Edgewood closes the story of those figures who act as anchors, who are bound to the land and helps explain the ritualistic aspects of the marriage between Smoky and Alice. He is the corn king, a character made by Alice with "his entrances and exits, contribute (ing) a line of dialogue now and then" (96). He has no control over the Tale. It ends when Alice declares it over: "It's been long enough, hasn't it?" (449). Smoky, as little a part of the Tale as ever, while simultaneously crucial to it, wonders, "How did she always come up with these un-answers, these remarks struck off with such an air of logical consequence, that meant nothing or as good as nothing?" (449). Which also, of course, forms a description of the conversational structure of the book.

One of the fascinating "tricks" Crowley deploys is the cross-cut conversation. This, more than almost anything else, creates the sense of a world of chiffon veils, parting to reveal meaning and as quickly closing, catching each protagonist in a different layer. Meaning becomes fragmented and trapped between the veils. There can be no true understanding because each person understands a different world. For example, George and Smoky's "I'll tell thee everything I can" interchange (book 2: Brother North Wind's Secret, chapter 3, "Up on the Hill," 151) is only one of a number of conversations in which cross-cutting is used to embed the fantastic. Incomplete exchanges—in which participants finish each other's sentences—are used to convey both meaning and confusion. As with Harrison's use of the technique, it leaves open what each gains from the conversation. In these conversations, Smoky's doubt, his own position on the threshold of belief, makes a portal for Auberon into belief.

Smoky becomes the Tale through which the characters are gathered, in his paternal contribution, and in his dying: "The something that had begun to open in his heart opened further; it let in great draughts of evening air, and swifts and bees in the hollyhocks; it hurt beyond pain, and wouldn't close. It admitted Sophie and his daughters, and his son Auberon too, and many dead" (531). And now as well as Tale, Smoky becomes portal. As so often in *Little, Big*, and in the fantasy novels explored in this chapter, the metaphor is literalized by the events of the fantastic.

In *Little, Big*, a counterarc of thickening reinforces and yet denies the thinning that John Clute has argued is usually a central characteristic of the fantasy novel. *Little, Big* begins rather ambiguously. In chapters 1 through 4, there is no evidence of the thinned world. It is only with the inward turning of Old Law Farm in book 3 and the rise of the reawakened Frederick Barbarossa in book 5 that we start to get a sense of a world decaying. When Sophie counts the remaining fairies toward the end of the text, we acquire a similar sense of the fairy world as thinned. But while the rise of Frederick Barbarossa and the sealing in of Old Law Farm (an act that closes off one of the portals into fairy) is the background to the Tale, it is not the Tale. The Tale is one of a gathering in.

Some of the thickening of the tale is conveyed in the descriptions of people, of landscape, and of the nature of magic. The burial of places and plots within the larger sense of place forms a liminality of geography. There is the obvious signaling: the Drinkwater family live in Edgewood, Edgewood lives in a pentangle of five towns. But people as well as place are mapped. Alice comments of growing larger, "Astonishing, astonishing that there could be no end to growing bigger" (286); Smoky considers that each charm "would only be the occasion for further charms, and anyway they had never been a causal chain but a series of removes, Chinese boxes one inside the other, the further in you went the bigger it got" (530). This is a novel in which the growing, rather than the having grown, is the Matter. With each corner turned and each story within a story, Crowley creates new worlds (such as George's world behind the walls of the tenement buildings) that lurk as *possible* worlds from which new universes can emerge.

Elsewhere, the thickening is one of knowledge, sometimes at variance to the world of fairy, but still part of the thickening of the tale. August's ruin comes from his attraction to this form of (perhaps false) thickening, an attraction to knowledge that denies stories, that he can pull on, "over the mad muddle of his childhood, as one draws on a duster over a suit of clothes" (102). Yet his assumption of the power of knowledge leads him to make wrong choices and requests in the belief that they will *not* be granted, and this is also part of the Tale. August's Fall is as much a part of the Thickening of the Tale as Lilac's kidnapping.

One irony is that this Thickening of the Tale is not to everyone's taste. For Smoky, the end of the Tale should have been a physical ending. Instead, the promise of new duties and a new future is a "horrid idea of some vindictive spiritualist" (516). For Smoky, the end of liminality promises to reinforce the sense of exclusion from the Tale. A reader and observer of the Tale, he "only wanted it to continue, not to stop, to go on being muttered out endlessly by whatever powers they were who spun it, putting him to sleep with its half-heard anecdotes and still going on while he slept in his grave" (517).

And although the Tale thickens, the portal Thins, both through the increasing visibility of the Powers (Mrs. Underhill and Lilac play a greater role in the later books) and through the physical thinning of the house: "At its perimeters, rooms had to be closed off: a tower, an extravagance, a glass orangery whose barley-sugar panes lay scattered amid the flower-pots. The kitchen-garden's was the slowest downfall and the longest decadence" (226). Yet this decay is conveyed through an accumulation of imagery: "Though whitewash flaked from the pretty cut out the porch and the grape-leaves strangled up the ogee arches, though the steps sagged and the flagstone path disappeared under dock and dandelion muscling up through its crevices" (226). The intensity of layering—so like that of Hope Mirrlees—is a defiance of the end times. As the house decays, our eyes are directed to the growing and Thickening that is taking place in the cracks of the old Tale. The new and next Tale is pushing through.

This layering of language creates an awareness of the baroque and a world overtaken by metaphor. The correlations between names and urtexts is fundamental to the density of the work. Yet while this creates the knowingness of the liminal fantasy, it merely scratches the surface of the degree to which metaphor creates dissonance and distance within the text. One of the best examples of this distancing is relatively early: Smoky's relationship with the Land—made metaphorical—is also created fantastical. Unrolling the map of the Land, Smoky can see, "There was a mighty double red line that went near there, proud with exits and entrances; he couldn't walk along that. A thick blue line (on the model of the vascular system, Smoky imagined all the traffic flowing south to the city on the blue lines, away on the red) ran somewhat nearer, extending the corpuscular access to towns and townlets along the way" (4). The Land is not a metaphorical body, it *is* a body, and one that will have its veins and arteries severed by the megalomania of the revived Emperor Barbarossa in the closing days of the Tale and of the book.

Liminal Fantasy and the Tension of the Slipstream

In the realms of liminal fantasy, we begin to approach another liminal space, the no-man's land in which exist (1) slipstream fiction (a term invented by

Bruce Sterling to refer to work that feels like science fiction but isn't marketed as such), and (2) a recent group of works that some people have designated the *interstitial* (to describe works of all kinds that mix genres; see the Web site of the Interstitial Arts Foundation).

Pinning these works down is rather difficult, but the first category includes the works of magic realists (who, I have already argued, should be considered as creating immersive fantasies) and such English-language writers as Jeanette Winterson, Andrew Greig, and Angela Carter. The second category seems to sweep up so many works it is hard to know where to begin. Heinz Feinkel regards his fictionalized biography as interstitial. Delia Sherman and Ellen Kushner describe their historical, romance fantasy *The Fall of the Kings* (2002) as interstitial. From my perspective, the latter book seems simply to reflect what most fantasy critics acknowledge: that fantasy has neither plot nor subject matter of its own and always borrows from other genres. *The Fall of the Kings* from this perspective is less interstitial than quintessential.

Nevertheless, there exist works by people who are self-identified as at least emerging from the worlds of fantasy who have been marketed as mainstream, and whose recent works I would describe as liminal fantasy but who would provide a test case for whether this term can be used interchangeably with "slipstream" or "interstitial." I believe it cannot: I believe that liminal is firmly within the genre that is called fantasy, while the other terms, slipstream and interstitial, are actually describing something else. Two works that contribute to this understanding are Christopher Priest's *The Separation* (2001) and Peter Straub's *lost boy lost girl* (2003), both of which could be claimed for the slipstream, but both of which seem to me to demand the reading codes of the fantastic, even while they stretch those codes. First, however, we need to consider the slipstream.

Slipstream is usually understood as hovering on the edge of the codes of science fiction and fantasy, combining them with the codes of the mimetic world to produce something else. The more I read of slipstream fiction, and of that kind of fantasy that relies on Todorov's hesitation—alongside "thrillers" written by sf writers—the less convincing this visualization, of an "edge place," seems to be. To take the relationship of thrillers to science fiction as an example, Gary K. Wolfe has pointed out that the emotional drive of the two genres is different ("Evaporating Genre"). To this we might add that the thriller almost always has an "against-time" narrative, while science fiction accepts that science can proceed no faster than it can work, no matter what the imperative. The result is that while each may use the wrapping of the other, readers can frequently see through the charade to underlying

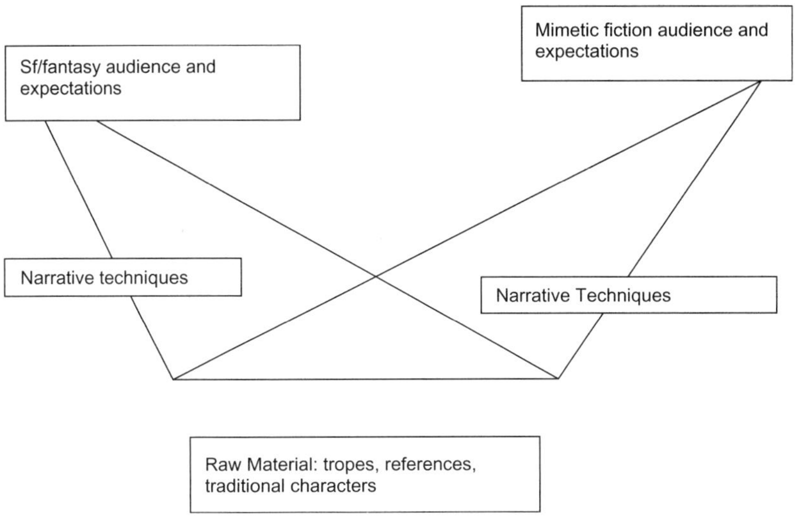

FIGURE 1. Genre = codes + narrative techniques + audience expectation

codes and know that it is not they who are being spoken to. Michael Crichton is a good example. His "futuristic thrillers" leave many sf readers ranting. Any idea that the two genres can "meet in the middle," can merge and provide something satisfactory to both groups may be a red herring that obscures an understanding of what genre *is*. This idea has profound consequences for this chapter, which has been all about manipulating both boundaries and liminal spaces.

A much better way of understanding the dynamic between the liminal fantasies and novels of the slipstream or the interstitial is to revisit the dialectical model of genre. In this model, *genre is the dialectical space between author intention and reader expectation*. What this means is that one can have a shared set of codes, the use of which alters according to who is being addressed. Figure 1 attempts to represent this dialectical space.

Andrew M. Butler has suggested the terms *convergence* and *emergence* for this envisioning, and these terms, embracing as they do a sense of movement toward and away from the reader, the sense of multiple valences, seem appropriate (discussion, ICFA, 23 March 2003). What figure 1 also does is to explain why some texts may be peculiarly open to multiple communities. One could construct a diagram that would look a lot like a Star of Texas in which *Star Trek* appeared in the middle, with a set of genre codes drawn from enough genres that they can be read from a range of audience positions. But figure 1 seems enough to illustrate what I'm trying to say: that when we consider liminal fantasy, we are not looking at something that is meant to bridge the gap between fantasy and mimesis, but a form of fiction that uses the expectations of the genre readers to which the text speaks in order to generate latency, constructed from the elements of equipoise and irony that I have discussed.

Peter Straub's *lost boy lost girl* and Christopher Priest's *The Separation* are particularly interesting *because* they draw attention to this issue by (I think) using more than one set of raw material and codes, deploying a range of genre-identified narrative techniques, and deliberately setting up their work to speak to more than one audience in a range of voices. Like Crowley, they work at the extremes of *knowingness*, but their multiplicity of codes allow them to construct narratives that contain and manipulate the polysemic uncertainties that are central to the liminal fantasy. They too are engaged in making liminality itself into story.

Peter Straub's *lost boy lost girl* is a murder mystery or horror novel in which Timothy Underhill's sister-in-law commits suicide and his nephew goes missing. The narrative is in part about a serial killer, but it is also a ghost fantasy in which the nephew is sucked into another world by the ghost of a murder/abuse victim. At issue is whether this book can be read as horror, as mimesis, or as both; the answers lie in the plotting, the actual structures of the novel, and the construction of the novel's emotional dynamic and diction.

The trick to the construction of *lost boy lost girl* is that the plot uses the juxtapositions of irony, while the construction of each individual paragraph is heavy with equipoise. The irony that is embedded in the plot plays very clearly on the reader's understanding of how horror works. So, for example, Straub's use of time belongs, in genre terms, less to fantasy than to the thriller or horror novel: time here is something that is running out, that is raced against. In *lost boy lost girl*, Timothy Underhill's nephew has gone missing; the story relates the events leading up to this, the events afterward, and also the events that take place while he is missing. In this book, time is an indicator of meaning. *When* things happened can be used by the reader to work out *whether* they happened.

Lost boy lost girl begins with the death by suicide of Timothy's sister-in-law. Timothy attends the funeral, attempts to comfort the brother he dislikes, and invites his nephew to visit him in New York. A few days after he returns to New York, his nephew Mark disappears. Timothy returns to try to find him and discovers that there is a serial killer in the neighborhood, and that his sister-in-law Nancy was the cousin of another serial killer, one whose house is very nearby and with which Mark was, purportedly, fascinated.

Lost boy lost girl can be read as a conventional horror story. There are at least two ghostly manifestations: Lily, the daughter of the earlier serial killer, and Lucy, the young woman who entraps Mark. There may even be a third: if Mark is dead, he may have sent Tim a posthumous e-mail. Or, neither Lucy or Mark may be ghosts; they may simply have eloped, either into the world, or into a fantastic otherworld—the second possibility taking us back to the questions we may have about Lucy's corporeality.

Part of the confusion centers around the presence of the third e-mail, which is part of the same narrative as Mark's presumed death. Tim, determined to believe his nephew is alive, regards the e-mails as evidence of his survival. Read in one way, and specifically read through the understanding of Timothy, Mark is not a victim of the current serial killer, but has instead slipped through the dimensions to join Lucy, apparently the now "grown up" daughter of the earlier killer.

But this is to assume that Tim is a reliable narrator of the tale, when Tim is not initially presented as the narrator at all. Most of the story, apart from Tim's journal entries and chapter 15, is told strictly in the third person and narrates scenes at which Tim is not present. At least initially, this style allows the reader to separate what Tim seems to know from what we know to be the real "hidden history" of Mark and his family. Nancy watching the little girl ghost, Mark exploring the "haunted" house, the red van that trails Mark—each of these is told as an apparent flashback, a return to a world that Tim has not seen.

But both Tim's point of view and the structure of the novel cast doubt upon this straightforward reading. If the scenes that play before our eyes are flashbacks, it is peculiar that we see them after Tim has heard about them. This point is easy to miss because it is so reminiscent of the narrative style of the police procedural that we forget the implications of the form: the officer conjectures, and we segue into, not the past, but a *constructed narrative* of the past. Straub plays on this: he is presenting us not with truth, but with *verisimilitude*, aware that this construction is not native to the horror genre. The construction of the past in the police procedural manipulates the belief in reason. The tone of the horror tale continually demands we reject reason and surrender to emotion. Yet the combination of the two generates two possible readings for the novel, one fantastical, one reasoned. If we use each to question the other, the readings become yet more complex. The speed with which the "solution" to the crime is wrapped up contains none of the tension or deliberateness of the crime novel: once an outside investigator, Tom Passmore, the world's greatest detective, establishes the correct thread to pull, the whole unravels. This technique (which Straub has used in many of his Millhaven novels) offers a mere sketch at genre.

Straub creates a text in which the third-person narration is not synonymous with creating a third-person omniscient position for the reader. We are not watching events unroll in omniscient flashback; instead we are (or may be) reading a narrative of events constructed by Tim, the novelist. The reader position may be far less close to the action than we imagined, far more intimate with the narrator. The flashbacks, told from that external, watching vantage point, offer a spurious intimacy to the reader. They are written, as Straub has argued, with "the solidity and immediate familiarity of *Middlemarch*" ("Horror's House" 66). The imagined past becomes more "real" by virtue of this intimacy than does the first-person present narrative of Timothy. Straub has used reader positioning to create the illusion of veracity.

We are told repeatedly, in a number of different ways, that Tim writes his journal as if it were fiction. We are also told by Tim that Mark has expressed a desire to have a life more congruent with fiction. The result is that the relatively straightforward language of the novel, which only occasionally dallies with the indications of horror—when Straub describes the Kalendar house, or the descriptions of the Dark Man who "haunts" the park—hides the possibility that the whole, as it is constructed by the primary narrator, is a fantasy in which the secondary narrator, Mark, may actually be a narrative construct. Much of what we learn of Mark is through Tim and is essentially uncorroborated. This subjectiveness is clearest when we examine Tim's affection for Mark. Tim's relationship with his nephew may be almost entirely a construction of his own mind, and one that is to be constructed *in the future*. He bases his "closeness" on a relationship that he had planned—more e-mails, some visits—not on anything that has happened. The evidence in fact is that he has been a rather neglectful uncle. Seen in this way, Tim's "construction" of the reasons behind Nancy's suicide may be a guilt-stricken displacement of the sense that he had neglected the child of the brother he dislikes, refused involvement where such might have "saved" that child.

There are further clues to Tim's construction of the narrative. The repeated reappearance of chocolate chip cookies as a symbol of safety, first on the airplane, then in Mark's tale; or the actor from *Family Ties*, who sat in Tim's seat on a previous flight and who is mentioned as starring in the film that Tim sees being shot from his hotel window (his actual name,

Michael Gross, is never mentioned by anyone, even though it's Tim who can't remember it). The constructed narrative of the past has the effect of assembling a world that feels like interlocked boxes, one in which we are aware of a wrongness that we displace onto the supernatural because that is what we *expect* from the plot as it is presented to us. What we think we know of events in novels *like* this skews our perception of what is actually narrated. This expectation is reinforced by our position behind the eyes of Timothy, and Timothy's understanding of the world—which is, as he has admitted to his friend Maggie Lah, inherently fictionalized: "After reading a section of an early journal of mine, Maggie Lah said, 'You write your journal like it was fiction.' I said, 'What makes you think it isn't?'" Mark's e-mail similarly challenges the reader to recognize that we are within a text: "do u ever feel like u r in 1 of your own books?" (171).

Gary K. Wolfe, reading this section, suggested that there is "an interesting interpenetration of material fantasy—that is, the sort that makes the narrative genuinely fantastic—and moral fantasy, or that which is constructed out of the desires and anxieties of one of the characters" (in conversation, April 2005). Both Straub and Priest make extensive use of this technique—important in terms of my argument that these books are neither slipstream nor interstitial, because elsewhere Wolfe has suggested that the central and defining characteristic is that fantasy is a literature of desire. I have suggested that fantasy seeks to make the universe understandable in moral terms. Both constructions would place these novels, not at the edge of genre, but at its heart: in *lost boy lost girl*, the desires of Tim for his nephew to be alive, and the desires of the reader for genre fulfillment.

By the novel midpoint, Tim's explanation of events has become increasingly supernatural; ironically it is this, rather than close reading, that encourages the reader to doubt his veracity and our understanding. Timothy's arguments for a supernatural explanation serve mainly to highlight the "rational" evidence. Straub forces the reader to shift positions and to interpret the world and the supernatural within the world, differently from Timothy. From page 194 on, we are being asked to decide for ourselves how much is supernatural and how much is delusion, and to what extent we will look for "supernatural literality" (Straub, "Horror's House" 66). But the choices are multiple. In part the narrative structure feeds this: how much of what we see, do we "see" and how much of it is Tim's understanding or desire? How much of this is Mark's delusion? How much Ronnie's (the serial killer) even? Do people see Ronnie or do they see Kalendar (the first of the killers)? Where are the e-mails from? Each time we make a decision for the supernatural or for the mundane, we turn the corner into a new novel, and whether it is a fantasy or not, is essentially *up to us, the readers.* The result is a perpetually poised liminality in which the reader and the narrator remain estranged from each other.

While the desires of genre could suggest a range of endings, these are repeatedly refused. If this is a detective novel, Mark could be found alive, or found dead and the murderer discovered. If this is horror, the ghost would really exist, and Mark killed or subsumed by that power. Not only are neither of these resolutions truly "proved," but both would leave Tim with an ending, and Tim would prefer a possibility. To return to figure 1, if what was happening was the mixing of genres to create something new, something interstitial, the vision might be more of tectonic plates, merging to create a magma of new expectations and a new genre. The reading would be monosemic; there would be a *correct* reading that might validate or invalidate Tim's understanding of events. Instead, there is a strong sense that all the readings of this novel should be held both simultaneously and *distinctly.*

So far I have discussed how this ambiguity is built into the plot. In addition to these very obvious signals that the narrative is in fact a story told by Tim, the ways in which Tim writes himself also clues us to genre. Tim sees himself as a character in a genre novel and his internal narrative is structured appropriately. Tim sees his world in terms of destiny. Consider this extract from the beginning of the novel when he is trying to work out how he will approach writing the book for a chamber opera about the serial killer, Dr. Herman Mudgett:

> He knew when he had first begun to see his own access into it. The moment had been the result of various unrelated objects producing a small but vital electrical pulse when accidentally joined together. He had gone out to loaf through the St Mark's bookstore and pick up a cup of coffee at Starbucks, and the first element of his inspiration had been an odd slogan stencilled atop a high, rounded Spring Street gutter passed on his eastward trek. The stencil had just been applied, and the ink glistened. It consisted of four words, all lower case: *lost boy lost girl.* Downtown indie-rock bands some-times advertised themselves by stencilling their names on sidewalks. . . . Whatever it was, he liked the phrase and hoped he would remember to notice where it might crop up again. (9–10)

The paragraph can of course be seen as simply a description of the inspirational process, and it is this I mean when I suggest that the style is essentially mimetic. But to the reader of genre, buried in Straub's words are the formulations of genre. The emphasis on the moment of recognition, of the sense of destiny. Its occurrence at the end of a quest (if only for coffee), and its revelation in cryptic prophecy, applied *just in time* for the protagonist hero to see it, the ink "glistening" with promise and portent. The image is resonant of the writing on the wall that condemned Nebuchanezzer. Later "the slogan had disappeared, as though the fresh ink has melted into the smooth concrete of the curb. *Impossible*, he thought, *I'm on the wrong corner*. It was not the wrong corner, he knew, but for three blocks he kept looking at the curb, and abandoned the project only when he began to feel foolish" (10–11). The slogan is meant for him, is, in a sense, the portal into fantasy should the reader wish to take it—doubly significant because the narrative that will be spun around Mark creates the possibility of a portal as salvation from a particularly nasty reality.

Within the paragraph, Straub writes destiny by linking the seemingly incidental. Jack Cohen, the sf critic and scientist, once told an audience that coincidence would be proof that God did not exist, as everything in God's world would be unique. Tim's understanding of every occurrence in his life as significant is an acceptance of destinarianism even while he might regard himself as rational. Thus, when a real killing becomes connected to him, he switches the application of the prophecy rather than abandoning it: his writing of Mark can be seen as the attempt to fit his life into this apparent foreordained structure.

The clue to who is telling what tale is similarly in the recognition of genre style. Although almost all of the book is told in the third person, this telling is handled very differently from section to section. The sections on Mark, and on his mother, are told intimately, with a deep attention to the diction of the story. The impression is much more of a tale told. We can see this first in the way Straub repeats words. Chapter 7 begins with a factual statement, "Mark's obsession had begun quietly and unobtrusively, as simple curiosity, with no hint of the urgency it would quickly acquire." But when the idea and phrases are repeated the tone changes, conjuring the "in the beginning" of the told tale:

> On the day Mark's obsession began, he had pushed himself past the entrance to the alley, rolled up Michigan Street, and given the board a good kick so that he could do the corner in style. . . . Mark swung around the corner in exemplary style. Then it took place, the transforming event. Mark saw something he had never really, never quite *taken in* before, although it had undoubtedly been in its present location through all the years he had been living around the corner. It

was a little house, nondescript in every way, except for the lifeless, almost hollowed-out look of a building that had long stood empty. (56)

So we have (a) the building that was never seen before, (b) the insignificant building that holds potential, and (c) the haunted house. Mark knows he must have seen it, but "until now, the building had receded into the unremarkable back-ground. He found this so extraordinary that he stepped backward off his board, pushed sharply down on its tail, and booted it up off the street. For once this stunt worked exactly as it was supposed to" (57).

The house transitions in front of our eyes as it moves from point *a* to point *c*. Its previous absence conjures the presence of all the magical shops and buildings that are only there once. It also becomes the locale of the portal, the place of transition itself. John Clute, discussing Elizabeth Hand's work on convention panels, has described a portal achieved as a kind of love death, and in the way in which Peter Straub handles the role of the house—a house that has held the machines and works of torture—and Tim's relationship to it, the phrase seems apt here. The descriptions of the house, and later what is found there, are *loving*.

To return to the quotation, the fabulous is in both the house and the achievement of the stunt, but it is also in the way in which the external view of Mark is coupled with his inner landscape. It is as if we are looking at him with X-ray goggles. We see both skin and the emotional bones. The genre that I most associate with this style is the True Crime novel. If we hold in our minds the diction of *In Cold Blood*, we can recognize immediately that Mark's narrative is not Mark's inner voice. The number of Mark sections that start with a temporal placement ("On the day . . .") or a sense of recognition ("By speaking when he knew he should have remained silent . . .") might alert us to the omniscience of "faction." It is probably helpful to know at this point that Tim's original topic, Herman Mudgett, really does exist. We may have moved from the fictionalizing of a real person within a fictional text, to the fictionalizing of a fictional person within a fictional text with that person, Mark, created twice: once by Straub and once by Tim, who pretends to an impossible intimacy with the motivations and inner thoughts of his nephew (itself characteristic of the true crime genre).

Such play with intimacy, with evidence, and the creation of complex layers of fiction similarly typifies Christopher Priest's *The Separation*, an alternative history in which two brothers leave behind them different memories and experiences of World War II. Jack Sawyer is a pilot who is commanded to serve with Churchill for a time, only to suspect he is serving a body double. Joe Sawyer is a conscientious objector. The first helps win the war; the second helps to end it, but not in the same universe. Only one of them can survive and leave behind a world. Here the issues of genre are a little different.

Priest plays both to the audience of fantasy and to a known readership of World War II history (and World War II alternate history) buffs. The effectiveness with which Priest deploys the conventions of evidence and reliability in True War novels to construct the veracity of both Jack and Joe's narration of the world is tied in with the determination of the novel to remain open to multiple interpretations that embrace both clear-cut alternate history, and the possibility of something rather more fantastical. At stake in any reading of *The Separation* is, as with *lost boy lost girl*, the nature and reliability of subjective reality.

The story is framed by the writer Stuart Gratton. Gratton has published a book on people's memories of 10 May 1941, the day the war ended in the world of the book. And he has discovered in it a small mystery: J. L. Sawyer, who was a lieutenant in the RAF (who met Churchill) but who also appears to be a conscientious objector—the issue of twinning, and doubling, runs through the book. Two breakthroughs are achieved: the first when he receives the memoirs of J. L. Sawyer from his daughter, Angela Chipperton, from which we realize that there are two brothers, Jack and Joe; the second when he receives letters from a Sam Levy, a navigator on J. L. Sawyer's crew.

By the end of the book, one of the realizations we *may* have had is that Angela Chipperton and Stuart Gratton are both descended from the twins, but that only one of them can actually exist in the world. It becomes clear that what happens to each of the twins is contingent on what happens to the other. Only one of the two Sawyer boys can survive, Jack Sawyer in a world like ours, where Churchill refuses to make a separate peace with the Nazis and retains control of Parliament; or Joe Sawyer, in a world in which the Red Cross negotiate a peace behind Churchill's back in 1941 and release Germany to conquer the Soviet Union. Two possibilities of time are existing side by side. However, to take this at face value is to ignore the degree to which, like Tim in *lost boy lost girl*, Stuart is engaged in constructing a story. True War writing, like True Crime, constructs intimacy to support interpretation.

Jack's story is communicated as memoir, and it is his narrative that most accords with ours. But this first-person narrative, in its creation of collusion between the reader and the narrator, is then undercut by the first part of Joe's story, which is reconstructed from scraps in the official histories, public records documents, and family letters (179–216). This juxtaposition of sources is important because in the True War genre, first-person reminiscence is generally accorded much greater reliability than it is by university-trained historians. At the same time, the marginalia of "official documents" form the only kind of third-person evidence that the True War genre will accept as competition (a form of conspiracy theory). It is a curious tension that holds the incidental at one end of the spectrum and the personal narrative at the other as the highest forms of truth, while frequently discarding much of the reportage, and mainline history as somehow tainted by its centrality.

It is in the interstices of this tension that Priest sites his tale and generates both the irony of dissonance—the distinctions between known history and the fantastic possibilities—and the equipoise of the possibility that is Joe's future. However, knowingness here rests on twin pillars of understanding: (1) of the war and how True War fiction functions, and (2) of the degree to which the fantastic believes that anything sufficiently narrated or found might be true. The assembling of Joe's history from scraps, because it is thus an incidental history, functions not just to create Joe in the reader's eye, but to support Joe's understanding of history, (despite its variance from our own knowledge and even when it might become clear to a nongenre reader that Joe is unstable). Joe's is a hidden history—in fantasy terms, "found" history—and therefore infinitely more intriguing than that of his brother.

The Separation is more uneven in its tension than is *lost boy lost girl*. Those multiple valences in figure 1 are pointed at potentially incompatible audiences. The instability of Joe is communicated in ways that are more understandable—I suspect—to the fantasy reader, than to the True War reader. The True War reader will be interested in how an alternate world works out. The fantasy reader is concerned as to whether it really *is* an alternate world. Our clues are mostly in Joe's behavior. It is unclear whether the brothers actually meet; however, whereas Jack always understands these meetings as real, Joe denies their reality and with them, in one sense, Jack's reality (a pattern he continues in his refusal to clarify the situation when he is mistaken for Jack).[7] It is as if Jack exists primarily in his relationship to Joe's anxieties and concerns; becomes Joe's counterbalance and foil, the thing against which Joe contrasts himself. Joe, on the other hand, believes in a world centered on him.

Joe continually analyzes both past and future. He sees too many possibilities, and in the end, can only choose between them by focusing on the future as a very personal thing. His pacifism is solipsistic: he is aware of what is happening in Germany, he understands that a Germany free of the war with Britain will almost certainly attack the U.S.S.R., but when Joe says he desires peace, it is *his* peace he desires. It is not simply that Joe is an absolute pacifist: absolute pacifists do not negotiate their peace at the expense of someone else's. There is something awry here.

Denying the reality *of* Jack leads easily to refusing that reality of which Jack is a part. Joe's solipsism is in direct contradiction to the polysemy of the novel, and it is in the interstices this creates that the element of the fantastic enters the text. As we move further away from the "real" world of Jack as we know it, we move further into a world that Joe may have created, not in the usual alternative history sense of a choice taken or not taken, but as a supernatural act. Like Tim, he may have literally *written* his alternate world, but in this case may (or may not) have brought this possibility to life. This alternate world we are in is one conjured by fantasy (in all senses of that word) rather than by physics. But this is a strategy that does not deny the nongenre reading strategy; indeed, it actively builds upon and within it. E. H. Gombrich wrote of the figure-ground puzzle: "What is interesting is not so much the flexibility of our interpretations as their exclusiveness. It is easy to see the bull's-eye as a head facing us, as a button, or as a letter. What is difficult—indeed impossible—is to see all these things at the same time" (198). Yet this is precisely what Priest asks of us. *The Separation* is at its most effective if the reader can hold more than one reading of the text in his head.

This latency, this equipoise, is built within the plot by the ironies of the relationship between Jack and Joe, but, as with *lost boy lost girl*, it is also marked in the writing of certain passages. Once Joe's life is put together through fragments, Priest allows us into Joe's head. This is a much more intimate position than was permitted with Jack, for whom we were simply audience, and it takes us right back to the form of irony that we first saw in Joan Aiken's "Yes, But Today is Tuesday." We sit in Joe's head, we see what he sees. But our understanding of it is very different.

Joe's confrontation with himself, dressed in RAF uniform, in a mirror (226–227), is a key moment that plays with the multiple ways of reading the text and the dissonance created by the reader's position as contrasted to the narrative position. The reader registers it as a reflection, but Joe, even when he becomes aware that there is a mirror there, insists on understanding the incident as a more spiritual connection with Jack. If we accept this, we are forced into fantasy, into a world where twinning is meaningful, and shapes how we read the next meeting/delusion:

My heart was drumming. I looked around: daylight was glancing in through the open hatch, and beyond the broad white spread of the wing I could see the backs of the men I had been flying with, as they walked towards the low buildings a couple of hundred yards across the apron. The co-pilot was following them. Behind me was the confined compartment of the plane: the utilitarian metal floor littered with discarded papers, cigarette ends, pieces of bread-crust dropped from sandwiches. It was plausibly real and actual, but I was gripped by the conviction that I was trapped in another lucid imagining. (Joe, 235)

Note the emphasis both on factual description, coupled with the intensification of emotion (the focus on the inner landscape, if you will) and the way in which, at the end, the readers are offered a way out. If they want to reject the idea that this could be fantasy, in which Joe is living Jack's life, they can choose to believe that this is just delusion.

Overall, this leaves readers with several options, each of which changes the generic direction of the novel. If Joe is genuinely swapping places with Jack, we are in a fantasy. If he is delusional, then there may be no fantasy at all; we are in our world and this Joe died in an air raid. But there is a third possibility that takes us back to Todorov's hesitation and to liminality: that the book ends at the moment of choice, when Joe can decide for us how to read the text he has written.

In these two books we can see that the ideological determinism of liminal fantasy is essentially polysemic. While the quest fantasy requires the closed view of the club narrative, the success of the liminal fantasy consists of, or invites, the reader to accept truth behind multiple and competing narratives while refusing to explain which truth it is we should discover.

In both cases, one could make an argument that the books are less written *within* genre, than are written *about* it, and both books demand that the reader take onboard more than one set of genre codes if they are to be fully appreciated. The liminality is maintained through both equipoise and through irony, the manipulation of different kinds of genres in ways that present as full "generic" reading, yet rest their genreness precisely on that refusal. In this they differ from, say, a novel like David Mitchell's *Cloud Atlas*, which, while it includes short sf passages, resolves itself by pointing to an inner, and more true, frame story that precludes an overall genre understanding. Specifically, it resolves. The two books I have looked at here depend on the refusal of resolution. The liminal fantasy, generally, can be typified as the novel of refusal.

We can see that this difference is consistent by considering a range of slipstream novels. Liminal fantasy is supported by buttresses of genre expectation: the fantastic exists because of the weight of expectation leaning against that space where the fantastic should be. These fantasies depend for the maintenance of their liminality on the knowingness of their readers, and, specifically, the degree to which their readers are versed in the codes of the fantastic. Without an understanding of the traditions of twinning, doubling, and of the role of delusion in the fantastic, Joe's narrative can only be understood in terms of true or false. Slipstream material also depends on knowingness, but, if we think back to figure 1, the direction of that knowingness points elsewhere. What is *known* are the codes of mainstream fiction, and it is these that support the assumption of metaphor in the context of the fantastical elements of the text.

When the fantastic is incorporated into this, it is frequently signposted, as in the dream sequences of Jeanette Winterson's *Oranges Are Not the Only Fruit* (1990); deployed as metaphor, as in Andrew Greig's *When They Lay Bare* (1999); or is used to discuss something quite other than the nature of the fantastic or the possibilities of the fantasy realized, as in the metafictive *Cloud Atlas* (2004) by David Mitchell. In this next section, it is important to be aware that all the books I discuss are books I like. My argument, however, is that the narrative strategies with which they engage—at the level of both plot and rhetoric—position the reader differently to the reader of the liminal fantasy; although they frequently deploy the tropes of fantasy (or science fiction), they do so with a quite different intention, and with an awareness of a different set of reader expectations.[8] In other words, they are not talking to *me*.

Cloud Atlas is structured in six parts and through six voices: the life of a lawyer missionary from San Francisco, moving through the New Zealand islands in search of the beneficiary to a will; a disgraced young musician in Belgium between the World Wars (easily the best realized of the sections); a young Pacific Islander from the far future; a "fabricant" from the islander's past but our future; a journalist in the 1970s; and a rather dilapidated publisher with a success on his hands and trapped in a convalescent home. All but the journalist's section is told in the first person, and this is the primary clue to what is going on.

Although Mitchell has used many of the tropes of genre, he is using them not to write within genre, but to write about it. Each of the sections contains its own set of genre codes: the first for example, the narrative of Ewing, the lawyer in New Zealand, references both Melville and Conrad. The journalist's section is built around what should probably be called the soft-boiled detective model: V. I. Warshawski rather than Philip Marlowe. Mitchell is writing about fiction and the construction of fiction: the hints of Conrad in the opening section are a clue to at least one understanding of the novel, which is a trip into the heart of darkness at the center of fiction writing. Most of these sections are not, fictively, "real." As we move through the book, we realize that it is an onion. At the heart of the book lies Cavendish, the publisher, who reads a manuscript about a journalist detective, Luisa Rey, who in turn reads the letters of Robert Frobisher, the composer, who in turn has discovered the memoirs of the lawyer, Ewing. In the other direction, Zakary, the Pacific Islander, and Sonmi, the fabricant, lie in the future in which Luisa Ewing prevents environmental disaster.

The use of the first person for all but Luisa Ewing's tale becomes a technical master stroke that controls the degree of distance the reader is asked to maintain from each character and from each microfiction. This control is particularly noticeable in those sections set in contexts least familiar to the reader, because it breaks the established ground rules for modern science fiction, reducing rather than heightening the degree of immersion in the created world.

The choice of the first-person narrative in fantasy and science fiction offers two choices. One tends to take us to the political and predictive structures of the portal-quest fantasies. The other takes us toward the immersive fantasy with its relatively greater freedom from narrative imprisonment (but deploys greater duplicity in the "objectivity" of cultural observation it deploys). Both methods hold to the idea of a story as "told." In the first strategy, the first-person narrator talks to the reader as if to a stranger, occasionally to a reader positioned as "posterity," but almost always to the reader as abstract. This permits a high level of exposition as the reader is assumed to be ignorant in all things.

In the second strategy—most commonly used in hard-boiled detective novels—the protagonist still talks to an abstract reader, but that reader is positioned as *knowing*. The first-person narrative creates a cozy objectivity, allowing much detail to be either elided or dropped in as material we all know but nonetheless observed in passing.

The overriding characteristic of the liminal fantasies is latency: the sense of the fantastic is encoded in refusal, a denial of interpretation. All the texts discussed so far—even *Lud-in-the-Mist*—remain ambiguous in some way not only until the end, but through and beyond the end. In contrast, all of the slipstream fantasies seem determined to tell us what to think. So, for example, in *Life of Pi* (2002), the narrator insists on the truth of his experience—in particular the talking tiger—and provides us with a decision to make in which we are pressured to accept the fantastic. The studied formalism of Indian English works well to reinforce the hermetic nature of the club story (reconstructed here by a speaker in a hospital bed with a very attentive audience of insurance agents). Andrew Greig's *When They Lay Bare*—a tale of lost heirs and ancient adultery structured around the "telling" of possibly magical story plates—concludes with a solution to the mystery that both reduces the fantasy and feels like an anticlimax. By the time the heroine leaves, her ambiguity has been dissolved. In the most severe example of this refusal to allow the reader to speculate, Jonathan Carroll's *The Marriage of Sticks* forces us into accepting the conclusions that the narrator states: that she is an egotist and that the metaphor of emotional vampirism has been translated into a real and fantastical creature.

Both liminal and slipstream writers want to control their readers, but the liminal fantasists are aiming at polysemic readings. The tendency of the slipstream writers to want to narrow their audience's interpretative strategies also explains the continual insistence of signposting. Liminal fantasies leave the fantastic in doubt in part because they deliberately elide the ways in which the fantastic and the mundane are written, frequently reserving the most baroque language for the mundane and the mimetic. They *play* with our expectations. The slipstream writers prefer that we remain aware of the distinction between the real and the not real. Although they are not writing portal fantasies in the way I have discussed elsewhere, the books are studded with moments in which we slide into fantasy. In Andrew Greig's *When They Lay Bare* the reading of the plates is set apart from the main narrative, signposted as part fantasy but possible metaphor. Jeanette Winterson, in *Oranges are Not the Only Fruit*, is even more didactic: her fables are introduced at the beginning of chapters. They explain the meaning of what we will read next, so that "Ruth" (the title itself an indicator) begins with a tale of education, adolescence, and family ties that is replicated in the tale of the child who returns to the home, changed, but still its product. Winterson uses the same technique in *The Powerbook* (2000); the use of metaphoric tales, or fables, holds open the promise of polysemy: "You can change the story. You are the story" (288). But it is a false promise: "Your Body is my Book of Hours / Open it. Read it. This is the true history of the world" (289).

The use of fables does not have to constrict meaning. Rarely discussed as a slipstream writer—and terming herself a fabulist—Suniti Namjoshi is, like the liminal fantasists, concerned with creating ambiguity. Although she still signposts her fantasy using a rhetorical technique common to the magic realists—narrating stories as "history" rather than as contemporaneous—her work insists on polysemy. In many ways, it is precisely *about* polysemy and (to return to fig. 1) is, like the works of Straub and Priest and some of the other texts in this chapter, concerned with combining genres in order to reach out to a complex audience—in Namjoshi's case, one that can combine fabulism, feminism and Hindu myth structures. In "The Life and Death of the Black Piglet" (*Building Babel*) the tale is not monosemic. With its staged interjections (set in brackets and italics) by members of the cast reading what Sister Solitude has written, the tale of the building of Babel is argued into being.

> Shy writes:
> [*Shy: Solitude! I see what you're doing. You're intent on proving that I was intent on killing The Black Piglet. But can't you see that you are responsible? You've written it into the logic of your language! You and The Black Piglet wanted to sit on a sand dune and dream of Crone Kronos. And not content with dreaming, you broadcast your tales. But ideas into action alter and falter. You can't build Babel and keep your hands clean. MYTHS MUTATE!!!*] (70)

As a slogan for the liminal fantasists, it works very well.

In chapter 1, I explained why I believe portal and quest fantasies to be essentially the same form. But portal/quest fantasies, and intrusion fantasies, are more intimately related to each other in structure and ideology than they are to the other categories for which I am arguing. Crucially, they appear to be shaped by a generic plot. Immersive and liminal fantasies do not have this level of predictability. I am no longer so convinced, however, by the neighborly placement of liminal fantasy and mimetic fiction. The liminal fantasy, far from being the least fantastical of my categories, may prove to be the most fantastical, in that it most thoroughly rests on the moment of recognition that Clute has argued in many places is fundamental to the fantasy and on a moment of recognition for the reader that some event or person is to be interpreted within the lines of the unwritten. My original mental construction placed the liminal on a trajectory toward mimetic fiction (see fig. 2).

		Portal/Quest fantasy		
Science Fiction	Immersive Fantasy		Liminal Fantasy	Mimetic fiction
		Intrusion Fantasy		

FIGURE 2. The Spectrum of Fantasy

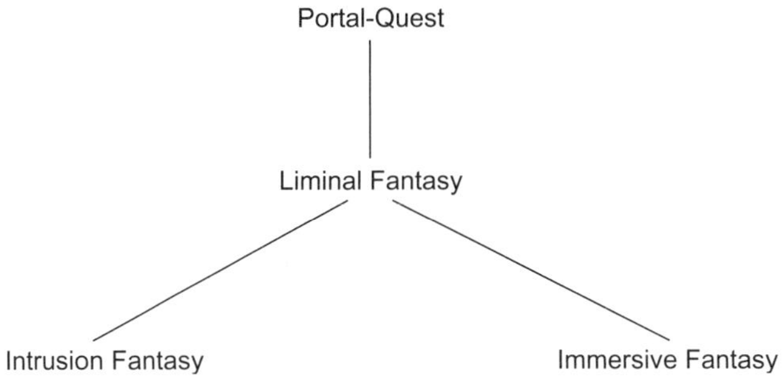

FIGURE 3.

However, in the process of working through this chapter, I have found it necessary to revise the spectrum of fantasy to reconsider where liminal fantasy fits in relation to the genre (see fig. 3).

With this image we can encompass Stableford's link to the intrusion fantasy, but also draw attention to the degree to which the liminal fantasy relies on the reading strategies constructed by each of the other forms. Rather than being a hybrid form, liminal fantasy, of all the forms of the fantastic, may be that which most requires that its readers be steeped in the conventions of fantasy, may indeed prove to be the purest form of the fantastic (or that most within the genre). In the next chapter, however, I shall discuss fantasies that *are* hybrids in my terms, texts that embrace more than one category in order to produce something other.

Chapter 5

"The Irregulars"

Subverting the Taxonomy

The only real purpose of any critical study such as this is to make it possible to open up new lines of inquiry and to lay down new challenges. In the previous four chapters, I have suggested some ways in which the English-language fantasy that has been written in the past hundred years can be understood; that there are certain types of fantasy and that to be effective, they need to be written in certain ways. In this chapter I shall draw attention to a few works that appear to break my "rules," novels that do not fit comfortably into my design. This chapter is not elective. If the first four chapters are to be regarded as descriptive rather than instructive, it must be possible to see their limits. Genre is a dialectic not a rubric, and the same should be true of genre analysis. The purpose of this chapter is to support my argument by undermining it.

The first four chapters of this book have considered how different modes by which the fantastic enters the text shapes the writing of those fantasies. It is quite feasible to overlap some modes (we saw this particularly with immersive fantasies, which frequently contain intrusions) or to segue from one to another, but all of these techniques essentially accord with the rhetorical structures I have outlined. In the case of immersive fantasies that contain intrusions, we need to consider whether the *location* and *story* of the fantastic is with the construction of the world, or with the intrusion. We can argue that with a novel such as *Jonathan Strange and Mr. Norrell*, it is not the world as we first meet it that we marvel at, but the intrusions that disturb this world. They are where the story *is*, and the chosen rhetorical strategy used to construct the fantastic is primarily that of the intrusion. Elsewhere, when the authors move a fantasy from an intrusion fantasy into a portal world (as in *Harry Potter and the Philosopher's*

Stone [*Harry Potter and the Sorcerer's Stone*]), the style changes to accommodate the shift. However, there are some authors—a very small number—who operate differently, whose work shifts from mode to mode without necessarily taking on the characteristics of each mode. In Hal Duncan's *Vellum* (2005), for example, Duncan constructs a portal fantasy in which only the reader, *but not the protagonist*, travels over the portals, so that while we enter world after world, we do so mostly through the eyes of the ensconced, frequently through the first person. The (deliberate) result is a dizzying disorientation with none of the expectation of eventual mastery that accompanied most of the portal fantasies. Duncan's rhetorical structure supports the "story of unbalance" that is also one way to interpret this eschatological novel. In the following discussion, the idea that structure replicates and intensifies story will be repeated. Other authors use the rhetorical structures I have outlined to mislead us into variant readings of the text—mislead in the sense that in some cases we misread the text, while in others all variant readings are simultaneously correct.

I shall begin with a set of novels that I originally placed in liminal fantasy: *The Legends of the Land* by Steve Cockayne. *The Legends of the Land* is written in three novels. The first, *Wanderers and Islanders* (2002), tells of Leonardo Pegasus, chief magician to the King; of Rusty Brown, a young boy in the hinterlands; of Alice, a child of the Islands; and of the renovation of a house. The second, *The Iron Chain* (2003), tells of Tom Slater, an abused and abandoned child who rises to become an entrepreneur, and also of Rusty's middle years. The final book, *The Seagull Drovers* (2004), follows Rusty's daughter Ashleigh, and then returns us to Leonardo Pegasus, and to the far north of the kingdom. In this book, prophecy is a dominant thread, but protagonists see themselves engaged in the more mundane tasks of fixing a computer network and overthrowing a tyrant. None of this tells the reader what the books are *about*.

Wanderers and Islanders and its sequels may provide the answer to a question that haunted chapter 4: is it possible to write a liminal fantasy within the immersive mode? In terms of the rhetorical structures discussed in chapter 2 (immersive fantasy), *The Legends of the Land* is clearly an immersive fantasy in that we are very much within the world, and are told the world from the point of view of familiarity. Dissonance is achieved through the casual mention of unfamiliar yet resonant technologies: steam-driven carriages, music rolls that record notes as colored lines, new apartment blocks without staircases, grey suits and heralds existing side by side, some accepted as normal by the characters, others as new to both them and us as might be the latest gadget in our streets.[1]

Although the plot element of the portal-quest fantasy is there—one of the characters, Rusty Brown, superficially follows the path into the "real world" and the adventure—the ideological structures of the portal-quest fantasy are consistently refused. Rusty is not wholly sheltered: he learns about the world outside his village from books and from the Wanderers; he doesn't meet the Guide figure (Leonardo Pegasus) until the end of the book. In addition, because the life of Pegasus is depicted separately—and from the point of view of an omniscient narrator—Pegasus is not in control of the narration of the world. Pegasus's position ironizes the structures of the portal-quest fantasy: his job at the start of the book is as a predictor and creator of the future, the very role ascribed to the mage. The trajectory of the trilogy, however, argues that the adventure may not even be his own.

The trajectory of this trilogy, and its consistent refusal of three of the dominant narratives I have outlined in this study, constructs a liminality of irony, while the role of magic, and its relationship to the irony of the plot—to the narrative of refusal—constructs the trilogy's equipoise. *The Legends of the Land* creates liminality through its *plot*, (a technique we have not seen before), using the rhetoric of immersive fantasy to support the expectation of genre—which it then refuses. Its equipoise is built on refusal, its irony on immersion.

In *Wanderers and Islanders*, Leonardo Pegasus finds himself in one of those periods of change that historians like to celebrate. The old King dies and is replaced by his son; with the new King, the guilds are dismantled, regalia is discarded, and automation and efficiency become the watchwords. With the passage of the old ways of doing things, the Land, we presume, will be thinned; the displacement of Leonardo Pegasus is asked to stand in for this. Leonardo, however, is displaced not by reason or rationalism, but simply by new technology and new ways of thinking about such technology: it is never clear in any of these books whether there is magic in the world Cockayne describes. Pegasus's Empathy Engine, a stage set on which dolls are moved in pseudowar games, is linked to with wires, nuts, and bolts. When Pegasus is replaced, it is with a machine like an abacus in which colored lights switch on and off under glass.[2] Cockayne succeeds in holding this uncertainty throughout the narrative. Even the conclusion of the trilogy does not wholly resolve the issue: Pegasus's "spells" are written on scrolls to be read by a cross between a jukebox and a pianola, and they feed directly into the "Network" created by the empathy engines, affecting the world within. This could be magic, or it could be cyberpunk.

For the fantasy reader the figures of Pegasus and Rusty are loaded with expectation. Rusty is cast very early on as the gifted child, emerging from the mists of legend: his father is a Wanderer, his mother from the Islands (and, as we learn later, is a cousin to the Wanderer Laurel). As a seven-year-old, Laurel gives him her Gift, the ability to see a person's past and future unravel in their eyes. Rusty seems intended to resolve the legends of the Wanderers and Islanders. When Rusty is admitted to the Brotherhood of Cartographers, he is admitted to the secrets of prophecy. Cockayne has posited geography, not history, as the sacred and arcane knowledge at the heart of his world; but when Rusty flees the Brotherhood, he rejects both his apparent destiny and the Scholasticism that haunts much genre fantasy.

Pegasus leaves the city and begins to wander, but no quest emerges, and he meets up with Rusty in a way both incidental and unmemorable (Rusty meets Alice in a similar way). Cockayne has denied us the meeting between "protagonist" and "mage" that would usually form one of the turning points of a quest fantasy (although Rusty and Pegasus do cross paths with people who have each come into contact with the other). We continually expect revelation, of the connections if not of anything more significant. Yet there is no moment of recognition. Even in the final book, the relevance of this thread is complex. It is not clear that the legends of the Wanderers and Islanders define the quest.

Wanderers and Islanders has yet a third thread: somewhere on a hill, a house is being renovated. Victor Lazarus, once a soldier of the King, is hired through an advertisement to supervise the renovation of an old house. Along with an accountant and a handyman, this he does, although increasingly tormented by a being (Lee) who seems to haunt the house. Lazarus's puzzlement shapes this section into an intrusion fantasy; the emphasis in the language is on the emotional experience of the intrusion; the telling of this tale seems to be haunted by the opening sequences of George MacDonald's *Lilith*. Eventually, Lazarus comes to terms with Lee, who emerges as a permanent inhabitant. The arrival, and the departure, of the owner is framed as both disruption and conclusion because his presence clarifies nothing.

The connection of this house to Pegasus and to Rusty is extremely unclear until very late in the book when Leonardo, recognizing that he has constructed futures for many other people but not for himself, begins to do so; his future he envisions as a house, and he begins his vision with the construction of the very advertisement that attracted Victor Lazarus. The house we have seen so carefully renovated is a vivid realization of the Renaissance Theatre of Memory. We have, apparently, a "conclusion" to the novel that, while leaving the Land in the process of thinning, and both

Pegasus and Rusty treading water, tells us that at least one element of the tale was "unreal."

The Iron Chain reorients much of what we have just read. To begin with, for much of the book Rusty is a character in someone else's story. When we do meet Rusty again, it is as a person treading water in the pool of middle age. He marries the daughter of his village doctor—his teenage, rather than childhood sweetheart—has two children, and founders on the usual stresses of middle age: boredom and temptation. But Rusty also sets up as the City's mapmaker, a job that requires him to walk the streets, to research, to reject the notion that cartography is somehow sacred. This emphasis on new ideas dramatically shifts Rusty's position and the ideology of the series. Unlike the roles of portal-quest fantasy protagonists, his is not a closed position. Rusty is learning to make knowledge, not find it.

In most middle books of quest fantasies, the middle book is the one in which the protagonist is most disassociated from his world, traveling through it as a tourist. In *The Iron Chain*, Rusty is very much a part of the thinned Land, not an observer of the process. Yet none of the usual hints of the portentousness of Rusty's background coalesce in the pattern of coincidences that construct fantasy's favored destinarianism. Rusty does rise to a high position, but essentially as an entrepreneur or bureaucrat. He stays resolutely middle-class. Some of this is shaped through his relative immobility in this novel.

If Rusty's story is of middle age, so too is the story of the Land itself. In the first book, the Land was quite nebulous, a feeling reinforced by the apparent lack of a name, and that there is only one city, the City. If portal-quest fantasies are typified by the real or metaphorical presence of a map, this sequence, which takes mapping as one of its themes, is curiously uncharted. But in *The Iron Chain*, the Land begins to come into its own as character, and as a character it is degrading. Under the young King, the states with which the Land has been at war are increasingly hostile, and the King must spend increasing amounts of time away. In his absence, the Land thins further amid a rising tide of violence, and the King, in an attempt to control it, takes the fatal step of legitimizing it, by transforming the feral Wolf Boys into the King's own Royal Wolf Boys Militia. Modernization, as in so much fantasy, seems to be under attack in this novel, but this is yet another misdirection.

Leonardo Pegasus's middle age is also of concern, but his middle age is in Rusty's past, during which he conceived a child with a female assistant. It is this child, Tom Slater, who is the central character of the book.

Slater, even more than Rusty, carries the attributes of an uncrowned king. Rejected by his mother, he is brought up by his putative father, who chains him to a table to keep him out of trouble. The short piece of iron chain becomes his security blanket; he takes it with him to the Academy of Cartographers, where he becomes a scholarship student and his life intersects with Rusty's. But where Tom is a one-page note in Rusty's life, Rusty's failure to complete a cartography field trip destroys Tom. He is forced into vagrancy and eventually ends up in the City where he creates for himself the role of superintendent of the Transport Interchange. When the Regent Fang decides Tom has become too powerful, his business—offering to list the timetable of coaches in return for commission—is refigured as corruption and Tom is destroyed once more. This time, he turns to Rusty for help but as a bitter Steerpike, determined to gain revenge on Rusty for the disparities in their fates.

The Iron Chain is a very strange book for a middle book in a trilogy. Even less than in *Wanderers and Islanders* do we get a sense of the fantastic at work in the Land. The fantasy in this book is almost entirely that of irony, the presentation of the technological marvelous as the fantastic marvelous. The incongruities of a changing society—and I can't think of another fantasy writer who has depicted so effectively that sense of past, present, and future existing together on the street that is real life—of a world in which elevators are still pulled by ponies (until a pony plague) but videophones are commonplace, constantly keeps the reader unbalanced, as do the elements that go unexplained, from the workings of the Empathy Engine to that pony plague (which may be a tiding of something worse, but if so we never know). In Cockayne's work, there are many unfinished stories; the tales are not contained within the pages. *The Iron Chain* extends the emphasis of the *Wanderers and Islanders* that our lives are lived in the everyday. The marvelous is contained within the mundane; it is not exterior to it.

But the novel is also strange because of that focus on Tom. First, there is the matter of his role in *Wanderers and Islanders*. The choice to write the second novel about a character who is merely background in Rusty's life, challenges the orientalism of much fantasy. Minor characters exist in most fantasy novels in order to provide lessons for the protagonist and to reinforce the sense that there is only one story, that of the Destiny. The structure of the *Iron Chain* both depicts this—Rusty is far less affected by Tom's reappearance in his life than the reverse—and challenges the notion that we can see the world as any kind of monosemic narrative. As with Mervyn Peake's *Titus Groan* and *Gormenghast*, and Peter David's *Sir*

Apropos of Nothing, there is a struggle in *The Iron Chain* for the control of the story. Consequently, it is a severe shock when Tom dies. It just is not done in fantasy to kill off the one who appears to have a destiny. Nor is it done for someone's death to have so little impact. By the time Tom dies, the trouble he has caused has, ironically, distracted Rusty from the "friendship." Tom fails to be the center of the narrative even when he writes it: he remains what Clute has called a fixed liminal, a character through whom the fantasy can be entered.

If *The Iron Chain* functioned as a metaphor for the lost direction of middle age, *The Seagull Drovers* tells of the liberation of old age and the passing on of mission to the young. In this it differs from many final books. Although there is completeness, that denial of explanation that haunted the first two books becomes, in the third book, the denial of closure and of the expectation of meaning.

The Seagull Drovers is narrated in part by Ashleigh Brown, daughter of Rusty, whose views of the events of *The Iron Chain* are rather different than those of her father: she knows both less and more than Rusty does; she is more attuned to the politics of the City and the condition of the Land. In this book, Ashleigh is, like most adolescents, in search of her life, but while she functions as one of the team within the story's arc, there is no conflation of bildungsroman with earth-shattering destiny. Ashleigh's story is of professional house decoration and the realization that love and compatibility aren't the same things. Once more, Cockayne forces us to pay attention to the mundane as the main concern of the characters.

Ashleigh's story undermines any understanding we may have gained from *The Iron Chain*. When we met Ashleigh first, it was as a victim, both of social dislocation and Tom's machinations. In *The Seagull Drovers*, that story is reconfigured into one of agency and opportunity, so that, for the second time we are forced to reconsider the story as a whole, to turn it around in our mind's eye. This story is polysemic, its meanings shifting according to perspective, and it is this as much as anything that structures its liminality. To this end, the quest—to which I have referred without explanation—remains to be discussed.

In *The Seagull Drovers*, Cockayne once more refuses to fulfill the ritual pointers. There are at least three potential quests: Charles and Sally Bannister's for the kidnapped King; the ragamuffin Seagull Drovers, for the seagulls (which they believe must return to the sea); and finally the quest of Leonardo Pegasus to, as he thinks, cleanse the Network.

However, when Charles and Sally Bannister find the King, he rejects restoration; we never do learn what the Seagull Drovers think they are saving the Land *from*, and Leonardo Pegasus is rather taken aback to discover that within the Network, he is merely a Companion, one of a number of attribute-defined players; Rusty is also merely a player. If there is an uncrowned king, it is Blaise, the waif in the Network, who may have created the world of the Land in the same way as Pegasus created his house of memory. The very lack of specificity, the limited geography of the Land, emerges to reinforce a moment of recognition that suggests unreality. At the same time as a counternarrative, the metanarrative of official history finds a comfortably plausible explanation for every oddity.

At the end of *The Seagull Drovers*, the trip to the mystical and utopian islands saves the Land, but Charles and Sally Bannister discover peat in the islands, which proves a viable substitute for the oil from the hostile states. As with Ashleigh's narration, the fantastic is contextualized by the mundane. The islands may be fantastical, but they are also a resource. The saving of the City and the ushering in of a new age is achieved at the expense of that which was central to the fantasy: there is no restoration, no healing. The Land will continue to be thinned, and in the process, be remade.

Throughout the trilogy, references and structures keep us off-balance: intensely resonant images that hold the promise of the fantastic never reappear; prophecy, when it manifests, is tatty and almost incidental; in *The Seagull Drovers*, music rolls codify human brainwaves and feed them into the Network, a fantasy novel becomes cyberpunk. Uncertainty is created through continual doubling: images of six-sided tower rooms repeat themselves, in Leonardo's house of the Mind, in the House of Rest, and in the Network; both Lee and the Islander Alice hang from a trapeze in the six-sided room. Who mimics whom? Lee, the imp in the Network, is doubled with Fang in the world. Rusty's dreams of an old man drowning in the river resonate in Pegasus's house of memory, and seem to come true in his own reality in the third book. Each world affects the other, but Blaise is convinced her world is the truly real.

Although the Land is saved at the end, very few of the participants are even aware that this is what is at stake: their own desires and narratives remain distinct from the metanarrative. And crucially, Cockayne's salvation has consequences: the Land cannot truly be healed. *The Legends of the Land* is a fantasy of refusal: every time we think we understand what is happening, or are offered moments of recognition, we are denied it or is recomplicated. The pattern of the full fantasy—wrongness, thinning, recognition, and healing/return—can be traced in the text, but the wrongness is not where we think. The thinned world promises new marvels, recognition is misleading, and there is no such thing as return, only a going forward. Steve Cockayne redefines the borderland of the fantastic; casual, cool, and unnervingly familiar, he plays with the expectations of his audience to create liminality almost entirely through the plotting and landscape of the sequence.

The next book to consider is Roderick Townley's *The Great Good Thing* (2001). Like *The Legends of the Land*, this is a book whose liminality is predominantly structured through the plot and a manipulation of the structures of the immersive fantasy, here encoded directly in the meaning of words. Townley creates concentric structures of immersion; unlike in *Legends of the Land*, these constructions are transparent, and it is in the transparency that we get the kind of dissonance that we saw in the work of Aiken and Mayne (see chapter 4). Townley's book is constructed of concentric circles of the Real, but these circles fracture and interact and reform, until finally they construct a figure-ground puzzle of the Real.

Sylvie is a twelve-year-old princess. She has been twelve years old for many years because she is a character in a book. But Sylvie is an *aware* character. Sylvie's own story is a quest fantasy in the pre-Lewis/Tolkien tradition, what I called in chapter 1 a *bracelet* fantasy, in which adventures are tacked on as links until the author runs out of inventiveness. As we later discover that Sylvie's book was written in 1917, this style is absolutely appropriate. But Sylvie is both bored by the fact that her book hasn't been read in some time, and bored by the story she is in.

Townley's fantasy is on one level quite clearly an immersive fantasy in that Sylvie takes her world utterly for granted. Yet the opening of the book immediately forces readers to reorient themselves: "Sylvie had an amazing life, but she didn't get to live it very often. What good were potions and disguises if no one came along to scare you or to save you or kiss you behind the waterfall?" (3). Later we will see her lean against a letter, take a short cut between descriptions to page 3 and tell a thief off for giving her a flower, because he is failing to stay in character while the book is unread. In most immersive fantasies, the reader is positioned in the hindbrain of the protagonist, conditioned to accept the world as the protagonist understands it and to work out the rest from hints. But usually the protagonist is herself utterly immersed; she believes in her world as the only world, and this is true even where other worlds are believed to exist. In Diana Wynne Jones's *Chrestomanci* series for example, the other worlds exist as an extension of the understanding that Chrestomanci's world is real; they reinforce it, rather than undercutting it.

Metatextual fantasies, where characters exist in an imaginary world within the real world are not unusual, nor is awareness qua awareness.

Cornelia Funke's *Inkheart* (2003), for example, is about book characters who, once released, want to be real. But Townley's Sylvia is multiply aware: she knows she is real, she knows her story is both a story and a real existence, and she constructs it as a "play." She even understands herself in philosophical terms: she and others are the tree that, if it falls in the forest when no one is looking, is *not* real, because there are no Readers to make it real. Later she will also accept that without herself, there is no story to be reconstructed. At the same time, Sylvie is aware of the Reader. The plot begins when she looks up and sees the Reader; there is a clear distinction between story (Sylvie's) and plot (the story we are reading), and Sylvie and many of her character-colleagues are aware of this.

When the book opens for a second time, Townley gives us a short piece that is a doubled irony, the irony of mimesis that is the immersive fantasy and a second irony of metonymy, which makes real the physical aspects of reading: "Everyone dived for cover, the jester closing himself inside two brackets, Queen Emmeline wedging herself into a dependent clause, and Sylvie racing to the Acknowledgements page, where she disappeared among a dozen names, including the author's pets and several friends without whose help this book could not have been written" (16–17). When the Reader wipes at a blob of strawberry jam with her spit, Sylvie thinks, "That's the last time I walk through *that* sentence!" (17). Sylvie is aware of world as an *interaction*. The only way I can think of describing this (although I shall contradict myself later) is that Sylvie is aware that she is the "other" side of the portal and that her side serves the "real" world. As in this scene:

> Sylvie heard her yawn several times and guessed that the girl was having her reading time before bed. Claire turned, as she often did, to the chapter in which Riggeloff's thieves chase Sylvie to the cliff. Rather than let herself be captured, Sylvie flings herself into the Mere of Remind and is sucked under by the whirlpool. . . . And that is where, on this particular evening, Claire drifted to sleep, her hand still resting on the edge of the page.
>
> Sylvie swam to shore and dried herself quickly with the monogrammed towel that hung just out of sight behind a bush. (70–71)

This interactivity between worlds has been inherent in portal fantasy since Mr. Tumnus inadvertently asserted the greater reality of Lucy in the world of Narnia (I say inadvertently because elsewhere it is clear that Lewis regards both Earth and Narnia as the shadowlands). But Sylvie *exists* in a state of interaction, and in a situated irony. As Sylvie goes through the movements of the story, she is aware of herself as performer and the reader as audience: "The princess could feel the cool shadow of the Reader overhead and hear her breathing. Story-book characters live for the sound of Readers breathing, especially as it softens and settles like the breath of dreamers. It gives the characters courage to go on through the most difficult plot twists" (18). And the more the Reader makes it clear that she is a committed reader (on completing it, the Reader turns the book over and starts from the beginning), the greater the effort the characters put into their roles (20). The boundaries between book and reality have grown permeable: while remaining in the book, Sylvie knows that what she and her colleagues do reaches beyond the portal into the Real world. Townley reifies the entire world of reader response theory. When the Reader first started, because the characters were unprepared, wrong things happened: a suit of armor fell over, parts were funny because rushed. On her second reading, these things aren't there, and the Reader "started opening and reading at random, trying to find the part that had made her laugh, but she could make no sense of what she read because the characters barely had time to arrive before she flipped to another page" (21).

Slowly the idea of the book as a fixed object shifts; the idea that there is a clear divide between Sylvie onstage/being read and Sylvie when the book is closed is undermined. All the while, Sylvie is aware of this philosophical conundrum and that her world is not quite real, but that her existence is in part dependent on a constructed and ontologically fragile reality. She acknowledges this construction when she tells off the nice thief: "Where would we be if we all started playing parts that weren't written for us?" (24). When the book is burned and Sylvie and the remaining cast flee into the Reader's dreams, this conundrum is precisely the challenge she must face.

But first, Sylvie breaks the boundaries of the immersive world. Straying one day into the forest, she finds a narrow strip of white and, beyond it, a world different from the ordered land in which she lived. Sylvie is written to want to explore, and explore she does, over the line and into a second portal world where she meets the new Reader. And here we have another flip. Although Sylvie is in the dream world of the Reader, and is herself a stranger, she remains immersed in the world, and becomes the guide figure for someone else's quest—a search for the Reader's grandmother who is in the hospital but whom the Reader configures as kidnapped. Sylvie experiences a profound shift of her position vis-à-vis Story: *she does not know how this story comes out*. Her realization that the Reader (Claire) does not know either destabilizes Sylvie's understanding of her own world. Even though Sylvie has been aware of how her world works, she has not been aware that its workings are specific to itself.

Instead of accepting her world, Sophie now questions it. Of Prince Rigelloff (charmer and evildoer) she says, "He's really a very interesting character. It's just that he's always interesting in exactly the same way" (33). When reminded that she shouldn't look at the Reader, she argues, "But nobody ever said why not" (47). Sylvie's awareness that her world is a manufacture becomes intense. As the book is repeatedly read, it begins to fall apart, and with it, the world changes, is *affected* by the world outside. The hinge becomes loose and the backup lights (which come on when the book is closed) stop working properly: "The sky came on green." Encoded in that short sentence is both the acceptance of the immersive fantasy (the sky came on) and *the awareness of existence* of the fantastic—which, properly speaking, does not belong in the immersive fantasy. This encoding is similarly expressed during the fire: "From what Sylvie could tell, the blaze had started in the west, near the front of the book" (73). Again, we have a moment of dissonance in which west is not quite what we understand west to be. Rather than creating liminality through juxtaposition, irony, or equipoise, this liminality is created by the overlaying of meanings within certain sentences.

Having fled the fire—and with the help of the dark blue–eyed girl, crossed a portal from the fixed fantasy world of the book—the family and their remaining courtiers must start a new life. This fate is terrifying: they are thrust from their immersion within the text into the new world of Claire's dreams, a very different kind of fantasy world and one to which they have a very different relationship. But they are not alone in this new world. Claire's grandmother, the girl with dark blue eyes, is there: "Come on, let's show you around" (89), she says. The casualness of this comment undercuts the pomp and estrangement of the portal-quest. The family is being introduced to somewhere they are expected to *live*, not somewhere they will pass through. We can see this orientation in the way in which the girl describes the place:

> "Where exactly are we?" asked the king.
>
> "In Claire's mind, of course. This is what you'd call the backstage area," she said, leading the bewildered family through the streets. "Up ahead there, where you see the bright spotlights, that's where Claire has her dreams." (90)

The girl has shown them the place as if it were a new house, exposing all the useful cupboards and showing them how to use the boiler. As the family become accustomed to this new place, it quickly becomes the location for their own understanding, delivered in a cozy rhetoric that emphasizes this as a place in which they live, not one in which they are tourists. However, the dreams with which they must now work are surreal and random. Worse, they require Sylvie and her family to *react*. Previously, they have spoken predirected lines; now they can no longer use spontaneity to distinguish their time on- and offstage. Furthermore, this need to react to a random landscape challenges their desire for immersion: they are no longer in a world they can take for granted, only one they can *pretend* to take for granted. The episteme of Sylvie's world has changed forever.

The crucial change is that where the book was a limited space the dream extends onward. When Sylvie becomes curious, she is told there is an entire hinterland to which dream characters retreat when no longer needed. Determined by this time to create an independent existence, Sylvie persuades her family to migrate. The migration leads the family into the wilderness where their certainty of place, their certainty of self, becomes vulnerable. "Occasionally, at royal command, a new production of *The Great Good Thing* would be staged. . . . Everyone needed to be kept in practice and up to performance level. After all, there was no book to refer to any more" (111). Yet slowly the text changes. Queen Emmeline can no longer remember all her lines. The characters are no longer in a fixed fantasy. Because they can no longer take their world for granted, they can no longer take themselves for granted. The rebellion, when it comes, is from a minor character (the jester), one who, in Sylvie's quest fantasy, is there to provide the color and variety through which she passes. The shift in fantastic structure shifts relationships. If we think back to the difficulty with which authors subverted the portal-quest fantasy we can see that this shift in relationships is inevitable. The monosemy of Sylvie's original story is broken as she becomes involved in the stories of Claire, of her own people, and of the metastory (which we shall come to in a moment).

In chapter 9, Sylvie's story changes yet again. The girl with the dark blue eyes appears and this time takes Sylvie into Claire's real life. But they do so (possibly in homage to both Lewis and Jung) by going down, "deeper towards the center" (121), and to a house containing a stairway that leads to Claire. This Claire is a grown woman, reading to her child (Lily), but unable to make up a story herself. She no longer remembers her dreams, "There were too many fires in them." So Sylvie whispers her story to Claire, who remembers the old book and tells Lily the story. Many years later, when Claire lies dying, the dark blue–eyed girl offers Sylvie the chance to survive the death of Claire's memories by moving over into Lily's dreams. Sylvie decides to take the chance but her family refuse, preferring to stay where they are. There is a crucial line here: looking at Fangl, the geometry teacher Claire remembered fondly and who has been adopted into the court, Sylvie remembers something he said to her, "*You can't solve a problem from inside it*" (173).

Sylvie finds herself at Claire's deathbed, while Lily explains that she could not find the book, and wonders if it was privately printed. Claire asks Lily to tell her the story, and this time Sylvie whispers into Lily's ears, prompting her where she forgets. Later that night, Sylvie slips into her dreams, but the dark blue–eyed girl cannot go with her. In her place is an elderly lady with stooped shoulders and a shawl. She is Claire's grandmother, and Lily has no memory of her.

Lily's mind is very different to Claire's. "It was much more orderly. . . . You didn't suddenly trip over yellow-eyed pythons or splash through ponds that a moment ago were windows. If you wanted pythons you went to the Reptile House. If you wanted ponds, you went to the Water Resource Center" (193). But while this new world has to be learned, again it is learned as a house to be moved into, somewhere to become established. It is never described as a place to be moved through. Sylvie is not a tourist and, like any new settler, she begins to miss her family. Here there is a moment of confusion. Sylvie wonders what the jester was up to, so she looks in the golden locket and sees her father on two canes, deteriorating steadily. Yet of course, if we think about what Townley has been doing, all of this is Sylvie keeping her family alive *by remembering them*; Claire no longer does, and they have sunk further back into Lily's mind, remembered only at second hand and with no illustrations to fix their images. Townley's concentric worlds have generated another, layered world: surrounding the bracelet fantasy structure of Sylvie's story with a matryushka doll.

So Sylvie, remembering once more Fangl's injunction, "*You can't solve a problem from inside it*," whispers to Lily, and Lily begins to write *The Great Good Thing*. But while Sylvie works hard to prevent Lily from including embellishments, "at times Sylvie was guilty of putting in extra words herself. She realised she had no choice, if she was ever to be happy again" (200). Sylvie is *writing her own world* and Townley writes this scene very differently from the cautious whispers from the edge of the fantastic that marked Sylvie's communications with Claire. Here there is argument:

> "I don't remember this stuff," the writer's voice echoed overhead as Sylvie dictated the new material.
>
> "Trust me!" Sylvie called back. (200)

The entire relationship between the worlds has shifted again, and we are hard put to it this time to work out on which side of the portal we are. Lily (the writer) and Sylvie (the character) are clearly now existing in the same momentary and multidimensional space we might call Creativity. Townley has created somewhere in which both are immersed and both are travelers; the result, however, is neither polysemic nor monosemic acceptance, but argument and negotiation. For me as reader, this new space is fascinating for the way in which neither questions it, but each absorbs it into their own immersion. Townley does not say this, but Sylvie has become that "character coming to life," who argues with her own tale in the way that authors in interview so often describe.

When the book is published and the family arrive they are bright and shiny, with no memory of the past. Lily, after all, didn't write that. And there are some other differences: costumes have changed, Queen Emmeline's nose is different. And the relationship between Reader and characters has shifted dramatically. When Lily opens the book, it is to greet the characters and to be greeted in turn by Sylvie. The barriers between the worlds have been *permanently* breached, and now both worlds are Real, for this moment at least. And, in an extension of the metaphor that Townley has slipped in throughout, the new book is a new residence to which one adjusts, noting what one needs to note to live, rather than to pass through: [Sylvie] . . . excused herself and set out for a walk. The Mere of Remind, she discovered, was no longer on page 35 but on page 42, and the illustration was much larger than before" (207). The scene is once more rather like checking where the cupboards are. Sylvie clearly understands the new world through the immersion of the old.

This Sylvie though is not the old Sylvie. She is no longer wholly within the story and the performance of story. She has found a place for Fangl in the new tale (as her tutor) and, as the book closes, the invisible fish opens its jaws and out steps the girl with the dark blue eyes. Sylvie has taken Fangl's injunction to heart and has written her into the book. Sylvie may be slow to realize it, but to the Reader, it is obvious: Reality has been inverted as the true Author becomes character.

Peter Beagle's *A Fine and Private Place* (1960) has an elusive quality. Its meaning, if it has one, does not speak itself aloud. The quest, if there is one, does not seem to belong to the protagonist. The ghosts are not frightening, and their issues are resolvable only by themselves. It is a novel that can only be understood if attention is paid to the *way* in which it is told, rather than what is narrated. The novel is written in a combination of the ironic mimesis of the immersive and liminal fantasies—the tone is cool, accepting the fantastic as somehow normal—but embraces within its conversational aspects the phatic discourse of the portal fantasy. There is no evidence of the naïveté of the intrusion fantasy (the expressions of surprise, or the sense that something must be worked out) even though in terms of the "icons" of the novel, it might be the most obvious category in which to place it. The success of the *acceptance* that Beagle builds into the telling is tied very directly to the degree to which Beagle plays on the expectation of the reader, an expectation that is continually sidestepped and redirected. The ironic mimesis of *A Fine and Private Place*—the cultivation of calm normality—fosters a very direct reading of the text, one that encourages an initial acceptance of the primary cues given by the author. Yet within that reading are secondary and tertiary cues, dependent on stylistic shifts, that redirect the meaning of the text.

Rebeck the tramp lives in the cemetery, where "the walls of the Yorkchester Cemetery mark it off as a secondary world surrounded by New York City" (Zahorski and Boyer 72). Rebeck can see and hear ghosts, but has become accustomed to their gradual disappearance as they lose their attachment to life. Having placed himself at the center of their universe as their "link" to life, their visible absence is interpreted by him to indicate their dispersal.

Rebeck has no goals and, apart from the visits of the raven who brings him food, and his conversations with the raven and the ghosts, there is little supernatural about this book. The raven is—at least initially—an accepted part of the scenery. So far, this is a fully immersive world; the otherworld of New York is kept safely at a distance. As Zahorski and Boyer observe, in this concrete sense, "the boundaries of the cemetery are very clearly defined; it is never difficult to determine where this land of the dead ends and the land of the living begins" (72). But while Rebeck takes for granted his own world in the conversations he has with the raven, he also describes the world to the newcomers as if he were observing it for us. The ghosts stand in our place to be explained to. This becomes a portal fantasy in which the main character is the guide rather than the usual reader-substitute, the hero.

This shift from Rebeck within an immersive fantasy to Rebeck as guide to the fantasy world is but the first. By the end of the novel, the ghosts have become more knowledgeable than Rebeck.[3] We are asked to consider just who is at home here, and the shift in style, from the accepting to the increasingly descriptive, parallels the content shift.

The crucial rhetorical strategy Beagle uses is to describe the fantastic locus from outside, or from above, while insisting that we follow, rather than identify with, the protagonist. This process begins with the raven:

> The baloney weighed the raven down, and the shopkeeper almost caught him as he whisked out the delicatessen door.
>
> . . . The raven flew lazily over New York, letting the early sun warm his feathers, A water truck waddled along Jerome Avenue, leaving the street dark and glittering behind it. A few taxi-cabs cruised around Fordham like well-fed sharks. (3)

As with the Seattle of Megan Lindholm's *Wizard of the Pigeons*, the world is made fantastical because of our distanced position from it (and this time also through the anthropomorphic construction of the raven). From the moment the raven is described as a "him" rather than an it, he is transmuted into a character and we are functioning in an immersive fantasy. Yet this is an immersion we sit outside and observe; we are *not* to take it for granted: "There was also a cemetery, and it was over this that the raven swooped. It was a very large cemetery, about half the size of Central Park, and thick with trees" (4).

In the copy I have this line is underlined, and the note placed beside it, "Bad." And in the ordinary course of the immersive fantasy this critic might be correct: this standing back to describe the cemetery *does* undermine the immersion. But if we consider the rest of the novel, this undermining is deliberate: the fantastical story of the novel is not the dealings between Rebeck and the ghosts per se, but the process by which Rebeck comes to accept that he is an alien in the world of ghosts, that he can only ever watch and describe. His immersion, his sense of place within the cemetery, is the false construction of a portal adventurer. The dynamic of the text circles around Rebeck's struggle to be central to the narrative of the ghosts, and the casual and uncaring development of the ghosts' own narrative as they do move fully into their new world. In the scene in which he welcomes Michael to the afterlife of the cemetery he sees himself as mage; from Michael's point of view, however, it is clear he is at best gatekeeper:

> Michael came slowly down the hill, and the man got up to meet him. He looked to be in his early fifties, for his shoulders were a little rounded and his hair was gray-white. But the smile he gave Michael was warm and youthful, and his eyes were the color of the earth. "How do you do?" he asked. "My name is Jonathan Rebeck." (18)

But Michael's hand goes through Rebeck and he recoils in horror, and, from that moment, knows that Rebeck cannot be a true guide.

The subject of the novel is, in part, Rebeck's Healing. He is the "Land" that is to be healed within the tale. For him to restore himself he has to accept his own alienness to this place, to understand that his own sense of belonging—depicted both through that ironic mimesis and the phatic discourse of the mage-guide—is itself illusory, that his *proper* narrative position within the fantasy is as alien. As the ghosts become more comfortable in the cemetery Rebeck becomes a mere hanger-on to their story and his interpretation/guidance becomes less reliable. Rebeck, in a dark corner of his mind, becomes more conscious of what is happening as a portal fantasy: he acknowledges his entry to the fantasy world, that he was not *always* there:

> "I got drunk enough for a wedding and a wake put together and I wandered in here, singing to myself—they just latched the gate in those days—and I fell asleep on the top step here and slept for a day."
>
> He shrugged. "And there you are. I stayed. At first I thought I'd just rest for a while, because I was very tired, but the raven brought me food—" He grinned suddenly. "The raven was there when I woke up, waiting for me. He told me he'd bring me food as long as I stayed, and when I asked why, he said it was because we had one thing in common. We both had delusions of kindness." (60)

As the novel proceeds, other elements conspire to undermine both the reader's and Rebeck's sense of immersion in the fantastic: we, like Rebeck, have no real place here. Rebeck, comfortable in his world, is intruded upon by Mrs. Klapper (or Klapper, as she titles herself), who, in her visits to her husband's grave, disturbs the equanimity of the cemetery. Rebeck must engage with Klapper as in an intrusion fantasy; he must work her out, negotiate with her, and eventually resolve the issues she had brought into his world. It is toward Klapper that Rebeck displays the characteristics of the naive protagonist. He reacts to her with astonishment, with continual surprise. When Klapper enters the cemetery and meets Rebeck, she intrudes on the orderliness of the "real" world. Her arrival is always loud and forceful: "Hey, Rebeck! It's Klapper!" (145). Her presence is important because it admits of his existence, and is one of the signs that he recognizes he might be in a place that is not his world: "Man searches constantly for identity, he thought as he trotted along the gravel path. He has no real proof of his existence except for the reaction of other people to that fact. . . . I'm glad Mrs. Klapper knows I exist. That should count for two or three ordinary people" (146).

Note that this is not stream-of-consciousness description of his place or movements, but philosophy, a standing back and considering, He can do this in part because he needs to justify where he stands; he needs to believe that the fantasy revolves around him. But what is important is that at this moment he places himself *twice.* He becomes the ghost who must be acknowledged to be real, *and* he is the protagonist rushing to meet the intruder.

Klapper is the element of intrusion in this novel that Rebeck must learn to negotiate with and "defeat." Klapper brings with her plans and aims and desires, all of which Rebeck has banished. Mrs. Klapper views the situation differently. For *her*, the graveyard is an otherworld. She steps through the portal—in this case, the subway exit—explores the world, and eventually withdraws, taking with her the Significant Object (Rebeck) that will ensure the restoration and healing of the portal-quest fantasy. With Klapper's entrance into the novel we can begin to see that Beagle is continuously forcing us to question whose novel this is, which protagonist offers us the point of reference that allows us to decide whether—for the purposes of fantasy—this is the frame world or the otherworld.

In the portal fantasy the protagonist, intruding into the other world, is usually (if not always) instrumental in resolving the problems of the world he visits. In *A Fine and Private Place*, this element is missing. Although Rebeck eventually moves Laura's coffin so that she can be with her ghostly lover, Laura and Michael have already resolved their own emotional problems (in the sense that is usually meant in ghost stories—the living soul resolving the unfinished business of the dead). But the element of negotiation with the intruder that I have suggested is fundamental to the intrusion fantasy *is* present in this novel if we position Rebeck as the intruder.

Our attention is drawn to this presentation of Rebeck repeatedly. The raven, Klapper, and Campos—all point out that the cemetery is not Rebeck's place. He resists because he cannot bring himself to leave, he feels a misfit in the real world. This alienation is a common characteristic of the protagonist of the more metaphoric portal fantasies (examples include *The Neverending Story* or the Thomas Covenant novels), but Beagle does not allow Rebeck to take on the mantle of a messiah in this alternate world. Instead, Rebeck becomes increasingly estranged from the fantasy. At the end, he is the intrusion, "defeated" and expelled from the fantasyland.

The tale is told as if Rebeck is fully immersed in the world, but reaches its conclusion by allowing the ghosts to create a more convincing "reality." We see this almost from the beginning; the air of ennui with which Michael contemplates his once-life reinforces its unreality. He and Laura talk as if they are *ex*-adventurers in a portal fantasy; now that they have left the "otherworld," they can only reminisce, can only reconstruct the

"the otherworld" from what they saw and heard and touched. There can be nothing new from there. Michael cannot even see Laura, "Just as a sort of general outline. Hair, shape—I know she's a woman, but that's about it" (61). And all of this is delivered in a rather dreary, depressed nostalgia. One of Beagle's achievements has been to construct the fantastic through the negation of wonder.

The location of the fantasyworld or otherworld shifts continuously within this novel. At its start, the "real" world is clearly that of the cemetery; it is described as if it is the frameworld, the place that *exists*. It is the city that the raven flies over that seems fantastic, the houses with their "stucco sailors, all left-handed and . . . [with] stucco pom-poms on their hats" (4), a fantasyworld to be found on the other side of the cemetery's literal portals. In comparison, the cemetery at the edge of Yorkchester is oppressively normal. Laid out in a grid, it mimics the American way of living. It even has good and bad neighborhoods. It is *predictable*. When Rebeck guesses where Klapper came from, he can anticipate a subway by the entrance: "Cemeteries were built like that" (38).

And Klapper, in the way she lives in the outside world, contributes to our understanding of it as a place of fantasy. To begin with, we hear Klapper's internal narrative: unlike as with Rebeck (whom we mostly see act even if that act is only sitting on the steps), Klapper is narrated in a stream of consciousness: 'If I go to Ida's I go past the butcher near the subway, and I could stop in and get maybe a pound of chopped meat and a couple of lamb chops.' She *would* go see Ida, then . . . Always, she remembered, always the look in the back of her eyes" (67–68). The world for Klapper is always moving, always to be commented on and described if only to herself. Klapper, while rooted in her world, describes it as if she is traveling through it, and the narrator does the same. The vision we get of New York in summer is meticulous, hyperreal: "The vendor buys an ice-cream cup for himself and sits down on the grass to eat it, or at least he thinks about doing it. The policeman sings to himself and stops to talk with the candy-store man. . . . And the old women move their chairs to follow the sun and do not speak to each other at all" (69). This world is stranger to us than the cemetery, which has its own realness created by the degree to which it is taken for granted by both the narrator and those who inhabit it.

The figure-ground slippage of the structure of the novel is also encoded into the plot. The Michael and Laura arc of the novel could be understood as a portal fantasy and as a romance. Michael's initial confrontation with the reality of his death is almost classically structured around the pattern of the quest fantasy: discovering a house (the mausoleum) and the old man (Rebeck), he immediately accepts Rebeck's understanding of the world. "Living is a big thing, and it's pretty hard to forget. . . . You find yourself becoming greedy of people; whenever they come to visit here you watch every movement they make, trying to remember the way you used to do that" (20). The subject matter, and Rebeck's own status as alien within this world disguises the degree to which he is acting as mage-guide in a form that mimics the many lectures delivered in the quest fantasies.

Only later, with the appearance of Laura, does he take on another's input—breaking that apparently impermeable narrative of the portal fantasy. The introduction of Laura is important because, with her arrival, Michael and Laura become settlers in the Land, rather than journeyers. And from the start, Laura emphasizes that *she* is the one who is real and inhabits the real space. Those who are alive are seen at a distance:

> The three people who had not left the cemetery stood over the grave. One of the men was less paunchy than the other. The woman's nails were broad and curved, the colour of old milk.
>
> "She was such a good girl," the woman said hoarsely. The men nodded.
>
> "Not exactly," said Laura Durand. She sat on the grass next to Michael and looked at the three people. "I was just tired." (44)

Michael and Laura are positioned differently with respect to the living world. Michael is still of it, his obsession with his wife and her trial, his need to have revenge—a revenge that turns out to hinge on a faked murder—all tie him to the world he has left. Yet the depiction of that world, his wife standing in front of his grave, is cinematic:

> As if she had heard, the woman knelt gracefully and put the rose back into line with the other flowers. Her long fingers had a slight tint of lemon to them, but her nails were the same shade as the roses. A little darker, perhaps; roses after rain.
>
> Thank you Sandra, Laura said. Good-by. She wondered where Michael was.
>
> "How much time do we have?" the woman asked. She and the man began to walk away from Michael's grave.
>
> "The trial's down for August eighth," the man answered. "Gives us almost a month." (130)

Beagle uses the proscenium arch to construct the relationship between worlds: is the audience or are the players more Real? And if Rebeck moves from one to the other, how Real is he? The dynamic between watched and watcher, Beagle's rhetorical construction of audience, throws the positioning of the fantastic into doubt. In this scene, in any scene where the ghosts watch the living, it is the living who seem fantastical.

Laura left the world with ease and without bitterness, and it is she that "creates" the world for both of them, makes it the "real" world and renders the otherworld a confused and confusing fantasy of what should have been. When Rebeck mentions that he has not seen her for some time, she comments that she was merely not wearing her body. "Sometimes I put my body back on. But not as often as I used to. It feels tight on me and makes me walk slowly. It always did. Some day, some day soon, I may just leave it and not come back" (92). Laura, by her way of being, challenges Rebeck's narration of the world. When she speaks, she almost always *describes* the world she has left. The world she is now in, she takes for granted.

The most significant incident is when Michael and Laura are sitting on the wall, Michael cannot hear the sounds of the city.

> [Michael] . . . smiled wryly at her puzzlement. "All the sounds we hear are sounds we remember. We know how talk and trains and running water should sound, and we're a little off in remembering, a little sharp or flat, nobody notices. But I just don't remember how Yorkchester sounded, all in all." (141)

Laura can. Because Laura paid attention to the city when alive, she knows what we, the readers know, that by describing one can make real. Paying attention, rather than location, is the key to being in a world, being aware of it to the degree that one can metaphorically give directions, but not so aware as to be continuously acknowledging it. As Michael learns to pay attention to Laura, he learns also to "live" in this otherworld. He himself moves from expressing the surprise, the curiosity, and the desire to work things out (the protagonist in the portal fantasy) to become a native of this world. One related issue is that he comes to recognize that his behavior in the living world—demanding attention, continually trying to win an ill-determined "quest"—made him an intruder in that world. Learning to love Laura is in part about learning to be fully of whichever world one is in. Eventually, both ghosts are able to reject the advice and philosophy of the mage-guide (Rebeck) and develop the native understanding of the rules of the fantasyland that forms the backbone of immersive fantasy.

Nevertheless, as we have seen in the chapter on immersive fantasy, the form is entirely compatible with intrusion fantasy, and from Laura and Michael's point of view, once immersed in this new world and no longer concerned with their journey through it, Rebeck takes on the form of an intrusion, that disturbance in the proper way of things that must be negotiated with and replaced in its own sphere. This intrusion is signaled when Rebeck exhibits his jealousy, interrupting their conversation: "He saw the childishly startled looks on their translucent faces and suddenly could think of nothing else to say. He had not shouted at anybody for a very long while" (49). Although we see it from Rebeck's point of view, rather than Laura or Michael's, Rebeck has registered that he is a mere side issue, when he had expected to remain the focus of their attention. He registers that the very source of his attraction for them—his life—is what ensures that he is not actually part of this world. But the choice of Rebeck as the viewpoint character means that the awe/surprise reaction usually encoded in the writing of intrusion fantasy is instead depicted only in the silence, the lack of response of the ghosts. Again Beagle constructs the fantastic through the absence rather than the presence of wonder.

If this is a ghost story, then Rebeck is the unsettled ghost. It is Rebeck's solipsism that positions Rebeck as the protagonist, his assumption that the crossroads in his lie are central to the story (118). Rebeck accepts that it is he who is the intrusion in this fantastic world. What he sees as his own space is actually the wrong side of the portal. What we are reading is an intrusion fantasy turned inside out, one that does not result in its apparent opposite, a portal fantasy. It is only when Rebeck, spurred by the ghostly Morris Klapper, leaves the cemetery that he truly begins his own portal fantasy; guided by his new mage, Mrs. Klapper, he enters a world that bears little resemblance to the one he once left.

When I began this book, its emphasis was on the way in which the fantastic entered the text. With the exception of the chapter on intrusion fantasies, there is a consequent emphasis on the way in which the reader enters the text. In my introduction, I emphasized that I would only regard this book, or this set of proposals, to have succeeded if it opened up more questions. Considering the books in this chapter, and particularly *A Fine and Private Place*, one new question to emerge is, How important is the leaving of the fantastic/the leaving of the story to the construction of the fantastic? To consider this in detail, I want to turn to Sean Stewart's *Galveston* (2000).

Galveston is an intrusion fantasy in which the intrusion has taken place in the past. In contrast to other intrusion fantasies, there is no surprise or awe, because those who were intruded upon are now old, and this tale is told by the second generation. The second generation has come to take for granted the conditions of the new world, but must still deal with the perspective of the older generation who are convinced they understand their world's narrative and rhetoric.[4] This tension drives the narrative in ways that double and redouble, the rhetoric of the fantastic paralleling the rhetoric of the story. This is not an intrusion plot within an immersive fantasy (as we saw in *Perdido Street Station*, in chapter 2), but a fantasy that is simultaneously an intrusion and an immersive fantasy, layered and entwined.

Galveston's first generation have held back the intrusion, placed a finger in the dike restraining the magic and pretended, as they dealt with the leaks, that they could hold it for ever, could reconstruct the pre–intruded-upon world. The older generation—Jane Gardner, the leader of the City; Odessa, the witch who holds back everyone's magic but her own; and Amanda Cane, the pharmacist—live their lives in an intrusion fantasy, in a constant state of fear and latency.

In contrast, their children accept the leaks and will, in the end, accept the flood: Sloane Gardner, Joshua Cane, and his friend Ham Mathers live in an immersive fantasy, but each exists in a different relationship to the fantastic. One element of both the fantastic and the mimetic rhetoric in this text is the difference between Ham, who is utterly immersed, and Joshua, who resists his own understanding of the world in a vain effort to preserve his mother's perspective. This resisting positions Joshua as a tourist in his own rhetorical world, which is doubled with a story line in which he refuses to accept that his social world is that of the poor to which he has descended, not that of the privileged from which he fell. And in this intrusion fantasy that is not an intrusion fantasy is—similarly—a portal fantasy that is not a portal fantasy: Sloane Garder, in an effort to save her dying mother, journeys into Krewes, the parallel and overlayed world in which the god Momus rules, a world that Odessa regards as utterly un-Real and that Sloane comes to realize is a felt absence from Galveston. Sloane's realization will be that magic accepted and lived with is utterly different from magic in the moment of arrival—This, of course, is one of the issues at stake in *this* (my) book.

The book opens perhaps thirty years after a tidal wave of magic has engulfed the city of Galveston, probably the entire United States, and perhaps the world: "Magic coalesced everywhere in the Flood, clotting around strong emotions, taking on flesh and will. Creatures born of survivor's joy and sufferers pain . . . had warred throughout the University of Texas Medical Branch, leaving the hospital a shattered ruin" (7). The result is trauma for the survivors. But as the book opens. this is already in the past and, crucially, the position of the reader is in the present, with the children of the survivors. *We* are not expected to take onboard this pain as our own, as we would in a traditional intrusion fantasy. The intrusion is *history* and is related in the kind of download we associate with history in the portal-quest fantasy: "In the spring of 2004 a cascade reaction began, magic kindling magic, the world awash in dreams. The bright rational day of the twentieth century was eclipsed, passing into a long night of spirits, here ghosts walked and a house or tree or road might wake to find its voice and will" (16). This history-intrusion is a deliberate rhetorical strategy, not a failure of immersion. The language Stewart deploys begins the construction of legend. The immersion is constructed in the tense struggle between the older generation to keep the Flood real and now and present, and the inevitability with which it becomes, to the younger generation, story and backdrop and, eventually, the very air they breathe.

At the end of the Flood, Jane Gardner and Odessa lead a city in which four of the five Krewes (originally guild-companies who sponsored the Mardi Gras parades) have agreed to keep what are now two Galvestons separate: the magic is confined to a world that exists both alongside and parallel to and overlaid with Galveston. It is a world of dark Carnival where the revelry never ceases, where those "gone to Krewes" go mad at the absence of time, and are trapped in the ever-present moment in yet an another irony, another inversion: this is precisely what, unknowing, the elders of Galveston have done to the city. Galveston is as much a fantastic world at odds with reality as is Carnival/Krewes.

As the book opens, the cracks are already appearing in Jane Gardner's consensus-Galveston. Her daughter Sloane muses, "if you felt God, or gods, you couldn't believe in Jane Gardner's world, could you? That great order the older generation had grown up with, before the Flood, was based on the idea that the world was inanimate. . . . But in a world alive, where that car might have a will . . . Jane Gardner would have said that the twentieth century was founded on reason, but Sloane wondered if vanity might be closer to the truth" (41). Sloane's musings direct our attention to a different way of understanding Jane Gardner's rhetorical position: to us, the readers, Jane is clearly the protagonist of an intrusion fantasy, but in her attempt to negotiate the new world, to make it (as Sloane notes) conform to twentieth-century perspectives, Jane positions herself as the protagonist in a portal fantasy. She *will* save the world, but what she is saving it from is itself and what she seeks to impose (as the four children impose the rule of Adam in Narnia) is a set of rules taken from another world. In so doing, she seeks to assert her old world as real, and her new world as somewhat less than real:

Sloane's mother always talked about magic as something impossible, something not real. The gods were wine or drugs that distorted your senses. Fever dreams and hallucinations. Nothing could be further than the truth. Standing before the hunchbacked god, Sloane knew that Momus alone was real. What she called life was a crayon drawing, crudely scribbled in a piece of paper, and Momus was the nail hammered through to pin it to the universe. (51)

One of the oldest philosophical threads in fantasy is this idea that the world we are in is the shadowland, that somewhere there is a Real place of which we are only copies. When Sloane enters Krewes after her first attempt to bargain fails, she does so wearing the mask that Odessa makes for her, a mask that does not disguise but renders her down to her essence, to *Sly*, the Sloane without the repressions, the girl she wished she was. And when Momus takes her heart into protective custody, he places it in the body of Scarlett, a fantastic creature in the shape of a small girl, perhaps ten years old but with the body of a two-year-old—a doll. Scarlett is "prettier, wilder, more exotic" but she is intensely *Sloane* (195).

While Sloane moves in and out of Krewes, Joshua moves in and out of his social world. When Sloane disappears, he and Ham are accused of rape and murder, and, because proof is circumstantial, they are expelled rather than executed. They survive capture by cannibals and a storm, and eventually return to Galveston where, at the exhortation of a ghost, Joshua saves the life of a boy by amputating his gangrenous leg. Where the blood splashes, Joshua's skin is washed milk-white. It is a portentous moment; this is not magic intruding into Galveston. As the ghostly Miss Bettie observes, "Our little sandbar has gone under the tide at last, Mr. Cane. Who is to say what miracles shall come to pass" (345).

As we reach the end of the story, we leave it in the direction of the magic. Galveston is moving further beneath the tide and, as the island is immersed, so too the strength of the immersive rhetoric increases. Those like Sheriff Denton who persist in framing the magic as an intrusion sound increasingly alien. When Joshua links hatred of the fantastic, of the *other*, with the age-old hatred of nonwhites (420–421), his is a doubled strategy: a calculated search for allies *and* a claiming of the world for a new generation. Denton does not look right-wing; he looks old-fashioned. The instantiation of the island took place within its children. The threat was from the inside, not the outside. In repudiating Denton, Joshua defines the immersive fantasy:

If this were 2004, I'd be in the streets with you, shooting any reveller you told me to. But it's not 2004. . . . The magic is coming and coming and coming, and there's no holding it back anymore. . . . *Those are our cards*, Sheriff. That's what

> life has dealt us this time around. And all we can do is play them as well as we can. (422)

I don't think Joshua's name is coincidental. If Moses took the children of Israel into the Wilderness, it is Joshua who leads them into the Promised Land, Joshua who says, this is what we have, make it work. Sean Stewart's *Galveston* is an antihorror. As Nalo Hopkinson wrote in response to this observation, "The scary world was mundane all along, not because you were seeing magic where there was none . . . but because you refused to accept the magic you could see perfectly well. You are not mad: the world is. Deal with it" (e-mail 14 December 2005).

Galveston is anti-intrusion fantasy, an inversion of the structure, not (as is the portal fantasy) its opposite. And this is why Joshua, Ham, and Sloane are, even as they usher in the period of immersion, not themselves fully immersed in the fantasy. As they construct it for those around them, they are themselves liminal figures. They and others of their age are Creole, with a foot in both the old age and the new:

> Bleakly Joshua tried to imagine what it would mean to live in a world where a dead woman might run the city's most powerful Krewe and a god could sit in on any hand of cards. Joshua's father would probably say it had been like that in the twentieth century, too. He'd say that tragedy had never been more than a car crash away, even before the flood. (449)

Joshua cannot "think" in the new language, but only in a hybrid of comparisons in which it is doubtful he understands either referent fully. It will be the next generation that will fully develop the language of Galveston, the language of immersion. His language (and it is with Joshua we are positioned at the end of the novel) is—like all creoles—a complex act of reluctant acceptance. At the end of this novel we are moving deeper into the fantastic: the portal is not a fixed space but a continuous process; the fantastic does not intrude once, but seeps over the land; the immersion is a state of mind, and it is one still developing.

Epilogue

Looking back over this book, I hope that I have drawn attention to a set of new questions to ask about fantastic literature. Emerging from the question with which I originally started—What happens if we consider fantasy from the way in which the fantastic enters the text?—have come issues of reader position and reader response; of character and story; issues of monosemy and polysemy; rather surprising (for me) conclusions about the apparent rigidity of ideological apparatus that surround the forms I identify; and an awareness that, while each form of fantasy plays the grammatical notes that Clute has identified, each shifts its emphasis to construct a set of variations of the fantastic. Elaborating on Attebery's original fuzzy set of fantasy, I have constructed four (or five) fuzzy sets, each of which yet looks to that common center that is so difficult to pinpoint, where mimesis ends and the fantastic begins. Perhaps the only thing at that center is the idea of *belief*, that however metaphoric a text may be, the fantastical must also contain a metonymic meaning, must be itself as much as it may be an enhancement.

If the schema I have outlined has any value at all, it will be in the questions it throws up about how authors use these structures and in the challenges it offers to writers of fantasy. Elsewhere I have used my own schema to interrogate the ways in which Diana Wynne Jones critiques fantasy in her fiction, while Brian Stableford has taken up other issues he feels are raised by these arguments in his *Historical Dictionary of Fantasy Literature* (xlvi–lxv and in many of the author entries therein).

This book was never intended to argue that the fantastic *should* be written in the ways I have outlined, but instead to say, "this is what I see, what else is possible?" It is an expression of faith in the narratological inventiveness of fantasy authors.

Notes

Introduction (pp. xiii–xxv)

1. A cursory consideration of the contents of the *Journal of the Fantastic in the Arts* will confirm this impression.

2. Karen Hellekson made the same decision when she constructed her taxonomy of Alternate History fictions ("Toward a Taxonomy" 251).

3. This itself is ideologically revealing. How many guests in utopia are shown the sewers?

4. Clute and I have had a number of discussions over which formulation of the grammar of Full Fantasy to use here. Clute being Clute, the formulation has gone through several revisions, rethinkings, and renamings. In the end, and knowing this is not his preference, I have chosen to go for the most physically accessible formula; that is, the version in the *Encyclopedia*.

5. For the importance and critical power of accepting the limits of individual theories, see my article, "Surpassing the Love of Vampires: Or Why (and How) a Queer Reading of the Buffy/Willow Relationship is Denied," in *Fighting the Forces: Essays on the Meaning of Buffy the Vampire Slayer*, ed. David Lavery and Rhonda Wilcox (Lanham, Md.: Rowman and Littlefield, 2001), 45–60.

6. At the end of *The Lord of the Rings* magic (in the form of grey dust from the Elves) is taken back to the Shire. It is made clear that magic is not normal to the Shire, that it is in fact an intrusion, made acceptable only because it smoothes the return to "normality."

7. In conversation over lunch in 2003.

1. The Portal-Quest Fantasy (pp. 1–58)

1. Although the first *Oz* book might more usually be thought of as a fantastical journey, in that the portal is patterned after the incredible journeys of the nineteenth century in which the actual adventures that occur are almost incidental to the text (the whirlwind might be seen as a facilitator rather than a portal).

2. A story that is clothed in the rationalizations of sf while adhering to the rules of fantasy. In this case, Darkover is a colony planet of Earth, whose

inhabitants practice matrix science manifesting as telepathy, telekinesis, and other psychic powers.

3. I shall not usually refer to non–English-language texts, given that language is precisely the issue of this book except where, as here, I am describing plot structures.

4. Although in *The Lord of the Rings* this figure is usually assumed to be Aragorn, Curtis Shoemaker has suggested that Sam also fulfills this role. "Just as Aragorn's presence renews the White Tree, Sam brings forth the new 'party tree': the Mallorn from Lorien, as well as all the other botanical wonders of the Shire's new age" (26 December 2002, International Association for the Fantastic in the Arts Mailing List).

5. Peter Nicholls writes of Katherine Kerr's work: "the central operating force is the destiny or Wyrd laid upon the major protagonists by the unseen forces of the universe. This is absolutely, centrally typical of the intellectual constructs found in genre fantasy . . . [but] . . . sooner or later [the reader] feels a sense of claustrophobia as he watches their characters become ever more trapped in their destinies" (34).

6. I am indebted to China Miéville for this succinct term, although he credits it to Guy Gavriel Kay. Its origins may be uncertain.

7. It is difficult to be sure without more research but this mistake appears to be predominantly American. The classic restoration fantasy in which the fated child reaches maturity and a crown is rare in the U.K. fantasy scene.

8. Brian Attebery alludes to this when he describes Dorothy as "aggressively, triumphantly American," but this is an America of the borderlands, not the more communitarian and conservative America of the cities (*Tradition* 96).

9. *Harry Potter and the Philosopher's Stone* [*Harry Potter and the Sorcerer's Stone*] (1997), *The Lord of the Rings* (1954–55), and *A Tale of Time City* (1997), respectively.

10. "We *live* our lives in chronological order. When we *remember* them, however, our mental movement is almost entirely associational" (Delany 42).

11. "The True State of Affairs" (Diana Wynne Jones [1995]), *Vurt* (Jeff Noon [1993]), and *The Iron Dragon's Daughter* (Michael Swanwick [1994]) in which the quest is for the portal.

12. "By far the most outstanding fact when looking at the titles of landscapes exhibited at the Academy in these early years [1770–1790] is the paucity of place-names. Most landscapes were compositions, John Rothstein's [1933] remark, 'a special aim of landscape painting is the reduction of the disorder of nature to an orderly design' is most obviously true in this period. Many artists saw no reason for this design to relate to a particular place, and frequently even to guess the subject matter with any confidence is difficult. . . . Such landscapes were constructed from a kit of parts" (Howard 31).

13. The issue of grandeur is complex but so many U.S. fantasies move through huge, imposing landscapes. To take just two U.K. equivalents discussed in this text, both *The Lion, the Witch and the Wardrobe* (C. S. Lewis [1950]), and

Mythago Wood (Robert Holdstock [1984]) take place in *woods*; the landscape is almost homely. The attempt to make the landscape of Lewis's tale imposing in the 2005 movie merely left the adventure looking a little lost and overwhelmed. See Steve Cockayne's *The Good People* (2006) for a discussion of the necessity of homely landscape as the appropriate foil for grand adventure.

14. Scholasticism rewrote history or science on the basis of what the ancients wrote, assuming that in a fallen world, knowledge diminished in the world rather than expanded.

15. In Rebecca Lisle's *Copper* (2002) the wardrobe is the way in, but is only found as the way out. It's a nice homage to *The Lion, the Witch and the Wardrobe*.

16. See Jones, *Howl's Moving Castle* (1986) and Hambly, *The Magicians of Night* (1991) respectively.

17. One concern here is that the way in which he is treated is almost classic brainwashing technique. In this case, it is used entirely on the side of good. C. S. Lewis will use it in *The Silver Chair* for evil ends. In the second sequence, the most lengthy, much of the narrative is straightforward even while confusing (although there are two set pieces to which I shall return), while the final sequence, the least successful, is the most allegorical, as if at this point MacDonald lost courage in the power of the fantastic and in the willingness of his readers *to stay confused*.

18. Among the metastories are his two encounters with the skeletons. In some ways, the most affecting tableaux in the text, they are entirely *watched*. Vane plays no part in them. In the first, skeletons only partly clothed in flesh dance. In the second, we meet a skeleton couple on the road, and the intention is clearly to construct a ghost story. That this is not effected is because the narrative tone remains that of description: it lacks the intensity and the naïveté essential to horror, and there is no sense of Vane's response (120–126). It is undermined further by the raven's explanation of what is witnessed (126–129). This narrative pattern is repeated when he describes the fights between the two cats (187–188). He is always observer, not participant. Pages 195–199 are entirely devoted to the raven explaining to Vane the "story" of his time with the Lovers. He cannot interpret these tableaux for himself, but must have them interpreted for him. And Lilith is explained, not by his own discoveries, but by the raven's narration of her history (including the link with Nona) which biblifies her (204–207).

19. Unlike Dorothy, who is never described in much detail as we are more interested in her impressions than her appearance, the Scarecrow, being all outside, as it were, is described quite exactly, and with frequent subsequent references to his peculiar looks.

20. For example: "This worried Dorothy a little, but she knew that only the great Oz could help her get back to Kansas again, so she bravely resolved not to turn back" (36).

21. Several readers of this chapter reminded me that Kansas is heartland America. To which all I can say is "in 1900 it wasn't."

22. Given the many editions available, I have thought it best to reference this book to chapter titles.

23. Most sword and sorcery novels, although sometimes structured around a search, are not quest novels: the object sought is rarely intended to change the world, and frequently becomes merely a plot token. "Deliciously pointless" might be the best way to describe these "quests."

24. For a particularly detailed description of the Vale that assumes newness and negotiation with the landscape, see p. 7.

25. See also p. 518 in which a rope can only be "pulled violently."

26. "Semantic material is always given to the hero's consciousness all at once and in its entirety, and given not as individual thoughts and propositions but as the semantic orientations of whole human beings, as voices; it remains only to make a choice among them. . . . This is why it is so common for heroes (or for a narrator speaking about a hero) to announce, after a catastrophe, that they had known and foreseen everything in advance" (Bahktin 239).

27. Incidentally placing the story as sf, not fantasy, or at least as rationalized fantasy. The story takes place after a nuclear war.

28. Shea declares: "Allanon can't tell us what to do forever. . . . Besides, I'm still not convinced that he has told us the truth about himself" (114). Unfortunately for any kind of tension, Shea is wrong.

29. The prophecy is downloaded from Nisses's book, cited by Morgenes, whose book is a bringing together of all known scholarship (661; see also 665 where knowledge is, of course, found in the past).

30. There are only two books in this sequence, although Hambly's most recent book, *Sisters of the Raven* (2002), seems to be set in the same universe as *The Rainbow Abyss* but sometime in the future.

31. In conversation, lunch sometime in 2003.

32. There is an implication that Smeagol is tortured for the truth of the ring (*Fellowship*: "The Council of Elrond" 332).

33. The yellow bricks coming into the city are mentioned only twice. This may be coincidental but it caused me to pause.

34. We see the same techniques in William Goldman's *The Princess Bride* (1973).

35. Pullman manages to pull off the reverse. In the *Northern Lights* [*The Golden Compass*], we are continually told that Lyra is central, but in this and its sequels we are rarely *shown* that she is, and in *The Amber Spyglass* (2000) she becomes obscure.

36. In his exchange with Justina Robson, Miéville wrote of New Weird fiction (a rather amorphous category label that emerged around 2003 and that was debated extensively on mailing lists and at conventions), that the traditional shape of the book might be necessary to the Weird: "Narrative/story is intrinsically comforting, because it is the imposition of structure (and thus implied meaning) on a contingent mass of stuff—narrative arc does violence to the chaos

of the Real" (Miéville, on M. John Harrison's message board at http://www.ttapress.com, 20 May 2003).

2. The Immersive Fantasy (pp. 59–113)

1. Even within mimetic literature, the extent to which the bible is shared may vary. Novels set in distant lands may have to engage in some of the world-building techniques we associate with sf. Novels written one hundred years ago may come to require more contextual reading from their audience than was intended.

2. Paul McAuley, discussing the New Weird (a movement in fantasy that began with the publication of China Miéville's *Perdido Street Station* in 2000): "the ordinariness of the frame-of-reference of any narrative discourse is culturally relative . . . what was once ordinary to the reader can with time become if not fantastic then at least unsettlingly different which is why my Penguin editions of Dickens's novels have footnotes that recontextualise for the modern reader the ordinary cultural framework of Victorian London" (on M. John Harrison's message board at http://www.ttapress.com, 4 June 2003).

3. Interview at the British Science Fiction Association, March 2004.

4. The closest predecessors to these novels may be Jack Vance's Big Planet stories and Robert Silverberg's *Lord Valentine's Castle*, both of which are popularly read as science fiction.

5. For a more extensive discussion, see E. H. Gombrich, *Art and Illusion: A Study in the Psychology of Pictorial Representation* (London: Phaidon Press, 1959).

6. One of the most powerful uses of immersive perspective is in David Inshaw's landscape, *The Cricket Game* (1979). Michael Benton writes:

> It was some minutes after first coming across David Inshaw's painting, *The Cricket Game* (1976), before I realised how I had been neatly positioned by the artist. Initially, my attention was caught by the atmosphere of an evening landscape, the vibrant greens of the rolling Dorset hills, a pale half-moon and lengthening shadows signalling that the sun was dropping out of sight somewhere to the right. . . . Cricket, I reflected, must be David Inshaw's religion. Then I realised how he had drawn me in: my perceptions adjusted from the sublime to the mundane, from the intertextualities of high culture to the banalities of "Spot the ball"! Where is it? The fast bowler is on. . . . An aggressive field is set . . . the left-hand batsman has swung and missed. . . . The keeper takes the ball: that's the moment of the picture. But, if the batsman had connected, the ball may well have skied on the leg side, if silly mid-on's movement is anything to go by; skied, in fact towards me, the invisible fielder at deep mid-wicket. I checked the figures just to be sure: two umpires, two batsmen, but only *ten* on the fielding side. As a spectator, I had been accommodated as someone to make up the number. What's more, I had been given

a pretty big area of the outfield to patrol—from a fielding position that afforded a central view of the action like that of a wide-angled lens; and from a vantage point just inside the boundary where the ground must rise, as it does under the trees beyond the bowler. (1–2)

7. Discussing the New Weird with M. John Harrison on his message board, I extended this perspective: "The New Weird is written as if by someone who has been commissioned to write a travel guide but who has no idea what a travel guide is, has never met a tourist, and didn't actually know that there were people out there" (on M. John Harrison's message board at http://www.ttapress.com, 7 June 2003). Miéville responded: "*Perdido Street Station: or, a Guide to New Crobuzon By a Local Moron with No Sense of Perspective*" (7 June 2003).

8. This book is itself a critique of the portal-quest fantasy and the politics of "tourists in fantasyland." It could be read alongside two essays, Ann Bermingham's "System Order, and Abstraction: The Politics of English Landscape Drawing around 1795" (77–102) and Elizabeth Helsinger's "Turner and the Representation of England" (103–126) in *Landscape and Power*, ed. W. J. T. Mitchell (Chicago: University of Chicago Press, 1994).

9. For the full discussion of Jones's techniques, see chapter 6 of Mendlesohn, *Diana Wynne Jones: Children's Literature and the Fantastic Tradition* (New York: Routledge, 2005).

10. Although author motivation is not really the subject matter of this book, I think it is no coincidence that *The Iron Dragon's Daughter* came out of an attempt to locate a fantasy in personal experience of the landscape. In the *New York Review of Science Fiction* Swanwick wrote scathingly of the "nostalgic hunt for authenticity" in the presumed-static culture of others. His moment of revelation came in Ireland:

> My wife and I were in Ireland, looking at an old ring fort, and a ten-year-old boy came out of his house to ask what we were doing. "Photographing the fairy ring." Marianne said. The kid looked disgusted and said, "Don't tell me you still believe in fairies!"
>
> Where I came from we don't have castles, cairns, holy wells or standing stones. Seeing them for the first time, they looked completely different from how I'd imagined them. I realized then that this is why so much of the best fantasy comes from the British Isles, and why so much American fantasy is so bad. Their writers grow up with ring forts literally in their back yards sometimes, while ours grow up reading their books. . . .
>
> Sometime later . . . I was driving to Pittsburgh and talking with my wife about fantasy novels and steam locomotives. I made a joke about the dragon at the Baldwin Steam Dragon works . . . (8)

All of the writers in this chapter write in the landscape that belongs to *them*. There is no reason that this should have to be the case, and there are not enough examples here to truly make an argument, but I think Swanwick's point may lurk as one of the hidden ideologies of the immersive fantasy (December 2003).

11. This book has also been turned into a Broadway musical. Although some of its popularity has almost certainly been founded on the popularity of *The Wizard of Oz*, its political messages are particularly relevant to George W. Bush's social policies, which seem to be trying to roll back the advancement of minority groups. Although written in 1995, the book may yet gain the stature of *The Crucible* as a barely veiled attack on social injustice.

12. *The Tale of the Ugly Stepsister* (1999) and *Mirror Mirror* (2003) respectively.

13. See the interview with Nalo Hopkinson at sci.fi.com: http://www.scifi.com/sfw/issue232/interview2.html.

14. This story was supplied in manuscript by the author. I have been unable to source the printed copy.

15. This story was also supplied in manuscript. The quotation is from page 1.

16. "Alien Sex Acts in Feminist Science Fiction: Heuristic Models for Thinking of a Feminist Future of Desire," *PMLA* 119, no. 3 (May 2004): 442–456.

17. Greer Watson in her article, "Introduction to a Multivariate Approach to Analyzing the Fantasmatic." *New York Review of Science Fiction*, issue 183; 16, no. 3 (November 2003): 14.

18. In *The Dream of Arkady*, MacKethan discusses in chapter 1 the way in which the voice of nostalgia is placed in the mouth of the ex-slave, especially in the work of Joel Chandler Harris. Her chapter 9, which focuses on Eudora Welty's fiction, is also pertinent to this discussion.

3. The Intrusion Fantasy (pp. 114–181)

1. Moss also points out that in the vampire genre as it developed in the nineteenth century, skepticism was the originating context that the vampire was able to exploit, and that in contemporary horror, the characters frequently revert to skepticism despite everything they have experienced (e-mail 16 September 2005).

2. Although it is not this book's business to explore the market, this issue may explain the astonishingly cyclical market presence of horror fiction. Each generation learns, is disillusioned, and passes away, leaving the genre to await the next entry of naive readers.

3. Guy Barker, commentary on "Dizzy Gillespie," episode of on *Ken Clark's Jazz Greats*. BBC Radio 4. 22 May 2005.

4. This may be merely coincidental, but that other Lucy, in chapter 5 of *Prince Caspian*, has a similar engagement with an older sibling when she insists that she has seen Aslan:

> "Where did you think you saw him?" asked Susan.
>
> "Don't talk like a grown-up," said Lucy, stamping her foot. "I didn't *think* I saw him. I saw him." (chap. 5, "What Lucy Saw")

5. When the witches defeat the vampires in Terry Pratchett's *Carpe Jugulum*, one aspect of their rage is the way the vampires have constructed a consensus reality that encourages humans to believe a "consensual" donation of blood is better than fighting the vampires.

6. Although the evidence of the texts in this chapter suggests that the more personal the better, I suspect that this is a function of the selection made, not of the category.

7. See McWilliams again, chap. 7, "Till a Better Epic Comes Along."

8. McWilliams, "Prospect," 238–239.

9. The trend in later American epic poetry—such as Daniel Bryan's transfiguration of Daniel Boone into a sort of Norse god in *The Mountain Muse*, carried on the back of a bear—may have fed straight into American heroic fantasy, providing the link between heroic folk tales and the likes of Conan the Barbarian.

10. Moss points out that Lovecraft frequently uses a landscape that really exists for his mythical towns: "the illusion of verisimilitude, is exactly what creates the terror. He turns a mundane world known by the reader into a horrific world that exists underneath" (e-mail 16 September 2005). This technique is emulated by many modern horror writers.

11. Personal conversation, June 2005.

12. Telephone conversation, 21 July 2006.

13. *Neverwhere* and *King Rat* are both portal fantasies although they begin with intrusions. The protagonists in both are pulled into the other world where they become involved in its needs. There is no threatened intrusion into the origin world.

14. Emma Bull's *War for the Oaks* is referenced to the citations from the 2001 edition.

15. Nalo Hopkinson, e-mail to author, 17 August 2005.

16. Although the primary structure of *King Rat* is formed around Saul's exploration of his new world, the intrusion of the Piper is marked in ways we understand in this chapter, with the Piper looming larger, more intimate, louder, and eventually in more than one line of flute music. (see chapter 5, this volume, for discussion of this incorporation).

17. See 71: "I wanted her. *Her.* The girl from the wildwood who had obsessed my brother."

18. This is a common misapprehension in the arts.

19. See 93, *Whose Mythago was she?* with its assumption that mythagos are something owned because they are something created.

20. For more comments on the intense Englishness of the novel and its contribution to the novel's internal structure, see Henry Farrell, "Return of the King," in *Jonathan Strange and Mr. Norrell: A Crooked Timber Symposium* (2005).

21. The name seems to be "stare-across," as in stare across worlds.

22. As during his visit to the King (355).

23. Ray Bradbury's "Referent" (1948) uses this idea.

24. M. John Harrison, conversation on a train, 14 October 2006.

4. The Liminal Fantasy (pp. 182–245)

1. Such legal fictions are not confined to fantasy; in the early years of the American Civil War, the Union, reluctant to free runaway slaves while they still hoped for early reunification, termed such people "contraband" and confiscated property.

2. So that the slake moths in Miéville's *Perdido Street Station* (2001) do not fit this category because although unusual, they are not alien.

3. This book does not consider television and film, as I am suspicious of attempts to create universal critical tools that apply to all creative forms. Still, it is interesting to note that *Buffy the Vampire Slayer* adopts an almost identical format from around season 5.

In seasons 1 to 3, *Buffy* is a classic intrusion fantasy. Although Buffy has accepted that there are nasty things out there, and they are breaking into the world, each of them is new and must be negotiated with. In season 3, our sense that Buffy lives in a world parallel to that of most people in Sunnydale is broken with the graduation scene, when her classmates acknowledge that there is something wrong with their town. But in seasons 5 and 6, Whedon uses this new situation to "flip" the horror, so that as the supernatural becomes more accepted and ordinary, the real horror comes from the everyday (such as the death of Joyce Summers from a brain tumor—no supernatural element required). In season 6, when Buffy is "doing things by numbers, going through the motions," the interaction of sardonic flippancy in the face of demons, hellholes, and the end of the world replicates Aiken's forms. No one is surprised any more by the supernatural. It's real life that is the real source of absurdity.

4. China Miéville uses this idea particularly effectively in *The Tain* (PS Publishing, 2003), maintaining equipoise as I have described it here for most of the novella.

5. That Kate's story of the lover torn to pieces is the story of Isis and Osiris may or may not be relevant here.

6. William Allingham's poem *The Fairies*, for example, furnishes the idea of an aging fairy kingdom and the accoutrements of fairy with which the newly married Smoky is garbed.

7. Jack always explains that he has a brother who is a CO. Joe simply replies, until very late, that he is not an RAF officer.

8. Dan Harland, in an online argument put it this way; "a reader of SF will expect—nay, demand and place a clear value on—a certain level of, well, earnestness to a novel's confected scenarios; a sense from the world depicted that it is *real*, not a counter-factual exercise or cowardly metaphor" On *Internal Oppressions*, http://fjm.livejournal.com/143590.html (12 November 2005).

5. "The Irregulars": Subverting the Taxonomy (pp. 246–272)

1. Of course, what Cockayne actually describes is a *real* world. No real world is ever "consistent" in its periodicity; it is always an overlay of the old-fashioned with the contemporary, with the incredibly new.

2. Rereading this, and now aware of Cockayne's background as a TV cameraman, I realize that this is of course Orac from the BBC's 1970s sf series, *Blake's 7*.

3. We discover, for example, that ghosts do not necessarily, as Rebeck believes, diffuse; they merely decide their bodies are no longer comfortable.

4. A common issue in utopian studies, and in studies of the religious colonies of colonial America, is how the children of the driven cope with a story of travail that is not their own. This may even be considered one of the *über* stories, even though it is not a common one; it is, of course, also the story of the Israelites in the wilderness.

Bibliography

Nonfiction

Ansley, William H. "Little, Big Girl: The Influence of the Alice Books and Other Works of Lewis Carroll on John Crowley's Novel, *Little, Big or, the Fairies Parliament.*" In *Snake's Hands: The Fiction of John Crowley*, edited by Alice K. Turner and Michael Andre-Driussi, 165–204. Holicong, Pa.: Cosmos Books, 2003.

Attebery, Brian. *The Fantasy Tradition in American Literature: From Irving to Le Guin*. Bloomington: Indiana University Press, 1980.

———. Reader's report for Wesleyan University Press, 2006.

———. *Strategies of Fantasy*. Bloomington: Indiana University Press, 1992.

Avery, Derek. *Antoni Gaudí*. London: Chaucer Press, 2004.

Bakhtin, Mikhail. *Problems of Dostoevsky's Poetics*. Edited and translated by Caryl Emerson. With an introduction by Wayne C. Booth. Theory and History of Literature, vol. 8. Manchester: Manchester University Press, 1984.

Barker, Guy. Commentary on "Dizzy Gillespie." Episode of *Ken Clark's Jazz Greats*. BBC Radio 4, 22 May 2005.

Barnes, Hazel E. *The Literature of Possibility: A Study in Humanistic Existentialism*. London: Tavistock Publications, 1961.

Barthes, Roland. "To Write: An Intransitive Verb." In (*The Languages of Criticism and the Sciences of Man:*) *The Structuralist Controversy*,' edited by R. Macksey and E. Donato, 134–154. Baltimore, Md.: Johns Hopkins University Press, 1970.

Benton, Michael. *Studies in the Spectator Role: Literature, Painting and Pedagogy*. New York: Routledge, 2000.

Bermingham, Ann. "System, Order, and Abstraction: The Politics of English Landscape Drawing around 1795." In *Landscape and Power*, edited by W. J. T. Mitchell, 77–102. Chicago: University of Chicago Press, 1994.

Booth, Wayne C. *The Rhetoric of Fiction*. 2nd ed. Chicago: University of Chicago Press, 1983.

———. *A Rhetoric of Irony*. Chicago: University of Chicago Press, 1974.

Boruah, Bijoy H. *Fiction and Emotion: A Study in Aesthetics and the Philosophy of the Mind*. Oxford: Clarendon Press, 1988.

Bosky, Bernadette. E-mail to the author, 10 March 2005.

Branham, Robert J. "Fantasy and Ineffability: Fiction at the Limits of Language." *Extrapolation* 24, no. 1 (1983): 66–79.

Butler, Andrew M. E-mail to the IAFA mailing list, 23 March 2003.

Cameron, Eleanor. *The Seed and the Vision: On Writing and Appreciation of Children's Books*. New York: Plume, 1993.

Clarke, Arthur C. *Profiles of the Future: An Inquiry into the Limits of the Possible*. 2nd ed. New York: Harper and Row, 1973.

Clute, John, "Beyond the Pale." In *Conjunctions 39: The New Wave Fabulists*, edited by Bradford Morrow and Peter Straub, 420–433. Annandale-on-Hudson, N.Y.: Bard College, 2003.

———. E-mail to author, 9 September 2004.

———. E-mail to IAFA mailing list, 4 September 2002.

———. *Scores: Reviews 1993–2003*. Harold Wood, Essex: Beccon Publications, 2003.

———. *Strokes: Essays and Reviews, 1966–1986*. Seattle: Serconia Press, 1988.

———, and John Grant, eds. *The Encyclopedia of Fantasy*. London: Orbit, 1997.

Csicery-Ronay, Istvan, Jr. "On the Grotesque in Science Fiction." *Science Fiction Studies*. 29, no. 86 (2002): 71–99.

Delany, Samuel R. *About Writing: Seven Essays, Four Letters and Five Interviews*. Middletown, Conn.: Wesleyan University Press, 2005.

Farrell, Henry. "Return of the King." In *Jonathan Strange and Mr. Norrell: A Crooked Timber Seminar*. <http://crookedtimber.org/2005/11/29/>. PDF download: 33–37.

Fish, Stanley. *Is There a Text in This Class? The Authority of Interpretive Communities*. Cambridge, Mass.: Harvard University Press, 1980.

Frye, Northrop. *Anatomy of Criticism: Four Essays*. Princeton, N.J.: Princeton University Press, 1957.

———. *The Great Code: The Bible and Literature*. New York: Harcourt Brace, 1982.

Genette, Gérard. *Narrative Discourse: An Essay on Method*. Translated by Jane E. Lewin. With a foreword by Jonathan Culler. Ithaca, N.Y.: Cornell University Press, 1982.

Gilman, Greer. Livejournal *Nineweaving*. 23 August 2005.

Gombrich, E. H. *Art and Illusion: A Study in the Psychology of Pictorial Representation*. London: Phaidon Press, 1959.

Gullon, Ricardo. "Gabriel García Márquez and the Lost Art of Storytelling." Translated José G. Sanchez. *Diacritics* 1, no. 1 (Autumn 1971): 27–32.

Harland, Dan. *On Internal Oppressions*, 12 November 2005. <http://fjm.livejournal.com/143590.html>.

Hayakawa. S. I. *Language in Thought and Action* [c. 1939]. London: Allen and Unwin, 1974.

Hellekson, Karen. "Toward a Taxonomy of the Alternate History Genre." *Extrapolation* 41, no. 3 (Fall 2000): 248–256.

Helsinger, Elizabeth. "Turner and the Representation of England." In *Landscape and Power*, edited by W. J. T. Mitchell, 103–126. Chicago: University of Chicago Press, 1994.

Holbo, John. "Two Thoughts (About Magic Christians and Two Cities)." In *Jonathan Strange and Mr. Norrell: A Crooked Timber Seminar*. <http://crookedtimber.org/2005/11/29/>. PDF download: 15–32.

Hopkinson, Nalo. E-mail to author, 17 August 2005.

———. E-mail to author, 14 December 2005.

———. Interview. <http://www.scifi.com/sfw/issue232/interview2.html>.

Howard, Peter. *Landscapes: The Artists' Vision*. New York: Routledge, 1991.

Hume, Kathryn. *Fantasy and Mimesis: Responses to Reality in Western Literature*. New York: Methuen: 1984.

Huntington, John. *Rationalizing Genius: Ideological Strategies in the Classic American Science Fiction Short Story*. New Brunswick, N.J.: Rutgers University Press, 1987.

Irwin, W. R. *The Game of the Impossible: A Rhetoric of Fantasy*. Urbana: University of Illinois Press, 1976.

Jackson, Rosemary. *Fantasy: The Literature of Subversion*. London: Methuen, 1981.

James, Edward. *Science Fiction in the Twentieth Century*. Oxford: Oxford University Press, 1994.

Jameson, Fredric. *The Political Unconscious: Narrative as a Symbolic Act*. London: Methuen, 1981.

Jones, Diana Wynne. *The Tough Guide to Fantasyland*. London: Vista, 1996.

Keeble, N. H. Introduction to *The Pilgrim's Progress* [1678 and 1684]. By John Bunyan. Oxford: Oxford University Press, 1984.

Laskar, Benjamin. "Suicide and the Absurd: The Influence of Jean-Paul Satre's and Albert Camus's Existentialism on Stephen Donaldson's *The Chronicles of Thomas Covenant the Unbeliever*." *Journal of the Fantastic in the Arts* 14, no. 4 (Winter 2004): 409–426.

Leffler, Yvonne. *Horror as Pleasure: The Aesthetics of Horror Fiction*. Stockholm: Almqvist and Wiksell International, 2000.

MacKethan, Lucinda Hardwick. *The Dream of Arcady: Place and Time in Southern Literature*. Baton Rouge: Louisiana State University Press, 1980.

Maisano, Scott. "Reading Underwater; Or, Fantasies of Fluency from Shakespeare to Miéville and Emshwiller." *Extrapolation* 45, no. 1 (Spring 2004): 76–86.

Manlove, Colin. *The Fantasy Literature of England*. Basingstoke: Macmillan, 1999.

———. *The Impulse of Fantasy Literature*. Basingstoke: Macmillan, 1983.

Mathews, Richard. *Aldiss Unbound: The Science Fiction of Brian W. Aldiss*. San Bernardino, Calif.: Borgo Press, 1977.

McAuley, Paul. Post on M. John Harrison's message board, 4 June 2003. <http://www.ttapress.com>.

McCabe, Allyssa, and Carole Peterson, eds. *Developing Narrative Structure*. Hillsdale, N.J.: Erlbaum, 1991.

McHale, Brian. *Postmodernist Fiction*. New York: Methuen, 1987.

McWilliams, John P. *The American Epic: Transforming a Genre, 1770–1860*. Cambridge: Cambridge University Press, 1989.

Mendlesohn, Farah. "*Perdido Street Station* and Strategies of Fantasy." *SFRA Review* 262 (January–February 2003): 9–13.

———. Post on M. John Harrison's message board, 7 June 2003. <http://www.ttapress.com>.

———. "Surpassing the Love of Vampires: Or Why (and How) a Queer Reading of the Buffy/ Willow Relationship is Denied." In *Fighting the Forces: Essays on the Meaning of Buffy the Vampire Slayer*, edited by David Lavery and Rhonda Wilcox, 45–60. Lanham, Md.: Rowman and Littlefield, 2001.

Miéville, China. E-mail to author, 16 January 2003.

———. Post on M. John Harrison's message board, 20 May 2003. <http://www.ttapress.com>.

———. Post on M. John Harrison's message board, 7 June 2003. <http://www.ttapress.com>.

Mitchell, W. J. T. *Landscape and Power*. Chicago: University of Chicago Press, 1994.

Moorcock, Michael. *Wizardry and Wild Romance*. London: Gollancz, 1987.

Moss, Stephanie. E-mail to author, 16 September 2005.

Nicholls, Peter. "Trapped in the Pattern: Science Fiction vs Fantasy, Open Universes vs Closed Universes, Free Will vs Predestination." In *The Fantastic Self: Essays on the Subject of the Self*, edited by Janeen Webb and Andrew Enstice, 28–36. North Perth, Australia: Eidolon, 1999.

O'Brien, Raymond J. *American Sublime: Landscape and Scenery in the Lower Hudson Valley*. New York: Columbia University Press, 1981.

Olsen, Lance. *Ellipse of Uncertainty: An Introduction to Postmodern Fantasy*. Westport, Conn.: Greenwood Press, 1987.

Punter, David. *The Literature of Terror: A History of Gothic Fictions from 1765 to the Present Day*. New York: Longmans, 1980.

Rahn, Suzanne. *Rediscoveries in Children's Literature*. New York: Garland, 1995.

Reed, Julia. *Queen of the Turtle Derby and Other Southern Phenomena*. New York: Random House, 2004.

Rifaterre, Michael. *Fictional Truth*. Baltimore, Md.: Johns Hopkins University Press, 1980.

Rimmon-Kenan, Slomith. *Narrative Fiction: Contemporary Poetics*. New York: Routledge, 2002.

Ringel, Faye. E-mail to author, 7 January 2005.

Robson, Justina. Post on M. John Harrison's message board, 20 May 2003. <http://www.ttapress.com>.

Rogan, Alecena Madelaine Davis. "Alien Sex Acts in Feminist Science Fiction: Heuristic Models for Thinking of a Feminist Future of Desire." *PMLA* 119, no. 3 (May 2004): 442–456.

Ryan, Marie-Laure. *Narrative as Virtual Reality: Immersion and Interaction in Literature and Electronic Media*. Baltimore, Md.: Johns Hopkins University Press, 2001.

Sage, Victor. *Horror Fiction in the Protestant Tradition*. Basingstoke: Macmillan, 1988.

Schiffman, Smadar. "Someone Else's Dream? An Approach to Twentieth Century Fantastic Fiction." *Journal of the Fantastic in the Arts* 13, no. 4 (2003): 352–367.

Schlobin, Roger C. "'Rituals' Footprints Ankle-deep in Stone': The Irrelevancy of Setting in the Fantastic." *Journal of the Fantastic in the Arts* 11, no. 2 (2000): 154–163.

Scholes, Robert. *Structural Fabulation: An Essay on Fiction of the Future*. Notre Dame, Ind.: University of Notre Dame Press, 1975.

Sedgwick, Eve Kosofsky. *The Coherence of Gothic Conventions*. New York: Arno Press, 1980.

Senior, W. A. *Stephen R. Donaldson's Chronicles of Thomas Covenant: Variations on the Fantasy Tradition*. Kent, Ohio: Kent State University Press, 1995.

Shoemaker, Curtis. E-mail to IAFA mailing list, 26 December 2002.

Sleight, Graham. E-mail to IAFA mailing list, 21 October 2003.

Slusser, George, and Eric S. Rabkin, eds. *Styles of Creation: Aesthetic Technique and the Creation of Fictional Worlds*. Athens: University of Georgia Press, 1992.

Spencer, Kathleen. "Naturalizing the Fantastic: Narrative Technique in the Novels of Charles Williams." *Extrapolation* 28, no. 1 (Winter 1987): 62–74.

Stableford, Brian. *Historical Dictionary of Fantasy Literature*. Historical Dictionaries of Literature and the Arts, vol. 5. Lanham, Md.: Scarecrow Press, 2005.

———. *The Way to Write Science Fiction*. London: Elm Tree Books, 1989.

———. *Writing Fantasy and Science Fiction: And Getting Published*. Los Angeles: NTC/Contemporary Publishing, 1998.

Staley, Allen. *The Pre-Raphaelite Landscape*. New Haven, Conn.: Yale University Press, 2001.

Straub, Peter. "Horror's House." *Locus*, issue 507; 50, no. 4 (April 2003): 8 and 66.

Suvin, Darko. "Considering the Sense of 'Fantasy' or 'Fantastic Fiction': An Effusion." *Extrapolation* 41, no. 3 (Fall 2000): 209–248.

———. *Metamorphoses of Science Fiction: On the Poetics and History of a Literary Genre*. New Haven, Conn.: Yale University Press, 1979.

Swanwick, Michael. "The View From the Top of the Mountain." *New York Review of Science Fiction*, issue 184; 16, no. 4 (December 2003): 1 and 6–9.

Tannen, Deborah. *Conversational Style: Analyzing Talk Among Friends*. Norwood, N.J.: Ablex, 1984.

Todorov, Tzvetan. *The Fantastic: A Structural Approach to a Literary Genre*. Translated by Richard Howard. Ithaca, N.Y.: Cornell University Press, 1973.

———. *Introduction to Poetics*. Translated by Richard Howard. Brighton, England: Harvester Press, 1981.

Toohey, Peter. *Reading Epic: An Introduction to the Ancient Narratives*. New York: Routledge, 1992.

Van Belkom, Edo. *Writing Horror*. Bellingham, Wash., and N. Vancouver, Canada: Self-Counsel Press, 2000.

Walton, Kendall L. *Mimesis as Make-Believe: On the Foundations of the Representational Arts*. Cambridge, Mass.: Harvard University Press, 1990.

Watson, Greer. "Assumptions of Reality: Low Fantasy, Magical Realism, and the Fantastic." *Journal of the Fantastic in the Arts* 11, no. 2 (2000): 164–172.

———. "Introduction to a Multivariate Approach to Analyzing the Fantasmatic." *New York Review of Science Fiction*, issue 183; 16, no. 3 (November 2003): 13–15.

Watt, James. *Contesting the Gothic: Fiction, Genre and Cultural Conflict, 1764–1832*. Cambridge: Cambridge University Press, 1999.

Wendland, Albert. *Science, Myth, and the Fictional Creation of Alien Worlds*. Ann Arbor, Mich.: UMI Research Press, 1985.

Westfahl, Gary. "Words of Wisdom; The Neologisms of Science Fiction." In *Styles of Creation: Aesthetic Technique and the Creation of Fictional Worlds*, edited by George Slusser and Eric S. Rabkin, 221–244. Athens: University of Georgia Press, 1992.

Wilson, Rob. *American Sublime: The Genealogy of a Poetic Genre*. Madison: University of Wisconsin Press, 1991.

Wilton, Andrew. "The Sublime in the Old World and the New." In *American Sublime: Landscape Painting in the United States, 1820–1880*, by Andrew Wilton and Tim Barringer, 11–37. Princeton, N.J.: Princeton University Press, 2002.

Wolfe, Gary K. *Critical Terms for Science Fiction and Fantasy: A Glossary and Guide to Scholarship*. New York: Greenwood Press, 1986.

———. "Evaporating Genre: Strategies of Dissolution in the Postmodern Fantastic." In *Edging into the Future: Science Fiction and Contemporary Cultural Transformation*, edited by Veronica Hollinger and Joan Gordon, 11–29. Philadelphia: University of Pennsylvania Press, 2002.

———. *Soundings*. Harold Wood, Essex: Beccon Publications, 2005.

Zahorski, Kenneth J., and Robert H. Boyer. "The Secondary Worlds of Fantasy." In *The Aesthetics of Fantasy Literature and Art*, edited by Roger C. Schlobin, 56–81. Notre Dame, Ind.: University of Notre Dame Press, 1982.

Fiction Cited

Where possible I have used first editions. Occasionally these could not be secured or—as in the case of "classics"—I deliberately chose instead easily obtainable Oxford or Penguin editions.

Aickman, Robert. "Ringing the Changes." In *The Third Ghost Book*, edited by Lady Cynthia Asquith, 85–112. London: Pan, 1955.

Aiken, Joan. "Humblepuppy." In *A Harp of Fishbones*, 170–177. London: Jonathan Cape, 1972.

———. "Yes, But Today is Tuesday." In *All You've Ever Wanted*. London: Jonathan Cape, 1953. Repr. in *All and More*, 17–26. London: Jonathan Cape, 1971.

Alexander, Lloyd. *The Black Cauldron*. New York: Laurel-Leaf (Dell), 1965.

Alexander, Lloyd. *The High King*. New York: Holt, 1968.

Allende, Isabel. *The House of the Spirits*. Translated by Magda Bogin. London: Black Swan, 1986.

Asquith, Cynthia. "Who is Sylvia?" In *The Third Ghost Book*, edited by Lady Cynthia Asquith, 241–253. London: Pan, 1957.

Austen, Jane. *Northanger Abbey and Persuasion*. London: John Murray, 1818.

———. *Pride and Prejudice*. London: T. Egerton, 1813.

———. *Sense and Sensibility*. London: T. Egerton, 1811.

Banks, Iain M. *The Algebraist*. London: Orbit, 2004.

Baum, L. Frank. *The Wonderful Wizard of Oz*. Chicago: George M. Hill, 1900.

Beagle, Peter. *A Fine and Private Place*. New York: Viking, 1960.

Bishop, K. J. *The Etched City*. Canton, Ohio: Prime Books, 2003.

Borges, Jorge Luis. "The Library of Babel" [1941]. Repr. in *Labyrinths*, 78–87. Harmondsworth, England, Penguin, 1970.

Bradbury, Ray [under pseudonym Brett Sterling]. "Referent." *Thrilling Wonder Stories*. (October 1948).

Bradley, Marion Zimmer. *The Spell Sword*. New York: DAW, 1974.

———. *Thendara House*. New York: DAW, 1983.

Brooks, Terry. *The Sword of Shannara*. New York: Random House, 1977.

Brown, Richard P. *Golden Armour: The Helmet*. London: Scholastic, 2000.

Brunner, John. *The Compleat Traveller in Black*. London: Methuen, 1987.

Bull, Emma. *War for the Oaks*. New York: Ace Books, 1987.

Bunyan, John. *The Pilgrim's Progress* [1678 and 1684]. With an introduction by N. H. Keble. Oxford: Oxford University Press, 1984.

Capote, Truman. *In Cold Blood*. New York: Random House, 1966.

Carroll, Jonathan. *The Marriage of Sticks*. New York: Tor, 1999.

Carroll, Lewis. *Alice's Adventures in Wonderland*. London: Macmillan, 1865.

———. *Through the Looking-Glass and What Alice Found There*. London: Macmillan, 1872.

Clarke, Susanna. *Jonathan Strange & Mr. Norrell*. London: Bloomsbury, 2004.

Cockayne, Steve. *The Good People*. London: Orbit, 2006.

———. *The Iron Chain*. London: Orbit, 2003.

———. *The Seagull Drovers*. London: Orbit, 2004.

———. *Wanderers and Islanders*. London: Orbit, 2002.

Conrad, Joseph, "Heart of Darkness." *Blackwood's Edinburgh Magazines* (1899).

Crowley, John. "The Girlhood of Shakespeare's Heroines." In *Conjunctions 39: The New Wave Fabulists*, edited by Bradford Morrow and Peter Straub, 9–52. Annandale-on-Hudson, N.Y.: Bard College, 2003.

———. *Little, Big*. New York: Bantam Books, 1981.

David, Peter. *Sir Apropos of Nothing*. New York: Pocket Books, 2001.

Delany, Samuel R. *Neveryóna*. New York: Bantam Books, 1983.

De Lint, Charles. *Drink Down the Moon*. New York: Ace Books, 1990.

———. *Jack, the Giant Killer*. New York: Berkley, 1987.
Donaldson, Stephen R. *Lord Foul's Bane*. New York: Holt, Rinehart and Winston, 1977.
Duncan, Andy. "The Big Rock Candy Mountain." In *Conjunctions 39: The New Wave Fabulists*, edited by Bradford Morrow and Peter Straub, 211–231. Annandale-on-Hudson, N.Y.: Bard College, 2003.
Duncan, Hal. *Vellum*. Basingstoke: Pan Macmillan, 2005.
Eager, Edward. *Seven Day Magic*. London: Macmillan, 1963.
Eddings, David. *Castle of Wizardry*. New York: Ballantine Books, 1984.
———. *Enchanter's Endgame*. New York: Ballantine Books, 1984
———. *Magician's Gambit*. New York: Ballantine Books, 1983.
———. *Pawn of Prophecy*. New York: Ballantine Books, 1982.
———. *Queen of Sorcery*. New York: Ballantine Books, 1983.
Ende, Michael. *The Neverending Story*. 1979. London: Allen Lane, 1983.
Ford, Jeffrey. *The Physiognomy*. New York: Avon/Eos, 1997.
Funke, Cornelia. *Inkheart*. London: Scholastic, 2003.
Gaiman, Neil. *Neverwhere*. New York: Avon Books, 1996.
———, and Dave McKean. *The Wolves in the Walls*. London: HarperCollins, 2003.
Garner, Alan. *Thursbitch*. London: Harvill Press, 2003.
Gentle, Mary. *Ash*. London: Victor Gollancz, 2000.
Gilman, Greer. "A Crowd of Bone." *Trampoline*, 73–148. Northampton, Mass.: Small Beer Press, 2003.
———. "Jack Daw's Pack." *Century* (Winter 2000): 77–95.
Goldman, William. *The Princess Bride: S. Morgenstern's Classic Tale of True Love and High Adventure; The "Good Parts" Version, Abridged by William Goldman*. New York: Harcourt Brace Jovanovich, 1973.
Greig, Andrew. *When They Lay Bare*. London: Faber and Faber, 1999.
Hambly, Barbara. *The Magicians of Night*. New York: Ballantine, 1992.
———. *Sisters of the Raven*. New York: Warner Books, 2002.
———. *Stranger at the Wedding*. New York: Ballantine Books, 1994.
Hand, Elizabeth. "The Least Trumps." In *Conjunctions 39: The New Wave Fabulists*, edited by Bradford Morrow and Peter Straub, 341–391. Annandale-on-Hudson, N.Y.: Bard College, 2003.
———. *Mortal Love*. New York: Morrow, 2004.
Hamilton, Laurell K. *Guilty Pleasures*. New York: Ace, 1993.
———. *Obsidian Butterfly*. New York: Ace, 2000.
Harrison, M. John. *The Course of the Heart*. London: Gollancz, 1992.
———. "Entertaining Angels Unawares." In *Conjunctions 39: The New Wave Fabulists*, edited by Bradford Morrow and Peter Straub, 85–95. Annandale-on-Hudson, N.Y.: Bard College, 2003.
———. "I Did It." In *Travelling Arrangements: Short Stories*, 181–185. London: Victor Gollancz, 2001.

———. *Light*. London: Gollancz, 2001.
———. *The Pastel City*. London: New English Library, 1971.
———. *Viriconium*. London: Gollancz, 1982.
Herbert, James. *The Rats*. London: New English Library, 1974.
Hobb, Robin. *The Farseer: Assassin's Apprentice*. New York: Bantam Books, 1995.
Hodgson, William Hope. *The House on the Borderland* [1908]. In *The House on the Borderland and Other Novels*, 107–202. London: Gollancz, 2002.
Holdstock, Robert. *Mythago Wood*. London: Victor Gollancz, 1984.
Hopkinson, Nalo. "Red Rider." A monologue written in Jamaican vernacular for *Tellin' it Like It Is: A Compendium of African Canadian Monologues for Actors*, edited by Djanet Sears. 1st chapbook ed. Toronto: Playwrights Union of Canada, 2000.
———. "Riding the Red." In *Black Swan, White Raven*, edited by Terri Windling and Ellen Datlow, 45–60. New York: AvonNova, 1997.
———. "Shift." In *Conjunctions 39: The New Wave Fabulists*, edited by Bradford Morrow and Peter Straub, 149–161. Annandale-on-Hudson, N.Y.: Bard College, 2003.
Howard, Robert E. "The Hyborian Age." *The Phantagraph* (February, August, and October–November 1936).
———. "The Tower of the Elephant." *Weird Tales* (March 1933): 306–322.
———. *The Tower of the Elephant*. West Kingston, R.I.: Donald M. Grant, 1975.
———, with L. Sprague de Camp. "The Hall of the Dead." *Magazine of Fantasy and Science Fiction* (February 1967): 5–23.
Irvine, Alexander. *A Scattering of Jades*. New York: Tor, 2002.
Irving, Washington. "The Legend of Sleepy Hollow." In *The Sketchbook of Geoffrey Crayon, Gent., as by Geoffrey Crayon*. London: John Murray, 1820.
Jackson, Shirley. *The Haunting of Hill House*. New York: Popular Library, 1959.
Jones, Diana Wynne. *Archer's Goon*. London: Methuen's Children's, 1984.
———. *Black Maria* [U.S. title, *Aunt Maria*]. London: Methuen, 1991.
———. *The Crown of Dalemark*. London: Mandarin, 1993.
———. *The Dark Lord of Derkholm*. London: Gollancz, 1998.
———. *Howl's Moving Castle*. London: Methuen's Children's, 1986.
———. *A Tale of Time City*. London: Methuen, 1987.
———. *The Tough Guide to Fantasyland*. London: Vista, 1996.
———. "The True State of Affairs." In *Everard's Ride*, 213–303. Framingham, Mass.: NESFA Press, 1995. Repr. in *Minor Arcana*, 153–287. London: Gollancz, 1996.
Jordan, Robert. *The Eye of the World*. New York: Tor, 1990.
Joyce, Graham. *The Tooth Fairy*. New York: Tor, 1996.
Kay, Guy Gavriel. *The Summer Tree*. Toronto: McClelland and Stewart, 1984.
Kindl, Patrice. *The Woman in the Wall*. New York: Houghton Mifflin, 1997; New York: Puffin, 1998.
King, Stephen. *Carrie*. Garden City, N.Y.: Doubleday, 1974.

Klasky, Mindy L. *The Glasswright's Apprentice.* New York: ROC, 2000.

Kushner, Ellen, and Delia Sherman. *The Fall of the Kings.* New York: Bantam Books, 2002.

Leavitt, Martine. *The Dollmage.* Calgary, Alberta, Canada: Red Deer Press, 2002.

Lee, Tanith. *Faces Under Water.* New York: Overlook Press, 1998.

Leiber, Fritz. "Ill Met in Lankhmar." *The Magazine of Fantasy and Science Fiction* 38, no. 4 (April 1970): 5–46. Repr. in Leiber, *Swords and Deviltry*, 165–254. New York: Ace, 1960.

Lethem. Jonathan. "The Dystopianist, Thinking of His Rival . . ." In *Conjunctions 39: The New Wave Fabulists*, edited by Bradford Morrow and Peter Straub, 163–171. Annandale-on-Hudson, N.Y.: Bard College, 2003.

Lewis, C. S. *The Last Battle.* London: Geoffrey Bles, 1956.

———. *The Lion, the Witch and the Wardrobe.* London: Geoffrey Bles, 1950.

———. *Prince Caspian.* London: Geoffrey Bles, 1951.

———. *The Silver Chair.* London: Geoffrey Bles, 1953.

———. *The Voyage of the Dawn Treader.* London: Geoffrey Bles, 1952.

Lindholm, Megan. *Wizard of the Pigeons.* New York: Ace, 1986.

Lindsey, David. *Voyage to Arcturus.* London: Methuen, 1920.

Link, Kelly. "Lull." In *Conjunctions 39: The New Wave Fabulists*, edited by Bradford Morrow and Peter Straub, 53–83. Annandale-on-Hudson, N.Y.: Bard College, 2003.

Lisle, Rebecca. *Copper.* London: Andersen, 2002.

Lovecraft, H. P. "The Call of Cthulhu." *Weird Tales* 11, no. 2 (February 1928): 159–178.

———. "The Shadow Over Innsmouth." *Weird Tales* 36, no. 3 (January 1942): 6–33.

Lynn, Elizabeth. *The Northern Girl.* New York: Berkley/Putnam, 1980.

MacDonald, George. *Lilith: a Romance.* London: Chatto and Windus, 1895.

MacLeod, Ken. *Newton's Wake.* London: Orbit, 2004.

Maguire, Gregory. *Confessions of an Ugly Stepsister.* New York: Regan (HarperCollins), 1999.

———. *Mirror Mirror.* New York: Regan (HarperCollins), 2003.

———. *Wicked: The Life and Times of the Wicked Witch of the West.* New York: Regan (HarperCollins), 1995.

Márquez, Gabriel García. *One Hundred Years of Solitude.* Translated by Gregory Rabassa. London: Jonathan Cape, 1970.

———. "A Very Old Man With Enormous Wings." In *The Collected Short Stories of Gabriel García Márquez*, 203–210. New York: Harper Perennial, 1993.

Martel, Yann. *Life of Pi.* Edinburgh: Canongate Books, 2001.

Mayne, William. *Tiger's Railway.* London: Walker Books, 1987.

McAuley, Paul. *White Devils.* London: Simon and Schuster, 2004.

McKinley, Robin. *Deerskin.* New York: Ace, 1993.

———. *Spindle's End.* New York: Putnam, 2000.

———. *Sunshine.* Berkeley, Calif.: Berkeley Publishing Group, 2003.

Miéville, China. *The Iron Council.* New York: Ballantine, 2004.

———. *King Rat*. New York: Tor, 1998.
———. *Perdido Street Station*. London: Macmillan, 2000.
———. *The Scar*. London: Macmillan, 2002.
Mirrlees, Hope. *Lud-in-the-Mist*. London: W. Collins, 1926.
Mitchell, David. *Cloud Atlas*. London: Sceptre, 2004.
Morrow, James. "The Wisdom of the Skin." In *Conjunctions 39: The New Wave Fabulists*, edited by Bradford Morrow and Peter Straub, 133–147. Annandale-on-Hudson, N.Y.: Bard College, 2003.
Namjoshi, Suniti. *Building Babel*. Melbourne, Australia: Spinifex Press, 1996.
Nesbit, E. *Five Children and It*. London: T. Fisher Unwin, 1902.
Noon, Jeff. *Vurt*. Stockport: Ringpull, 1993.
O'Leary, Patrick. "The Bearing of Light." In *Conjunctions 39: The New Wave Fabulists*, edited by Bradford Morrow and Peter Straub, 267–275 Annandale-on-Hudson, N.Y.: Bard College, 2003.
Parker, K. J. *The Belly of the Bow*. London: Orbit, 1999.
———. *Colours in the Steel*. London: Orbit, 1998.
———. *The Proof House*. London: Orbit, 2000.
Peake, Mervyn. *Gormenghast*. London: Eyre and Spottiswoode, 1950.
———. *Titus Groan*. London: Eyre and Spottiswoode, 1946.
Poe, Edgar Allen. "The Pit and the Pendulum" [1842]. In *Selected Tales*, 252–266. London: Penguin Popular Classics, 1994.
Pratchett, Terry. *Carpe Jugulum*. London: Doubleday, 1998.
———. *Feet of Clay*. London: Gollancz, 1996.
———. *The Fifth Elephant*. London: Doubleday, 1999.
———. *Guards! Guards!* London: Gollancz, 1989.
———. *Jingo*. London: Gollancz, 1997.
———. *Monstrous Regiment*. London: Doubleday, 2003.
———. *Nightwatch*. London: Doubleday, 2002.
———. *The Truth*. London: Doubleday, 2000.
———. *Witches Abroad*. London: Gollancz, 1991.
Priest, Christopher. *The Separation*. London: Scribner, 2002.
Pullman, Philip. *The Amber Spyglass*. London: Scholastic Press, 2000.
———. *Northern Lights*. London: Scholastic Press, 1995.
———. *The Subtle Knife*. London: Scholastic Press, 1997.
Radcliffe, Ann. *The Mysteries of Udolpho* [1794]. Oxford: Oxford World Classics, 1998.
Rice, Anne. *Interview with a Vampire*. New York: Knopf, 1976.
Rowling, J. K. *Harry Potter and the Chamber of Secrets*. London: Bloomsbury, 1998.
———. *Harry Potter and the Philosopher's Stone*. London: Bloomsbury, 1997.
Sachar, Louis. *Holes*. New York: Frances Foster Books/Farrar, Straus and Giroux, 1998.
Shelley, Mary. *Frankenstein* [1818]. Penguin Classic. Harmondsworth, England: Penguin, 1985.

Stevenson, Robert Louis. *The Strange Case of Dr Jekyll and Mr Hyde and Other Tales of Terror*. Penguin Classic. London: Penguin, 2002.

Stevermer, Caroline. *A College of Magics*. New York: Tor, 1994.

Stewart, Sean. *Galveston*. New York: Ace, 2000.

Stoker, Bram. *Dracula*. 1897. Penguin Classic. Harmondsworth, England: Penguin, 1993.

Straub, Peter. *In the Night Room*. New York: Random House, 2004.

———. "Little Red's Tango." In *Conjunctions 39: The New Wave Fabulists*, edited by Bradford Morrow and Peter Straub, 97–131. Annandale-on-Hudson, N.Y.: Bard College, 2003.

———. *lost boy lost girl*. New York: Random House, 2003.

Swainston, Steph. *The Year of Our War*. London: Gollancz, 2004.

Swanwick, Michael. *The Iron Dragon's Daughter*. London: Orion, 1994.

Swindell, Robert. *Brother in the Land*. Oxford: Oxford University Press,1984.

Taylor, G. P. *Shadowmancer*. London: Faber, 2003.

Tepper, Sheri S. *Marianne, the Madame, and the Momentary Gods*. New York: Ace Books. 1988.

———. *Marianne, the Magus, and the Manticore*. New York: Ace Books, 1985.

———. *Marianne, the Matchbox, and the Malachite Mouse*. New York: Ace Books, 1989.

Thurber, James. "The Unicorn in the Garden." In *Fables for Our Time and Famous Poems Illustrated*, 65–66. New York: Harper and Brothers, 1940.

Tolkien, J. R. R. *The Fellowship of the Ring*. London: Allen and Unwin, 1954.

———. *The Return of the King*. London: Allen and Unwin, 1955.

———. *The Two Towers*. London: Allen and Unwin, 1954.

Townley, Roderick. *The Great Good Thing*. London: Simon and Schuster, 2001.

Traviss, Karen. *City of Pearl*. New York: Ace, 2004.

VanderMeer, Jeff. "Dradin in Love." In *City of Saints and Madmen*, 15–72. Canton, Ohio: Prime, 2002.

———. "Secret Life" [2002]. In *Secret Life*, 3–23. Urbana, Ill.: Golden Gryphon Press, 2004.

Walpole, Horace. *The Castle of Otranto* [1764]. Penguin Classics. Harmondsworth, England: Penguin, 2002.

Wells, H. G. "The Door in the Wall" [1906]. In *The Short Stories of H.G. Wells*, 164–183. London: Ernest Benn, 1906.

Welty, Eudora. *The Golden Apples*. New York; Harcourt, Brace, 1945.

Westerfield, Scott. *The Midnighters: The Secret Hour*. New York: Eos, 2004.

Williams, Tad. *The Dragonbone Chair*. New York: DAW, 1988.

Winterson, Jeanette. *Oranges Are Not the Only Fruit*. London: Pandora, 1985.

———. *The Powerbook*. London: Jonathan Cape, 2000.

Wittig, Monique. *Les Guérillères* [1969]. Translated by David Le Vay. London: Peter Owen, 1971.

Index

Farah Mendlesohn lectures in science fiction and fantasy at Middlesex University, London. She has been editor of *Foundation: The International Review of Science Fiction* for six years, and is the author of *Diana Wynne Jones: Children's Literature and the Fantastic Tradition* (2005) and coeditor of *The Cambridge Companion to Science Fiction* (2003), winner of a Hugo Award.